MAKING THE JESUITS MORE MODERN

Thomas Philip Faase

UNIVERSITY
PRESS OF
AMERICA

PREFACE

Making Jesuits more modern can be viewed in many ways. So a methodological note is given here to orient the reader to the approach taken in this study. It is a study of Jesuit values. That is, it investigates what the Jesuit Order considers important enough to selectively influence its long-run decisions.

Ten years ago, a review of many research reports comprising the American contribution to a sociological survey of the entire Society of Jesus convinced this writer of two requirements for a proper assessment of the Jesuits: to be adequately intensive, it must focus on values; to be adequately extensive, it must study Jesuit membership overall. The present research attempts this overall study of Jesuit values, the values of the Jesuit membership as object of the deliberations and legislation of the Thirty-Second General Congregation.

This empirical study of values is not narrowly proscribed. "Description and analysis of values by social scientists rest on the use of several lines of evidence."[1] The lines of evidence suggested are testimony, choices, directions of interest, content analysis, and rewards and punishments.

> The sources of evidence mentioned above indicate just so many "operational definitions" of value: value as overt choice or preference, as attention or emphasis, as statement or assertion, as implicit premise, as a referent of social sanctions. These various evidences are "pointers" that say "this is what is meant." Not all are of equal usefulness for every purpose, but all are useful. When used in combination, these several different approximations

gain reliability in so far as they are mutually consistent.[2]

The validity of this set of mutually consistent pointers derives from a procedure that has been called "methodological triangulation," i.e. employing several different methodological approaches to get at the same variable or dimension or continuum or concept.[3]

> No single operation is taken as perfectly defining the distal construct. Instead, the firmness and relative unequivocality of our knowledge of distal constructs comes through a triangulation of two or more operations, no one of which has priority as the criterion or the definition, and no one of which would be unequivocal without the other.... The joint employment of maximally independent methods focused upon the same construct greatly reduces the number of tenable rival interpretations for both sets of measures, and thus indicates the degree of success of the constructual enterprise. Fiske and I have referred to this aspect of validation as convergent validation. It constitutes a methodological triangulation.[4]

As it happens, this research employs all of the lines of evidence suggested above. These various sources build like layers one upon the other in support of a hypothetical model of modernization developed in this study. The testimony of numerous commentators on Jesuit activities, assemblies, and legislation augments participant observation and scholarly accounts of Jesuit life and history. The choices taken by the Society of Jesus are measured by the voting by delegates to its highest level legislative assembly. The directions of interest are evidenced by changes throughout the past fifteen

iv

years and by questionnaire responses by delegates and a non-delegate Jesuit sample. Content analysis is employed on documents from two general congregations a decade apart to determine changes in orientation. Rewards and punishments are reported as the consequences and trade-offs experienced by the Jesuit Order and its administrators resulting from policies they have set and adhered to.

FOOTNOTES

[1]Robin M. Williams, Jr., "Values: The Concept of Values" in International Encyclopedia of the Social Sciences, New York, 1968, p. 285.

[2]Robin M. Williams, Jr., American Society: A Sociological Interpretation, Third Edition, New York, 1970, p. 447.

[3]Donald T. Campbell, Leadership And Its Effects Upon the Group, Columbus, Ohio, 1956, p. 73-74.

[4]Donald T. Campbell, "Methodological Suggestions From a Comparative Psychology of Knowledge Processes," Inquiry, Vol. 2, No. 3, (Spring, 1959) p. 176-177.

ACKNOWLEDGMENTS

I have learned slowly but surely that
sociological research is not "metaphysical."
Nonetheless, there is something very basic and
intangible about the community of ideas, instruction, encouragement, companionship and
lasting value that surrounds a study like this
one.

Before all, I thank the Society of Jesus
for providing requisites of every kind for this
research. I am grateful to the General Congregation and its administration, to Fathers Bruce
Biever, John Padberg, and John Swain who were
instrumental in my gaining access to the assembly
and responses of the delegates. Although I was
officially authorized by the Congregation to
attend its sessions, this account of what transpired is my interpretation and analysis and is
not to be taken as an account officially
authorized by the Society of Jesus. Fathers
Marc Brousseau and Hernando Ramirez generously
provided the French and Spanish translations.
Joseph Barton and Peter Marchetti organized,
assisted, consuled, and endured my work and
prompted my best efforts by their tremendous
help and encouragement. The assistance of Chris
Rupert and printing skills of Robert Finaly were
indispensable. Many other Jesuits have helped
and supported me and I specially thank the
Wisconsin Province and the Regis College Jesuit
Community.

My gratitude to my Graduate Committee at
Cornell - Professors Robin Williams, Urie
Bronfenbrenner, William Lucas and Donald Hayes -
is immense and must continually be expressed by
what I make of all they have given me profession-
ally and personally. The congenial and excellent
programming and analysis work by James Wert and
John Tibert of York University is greatly ap-
preciated. The consent to use materials of

Professor Milton Rokeach and Reverend Richard Rashke, and the translating of Dr. Hartmut Guenther, Mrs. Shirley Edwards, Mrs. Sharon Staples, Professor Victoria Muller Carson and Ewald Schaefer are gratefully acknowledged.

The manuscript has been prepared for publication by Diane Streich. Her excellent ability, helpful initiative and patience freed me from all concern and I deeply appreciate that. The encouragement and help of so many people has gone into the making of this work and I am grateful.

TABLE OF CONTENTS

Table of Contents - continued

Table of Contents - continued

Table of Contents - continued

CHAPTER NINE - continued

LIST OF TABLES

List of Tables - continued

List of Tables - continued

List of Tables - continued

List of Tables - continued

List of Tables - continued

                  xviii

List of Tables - continued

CHAPTER ONE

CATHOLICISM AND THE SOCIETY OF JESUS

IN TIMES OF CHANGE

Catholicism throughout the world is in a state of religious revolution. The changes that have occurred during the past fifteen years affect every aspect of Catholic life and practice. They are so drastic as to have created an aura of disorientation and sustained unfamiliarity in persons who have been Catholics for many years. These changes form the background for this report, which is a sociological account of the aggiornamento of the Society of Jesus.

The Society of Jesus is the largest religious order in the Catholic Church. It consists of 28,856 members,[1] all male and all committed to the organization by life-long promises (vows) of poverty (not to own any property), chastity (never to marry) and obedience (submission to the authority of superiors in the Society). Of the total number of Jesuits, 20,627 are ordained priests, 3,770 are studying for the priesthood, and 4,459 are brothers.[2]

Within the Church, the largest role played by Jesuits is in education. The Jesuits run educational institutions in sixty-four countries: fifty-three universities, forty-five colleges, more than 350 high schools, and some 4,300 primary schools.[3] In secondary education alone, the Jesuits are responsible for nearly 400,000 students.[4] One-third of all Jesuits work in "missionary territories" designated as such by the Vatican. More than 600 Jesuits work in television and radio, including the direction of the Vatican radio station. Scholarly publications, research, retreat direction, and parochial ministry are other "usual" Jesuit apostolates.

The role of the Society of Jesus in the

1

Catholic Church was authoritatively described by
the Pope himself in his address to all of the
members of the Thirty-Second General Congregation
on December 3, 1974:

> You are at the head of that interior re-
> newal which the Church is facing in this
> secularized world, especially after the
> Second Vatican Council. Your Society is,
> we say, the test of the vitality of the
> Church throughout the centuries; it is
> perhaps one of the most meaningful cru-
> cibles in which are encountered the
> difficulties, the temptations, the ef-
> forts, the perpetuity and the successes
> of the whole Church.[5]

Chapters One and Two portray a background
for the research detailed later in this report.
This background material consists of the
following: (1) a brief overview of the nature of
changes in Catholicism over the last century; (2)
an account of the Second Vatican Council; (3)
description of changes in the Catholic Church set
in motion by Vatican II; (4) an account of the
Thirty-First General Congregation; (5) description
of changes in the Society of Jesus as a result of
that congregation; and (6) an account of the
preparation for and the dynamics and legislation
of the Thirty-Second General Congregation.

The sources for this background account are
two-fold, published materials and personal observation. The historical overview of the past
century relies mainly on the work of Thomas O'Dea.
The account of the Second Vatican Council relies
on O'Dea, Rock Caporale, Andrew Greeley, and the
Council documents. Description of the Thirty-
First General Congregation of the Jesuits relies
on numerous articles from Woodstock Letters, a
publication of the Jesuits of Woodstock College.
These articles include the minutes of the Congregation sessions reworked as an historical record,
and commentary and observations written by
delegates during the Congregation. The brief

history of the General Congregations by John
Padberg, S.J. is also source for this account.
Numerous articles, comments and observations from
delegates to the Thirty-Second General Congregation are published and cited as sources for the
description of this latest Congregation. Personal
participation in the Jesuit Order for seventeen
years and observation of the Thirty-Second
General Congregation are primary sources of information throughout this portrayal of the background of Jesuit aggiornamento.

The Catholic Church Prior to Vatican II

The Catholic Church throughout the nineteenth and first half of the twentieth centuries
concentrated on the defense of the faith. Since
the Protestant Reformation and the Council of
Trent, it developed largely in reaction to
changes and developments in Protestantism, in
science and in culture generally.

The earliest attempts in the nineteenth
century to change a defensive status quo concerned the question of church and state.
Sympathetic to the French Revolution, French
liberal Catholic thinking favored abandoning
support of monarchies and supporting liberalism
and democracy. The French hierarchy denounced
such thinking. Such concepts as freedom of
conscience, separation of church and state, and
alliances of men of varied faiths for the common
good were denounced and condemned.

In Germany, Catholic liberalism of the
nineteenth century stressed a dynamic theology
based on process philosophy and the advances of
science. These ideas were frowned upon by ecclesiastical authority. The suggestion of
Scholastic Theology as a "thing of the past," and
avowals of freedom for intellectual inquiry were
hailed by Catholic liberals, but criticized by
the official Church.

3

Other liberal currents emanated from Belgium, England, France and Italy. However, in 1864, Pius IX issued the <u>Syllabus of Errors</u> "which led to the total eclipse of liberal Catholicism."[6] In 1870 the First Vatican Council convened. Its main accomplishment was to define Papal Infallibility as a dogma. This strengthened the Church's defensive posture.

Some liberal thought persisted despite setbacks. At the beginning of the twentieth century, Pope Leo XIII urged the recognition of the French Revolution and wrote an enlightened critique of industrialization. Henry Cardinal Newman emerged at this time; he was a bright and open-minded thinker who was also orthodox and devout. American Catholicism affected the Church at the beginning of this century as well.

> The Catholic Church in America came to combine a kind of liberal spirit about politics and community with a kind of integralist conception with respect to its own inner life, its own ideas, and its own place in the society.[7]

Great advances were being made by Protestant scholars in biblical research. But as some Catholics began to attend to this scholarship, the hierarchy grew defensive. The "tools" of modern historical criticism were too new to be accepted by the magesterium. Similarly historicist and psychological emphases were introduced as approaches to systematic theology in works of such men as Tyrrell and Blondel. Tyrrell stressed the primacy of experience and relationship over definition, suggesting that "Revelation itself was a matter of experience - experience that transcended its verbal description or statement."[8] In a complementary vein, Blondel was advocating a religiosity of "becoming" and experience.

Other thinkers followed these liberal lines, including further developments in political philosophy supporting the Christian democratic

4

movements. But Pope Pius X in a series of pronouncements denounced these liberal tendencies
of the first decade of this century. In a moto
proprio of December 18, 1903, Pius X said that
it was "in conformity with the order established
by God that there should be in human society,
princes and subjects, patrons and proletariat,
rich and poor, learned and ignorant, nobles and
plebeians."[9] In a letter to French bishops of
August 25, 1910, Pius X quoted his predecessor
Leo XIII who said that "a Christian democracy
should maintain that distinction of classes
which is proper to a well-constituted city."[10]
The liberal trends of the era were then condemned
in the encyclical Pascendi Gregis as "modernism."
Modernism was liberal thought seen as tainted
with agnosticism and immanentism. After this
encyclical there was a minor inquisition over
the next few years up to the First World War.
Disciplinary measures again stifled liberal
Catholicism.

Theological positions and trends which are
today taken for granted as development of dogma
emerged throughout this time and into the thirties
and forties. Repeatedly they were submerged by
the criticism and censure of a conservative
magesterium.

Yet always suspect by the conservatives
and always in danger of calling down upon
themselves the censures of authority,
the Catholic theological intelligentia
continued the work of proto aggiornamento.
The years following the Second World War
saw a veritable Catholic renaissance.
In this period there developed the men
who were to become the strategically
influential periti of the Second Vatican
Council. Despite their skirmishes and
clashes with traditional authority, they
carried on. In the early 1950s, their
work brought from Pius XII the encyclical Humani Gereris, but though slowed
down it did continue.[11]

5

Table One summarizes the issues upon which liberals and conservatives diverged.

Behind the revolution of the Church can be seen an explicit shift in culture. The Church changed within its own precincts in order to "catch up" with the shift already experienced by most of Western civilization, a shift from classicist to modern culture, from an Aristotelian to a Galeleian mode of thought.[12]

> Classical culture has given way to modern culture, and, I would submit, the crisis of our age is in no small measure the fact that modern culture has not yet reached its maturity. The classical mediation of meaning has broken down.[13]

This drastic change and disorientation has caused a distinct crisis in the Church. After so many years of taking an embattled stance, the full transformation to new forms is not an easy adaptation.

> There is a crisis of the first magnitude today. For a principle duty of priests is to lead and teach the people of God. But all leadership and all teaching occurs within social structures and through cultural channels. In the measure that one insists on leading and teaching within structures that no longer function and through channels that no longer exist, in that very measure leadership and teaching cease to exist.[14]

To this crisis Pope John XXIII was responding when he asked that "the windows be opened" and the Church be updated. He instituted aggiornamento and set it in motion by convoking the Second Vatican Council.

6

TABLE ONE

CONTRASTING EMPHASES AND PATTERNS OF
BELIEF BETWEEN INNOVATORS AND ESTABLISHED
POSITIONS IN EARLY TWENTIETH CENTURY CATHOLICISM

Source: Thomas O'Dea The Catholic Crisis pp. 62-65

"INNOVATORS"	"THOSE WHO HELD ESTABLISHED POSITIONS"
1. emphasized experience	1. gave priority to codified definitions
2. recognized significance of emotion and feeling	2. rested faith on assent to intellectual formulas
3. held that life was in some basic way a process	3. saw life as an interaction of fixed intellectual, cultural and social forms
4. saw the coming victory of democracy and relativized social forms	4. saw the world as a substantial hierarchical order, within which particular forms were sacral
5. suspected the vast implications of the historically specific and non-absolute	5. held to general statements embodying older ideas seen as self-evident to right reason
6. saw importance to immanent forces and tendencies in social life, modes of expressing these, and their relation to present state of things	6. saw codified formulas as timeless embodiment of the transcendent and understood transcendence in highly rationalized way
7. saw life as open-ended	7. seemed to see nothing new under the sun
8. saw inconsistency in the Church basing its propaedeutic to faith upon reason and history and yet making rules to curtail reason and enclose history	8. saw no problem in the circularity of basing propaedeutic to faith upon reason and history while curtailing reason and enclosing history

9. saw the approach of a greater equality and a coming of age for modern man

9. saw submission of inferior to superior as part of the divinely ordained nature of things and emphasized the religious importance of obedience

10. suggested that no historically evolved conceptions of being and value could be final and definitive

10. tended to see both being and value and their human formulations as fixed and complete

11. began to appreciate that men act out, in their lives and generation in history, complex and subtle dramas, whose script is original and whose source and consummation are obscure.

11. were prone to see the activity of the laymen as having meaning only in its moral aspects, and to see in their own highly conventionalized presentation of the religious experience the only noble human end.

Vatican II and the Changing Church

On January 25, 1959, Pope John XXIII
stunned most of the Catholic Church hierarchy and
its experts when, only three months into his papacy, he announced that he would convoke a world-
wide Ecumenical Council, that is, to summon all
of the nearly 2,300 bishops of the world to form
the highest level legislative body of the
Catholic Church. On Christmas Day, 1961, after
commissions had been set up to see to the Council's preparation, Pope John formally convoked
the Second Vatican Council.

The Council met in four distinct sessions.
It began on October 11, 1962. Session one ran
until December 8, 1962. Pope John XXIII died on
June 3, 1963 before the second session. Pope
Paul VI formally continued the Council. The
second session ran from September 29 until
December 4, 1963. The third session began
September 14, 1964 and ended November 21 of that
year. Finally, the fourth session, begun on
September 14, 1965, was formally adjourned by
Pope Paul VI on December 8, 1965. In that three
year span, the impetus, orientations, and some
of the machinery for fundamental change in all
Catholicism originated. Pope Paul VI on closing
the Council said:

The Second Vatican Ecumenical Council
...must be numbered without doubt among
the greatest events of the Church. In
fact it was the largest in the number of
Fathers who came to (Rome) from every
part of the world.... It was the rich-
est because of the questions which for
four sessions have been discussed carefully and profoundly. And last of all
it was the most opportune because,
bearing in mind the necessities of the
present day, above all it sought to meet
the pastoral needs and...it has made a
great effort to reach...the whole human
family.[15]

9

The Second Vatican Council is the structure which instigated revolution in the entire fabric of Catholic thought and institutions. Andrew Greeley, priest-sociologist, suggests that there were four principal accomplishments. They are:

1. The fixed, immutable, unquestionable structure of the Church's organization and theory that had persisted for centuries was definitely opened up.

2. The principle of collegiality provided the Church with an organizational theme which, on the theoretical level, can serve as the basis for profoundly changing the routinized patterns of behaviour that had given shape and form to the Church for several centuries.

3. With the Pastoral Constitution on the Church in the Modern World, Catholicism officially opened itself up not merely to the possibility of dialogue with separated brother Christians, but to the whole vast culture that we call the modern world.

4. The Constitutions on the Church and on Divine Revelation created the beginnings of a theological context within which Catholicism could address the modern world and also address its own membership to the extent that the membership is deeply involved in the modern world.[16]

The judgment of this Council was a turning away from the defensive, juridical, and self-proclaiming approach typical of an earlier Church. Indeed, this accomplishment is mainly at the level of culture. Yet the documents give direction and erect machinery for the structures which evidence that changing mentality. "Even if the Church organization of the future has not yet come into being, at least the principle is there according to which it can begin."[17] Much remains to be done

to implement the changes of culture. The socialization of new generations of Catholics must be
prepared through the emergence of new channels
of meaning and new symbols. Although the Council
has transformed the culture and the approach to
all vital church questions, the means to uncover
and transmit and internalize these "new truths"
are presently inadequate.[18]

The changes in culture effected from the
Council could be summarized under the following
headings which are taken from an analysis of one
of the most important documents of the Council,
the Dogmatic Constitution on the Church.

1. The different and to some extent un-
   harmonized conceptions of the Church
   found in the document;

2. the contrasting conceptions of the
   world with their implications for the
   Church's mission;

3. a new emphasis upon the dignity of the
   lay state and a new emphasis upon the
   priesthood of believers together with
   an older stress upon hierarchy and
   upon special clerical status as central
   to the Church's structure;

4. the new idea that all callings, worldly
   as well as religious, share equally
   in God's plan, as against the older
   special recognition of the formally
   religious and quasimonastic religious
   roles as central and exemplary;

5. the use of scriptural concepts in preference to the established scholastic
   vocabulary to describe the content of
   faith and the equally important reliance
   at certain junctures upon the scholastic
   conceptions; and

6. the expression of a genuine and

11

> enthusiastic ecumenicity and the
> endeavour to reconcile it with a
> reformed version of the older ex-
> clusiveness of Catholic claims.[19]

Two processes characteristic of the changes in the Second Vatican Council are important to isolate and examine. These processes are (1) the development of dogma by means of "context theologizing" and (2) the transformation of culture through the forum of an ideational Council.

The first process is that of the development of doctrine through "context theologizing." This is a process of changing the meaning of previous time-honored statements by situating them in a context that changes emphasis and attention to aspects of the message. New meanings and new elements are introduced in conjunction with older traditions. This conjunction changes the older tradition at the same time as it legitimizes the new message by its association with the older. This is a process whereby the principles and values underlying the enormous ediface of a 2000-year old institution can be called upon as part of the legitimizing of changes in principles and values. It is an intellectual, ideational device that harmonizes change with continuity. In tandom with a mechanism in which the ideational is paramount, this process is enabled to instigate a revolution just as we recognize Vatican II to have done.

The second process is the ideational process of a Council and the way it influences transformation. The Council is a deliberate, discursive, intellectual body. It is a forum in which ideas are supreme, and in such a forum ideas are the facilitator of all subsequent policy decisions. Through its deliberations, discussions and thought, the changes are legislated. That is to say, through the medium of the Council the culture is given impetus and substance for transformation. There remains the far more difficult course of changing the whole network of reenforcing

12

structures, attitudes and the like. Nevertheless, it is precisely by reason of a Council being an intellectual forum that, given the proper shared disposition in favour of renewal and <u>aggiornamento</u>, such drastic and far-reaching changes in culture could be achieved.

> The context (of the Council) threw the balance in favor of the intellectuals, but conservative theologians were prepared to do scarcely more than repeat the older positions. They had little to offer except further condemnations of the well-known sources of threat; communism, atheism, etc. Yet John XXIII had called the Council in the spirit of dialogue, of pastoral concern, of updating the Church, and not of polemic and anathema. The conditions within the Church and the position of the Church in the world - the total context - new theologians - those who, under official discouragement and disapproval, explored the theology of the secular world, of the Church, of history and the Bible - had something to offer. Not surprisingly, they were more and more called upon. It was a great moment of fulfillment for a century and a half of unsuccessful efforts at <u>aggiornamento</u> when the progressive theologians emerged as the most influential periti at the Council.[20]

The Council changed the thinking and expectations of Catholics by reason of developments in the thinking and expectations of the Church's leaders. These leaders were influenced by the charisma of Pope John XXIII and by the expertise of specialists.

Of seventy-three bishops interviewed by a Columbia University sociologist, sixty-four were in deep-felt admiration and praise of Pope John. He was more frequently applauded for spiritual gifts of humility, simplicity, and kindness. He

13

was further characterized as charismatic and intuitive. There was also some criticism: "John lacked both method and organization. His method was good for a time, but now a new development is called for." Another referred to his calling the Council as "a supernaturally motivated caprice, or you may say, a studied caprice. John was humble, and only humble people can afford to be capricious."[21]

The experience of the almost 2,300 bishops would, of course, vary. Nevertheless a common experience was that of sharing with their peers. At no other time could bishops congregate in so extensive a peer-group. The greatest solidarity was evidenced by the French, German, Spanish and Belgium bishops.

Three factors existed as particularly influential in the determination of informal relations among bishops at the Council. These were "1) the language areas to which the bishops belonged; 2) the schoolmate links (generally in Roman Colleges); and 3) the position occupied and the international experience already gained."[22]

Periti were very important to Vatican II. They are the experts and specialists in various fields.

At the First Session 280 _periti_ participated or were officially appointed. A few more were added at the Second Session. More important than knowing their exact number is the realization that by far the majority of them came from Europe and North America.[23]

Generally the bishops of the Council were very open and receptive to these experts and their work clearly paved the way, set the style and provided the substance for the changes effected by the Council.

More than all other groups the Italian

14

bishops resisted and avoided recourse to non-Italian periti. The Italian periti were not of much assistance to the whole Council.

> The Italian periti, forming a considerable group and a large percentage of the total number of periti were "the most conspicuous for their silence and their absences from tangible contribution." Never did any Italian peritus venture to participate in any of the series of lectures and conferences given to the bishops at the international level.... Foreign periti were never invited to address the Italian episcopal body.[24]

In contrast to the availability of European and North American experts, and to the intransigence of the Italian experts, the developing nations would have liked to avail themselves of experts but experts in the affairs of these nations were unavailable.

> The approach and specialization of the majority of periti was thoroughly Western, and consequently did not respond to the needs of missionary areas. Said one bishop from Asia: "By and large, the topics raised at the Council referred to the Western countries. When we asked the periti our questions and our problems, they had no answers. They make laws for our regions, too, but without knowing the actual situation there."[25]

Contact, discussion and voting increased the understanding and the consensus of the Council Fathers. Much of the vitality of implementation after the Council can be attributed to what the leaders had learned and experienced and how thoroughly they had been "won over" to the culture of a changing Church.

> By means of a succession of polls, the outcome was the formation of a strong

15

majority and a steady diminution of the
"non placet" (negative) vote. The opinions
of the bishops were gradually crystallizing
in one direction and a consensus was being
achieved, which was a far cry from the very
divergent positions of the first days of
the Council.[26]

Out of a very human and very large, un-
wieldly mechanism, sixteen documents (See Table
Two), vastly more open and forward-looking
orientations, greater tolerance and accommodation,
and unprecedented change in Catholicism came
about. The entire process of deinstitutionalizing and reinstitutionalizing Catholicism to
transform it in terms of modernization had begun.
Pope John XXIII inspired this and the Second
Vatican Council he summoned set the aggiornamento
he asked for in motion. The Council is for
Catholicism and the entire institution of religion
a major watershed.

The Council marked the decisive beginning
of the aggiornamento, it established the
renewal, it called us to the ever necessary repentence and return; in other words,
it was only the beginning of the beginning.[27]

The Catholic Church After the Council

In the religious jargon the Catholic Church
has been referred to as the "Post-Tridentine"
Church. It was so named as bearing characteristics of the Counter-Reformation and the Ecumenical
Council of Trent which ended in 1563. Today the
Church is referred to as "Post-Conciliar" to de-
note it as no longer a Church of the Counter-
Reformation or Trent but a Church of the spirit
of the Second Vatican Council.

The Council of Trent and the subsequent 400
years confirmed and sanctified the structures and
organization of the Church that had been so

16

TABLE TWO

DOCUMENTS OF THE SECOND VATICAN COUNCIL

Document	Length
1. Dogmatic Constitution on the Church	16,200 words
2. Dogmatic Constitution on Divine Revelation	2,996 words
3. Constitution on the Sacred Liturgy	7,806 words
4. Pastoral Constitution on the Church in the Modern World	23,335 words
5. Decree on the Instruments of Social Communication	2,225 words
6. Decree on Ecumenism	4,790 words
7. Decree on Eastern Catholic Churches	1,806 words
8. Decree on the Bishops' Pastoral Office in the Church	5,982 words
9. Decree on Priestly Formation	2,987 words
10. Decree on the Appropriate Renewal of the Religious Life	3,189 words
11. Decree on the Apostolate of the Laity	7,016 words
12. Decree on the Ministry and Life of Priests	7,896 words
13. Decree on the Church's Missionary Activity	9,870 words
14. Declaration on Christian Education	2,604 words
15. Declaration on the Relationship of the Church to the Non-Christian Religions	1,117 words
16. Declaration on Religious Freedom	3,195 words

"What the Second Vatican Council said is what it said in its official latin texts.   Exclusive of 992 footnotes of varying length the sixteen promulgated texts run to approximately 103,014 words."

Source: Very Reverend Msgr. Joseph Gallagher, translation editor.   The Documents of Vatican II, "Preface to the Translation," p. IX.

strictly defined and enforced in the face of the
Protestant Reformation. It was a monolythic,
highly authoritarian, hierarchical organization.
Its world-wide parochial structures, auxiliary
formal organizations, parent-child relationships
between bishops and priests, pastors and assistants, priests and people and a heavily dogmatic,
prescriptive, and unchanging solemn atmosphere
all mirrored Rome's relationship to the rest of
the Church.

The cultural variables such as doctrine,
or morale, or religious observance were all
firmly routinized. Doctrine was defined and prescribed and communicated exclusively to students
of the priesthood in seminaries bound by Canon
Law to teach only scholastic philosophy and
theology. Morale was often the reiterative
phenomena of boarding schools and annual
gatherings - rarely changing because rigidly
formalized and structured. Religious observance
was bound in by sanction of sin (or excommunica-
tion in serious matters). In even so ideational
an institution as the Church, the ideas were
dominated by the structures in which they were
cast.

With the brief flourishing of Pope John all
this changed to a spirit of renovation and
aggiornamento. A definite, idealistic triumpha-
lism seized the Catholic Church. In the United
States a Catholic, John F. Kennedy, was elected
president for the first time in history and an
immigrant church saw itself as "arrived." Pope
John published his encyclical, Pacem in Terris,
the first Roman Catholic encyclical ever addressed "to all men of good will." Acclaim for this
document and renown for the person of Pope John
came from all denominations and the international
community. The dramatic event of the Vatican
Council itself warranted publicity and attention
for the changing Church. With the death of Pope
John, Pope Paul VI showed evidence of continuing
the thrust of this innovative spirit. Two years
after his election and in the midst of the

Council, Pope Paul journeyed to the United States and formally addressed the United Nations General Assembly on October 5, 1965. His trip and address were given complete television and radio coverage which included the liturgically revised celebration of the Mass at Yankee Stadium in New York.

Precisely under this burst of triumphant enthusiasm, a great thrust of cultural innovation began to spread through the institutional Church. The cultural sphere came to dominance in a rising level of expectations, awakened pride and involvement of the laity, increasing attendance, vocations and conversions, and rapproachement to other faiths. But the entrenched and routinized structures could not support this increased salience and intensity.

> Within two years, the glory of Vatican
> II had changed into the crisis of reform.
> The Church, which had won new admiration
> from non-Catholics for its attempt at
> updating, suddenly came under a barrage
> of attacks from within.[28]

The irony of renewed respect and support coming from outside the Church and the simultaneous rebellion of the faithful within the Church seems best understood in terms of the "Conciliar" culture surpassing the structures reenforced by the Tridentine Church. The complaints, defections, and revolution were carried on "in the name" of the values transmitted by the very Church presently under attack. The integration of culture and structure was fractured. Culture came into dominance. "The Catholic Church, which had traditionally presented a united front to the world, suddenly became a house divided."[29]

The decade from the end of the Council to the present was the most extensively turbulent decade for the Church since the Reformation. The Church had worked at the Council to update, to modernize its message, to present Catholicism as

19

more attractive and more relevant to mankind. And yet, every facet and feature of Catholic life experienced convulsive rending and reordering.

This convulsion is evidenced by the statistical indicators of traditional Catholic growth. In the United States, for example, the number of converts was reduced by one-half between 1960 and 1975 (from 146,000 to 75,000). The number of seminarians dropped drastically (from 49,000 to 18,000). The number of nuns dropped by a quarter (from 181,000 to 135,000).[30] World-wide the number of male religious dropped by eighteen percent.

The Post-Tridentine Church had been integrated by an aura and mystery and sense of the sacred which was reenforced in every structure prevailing in the Church. But as these structures fell into disuse because of cultural reorientation and some structural reform, the aura and mystery and sense of the sacred lost their more popular and prominent vehicles. This loss further fractured the integration of the Church. A desacralized and clearly pluralist spirit took hold and became loudly and, often rebelliously, asserted. The older structures were called "bare ruined choirs."[31]

With the destruction of this integration, the Church was exposed to a profound crisis of authority at many levels, most notably at the level of allegiance to the teaching and moral authority of the Pope. More than any other sign, the failure of the Pope's authority in the area of family planning and birth-control evidenced the Church in revolution.

The matter of birth-control was crucial and uppermost in the mind of many bishops at the time of the Council. A fateful decision was made when, thinking the question to be so complex and so fraught with turmoil, the Council Fathers agreed with the Pope to remove discussion, debate and decision on the matter from the Vatican Council deliberations. Consequently, the Pastoral

Constitution on the Church in the Modern World
treated the issue by saying only: "Relying on
these principles, sons of the Church may not
undertake methods of regulating procreation which
are found blameworthy by the teaching authority
of the Church in its unfolding of the divine
law."[32]   But this reference included the footnote
which read:

> Certain questions which need further and
> more careful investigation have been
> handed over, at the command of the Supreme
> Pontiff, to a commission for the study of
> population, family, and births, in order
> that, after it fulfills its function, the
> Supreme Pontiff may pass judgment. With
> the doctrine of the magisterium in this
> state, the holy Synod does not intend to
> propose immediately concrete solutions.[33]

On June 23, 1964, Pope Paul established
this special commission to study the issue.   The
commission met in at least five lengthy sessions
over more than a year.   Two distinct viewpoints
emerged, and secret working papers bearing the
contrast of these two views were "leaked" and
published by the National Catholic Reporter.   The
majority of this commission favored a change in
the Church's traditional teaching on birth-control.
In the document of this group, "context theology"
was employed.   The document argued that "this
truly 'contraceptive' mentality and practice has
been condemned by the traditional doctrine of the
church and will always be condemned as gravely
sinful."[34]   It argued further: "The true opposition is not to be sought between some material
conformity to the psychological processes of
nature and some artificial intervention."[35]   On
the basis of this departure from the traditional
deductive method of "natural law," this view
advised:

> "...let couples form a judgment which is
> objectively formed, with all the criteria
> considered.... Well instructed and

prudently educated as Christians,
they will prudently and serenely
decide what is truly for the good of
the couple and of the children, and
does not neglect their own personal
Christian perfection, and is, therefore,
what God revealing himself through the
natural law and Christian revelation, sets
before them to do."36

When the Pastoral Constitution prohibited
regulation of births in ways "which are found
blameworthy," it previously had said "the parents
themselves should ultimately make this judgment
in the sight of God"37 in reference to the size
of the family that was desirable for a married
couple. Bernard Haring wrote that the Vatican
Council "teaches the principle of responsible
parenthood in article 50, in spite of the loud
warning of Cardinal Ottaviani, that by doing so
the Church would also have to change her doctrine
on infallibility."38 He was correct. Ottaviani
was head of the minority report that concluded
that loyalty to the infallible magesterium made
it impossible to do otherwise than prohibit con-
traception altogether. Ottaviani submitted a
further report beyond those of the Commission and
contributed with his theologians to writing the
actual text of Humanae Vitae.39

This encyclical which ignored the context
theology and stressed strict and conservative
orthodoxy, was issued July 29, 1968. The reaction was intense and polarized. A group of
theologians at the Catholic University of America
published a statement denying the binding effect
of the encyclical. Eventually 650 professionals
signed this statement. A noted moralist, once
the Pope's retreat-master, denounced it as "the
product of the closed minds of Vatican functionaries" and he called for the church to "rescue
the Pope from isolation." Numerous priests were
suspended from teaching posts or from their
priesthood for defiance of the encyclical. A
poll in the United States found only twenty-eight

22

out of every 100 Catholics in agreement, and a
survey in Catholic Italy found only thirty-two
out of every 100 in agreement.

Humanae Vitae in the minds and subsequent
experience of innumerable churchmen had the effect
of disenfranchising the ordinary pastor or local
priest from requests by the laity on matters of
sexuality or conjugal love. It was too apparent
that the Church's position was in defense of
tradition and papal infallibility.

A further stage in the outcome of this
crisis of authority occurred even in the midst
of the time the Jesuits met for their Thirty-
Second General Congregation. For during that
period, a censure was pronounced against Hans
Kung, a Swiss priest and theologian (not a Jesuit)
for his recent book which severely questions and
challenges the infallibility of the papacy. In
this and many other respects, the Church has
incurred the loss of obedience and affective
loyalty on the part of a vast number of Catholics
world-wide.

> The Council "demythologized" the Church
> in that it brought about a revolutionary
> change in attitudes for large segments of
> the American Catholic laity. This has
> helped produce current dual crises of
> faith and identity gripping the lives
> of untold numbers of laymen today.[40]

If the loss of integration in the Church
and, of course, the resulting loss of unquestioned
status and prestige to her functionaries, the
priests, was a psychological letdown to the laity,
it was far more so to the ordinary priest, sister,
or seminarian. The members of the Society of
Jesus were themselves facing this crisis. The
Society's own organizational and legislative
apparatus would attempt to handle the task and
to reunite and update its ranks by means of its
Thirty-First General Congregation.

The Thirty-First General Congregation
and Jesuit Renewal

In the course of the third session of Vatican II, on October 5, 1964, Father John Baptist Janssens, superior general of the Society of Jesus, died. Thus the Vicar General, Father John Swain, sent out the announcement of the convocation of the Thirty-First General Congregation.

Nine years had passed since the Thirtieth Congregation, a post-Tridentine kind of Congregation. Although some modernization had been intended, that Congregation was sobered by a harsh, restrictive allocution to the delegates by Pope Pius XII.[41] The Thirty-First General Congregation was the first to be held in the time of Vatican II.

An early indication of the nature of this Congregation is seen in its delaying the election of the General in order to determine whether or not to change the legislation concerning the General's term of office from a life term to one of some specified period of years. This was a concrete specifiable issue which, in its own way, set the tone to much of the deliberations and accomplishments of the First Session of the Congregation.[42] It had the symbolic value, as well, of indicating that "there was a willingness to discuss and a desire that all be free to express their opinions."[43] The Vicar General told the delegates that the Pope himself lifted any restrictions on matters to be discussed and said "let them be free."[44]

Early in the Congregation, the delegates were proposed certain criteria which, considering the state of the society at the time, they might consider in electing the General. The new leader must be discerning and enlightened, striving to overcome class-struggles and national rivalries. Facing the uncertainties of a transition from older forms and the old order to the new, the Society of Jesus and the new General were exhorted

24

to recognize humanity's "deep restlessness" and
"boldly to penetrate these new movements, to
evaluate their widespread hopes in order that the
Divine Will may be made clear to us in this
reordering."[45] A General was asked for who would
keep the Society united to the world, not only by
enlarging or continuing particular works, but
through a vision "fixed on the universal good."
Furthermore:

> At this time above all others, it is the
> Society's most important task to embrace
> freely and uphold strongly this renewal
> of the Church, and with its whole
> strength to work for its increase, re-
> newing itself so as to be readier and
> better equipped to serve Jesus Christ
> in his Church.[46]

Aware of the difficulty of the times and the
transition, it was said that "we expect our
Father General to assist the whole Society and
each of her children to enter deeply into that
mystery of death which brings fulfillment, so
that we will be able in the difficult circumstances of today to bring a salvation to the
world...."[47]

The Congregation elected Father Pedro
Arrupe as Superior General. He was a fifty-seven
year old Spaniard, from the same Basque territory
as Saint Ignatius Loyola. His training had been
world-wide and his apostolic work centered in Asia.
For ten years previous to his election, he was
Provincial to Japan. His sentiments coincided
with those of the Congregation.

The thrust of the Congregation was renewal.
Its inspiration and atmosphere were the Second
Vatican Council. It asserted its resolve in this
direction in the first decree, situating itself
with the Church in a "new age." The Congregation
resolved, for the Society:

...to take a very close look at its own

> nature and mission in order that,
> faithful to its own vocation, it can
> renew itself and adapt its life and its
> activities to the exigencies of the
> Church and the needs of contemporary
> man.[48]

The documents are replete with citations from the documents of Vatican II. The Council is cited in footnotes 200 times. Most often cited is _Perfectae Caritatis: Decree on the Adaptation and Renewal of Religious Life_, next most often cited is _Lumen Gentium: Dogmatic Constitution on the Church_ and the 1966 Moto Proprio _Ecclesiae Sanctae_. The two decrees on priesthood, _Presbyterorum Ordinis: Decree on the Ministry and Life of Priests_, and _Optatam Totius: Decree on Priestly Formation_ are often cited. _Gaudium et Spes: Pastoral Constitution on the Church in the Modern World_ and _Ad Gentes: Decree on the Church's Missionary Activity_ are also often cited. Clearly, beyond the cited references to the Vatican Council, the entire inspiration and acceptance of the revolution implied by it are present and operative in this General Congregation.

The resolves and documentation, however, manifest an anxiety and anguish underneath. The Society was suffering through changes and many Jesuits were likely to lose heart. There was actually a crisis of identity for many. Both within the Congregation and in the communities of the Society, a clear resounding sign of hope for the future was badly needed. To a certain extent at the Congregation this need was met in the person of the man they had elected as leader of the whole Society.

The influence of Father Arrupe as General was evident from the very start. His boundless energies and enthusiasm are noted in several discussions of the Congregation. In his first address as General, he spoke of change - in society, the Church, the Jesuits. He called for

26

sincerity, objectivity, insight, courage and
liberty of spirit. He insisted that Jesuits must
discriminate the lasting from the transitory, the
essential from that which is subject to change.
He faced the faults of the Society and likened
the times to the sixteenth century in which St.
Ignatius founded the Society.

He decried the lack of enthusiasm and con-
fidence shown by many. "Often enough they say
'I cannot advise our students to enter the
Society.' These are indeed very sad words!"[49]

In vivid contrast to hesitancy about the
Society's future, the General urged that the
Society present a new image to its young men.

This indeed is the most serious business
of our Congregation; to distill all the
good contained in the numerous proposals
and requests of our young men and to
properly channel that force and dynamism.
This is an absolute necessity. We are
dealing with a biological or social law
which is irresistible. We should not
try to resist it unless we wish to bring
complete upheaval.[50]

In this time of uncertainty there had
developed within the Jesuit communities world-wide
a generation gap. The changes prescribed by the
Congregation for the formation of the young could
only intensify the differences between young and
old. The option taken by the General, and
ratified in much legislation by the Congregation,
was in full support of change and complete alliance with the younger side of the Society.
This is the most important decision of the Thirty-
First General Congregation, and its effects are
seen most significantly in its legislation on
formation and on Province Congregations.

The major contribution of the decree on
formation from this Congregation was to remove
much of the structure which would have otherwise

27

prohibited a real adaptation to changing times and the modern world. The Congregation gave a set of broad principles requiring implementation in diverse situations. It called for much experimentation at the local level. Five distinct decrees dealt with areas of formation.

The documents ask for emotional balance, self-acceptance, trust and freedom in contrast to traditional exhortations to self-denial and mortification. It is explicitly stated that novices and scholastics need leeway in order to gain responsibility. They must be allowed to make mistakes rather than be totally controlled. "Sufficient social contact" (both within and outside the Society) was explicitly demanded. Instead of a rarified atmosphere for beginners, the novitiate is to be conducted according "to the manner of life proper to the Society."[51] New experiments, i.e., tasks to give and evaluate experience, which fulfill the purpose of letting all novices exhibit "what they really are" ..."ought to be prudently and boldly pursued."[52]

In the course of studies, learning, spiritual growth and apostolic action were to be combined and integrated. Training in the emotions, with the advice of psychologists, was called for. Individual talents must be stimulated. True dialogue between superiors, faculty, and students should occur.

Extensive revision of the curricula was demanded. Methods were to be changed, hours lessened, private tutorial courses encouraged, segregated courses for brighter students no longer mandatory, final oral exams shortened. Furthermore, technology was to be taken account of, the positive sciences to be learned, foreign study encouraged, and schools located in urban centers instead of secluded countryside locations. Diversity and adaptation, trademarks of the Jesuit Order but absent from prior structures of formation, were now desirable and legislated.

> Our teaching should faithfully adhere
> to what "was once given to the holy men
> of the faith" (Jude 3), and should be
> such that, accommodating itself to diverse
> cultures of the whole world, it can
> continually revivify that faith in the
> hearts of men.[53]

The second matter of definite change of
structures favorable to the younger Jesuits was
the change in legislation concerning eligibility
for participation in Province Congregations. The
Province Congregations are the threshhold to the
General Congregations; they prepare for it, present postulates to it, and most importantly,
designate the delegates other than the Provincial
who will attend and be empowered as Society-wide
legislators at the General Congregation.

The Provincial Congregation was originally
intended to be comprised of "all the professed
who can come, the superiors of the house, the
rectors of colleges, and the procurators, or
those whom they send in their place."[54] The Fifth
General Congregation, which met in 1593, limited
the composition of the Province Congregations to
all Provincials and all local superiors appointed
by Rome with the addition of enough members of
the Province chosen strictly according to
seniority to form a group of forty members.
Thus, only the oldest members of the Province
would rule on who would represent the Province
at the General Congregation and what postulates
would be submitted in the Province's name. The
legislation of 1593 remained intact until this
Thirty-First General Congregation.

This Congregation legislated that participants in the Provincial Congregations were to be
elected by Province vote. Half the members had
to be "professed of four vows," i.e., the top
grade in the Order. No seniority rule applied.
Brothers were eligible to attend. The Provincial
and Rectors attended ex officio. This legislation
- as the Thirty-Second General Congregation would

29

clearly illustrate - insured a broader representation of Jesuits and thus encouraged a younger
delegation and more liberal set of postulata as
constitutive of future General Congregations.

An important decision was made on the issue
of the "substantials" of the Institute. The
matter of "substantials" concerns the strategy
of protecting and preserving the character of the
Order.

> Here, as in many other instances in the
> Congregation, the serious differences
> became apparent in the way two groups
> approached the problem of preserving
> the genuine spirit of the Society, an
> overriding goal to which both subscribed.
> Briefly, some would find solution in
> fidelity to documents and to legal pre-
> cedents; others would find it in the
> study of and adaptation to concrete con-
> temporary circumstances.[55]

After long discussion in both sessions, the
General Congregation stated: the "Congregation
can declare the meaning of the Substantials."
Regarding non-substantials, "the Constitutions
can and sometimes should be changed by the
General Congregation," and that it is the Congregation's duty "to provide for the continuing
adaptation of them to the needs of the times,"
(decree 4).[56]

The Congregation went on to use this power
when they definitively stated the substance of
one of the most historically thorny questions of
the Society, that of Poverty. All Professed
Jesuits take a life-long vow never to relax the
statutes and matter of Jesuit poverty. But am-
biguities have abounded in the interpretation of
the vow. This Congregation boldly asserted its
new prerogative to define the substance of that
vow in completely unequivocal terms. The Congregation also opened an entirely new category of
interpretation of the style of living the vow of

poverty by declaring that "gain from or remuneration for work done according to the Institute is a legitimate source of material goods which are necessary for the life and apostolate of Jesuits."57

Another consequence of the spirit of reform and renewal in this Congregation was the vast attention paid to "the Better Choice and Promotion of Ministries." The Congregation stated that despite the hard work of Jesuits, the labour has not produced "all the results that we could rightly expect." It called for the renewal of works, increase of flexibility in tasks undertaken and assignments made, new kinds of cooperation, and acceptance of regular and effective processes for continual renewal and adaptation of apostolic work. It instituted in every Province of the world the structure of a "Commission for Promoting the Better Choice of Ministries." This structure served in the tumultuous years that immediately followed as the vehicle to instigate, legitimate and effectively accomplish significant changes in personnel placement and kinds of work pursued by Jesuits in various local situations.

One issue that met with great controversy in both the first and second session of this General Congregation was the matter of grades in the Society. Presently there is a hierarchy of membership in the Jesuit Order. The highest echelon, which consists of between one-third and two-fifths of all the priests, is the level of the Professed of Four Vows. The second echelon, conceived of in name as helpers to the Professed in spiritual matters, is the grade of Spiritual Coadjutors, who are priests with last vows but not professed. This consists of more than half of all the priests. Another echelon is that of approved scholastics, namely scholastics already ordained but not yet in final vows. They comprise about one-fifth of the priests; whether these will be admitted to the grade of Professed or not is a decision considered particularly "weighty" and made by the Provincial and his consultors.

31

Another echelon is the grade of temporal Coadjutors (or Brothers); this consists of men who
have entered the Jesuits without the intention of
being ordained. The unordained scholastics and
the brothers not yet in final vows comprise the
echelon of Jesuits in formation.

Practically the argument concerned whether
there should be a grade of Spiritual Coadjutor.
Many argued that the grades were discriminatory
and should be done away with. The controversy
was resolved in a three-fold action; first the
decision not to abolish the grades, second, the
reworking of the criteria for granting Profession,
and third, a two paragraph decree asking that a
commission should be set up to "study the whole
matter of suppressing the grade of spiritual
coadjutors, either in law or in practice" and if
need be to convoke another General Congregation
to finally decide the issue. The second paragraph
recommends that the same commission consider extending solemn profession to the temporal Coadjutors.[58] Unknown to the delegates of the
Thirty-First General Congregation, their specification of this issue for a later General Congregation would bring the matter of highest controversy and crisis before the Thirty-Second General
Congregation.

Of lasting impact was the matter of an
allocution by Pope Paul VI to the delegates. In
this address, the Pope imposed a new concern, a
new "mission," upon the Jesuit Order in virtue
of the special relationship that professed
Jesuits have through their vow of obedience to
the Pope in regard to missions. The Pope declared
that the fight against atheism was the new mission
of the Society. He stated:

The most terrible form of atheism is
that which is wickedly aggressive not
only in denying the existence of God
in theory and practice, but in deliberately using its weapons to destroy
at the roots all sense of religion and

32

all that is holy and pius.... It is
the special task of the Society of
Jesus to defend religion and holy
Church in the most tragic times. We
entrust to it the charge of opposing
atheism with its total, concentrated
effort, under the protection of Saint
Michael, the prince of the heavenly
hosts.[59]

The manner in which this mandate was accepted by the Society is an instance of "context
theologizing." This is evident from the more
universalistic tone of the document to combat
atheism that the Congregation wrote. This same
tone is evident in a press conference on the subject given by Father General. He explained:

Atheism is in fact one of our basic
and gravest problems. This is true
for all the faithful, but especially
for us and for all whose vocation is
apostolic. The Pope's call must make
us direct our efforts to believers as
well as unbelievers. There are no
believers today whose faith is not
tested by the great problems set by
the rapid evolution of the world, of
science, and of society. We must help
the faithful to understand and purify
their faith, to resist better the
temptations of our times, and we must
draw closer to unbelievers than in the
past, to help them to overcome the pre-
judice which keeps them from the faith....
We must, for pastoral reasons, try to
penetrate the mind of the modern atheist,
and look for the motives of his confu-
sions and denials. They will prove to
be manifold and complex. A better
knowledge of them will make us more
prudent in our judgments and more effective in our work.[60]

Another element that heavily burdened the

delegates in the second session was a distressing relationship with the Holy See. The Pope found fault with the Society of Jesus. The content of the Pope's message to the Congregation - reported on September 21, 1966, two weeks into the second session - is secret. One account says only this:

> From the reports coming from the nuncios and apostolic delegates throughout the whole world, the Pope gave the General a sketch of the image which the Society projects at present, and this image needs serious retouching.... For a quarter of an hour, the General exposed for us, point by point, what the Pope had told him.[61]

The "fault finding" continued in terms of "clouds on the horizon" that the Pope made reference to in his closing allocution to the delegates of the Congregation. In this talk, along with expressions of devotion and confidence, the Pope "noted certain rumours that he had detected relative to the possible loss of the spirit of obedience handed down by the founder of the Society of Jesus."[62]

> Pope Paul spoke of "arbitrary novelty," "free and irresponsible initiatives," of substitution "for sure doctrines, new theories and conceptions that are personal and arbitrary," "the changeable and worldly current opinions of our time," "historically relativist adaptations and subjective interpretations." "One cannot," he declared, "demolish a Church of yesterday to build a new one today."[63]

In various ages, the Holy See has reprimanded the Society of Jesus. The most severe sanction was the suppression of the Society which lasted from 1773 until 1814. The gist of criticism has more often than not been for positions of a "liberal" slant, of certain

34

innovations and intellectual currents of thought
that challenge orthodoxy and tradition and structure. This was again the nature of the complaints
and reprimand made during the Thirty-First
General Congregation.

In a letter from Father General Pedro Arrupe,
dated July 31, 1965, two weeks after the closing
of the first session of the Congregation, he
quotes the Holy Father:

> Obedience will be expected of you, even
> when the reason for the command is not
> given, for your obedience is "like that
> of a dead body." But remember that Our
> esteem for you and Our trust are no less
> for that.[64]

This position would also be tested again in the
Thirty-Second General Congregation.

The remainder of the documents extend the
spirit of Vatican II into other concerns of
Jesuit life. They legitimated change in many
areas and fostered exploration and evaluation of
other areas with a view to future changes. Again,
they do this particularly in the cultural sphere.
"The documents are fundamentally pastoral, not
concerned with the passing of laws, but with the
renewal of spirit."[65]

The entire text of the documents is a book
of 122 pages in length, made up of fifty-two
decrees. The two longest decrees are on the
"Spiritual Formation of Jesuits" and the "Training
of Scholastics." There are seventeen decrees on
the apostolates, including specific decrees on
the Vatican radio station, the Arts, scholarly
work, and the "Social Apostolate" (a two-page
decree).

A striking contrast in the list of decrees
is that between the profoundly inspiring, relevant and ideational decrees on the one hand, and
the picayune, passing and insignificant decrees

on the other. Both are published side by side;
the revolutionary documents on formation along
with those on "Reading At Table" (now a defunct
custom) and a five line decree on "Journeys by
Missionaries."

This specificity is something of an indicator of what "used to be." It suggests that the
full transformation of the Society away from its
Post-Tridentine structures had not yet been
accomplished. The grander documents were un-
mistakable movements towards the transformation
of thought, culture, and tradition.

Summary and Conclusions

The Catholic Church was exposed to attempts
at innovation at various times since 1800. But
conservative government in the fashion of the
Council of Trent and the First Vatican Council
stifled these attempts. Structures of orthodoxy
and tradition prevailed over any ideas of momen-
tous change.

The Second Vatican Council reversed this.
Inspired by Pope John XXIII, it instituted revolutionary changes. A post-Conciliar culture
of adaptation and change developed and prevailed.
This culture fractured many prior structures and
dominated the Church. The demise of much piety,
mystique, and authoritarianism resulted. As an
ideational forum adapting the context of Catholic
doctrine, this Council accommodated the Church
to a rationalized, non-sectarian world in many
ways.

The Thirty-First General Congregation instituted these changes and undertook this accommodation for the Society of Jesus. It thoroughly
reflected the inspiration and modern directions
of Vatican II and had the power among Jesuits to
implement them in actual routines.

36

The mood of _aggiornamento_, abandonment of past restrictions, and high recruitment of new members were conditions that combined to arouse strong support of young Jesuits by this Congregation. Both formation and eligibility to Jesuit legislature were changed drastically in their favor. These changes momentously influenced the following decade and the next Congregation.

The Congregation elected Pedro Arrupe as General of the Society of Jesus. He cultivated adaptation and experimentation and personally encouraged a movement of social action and the struggle against social injustice. He enunciated Jesuit values in flexible, more generalized terms and exacted the qualifications for renewal from a Society-wide examination of "how we may penetrate more deeply into Ignatian principles and free the Society from those things which can be a barrier to its more effective work."[66]

Commissions were set up and granted legitimacy for revamping Jesuit ministries. Revered activities lost their following and the traditional basis they relied upon diminished. Unprecedented activities flourished with "experimental" sanction.

The Congregation made practical and unequivocal declarations regarding poverty and the substantials of the Institute replacing more religiously pleasing but vague formulas. Remuneration for work was given value equal to living from alms. The hierarchy of grades was challenged and a study geared to their transformation was inaugurated.

The Pope's mandate to fight atheism was accepted in a broader, more modern sense and his criticism for novelty had been preceded by the judgment that the substantials of the Institute were rightly changeable.

Amidst this revamping, novelty, and passing of old forms, painful upheaval, critical disbelief,

37

and relative deprivation variously stunned the
entire Jesuit Order. Over six thousand Jesuits
left the Society. Many others grew confused and
sorrowful. A decade of religious revolution
necessarily took its toll. Nevertheless, the
changes turned out by the Thirty-First General
Congregation provided the threads for a new
fabric of the Society of Jesus. Out of these
same unbroken threads, to quote a remark of the
Father General, the contributions of the Thirty-
Second General Congregation would be woven.

Footnotes

[1]This figure represents the total of all
Jesuits at the beginning of 1975. Source:
Supplementum Catalogorum Societatis Jesu: 1976
Romae, Apud Curiam Praepositi Generalis, 15 IUL.
1975, p. 10.

[2]Ibid.

[3]Thirty-Second General Congregation Society
of Jesus Press Pack, Rome, Society of Jesus Press
and Information Office, 1974, p. 78.

[4]Ibid.

[5]The Jesuit Conference, Documents of the
Thirty-Second General Congregation of the Society
of Jesus: An English Translation, Washington,
D.C., Jesuit Conference, 1975, p. 141. (hereafter
referred to as Documents: 32 GC.

[6]Thomas F. O'Dea, The Catholic Crisis,
Boston, Beacon Press, 1968, p. 54.

[7]Ibid., p. 61.

[8]Ibid., p. 76.

[9]Quoted in O'Dea, p. 78.

[10]Ibid.

[11]Ibid., p. 89.

[12]Kurt Lewin "Chapter 1, The Conflict
Between Aristotelian and Galileian Modes of
Thought in Contemporary Psychology" in A
Dynamic Theory of Personality, New York, McGraw-
Hill, 1935, pp. 1-42.

[13]Bernard Lonergan, S.J., in "Chapter 16,
Dimensions of Meaning" in Collection: Papers by
Bernard Lonergan, S.J., edited by F.E. Crowe, S.J.,
New York, Herder and Herder, 1967, p. 259.

[14]Bernard Lonergan, S.J., "The Response of the Jesuit, as Priest and Apostle, in the Modern World" in <u>Studies in the Spirituality of Jesuits</u>, Vol. II, No. 3 (September, 1970), p. 106.

[15]Pope Paul VI, "Papal Brief Declaring the Council Completed" in Walter M. Abbott, S.J., <u>The Documents of Vatican II</u>, New York, Guild Press et al, 1966, pp. 738-739.

[16]Andrew M. Greeley, "Myths, Meaning and Vatican II" in <u>America</u>, December 19, 1970, p. 538.

[17]<u>Ibid</u>.

[18]Greeley, "Myths, Meaning and Vatican II," pp. 538-542, passim.

[19]O'Dea, p. 18.

[20]<u>Ibid</u>., pp. 123-124.

[21]Rock Caporale, S.J., <u>Vatican II: Last of the Councils</u>, Baltimore, Helicon Press, 1964, p. 38, 42.

[22]<u>Ibid</u>., p. 82.

[23]<u>Ibid</u>., p. 87.

[24]<u>Ibid</u>.

[25]<u>Ibid</u>., p. 90.

[26]<u>Ibid</u>., p. 133.

[27]Karl Rahner, <u>The Church After the Council</u>, New York, Herder and Herder, 1956, pp. 19-20.

[28]Douglas J. Roche, <u>The Catholic Revolution</u>, New York, David McKay Company, Inc., 1968, pp. XV-XVL.

[29]<u>Ibid</u>., XV.

[30]The Official Catholic Directory: Anno Domini 1975, (1965), New York, P.J. Kennedy and Sons, 1975, "General Summary," pp. 1-4.

[31]Garry Wills, Bare Ruined Choirs: Doubt, Prophecy and Radical Religion, Garden City, N.Y., Doubleday Company, 1972.

[32]Vatican II Documents, p. 256.

[33]Ibid.

[34]The Birth Control Debate: Interim History from the Pages of National Catholic Reporter, edited by Robert C. Hoyt, Kansas City, National Catholic Reporter, 1968, p. 88.

[35]Ibid., pp. 90-91.

[36]Ibid., p. 95.

[37]Pastoral Constitution on the Church in the Modern World Article 50, in Vatican II Documents, p. 254.

[38]Bernard Haring, CSsR, "Marriage and the Family" in John H. Nuller, CSsR, ed., Vatican II: An Interfaith Appraisal, International Theological Conference, University of Notre Dame, March 20-26, 1966 (Notre Dame, Indiana, University of Notre Dame Press, 1966), p. 443.

[39]The Birth Control Debate, p. 23.

[40]Donald J. Thorman, "Today's Layman: An Uncertain Catholic," in America, January 14, 1967, pp. 39-40.

[41]John W. Padberg, S.J. "The General Congregations of the Society of Jesus: A Brief Survey of their History" in Studies in the Spirituality of Jesuits, Vol. VI, Nos. 1 and 2, January and March, 1974, pp. 70-71.

[42]Edward J. Sponga, S.J., "The General

Congregation: Its Atmosphere and Hopes" in
Woodstock Letters, Fall, 1965, pp. 396-406.

[43]Ibid., pp. 398-399.

[44]George E. Ganss, S.J., "Impressions of the
31st General Congregation" in Woodstock Letters,
Fall, 1965, p. 381.

[45]Reverend Maurice Guiliani, "Sermon delivered at election day Mass, May 22, 1965,"
quoted in "Thirty-First General Congregation:
The First Session," edited by James P. Jurich,
S.J., in Woodstock Letters, Vol. 95, #1, Winter,
1966, pp. 11-13.

[46]Ibid., p. 12.

[47]Ibid., p. 13.

[48]"The Mission of the Society of Jesus
Today" in Documents of the Thirty-First General
Congregation, Woodstock, Maryland, Woodstock
College, 1967, p. 5.

[49]James P. Jurich, editor, "Thirty-First
General Congregation: The First Session" in
Woodstock Letters, Vol. 95, #1, Winter, 1966,
p. 16.

[50]Ibid., pp. 16-17.

[51]"The Spiritual Formation of Jesuits" in
Documents of the Thirty-First General Congregation, p. 23.

[52]Ibid.

[53]"The Training of Scholastics Especially
in Studies," in Documents of the Thirty-First
General Congregation, p. 34.

[54]Saint Ignatius of Loyola, The Constitution
of the Society of Jesus, translated by George
Ganss, S.J., Saint Louis, The Institute of Jesuit

Sources, 1970, p. 296.

[55]John W. Padberg, S.J., "The General Congregation of the Society of Jesus: A Brief Survey of their History," p. 83.

[56]Ibid.

[57]"Poverty" in Documents of the Thirty-First General Congregation, p. 60.

[58]"The Distinction of Grades" in Documents of the Thirty-First General Congregation, p. 15.

[59]"The Jesuits in the Post-Conciliar Era: The Thirty-First General Congregation and the New General" in Herder Correspondence, November, 1965, pp. 356-357.

[60]Ibid., p. 357.

[61]James J. Jurich, S.J., editor, "The 31st General Congregation: Letters from the Second Session" in Woodstock Letters, 1968, September 21, 1965, p. 28.

[62]Edward J. Sponga, "Jesuits Face the Future," in America, February 11, 1967, p. 209.

[63]"Editorials - Pope and Jesuits: Invitation and Response," in America, December 3, 1966, p. 729.

[64]Pope Paul VI to the members of the Society of Jesus quoted by Reverend Pedro Arrupe, S.J. in "A Letter of Very Reverend Father General to the Whole Society on the 31st General Congregation," reprinted in Woodstock Letters, Vol. 94, Fall, 1965, p. 370.

[65]Edward J. Sponga, "Jesuits Face the Future," p. 209.

[66]Jurich, "The 31st General Congregation: The First Session," p. 16.

CHAPTER TWO

RENEWAL IN THE PRESENT DAY AND THE

THIRTY-SECOND GENERAL CONGREGATION

Chapter One portrayed the changing Church prior to, during, and after Vatican II. The Jesuit response to that Council, the Thirty-First General Congregation, was also discussed. This chapter will recount the interim period between that Congregation and its successor, and then concentrate on the latter, and its impact on modernization. Its sources are those mentioned in the previous chapter.

The Thirty-First General Congregation channeled the atmosphere and changes demanded by a Vatican II mentality to the Jesuit Order. The activities and reactions, the initiatives and their implementation, the enthusiasm and chagrin, progress and setbacks of these eight years affected the Society's ranks as profound reform and renewal. But there was also a crisis of staggering proportions.

To understand the crisis, it is necessary to understand the Jesuit role in the Church and the history of Catholicism. The Post-Tridentine Church was based on the model of the Jesuits of the Counter-Reformation.

(It) is undeniable that the "Tridentine era" of the Church was greatly dominated by the Jesuit spirit and organization (unless one wishes to say that the Tridentine Church found its most marked and congenial expression in the Jesuit Order). The centralization of the Order, with its tightly knit chain of command depending on the one general superior in Rome, was to become the general pattern of all modern congregations of religious.... But above all, in their pastoral, educational and

theological work in Europe and their vast
mission fields, it was the Jesuits who
were in a large measure the instruments
of the Church in the Counter-Reformation
which formed Catholics in the spirit and
discipline of Trent.[1]

If the Post-Tridentine Church had to pass
away, something of what was the Society of Jesus
had to pass away as well. If the meaning and
symbols of that Church had to fade, those same
meanings and symbols as characteristic of the
Jesuits had to fade and yield to new forms. The
time of transition for both Church and Society
has been turbulent, transforming and difficult.
But it was occasioned by demands of the time that
had to be met.

It is the challenge to move one - without
loss of essential identity - from the
attitudes, style and institutions suited
to the post-Tridentine age to the attitudes,
style and institutions of a radically new
world. No one can guarantee that so demanding and agonizing a transition will be
successfully carried out.... But we would
not be Jesuits - or Christians - if we did
not feel a certain zest for this adventure
we share with the whole contemporary
Church.[2]

The crisis would be "a proof of special
vitality and sensibility;" since when the rest of
the world was undergoing the turbulence of change,
the Society would have to be irrelevant to be
immune to it. "If in a time of peace and of
general enlightenment we were the only ones to
have problems, there would be cause for alarm;
but if we share in the problems of all, then with
all we must humbly seek the solution."[3]

The changes in the Jesuits involved legitimacy and integration. Regimentation gave way to
adaptability, or at least to uncertainty, compromise and experimentation. Social boundaries

and definitions of in-group and out-group changed. Along with them, situations and relations of power changed. The right of seniority gave way to the right of youthful potential.

Candidates for the appointments to Provincial were literally hand-picked by the General and his counsultors. They were scrutinized for the qualifications of "penetrating more deeply into Ignatian principles" and being able to help to "free the Society from all those things which can be a barrier to its more effective work." Consequently, leadership positions became increasingly filled with younger men.

The direction of power in practice then became a definite two-way process. The younger men could not rule as the older ones had, for the shift from older to younger entailed a shift in major values. The older form of authority went out with the older authoritarian Church.

Other changes caused strain and collapse in the Society's integration. Most Jesuits experienced crisis of one sort or another. The crises of belief, of authority, of identity all added to disintegration. Over and over again it was said of one sector in the Society by another, "I just cannot understand them" or "This is not the Society I joined." Between 1966 and 1974, more than 1,500 already ordained priests left the priesthood and the Society while the total number of Jesuits declined by 6,500 men. At the same time, the number of new recruits dropped to one-third its previous rate.

To counteract this malaise, various mechanisms of integration were instituted. Many new modes of communication were tried and either abandoned or adopted in Provinces throughout the world. The Thirty-First General Congregation is responsible for the creation of an information office in the Jesuit headquarters. The former General, Father Janssens, and the present General set up secretariats to facilitate communication

47

in various sectors. Correspondence, newsletters, historical studies of the Jesuits, seminars, theological renovations, conferences, group dynamic weekends, retreats, projects of innumerable kinds flourished.

Shortly after the Thirty-First General Congregation ended, Father General announced a world-wide "Sociological Survey." Thereafter, between 1966 and 1969, every Jesuit Province in the world was ordered to undertake a sociological investigation of its organization and services. Academic departments, management consultants, survey research units, innumerable methods and operations were marshalled one way and another to examine the state of the Society. In the United States alone, one hundred and forty sizeable research studies were compiled in a five volume report issued for Rome.[4] In a summary of the volume on research studies, John L. Thomas offered the following conclusion:

> The basic problems we are currently experiencing in the Society of Jesus stem from lack of agreement regarding the fundamental beliefs and rationales underlying our assumptions, values, attitudes, and practices relating to religious life. Research studies can reveal some of the dimensions of this lack of agreement, but only a profound, concerned, and continued rethinking of these beliefs and rationales can provide basis for the unity and consensus required for survival.[5]

A further instrument intended as integrative of the Jesuits was the elaborate preparation devised for the Thirty-Second General Congregation. This intent was indicated to the Congregation of Procurators in 1971 by Father General. He stated:

> It is not this next Congregation which will have the greatest importance in our spiritual and apostolic renovation; rather it is the renovation of the Society and

48

the apostolic zeal of all its members
which should lead up to a congregation
capable of giving new expression to the
primitive charism.... This Thirty-
Second General Congregation should be
nothing more than the final, juridical
expression of all the work of the provinces
and of the communal reflection of all
their members on the best means of assuring our spiritual and apostolic renewal.[6]

The deliberate manner of proceeding for the
entire preparatory stage of the Congregation bore
this intention out. It included Father General's
Christmas message of 1971 on "Communal Spiritual
Discernment." The head of the Preparatory Commission called for a "special effort of spiritual
preparation" addressing all Jesuits on May 2,
1972. Studies were pursued in all communities
revolving around fundamental integrative themes;
namely, The Vocation and Mission of the Society
of Jesus, Apostolic Service Today, and Jesuit
Religious and Community Life. Father General
asked that 1973 be considered by all Jesuits a
"Year of the Constitutions" and that all Jesuits
should "through study and meditation, strive to
rediscover the basic intuitions of the Ignatian
Constitutions."[7]

Therefore, the Thirty-Second General Congregation was inaugurated with the purpose given
all general congregations in the Constitutions by
Saint Ignatius, namely, to effect the "union of
persons" in the Society. ("Our Constitutions, in
fact, speak of the general congregations in the
section that treats of 'union' and not in the
section on 'government.'")[8] It was intended to
create "a profound spiritual interchange," to
serve as "the center of convergence of a vast
network of exchanges."[9]

In appraising the work and success of this
integrative mechanism served by the preparatory
stage, the head of that commission stated:

> Balance was constantly difficult to main-
> tain between the freedom of expression
> that was necessary and taking over direc-
> tion so as to bring out the imcompati-
> bility of such or such a proposal with
> certain essential aspects of our kind of
> life. Too much direction would compromise
> full and sincere participation. Too little
> direction would give to some the impression
> that authority did not contradict, or even
> that it favored, proposals which were un-
> acceptable...[10]

That the procedure was arduous and not entirely
an unmitigated success can be inferred from the
additional remark:

> Let us add in the same vein that it would not
> be a healthy procedure to expose a religious
> order too often to such a trial. To go this
> far was possible only for a general congre-
> gation of a rather exceptional character,
> one intended to transact its business at a
> particularly crucial moment in the life of
> the Church.[11]

Church officials at the Vatican and some
discontented Jesuits were not always ready and
willing to bear the uncertainty and contradictory
currents that such a process of integration entailed. Clearly, the bad publicity and wide-
ranging liberality of some of the voiced opinions
and positions of open dialogue upset Vatican officials and constituted another definite feature
of the upcoming Congregation.

One week after Father General announced the
convocation of the Thirty-Second General Congregation on September 8, 1973, a letter in response
was sent from the Pope to Father General and,
through him, to all of the Society. The letter
was written "to encourage you and to send you Our
best wishes for a happy outcome to the Congregation."[12]

50

The Holy Father expressed his happiness over the Society "making a great effort...to adapt its life and its apostolate to the needs of today's world," and found that adaptation corresponding to the norms of the Second Vatican Council. The Pope added:

Nor are We ignorant of the fact that over the past few years in several parts of the Society - and it is by no means absent either from the life of the Church in general - certain tendencies have arisen of an intellectual and disciplinary nature which, if fostered and given support, could lead to serious and possibly irreparable changes in the essential structure itself of your Society.[13]

The tone of this letter did not escape the world's press. Many newspapers emphasized the negative aspects of the letter rehearsing again the negative elements in various other correspondence from the Vatican to the Jesuits. It was pointed out that this letter was part of a growing friction. As Time magazine analyzed it:

Many conservative Jesuits have protested that during Arrupe's nine-year reign the order has been disintegrating, particularly in discipline and in loyalty to the Pope's teachings. In addition, Cardinal Villot (The Vatican Secretary of State) and his aides have passed on to the Pope complaints of conservative bishops throughout the world who were upset by the social radicalism of some of the Jesuits operating in their sees.

To embarrass Arrupe, Curia conservatives leaked several confidential dressing-down letters from the Pope to the Jesuit Superior General. The conflict erupted in public in the fall of 1973, when Villot's office prepared a letter about the forthcoming Congregation that Pope Paul sent

51

to Arrupe.   In it, the Pope urged Arrupe
to end the permissiveness of recent years.[14]

The political machinations of this period
were much discussed in the Press, and to some
extent, sensationalized.   Nevertheless they indicated an important aspect to the situation the
General and this Congregation would face.   To
some extent, at least, the latent purpose of the
Thirty-Second General Congregation was for the
Society to take a reading of support and vote of
confidence or non-confidence in their General.

The Constitutions of the Society of Jesus
specify the purpose of any General Congregation:

1.   ...on some occasions, a general congregation will be necessary, for
example, for the election of a
general...

2.   The second occasion arises when it
is necessary to deal with long-
lasting and important matters, as
would be the suppression or trans-
ference of houses or colleges, or
with other very difficult matters
pertaining to the whole body of the
Society or its manner of proceeding,
for the greater service to God our
Lord.[15]

Twenty-four of the thirty-two general con-
gregations were called to elect a new general.
One was called by a Congregation of Procurators
in 1608.   Three were called by mandate of the
Pope, usually for his own political reasons.
Three others were called by elderly or sick
Generals who wanted Vicars to aid them in govern-
ing the Order.   In 1923, the General, Father
Wlodmir Ledochowski, convoked the Twenty-Seventh
General Congregation in order to adapt the Jesuit
Constitutions to the newly revised code of Canon
Law.[16]   Therefore, the Thirty-Second General Con-
gregation was extraordinary as convoked by a

living General in good health. In convoking the
Congregation, Father Arrupe said:

> We must bend every effort to assure that
> the Congregation be for the Society an
> occasion to rediscover its own task under
> the guidance of the Holy Spirit and then
> to spend itself in the greatest service
> of God and of the Church "under the Roman
> Pontiff" and "for the salvation of souls."[17]

The Thirty-Second General Congregation

On the morning of December 2, 1974, two
hundred and thirty-six Jesuits convened at the
General Headquarters of the Society of Jesus in
a large rectangular room known as the "Aula" for
the beginning of the Thirty-Second General Congregation. It began by Father General referring
to it as an "hour of decision" and saying "I can
affirm that the greatest decision of my generalate
has been to convoke the General Congregation."[18]
The General spoke of "concrete, practical decisions" that had to be made concerning the interior
state of the Jesuits, the Jesuits in relation to
the world, and solutions to problems of Jesuit
spirituality, formation and structures.

The Congregation began with three days of
reflection and attention to the spiritual ramifi-
cations of the even. Father General gave three
talks which dealt with the themes of "the challenge of the world and the mission of the Society," "the guidance of the Holy Spirit," and "God
alone as our hope."

On the second day of the Congregation,
December 3, 1974, the delegates were received in
special audience by Pope Paul VI who delivered
an address to the delegates concerning the Congregation. The address was an even mixture of
encouragement and concern. It revolved around
three questions: Where do you come from, who are

53

you, and where are you going? The Pope answered
the first question in terms of the history of the
Order and the Order's founder. He answered the
second question as he had in the letter of 1973:
"You are members of an Order that is religious,
apostolic, priestly, and united with the Roman
Pontiff by a special bond of love and service, in
the manner described in the Formula of the
Institute."[19] In constant references to the
Formula of the Institute, the Pope insisted that
"This image must not be altered; it must not be
distorted."[20] The Pope asked near closing the
address that the Congregation "restate the essential elements of the Jesuit vocation," and
said that he would follow the Congregation with
"most lively interest."[21] During the Congregation the minutes of the sessions and the GC News
were delivered regularly to the offices of the
Secretary of State of the Vatican.

Over 1,000 postulata or requests had been
submitted to the Congregation. A task-force of
five delegates had assembled two weeks early to
organize procedures. They drafted a list of
forty-eight headings "that summarized or synthe-
sized the contents of the postulata."[22] From
reports of a series of small group meetings, in
twelve Assistancy groups and eighteen "Language
Circles," the delegates indicated which of these
forty-eight topics were most important. These
were: (1) criteria or directions for apostolates,
(2) the mission of the Society, (3) poverty, (4)
the promotion of justice, (5) the nature of formal
membership in the Society, i.e., the issue of
"grades," (6) the special vow of obedience to the
Pope, (7) the education of young Jesuits and (8)
spiritual facets of Jesuit community life.

When voting upon the priority of these
topics, the assembly was confronted with a crucial
decision. Many postulata had proposed the
recognition of social justice as a governing
horizon for all deliberations; this proposal was
handled as a motion to select a Priority of
Priorities.

"The result was a vote on the afternoon of
December 12 to spend two or three days in group
discussion, and possibly in plenary session, on
the joint theme of criteria for our apostolates
and the matter of promoting justice in the
world."[23] This decision by the Congregation in
a rather roundabout and spirited exchange of
viewpoints to select two of the previously
determined priorities as a Priority of Priorities
must be examined as one of the most significant
and influential decisions of the General Congregation. Its effects would be felt in many subsequent deliberations and would be cited as
fundamental in seven of the sixteen documents.
Only in documents of a brief or strictly technical nature is the Priority of Priorities not
mentioned.

The promotion of justice has a history in
the recent experience of the Society of Jesus.
Furthermore, there was concerted "lobbying" before the various Provincial Congregations on
behalf of this issue. The first Society-wide
representation of concern for social justice
was the General. Father Arrupe was present at
Hiroshima, Japan, during the tragic atomic bomb
attack of August 6, 1945. He was at the time
Novice Master and Rector at the novitiate at
Nagatsuka. "With his knowledge of medicine, he
organized the novitiate into an emergency hospital, and with the help of the novices assisted
the victims and wounded of the atomic bomb."[24]

As Father General, he has many times given
addresses on the topic of social justice. The
curia in Rome has given wide circulation of these
addresses throughout the Society. His address to
the 1971 Synod of Bishops, entitled Witnessing to
Justice, was printed by the Pontifical Commission
on Justice and Peace from Vatican City in 1972.
Other of his talks have been reprinted and circulated among Jesuits. In 1971, he traveled to
the United States for the opening of an office
staffed by Jesuits and supported by American
bishops for the promotion of Social Justice, The

<u>Center</u> <u>for</u> <u>Concern</u>. On the same visit he met
with U Thant, Secretary-General of the United
Nations. On that occasion, Father General
pledged:

> May I, as head of the Society of Jesus,
> identify myself with that same faith and
> hope in you and in what your organization
> is doing. For we Jesuits, relatively few
> but active in five continents, are pledged
> to work with right-minded men of all creeds
> and none, for a more truly human society.
> World justice and peace, a sense of family
> and of joint effort among the nations:
> These are the United Nations ideals to which
> many good men today devote the best of their
> lives. And these ideals take top priority
> among Jesuit aims and objectives.[25]

Perhaps more than any other, an address that
Father Arrupe gave on July 31, 1973, in Valencia,
Spain, stirred the imagination of Jesuits around
the world. The address was delivered to the
"Tenth International Congress of Jesuit Alumni of
Europe." It is a rebuke of Jesuit support for
the "status quo" in the face of social injustice
perpetrated by the established vested interests
of the world. The attraction of the message to
many Jesuits was the boldness of addressing the
affluent benefactors of Jesuit institutions with
a "radical" message of social justice. The address received wide circulation and was translated into English, French, Spanish and Italian.
Its title has become a watchword of Jesuit
aspirations to be "Men for Others."[26]

Another influence underlying the acceptance
of the Priority of Priorities at the start of this
General Congregation was an effective campaign in
its favor. Thirteen Provinces from around the
world and participants of an inter-Provincial
Brazilian meeting submitted postulata nearly
identical to one another. Other Province Congregations had postulata of similar emphasis. The
major theme of these is seen in the postulatum

submitted by the Mexican Provincial Congregation. It read:

1. That the General Congregation define explicitly, from the beginning of its deliberations, the Society's option as regards the problems of international injustice, in such a way that all the deliberations of the Congregation regarding our way of life and apostolic mission in the world today fall within the perspective of this fundamental option.

2. That the Congregation approve and commission Father General to put into practice a program of reflection for all members of the Society with regard to the problems of international justice.[27]

In January, 1974, five Mexican Jesuits wrote a sixty-page proposal concerning the role of Jesuits in the promotion of international justice. The document describes injustice in the world, economic and social inequalities, and political, military, and cultural domination. It explains these injustices "in terms of neo-colonialism, of economic, political, and cultural dependencies of developing and developed countries."[28] It concludes with an "interpretation of the facts in the light of faith and to a definition of the role of the Church and of the Society in the struggle against injustice, particularly at the international level."[29]

This document met high approval in Mexico and various other provinces. Two other young Jesuits condensed the report in a shortened version and distributed it widely. The proposal and its condensed version reached many provinces before they held their Provincial Congregations preliminary to the General Congregation. The result was an effective input at the level of different regions of the world that converged in the

assembly of the General Congregation. As further
attention and clarification in this process, the
Secretariat on socio-economic development at the
Jesuit headquarters prepared a twenty-three page
analysis of these postulata and translated it into the various languages of the Congregation.

It is evident that the promotion of the
issue of social justice greatly increased the
likelihood of its gaining the attention and
following that it had at the Congregation.
Clearly it spoke to an important and timely concern. It had the full sanction and obvious
backing of the Society's General. Even with this
support, the final impact of this concern on the
Congregation was far greater than expected.

When the General Congregation was asked if
it pleased them to select some priority to be
treated in a special way, namely as a Priority of
Priorities, two-thirds of the delegates were in
favor of this. Later the same day the various
options combining the main priorities were presented for a vote. The first choice presented to
the delegates was a combination of the first and
the fourth ranked priorities, namely, "Concerning
the criteria for our Apostolic Ministries Today"
and "On the Promotion of Justice." It passed
immediately.

The decision to put the combined themes of
criteria for apostolates and promotion of justice
together was a decision made, it appears, by the
Council of the President. Instead of voting
issues one by one, the combination of these
issues was presented and on the first vote it
received exactly a two-thirds vote.[30]

The discussions before the voting were intense and varied. No one denied the value of
promoting justice, but some refused to give it
"first place" as a "governing horizon." Many
considered it a source of division; many others
saw it as a source of "conversion of spirit."
Some delegates, cognizant of Vatican concerns, saw

it as distracting the delegates from a request of the Pope. Explicit reference was made in the discussion before voting to choose a Priority of Priorities to the fact that the Pope had given his own "postulatum" to the delegates. In his December 3, 1974 talk, the Pope said:

> We think that we are not asking too much when we express the desire that the Congregation should profoundly study and restate the essential elements (essentialia) of the Jesuit vocation in such a way that all your confreres will be able to recognize themselves, to strengthen their commitment, to rediscover their identity, to experience again their particular vocation, and recast their proper community union. The moment requires it, the Society expects a decisive voice. Do not let that voice be lacking.[31]

The "essentialia" were of great importance to the Pope. He had mentioned them in his letter of September, 1973 and repeated this in December, 1974. But to ask for a restatement "in such a way that all your confreres will be able to recognize themselves," is to ask for a consensual, conservative and orthodox statement. This request to discuss Jesuit identity in the juridical categories of a "religious, apostolic, priestly order," linked to the Roman Pontiff" as a first agenda necessarily conflicted with the Jesuit "groundswell" to discuss the more radical, unorthodox, challenging and divisive subject of social justice.

A compromise resulted. The Council of the President presented the combination of justice and criteria for apostolic ministries in the vote for a possible Priority of Priorities. The Pope's mandate to combat atheism, given to the Jesuits at the Thirty-First General Congregation, has since been a criteria for apostolic ministries. Its inclusion in the Priority of Priorities took regard of the Pope's request while it left the

Congregation free to choose justice as a governing
horizon. Eventually the "combating atheism" was
translated as evangelization and service of the
Faith which combined with justice in the decree:
"Our Mission Today: The Service of Faith and the
Promotion of Justice." It is a bold and challenging document, although not entirely consistent throughout to a single theme. It is a clear
instance of "context theologizing." Its implications and implementation can be predicted to
eventually change the expectations of the world-
wide Society of Jesus.

The decision next in sequence and equal in
importance to the Priority of Priorities was that
to attempt a renovation of grades. "Grades" refer
to the levels of membership in the Society,
especially as a consequence of the special vow to
the Supreme Pontiff in regards to Mission. About
forty percent of Jesuit priests are allowed to
take this "fourth vow." They thereby form an
internal elite within the Jesuits. At the Congregation there was strong pressure to eliminate
this distinction. Sixty-five postulata treated
the matter, forty-one of them asked for abolition
of the distinction. The former Congregation had
passed on the responsibility for change in this
matter to the Thirty-Second.

The abolition of grades would produce a
structural democratization in the Order. It
would have been achieved by extending the special
fourth vow to all Jesuits. As such, it was a
decision that changed an essential element of the
charter of the Society, the Formula of the
Institute. Approbation by the Pope is required
for such a change.

But the Pope wanted the elite status to continue. It is a reflection of the Post-Tridentine
shape of the Church and papacy. He saw a change
in this as a step toward secularization which
would undermine the "priestly character" of the
Jesuit Order.

> Supporting (The Holy See's) fears, the
> Italian Jesuit periodical Civilta
> Catholica carried an article shortly
> before the Congregation began which
> portrayed the proposed abolition of
> grades as part of a plan from the
> Society's left to turn the Order into
> a secular institute, indiscriminately
> composed of priests and laymen.[32]

After the vote on the Priority of Priorities,
Father General told the delegates that the Pope
had expressed reluctance. He reported a letter
of December 3, 1974, in which the Vatican Secretary of State said that such a change would "pose
serious difficulties which would prevent the
granting of necessary approval."[33]

Delegates believed the matter was still open
for discussion. As it was remembered by one
delegate:

> Even when we received the letter from the
> Secretary of State, Cardinal Villot, a
> week later, the matter was still vague.
> He said only that "there would seem to
> be serious reasons which might prevent
> the necessary approval," without stating
> what those "serious reasons" were
> (italics added by speaker).[34]

Vatican II had explicitly asked that all members
of a religious institute be admitted "on the same
basis and with equal rights and duties...."[35]
The Vatican office on religious orders confirmed
that. It was reasoned that there were conflicting
directives from the Vatican.

More than one month later the matter of the
Fourth Vow came up before a plenary session of
the Aula. Before discussing the matter, it was
necessary to have a vote on whether to treat a
matter which touches the Constitutions. Only
eight of the 236 delegates voted against discussion of the matter.

At that time the Commission dealing with this matter posed several questions to be voted on by the Congregation as an "indicative vote" or "straw-vote" procedure. This crucial indicative vote favored the abolition of grades by a majority of seventy-two percent. The aftermath of this vote is well summarized by one of the delegates:

> This unfortunate series of events precipitated a strong response from the Vatican. First there was a letter from Cardinal Villot in the name of the Holy Father expressing his consternation at the proceedings. Later there was a letter from the Holy Father himself, in which he expressed his wonderment, pain, disappointment. What the delegates found particularly difficult to understand in Cardinal Villot's letter was the strong language used about the failure of Father Arrupe to exercise the proper kind of leadership that could have headed off this series of unfortunate events.

> While the delegates were still reeling from this unexpected turn of events, they learned of the directive that had been given by Cardinal Villot to one of the officials to be given to the congregation. The official explained before the whole congregation that he had not understood that he was supposed to transmit this directive to the delegates in any official way.[36]

The Vatican was clearly keeping a day-by-day and very close watch on the events of the General Congregation. When the indicative vote on grades was passed, it took only two days for a forceful, one might say insulting, letter to come from the Vatican Secretary of State. It emphasized the displeasure of the Vatican with the leadership of Father Arrupe.

Much of the burden seemed to rest on the official who did not reveal the directive from Cardinal Villot to cease and desist discussing this matter. There is room for various opinions. One delegate considers the official's silence as "a costly mistake;"[37] an observer said "clearly the Congregation had misread the Vatican;"[38] another delegate bewailed "the process of dealing with the Vatican, its mode of communication and lack of dialog;"[39] another delegate said: "the humiliating modes of speech and writing which some Vatican officials (not the Holy Father) employ toward Father General, are profoundly disedifying, even unChristian."[40]

If the official had put an end to discussion, the burden for taking no action would have befallen the delegates. In the case of the Vatican's intrusion, the same result of no action occurred, but the Congregation clearly had reason outside itself for the decision. The Council of the President as official steering committee seems to have been in the precarious position of having to ward off serious onslaughts against the freedom of the Congregation to expose and to discuss an issue which had developed and matured in the Society for nearly a decade.

Fundamentally as a delegate points out there are two problems:

There is a serious historical and political issue here whose solution will tell enormously and importantly upon the future work of both the Society and the Holy See.

...But there is also a religious problem in the event itself, even within the progressive embroilment of men who found themselves unable to understand one another clearly and effectively.[41]

This rather unprecedented employment of power by the Vatican must be analyzed psychologically and politically on the one hand, and

religiously on the other to characterize its part
in the General Congregation.

Psychologically and politically this series
of events was the use of power that accomplished
for the Vatican its definite objectives, but con-
founded its meaning and credibility. The Congregation received the censure of the Holy See as a
painful blow and a humiliation. It came as a
stalemate, a failure and a paralysis. But in a
matter of days, the agenda was broadened to
consider the Vatican's demands and to meet them
in the continuance of the Congregation. The
demand to restate the "essentialia" which had been
circumvented prompted the formation of a special
ad hoc committee which worked to accommodate the
Vatican demands. The matter of grades was
shelved: since the Vatican would refuse, no request would be made. But the burden of this
failure to accomplish what half the Society
explicitly asked for fell to the Vatican, since
the Society had expressed its mind only to be
censured by the mind of the Holy See. The
Vatican demanded that all documents be presented
before their promulgation. This deprives the
Society of an exemption it has enjoyed; it is
probable the Vatican will not give the exemption
back lightly. But the manner of wresting control
was so elaborate and high-profile for the Vatican
that the "stock" in its demand loses much under-
pinning.

In sum, two very powerful tracks of
Catholicism are presently at odds. Reconciliation must occur in a fashion and persuasion
compatible with the twentieth century or else
the Holy See will have less flexible recourse to
a powerful ally and the Society of Jesus will be
intrinsically stifled in serving the Church.

The second level of analysis of this encounter between the Holy See and the Congregation
is the spiritual or religious sense. It is this
sense that the delegates emphasize in recounting
the experience of the Congregation. It is the

64

most personally poignant of all experiences of the Congregation.

An array of emotions crowded in upon the delegates. Impatience, frustration, boredom, anger, humiliation all exacted from the delegates the last ounce of energy and reserve. At precisely that point, the General of the Jesuits spoke, but with failing resources. He addressed the Congregation in an individualistic spiritual mode that took the blame for the events in disarray. He took the blame not only upon himself but upon them all. To nearly the last delegate, the address was unconvincing. However, it touched on a theme which reenforced the deepest sources of Jesuit socialization. In accepting the blame for the troubles, Father General likened the delegates to the faithful servant living and acting "under the standard of Christ" which Saint Ignatius sets before every Jesuit in the Spiritual Exercises.[42]

In the focal meditation of the "Two Standards" in the Spiritual Exercises, Saint Ignatius has written of a summons by Chirst in the words:

> Consider the address which Christ our Lord makes to all His servants and friends whom He sends on the enterprise, recommending to them to seek to help all, first by attracting them to the highest spiritual poverty, and should it please the Divine Majesty...even to actual poverty. Secondly, they should lead them to a desire for insults and contempt, for from these springs humility.

> Hence there will be three steps: the first, poverty as opposed to riches; the second, insults or contempt as opposed to the honor of this world; and third humility as opposed to pride. From these three steps, let them lead men to all other virtues.[43]

The dramatic entry into poverty, insult and humiliation to be with Christ in His sufferings in order to accompany Christ as well in His Resurrection represents for nearly every delegate of the General Congregation the most significant event of this Congregation. It was taken as an experience instead of an academic exercise of what it means to be a "companion of Jesus."

Through a process of approximately ten days, the delegates as one large group labored with only the most feeble and exhausted resources. They enlarged the agenda, accommodated to the Holy Father, viewed the recovery of Father General, continued more meaningful celebration of Eucharist together. All this primed them in common for a spiritual uplift which served to provide entirely new and formerly unavailable psychic and social resources and energy. These resources and energy saw them through completion of work they thought they would never finish, and with the management of the labor nearly completed there came, as well, a reconciliatory letter and a valuable antique gift from the Pope. In the brief conciliatory address the Pope said:

> For our part, We admit that We were impelled by the very spirit of love, by which We embrace all of you, to interpose our authority with the superiors of your Society - as you well know - in rather recent circumstances. We thought that this action had to be taken because of our consciousness that We are the supreme protector and guardian of the <u>Formula of the Institute</u>, as well as <u>Shepherd of the Universal</u> Church. Actually, at that time We were not a little pleased by the fact that the members of the General Congregation favorably understood the force and meaning of our recommendations and showed that they received them with a willingness to carry them out. Now we wish once again to cite the words of the

66

Apostle Paul: "I wrote (what) I did...
(confident that) you all know that I
could never be happy, unless you were.
When I wrote to you, in deep distress
and anguish of mind, and in tears, it
was not to make you feel hurt but to
let you know how much love I have for
you" (II Cor. 2:3-4).44

The reconciliation of the Holy See with the
delegates was an experience profoundly and very
personally felt by every one of them. It provided a sense of resolution to all that the
delegates had been doing for the previous ninety-
seven days. Because of its deep roots in Jesuit
tradition and its pervasive personal quality,
this encounter marked the most characteristic
value orientation to the delegates. In a letter
of Father Arrupe to the whole Society, he says:

I would make bold to say that the most
marked characteristic of this Congregation was the "metanoia" and purification
which took place in all of us who participated in it. This profound experience
of the General Congregation was at the
same time personal and communitarian.
Through the intimate experience of one's
own limitations (and those of the
Society), the General Congregation led
the way along the road of faith and the
typically Ignatian obedience to the Vicar
of Christ on earth.45

From their labors, the Thirty-Second General
Congregation produced sixteen decrees. The major
documents include "Jesuits Today" a well-wrought
document on Jesuit Identity. It is the product
of mainly one author who, with an ad hoc commission of five, wove together the major threads
of the entire fourteen weeks to spiritually and
dynamically characterize Jesuit identity in terms
of the event of the Congregation.

The larger documents include "Our Mission

Today - Service of Faith and Promotion of Justice"; "Poverty"; "The Formation of Jesuits, Especially with Regard to the Apostolate and Studies," and "The Union of Minds and Hearts in the Society of Jesus."

The document on Poverty is well suited to the tone and direction of the Priority of Priorities, and the major atmosphere of the Congregation. Its primary purpose is to adjust the legislation of the Society to make it accord more with the practice. At the same time, this document allows Provincials the power to control the budget of local houses more closely. Three elements characterize the document: (1) the source of support for Jesuits is more the earnings of Jesuits than charitable benefactions, (2) the Jesuit community can live off of earnings but not off of capital with which its institutions might be endowed, and these earnings can be spent only according to a budget approved by the Provincial, and (3) any surplus accruing to a community can be taken by the Provincial for uses other than that of the Community itself according to the Provincial's discretion and general authority.

The document on "The Formation of Jesuits, Especially with Regard to the Apostolate and Studies" builds upon the two documents of the Thirty-First General Congregation, "The Training of Scholastics Especially in Studies" and "The Spiritual Formation of Jesuits." The very fact that these elements are combined in a more general statement is characteristic of the approach taken which is a thrust for the integration of the various elements of Jesuit socialization and lifework situations.

Although the other documents are less lengthy, some of them are important. The three brief documents of interest to the dynamics of the Congregation are the "Introductory Decree," "Fidelity to the Magisterium and the Supreme Pontiff" and "The Work of Inculturation and the

Promotion of Christian Life."

The first two of these three documents were written in clear and deliberate accommodation to the pressure of the Holy See. "The Fidelity to the Magisterium" decree is a four paragraph statement to please the conservatives and the Vatican. It praises scholarship only to regret the failings of unorthodoxy which this scholarship has sometimes produced. The Congregation recommended firmness in applying the age-old rules for thinking with the Church, but in the next line by compromise, suggests that "Freedom should be intelligently encouraged." When the documents were promulgated, a criticism of that one sentence of a seven sentence decree was included by the Papal Secretary of State.

The third brief decree is entitled: "The work of Inculturation of the Faith and Promotion of Christian Life." It is only thirty-four lines long, yet some observors insist that it is the most revolutionary position legislated by the Congregation. It concerns Jesuit attempts to accommodate the message of Christ and the Gospels to the cultural milieu in which it is preached "especially in regions of Asia and Africa and in some countries of Latin America."[46] Rather than relegating the matter of inculturation to "missionaries," the Congregation insists that it "deserves the progressively greater concern and attention of the whole Society."[47] Finally, the document requests Father General to prepare an instruction to the entire Society on this matter and to promote it "in any other ways which seem to him more conducive to God's greater glory."[48]

The more legalistic documents and those documents normative of Jesuit religious life all show the trend to a greater democratization and decentralization along lines of personal, charismatic government. The model for government is clearly shifting to a more religious and less political model.

The Values of the Thirty-Second
General Congregation

What values emerged as predominant in the
Society of Jesus? Above all else, the relevance
and worth of the Spiritual Exercises of Saint
Ignatius was recognized as an integrative value
for the Jesuits. Secondly, the documents evidence a changing focus in Jesuit culture from an
urbane elite to a status of solidarity with the
victims of social injustice. Thirdly, the role
of the local community is seen as guarantor of
Jesuit life through affective and spiritual
sharing and common discernment of plans for the
apostolate. Fourthly, the vehicle for this
sharing and common discernment is given in the
revived tradition of communal discernment of
spirits.

Even the documents' repeated emphasis on
"spiritual discernment" as a dimension
of both the individual's and community's
everyday life means that the Congregation is urging the application of purely
religious norms of judgment in making and
evaluating what are normally taken to be
purely practical decisions.[49]

In his letter to the entire Society of Jesus
on the implementation of the decrees of the
Congregation, Father Arrupe lists concepts which
stand out in all the documents. These are:

The concept of mission by which the Jesuit
is sent out and concretizes for himself
the service he has to render - mission
which overrides other inclinations of
human compromises.

The concept of incarnation in human realities which include "inculturation"
or the assimilation of different cultures
in the expression of the universal faith.

The concept of integration in its various

70

aspects: integration among the different dimensions of our apostolic mission, personal and social; between the service of Faith and the promotion of justice; integration also in our apostolate at the inter-provincial and international levels; finally integration in the apostolic formation of the young Jesuit; between his spiritual and intellectual formation at the various states of studies, between his religious and community life and his gradual apostolic insertion in the world and in the body of the Society.

The concept of <u>union of minds and hearts</u> as a condition for the life and activity of the Society.

The concept of <u>community</u> of friends in Christ; that means the Ignatian community which has Christ and the Eucharist as its center and which is at the same time the source of human and fraternal support and of discernment and apostolic dynamism.

The concept of <u>authority</u> as service and as the source of apostolic mission in the name of Christ.

The concept of <u>poverty</u>, which while retaining all its ascetical significance presents also elements of "testimony," of apostolic value and of credibility; of solidarity with those among whom we live and with other communities, reaching out to other provinces and to all men, especially the most destitute and forsaken. Further, our poverty appears nowadays as a tacit condemnation of the consumer society, acquiring thereby a new value with a notable social impact.

The concept of a true sense of <u>humble collaboration</u> which averts the danger

of considering ourselves superior to
anyone in the Church of God.[50]

On March 7, 1975, the Thirty-Second General
Congregation adjourned. It had run a course
ninety-seven days long, through eighty-three
plenary sessions, deciding over 1,200 issues by
voting. Two hundred and thirty-six delegates
began the Congregation; two hundred and one
completed it. The other delegates were forced
to return to their native countries by other
responsibilities in the latter weeks of the Congregation.

There are two sides to the perception that
the delegates had of the Congregation, the experience of people and the experience of procedures. On the one hand, the experience of people
was worthwhile, enlarging, diverse, stimulating,
comforting, loving, prayerful, and supporting.
It was the experience of a community that
developed into a deep and true union of hearts.
On the other hand, the reactions to procedures
are broadly negative. One reaction described
the crucial problem:

On a more personal note, the many-sided
processes at work, including especially
God's grace, combined in me a humiliating
experience of the "under" side, the dark
side of my life, evidenced in my anger
at Vatican interventions, and in impatience, frustration, and boredom from
the legislative process. More persis-
tently, the unrelenting torrent of words,
spoken and written, along with hours of
sitting in a very structured atmosphere
built up and bottled up interior
resistances...[51]

Six days per week of meetings, tension, and
foreign surroundings took their toll. Delegates
seriously mention "getting through it" and "not
breaking down" as accomplishments of the Congregation. "On the one hand, it was the occasion of

the greatest consolation; on the other, I have
never in my life experienced such heaviness of
heart."[52]

The question can be asked whether the
Thirty-Second General Congregation, after four
years of preparation and over three months of
deliberation, was timely or premature. Considering the era of a Church struggling to become
consistently Post-Conciliar and to throw off the
clinging impediments of the Tridentine, did the
Society of Jesus organize itself and plan for
the next decade at the right time or was this
meeting premature?

The answer depends on the end according to
which the Congregation is judged. If the end to
which it is judged were the definitive reinstitutionalization of the Society of Jesus in
structures that will channel the energies and
expectations of 29,000 Jesuits in corporate and
concerted ways, structures that validly would
inform the culture in an organization right and
exemplary for this time of the Church's history,
then the judgment is necessarily that the Congregation was premature. Neither the insight, nor
the leeway, nor the common option were present
for the construction of such structures.

If the end to which the Congregation is
being judged is the integration of persons who
come from varied roles and expectations in times
that exhibit many contrary viewpoints simultaneously and provide for them a tentative
corporateness and communality with some clarification about a concerted thrust of ideas and
expectations that say "where we are going," then
the judgment must be that the Thirty-Second General Congregation was a success. As a legislative
process inclined to structures, it was premature;
as an integrative process beginning in the grass-
roots and culminating in actual symbolization and
affect on culture, it was timely.

Summary and Conclusions

The Thirty-Second General Congregation is old and new. It extended and resolved concerns of the Thirty-First General Congregation and operated in deliberate continuity with the Congregation. Yet it comes a decade later and even the continuity has a uniqueness shown in the documents, the methodology and the circumstances of a more developed and pluralistic context.

This Congregation insisted on its continuity with the former Congregation. It "makes its own and confirms all the declarations and dispositions of the 31st General Congregation."[53]

For the loss of piety, mystery, and authoritarianism, this Congregation stressed integration. Along side the youthful emphasis of the former, this Congregation strove for authenticity, to make the Society creditable to all its members. Its own youthfulness resulting from new rules for eligibility, this Congregation liberalized that eligibility slightly more.

The central document on faith and justice merges the emphasis of the former Congregation on adaptation, the concern of the General elected by the former Congregation for social justice, and the progressive concern for the problem of atheism mandated by the Pope to the former Congregation. The generality and flexibility conveyed in this document and others are predictable outcomes of the revamping and experimentation which has characterized the Jesuit Order since then.

Changes in the status of poverty instituted in the former led to the distinction between apostolates and communities in this latter Congregation. The challenge to grades and mandate for a rethinking of this matter given by the former Congregation resulted in the turmoil and papal interventions of this Congregation.

The continuity manifested between these two Congregations a decade apart in a time of religious revolution suggest a pattern of social change. It is as if the former Congregation served to "break down" elements opposed to new directions and provided the momentum and disposition for new forms to emerge. The latter Congregation could then "build up" a new context and methodology for the Society of Jesus to be implemented in the years ahead.

The new context and methodology does not resemble the old. It is more generalized, flexible, non-directive in detail. This Congregation portrayed the Society of Jesus in a younger mold than former Congregations. It was the result of far longer and more conscious planning and a two-way public airing of views and dispositions.

In other words, this was probably the most transparent Congregation in history. It is the first in history to allow a sociologist to observe and analyze its deliberations.

This transparency and publicity occasioned a confrontation with the papacy which was frank and forceful. The Jesuits evidenced loyalty while revealing a great difference in ecclesiastical styles. The loyalty shown is manifestation of an ability to conform while realizing simultaneously a deeper, different and more essential allegiance to values than possessed before. A "coming of age" or experience of deeper maturity was a consequence of the confrontation on the part of the delegates. It was an experience of growth rooted deeply in the fundamental traditions of the Society of Jesus.

The documents of this Congregation could not have been written a decade ago. They show a level of generalization and expansive concern that outreaches structures which were elemental for self-definition and religious practice a decade ago. Gone are many sectarian defenses and exclusive vocabulary. An opening to matters of social justice and the affairs of the family of man characterize this Congregation's thrust. It is a thrust which must operate as an expectation and a guage for the broadened perspective and activities of the rank-and-file.

This operation will be worked out by a process which is also a contribution of this Congregation. The process is communal discernment. Planning and solidarity are going to be pursued at a community level. Socialization, apostolate, and style of life are to be determined in this decentralized forum.

The stress on community is a step towards democratization. It also reckons with greater diversity and pluralism through a practice of subsidiarity. It is a rationalized, generalized procedure in concept. However, in implementation, it becomes a spiritualized and integrative use of tradition. Sources of Jesuit socialization and evangelical precedent are the basis for this change. A profound reordering of Jesuit values is urged by reference to root concerns of the Society in order to accomplish a modern transformation.

The Thirty-Second General Congregation is probably the last Congregation in the lifetime of this General. He quipped that he would be "in heaven" when the next Congregation is convoked. Perhaps a decade or two will pass before then. An understanding of what transpired prior to and during this event is important for recognizing today's religious institution and Catholic community. It is an important instance of how the Second Vatican Council is organizationally implemented in the Church. It evidences a process of change through the most tumultuous decade in Catholicism since the reformation. And the immediate future of Jesuit life will be lived in reference to the directions and identity set down by this Congregation.

Footnotes

[1]"The Jesuits in the Post-Conciliar Era:
The Thirty-First General Congregation and the New
General," in Herder Correspondence, November,
1965, p. 352.

[2]"Editorials: Pope and Jesuits: Invitation
and Response," (author not given) in America,
December 3, 1966, p. 729.

[3]Very Reverend Pedro Arrupe, S.J., "The
Society of Jesus in the World of Today" in Visit
of Father General to the American Assistancy -
1971: Talks and Writings, Washington, D.C.,
Jesuit Conference, 1971, p. 2, 3.

[4]Cf. Bruce F. Biever, S.J., and Thomas M.
Gannon, S.J., editors, General Survey of the
Society of Jesus: North American Assistancy,
Five Volumes, Oak Park, Illinois, National Office
of Pastoral Research, 1969.

[5]John L. Thomas, S.J., "Afterword," in
Biever and Gannon, Vol. 3, "Research Studies,"
pp. 295-319.

[6]Very Reverend Pedro Arrupe, "Address of
Very Reverend Father General to the Congregation
of Procurators, October 6, 1970) quoted at length
in Jean Yves Calvez, S.J., "A Critical Appraisal
of the Preparation for the Jesuits' Thirty-
Second General Congregation" in Review for
Religious, Volume 34, No. 6, November, 1975, pp.
938-939.

[7]Quoted in Calvez, Ibid., p. 941-942.

[8]Ibid., p. 938.

[9]Ibid.

[10]Ibid., pp. 942-943.

[11]Ibid., p. 944.

[12]Pope Paul VI, Letter of the Holy Father on the Convocation of the 32nd General Congregation, sent from Rome, General Curia of the Society of Jesus, October 4, 1973.

[13]Ibid., p. 3.

[14]"Extending the Vow," an account of the proceedings of the Thirty-Second General Congregation in Time Magazine, (Europe edition), February 10, 1975, pp. 32-33.

[15]Saint Ignatius of Loyola, The Constitutions of the Society of Jesus, translated by George E. Ganss, S.J., pp. 294-295.

[16]Thomas J. Reese, S.J., "The General Congregation: A Study in the Legislative Process," an unpublished paper written for the Department of Political Science, University of California at Berkeley, and circulated to the American delegates to the Thirty-Second General Congregation, p. 6.

[17]Very Reverend Pedro Arrupe, "Letter of Very Reverend Father General convoking the Thirty-Second General Congregation," Rome, General Curia of the Society of Jesus, September 8, 1973.

[18]As quoted in G.C. News, No. 1, December 4, 1974. The G.C. News, English edition, was written by Reverend Donald Campion, S.J. and provided a regular account of the proceedings of the General Congregation for Jesuits in English speaking countries. There were editions as well in French, German, Italian and Spanish. Over the fourteen week span of the Congregation, there were twenty-one issues of the G.C. News.

[19]Pope Paul VI, "Address of Pope Paul VI to the Thirty-Second General Congregation of the Society of Jesus, December 3, 1974," given in full as "Appendix A" of Documents of the Thirty-Second General Congregation of the Society of Jesus: An English Translation, Washington, D.C.,

The Jesuit Conference, 1975. (hereafter referred to as "Documents, 32 G.C.").

[20]Ibid., p. 141.

[21]Ibid., pp. 148-149.

[22]G.C. News, No. 4, December 12, 1974, p. 1.

[23]Ibid., p. 4.

[24]32nd General Congregation of the Society of Jesus - Press Pack Rome, S.J. Press and Information Office, 1975, p. 41.

[25]Very Reverend Pedro Arrupe, S.J., "Father General's Statement on the Occasion of His Meeting with the Secretary-General of the United Nations, New York, May 4, 1971," in Visit of Father General to the American Assistancy, Washington, D.C., Jesuit Conference, August, 1971, p. 631.

[26]Very Reverend Pedro Arrupe, Men for Others, Washington, D.C., Jesuit Secondary Educational Association, March, 1974.

[27]Quoted in Francis Ivern, S.J., "The Society's Commitment to the Promotion of Justice: Analysis of the Postulata Submitted to the 32nd General Congregation" an unpublished paper circulated among the delegates to the Thirty-Second General Congregation by the Secretariat on socio-economic development of the General Curia of the Society of Jesus.

[28]Ibid., p. 11.

[29]Ibid., p. 12.

[30]Two sources recounting this General Congregation provide conflicting testimony on the content of the vote to establish the Priority of Priorities. In one account, one of the major translators at the Congregation states: "At the

end of the second week the Congregation decided, after heated debates, that of all the urgent issues before it, the Society's attitude towards the promotion of justice should have the prioritas prioritatum, the pride of place," in Brian Daley, S.J. "Identifying Jesuits: The 32nd General Congregation." The Month, CCXXXVI, (May, 1974), pp. 146-151. This account is disputed by one of the delegates to the Congregation, who says in a footnote: "Here I should have to disagree with one assertion.... The Congregation never made the promotion of justice its priority of priorities. In fact, in a vote taken on the 12th of December, the Congregation specifically excluded that option. On that day, six priority items were selected by the Congregation, one of which was the promotion of justice. The Congregation did not want any of these singly to constitute its priority of priorities, but chose rather to combine number 28 (the promotion of justice) and number 26 (the principal criteria of our apostolate, which included the previous papal commissions regarding atheism) into a single focus given to the apostolic mission of the Society." This account in Michael J. Buckley, S.J., "The Confirmation of Promise: A Letter to George Ganss," in Studies in the Spirituality of Jesuits, Vol. VII, No. 5, November, 1975, p. 217. The "Acta" or minutes of the Congregation sessions do not indicate their ever "specifically excluding" any option but rather passing the first option presented them as set forth by the chairman at the direction of the Council of the President.

[31]Pope Paul VI, "Address of Pope Paul VI to the Thirty-Second General Congregation of The Society of Jesus, December 3, 1974," in Documents - 32 G.C., pp. 148-149.

[32]Brian Daley, S.J., "Identifying Jesuits: The 32nd General Congregation," p. 149.

[33]Quoted in Brian Daley, S.J., p. 149.

[34]Reverend Maurice B. Walsh, S.J.

"Highlights" in S.J. News, Vol. 5, No. 3, April, 1975, (monthly newsletter of the Society of Jesus of the New England Province), p. 3.

[35]"Decree of the Appropriate Renewal of the Religious Life" in The Documents of Vatican II, p. 478.

[36]John R. Sheets, S.J., "A Survey of the Thirty-Second General Congregation," in Review for Religious, Vol. 34, No. 5, (September, 1975), pp. 679-680.

[37]Ibid., p. 680.

[38]Brian Daley, S.J., p. 150.

[39]Reverend Paul T. Lucey, S.J., "Spiritual Dynamics" in S.J. News, Vol. 5, No. 3, April, 1975, p. 2.

[40]Reverend William G. Guindon, S.J., "Overview" in S.J. News, Vol. 5, No. 3, April, 1975, p. 2.

[41]Michael J. Buckley, p. 191.

[42]The Spiritual Exercises of Saint Ignatius comprise the fundamental socialization of every Jesuit. It is the experience of prayer over thirty days, usually spent in silence, that covers a set of experiences which Saint Ignatius himself experienced as part of his own conversion. Every Jesuit makes these "Spiritual Exercises," or "Long Retreat" as it is called, twice in his training, once shortly after entering the Jesuits, the second time around fifteen years later at the completion of the period of training. This socialization is reenforced by a repetition of the experience in the shortened form of eight days every year as an annual retreat. The central values of the Jesuit Order, its style of life, its Constitutions and the allegiance to the Pope as representative of Christ are all carefully consistent with the thrust of the Exercises.

[43]Saint Ignatius of Loyola, _The Spiritual Exercises of Saint Ignatius: A New Translation_, translated by Louis J. Puhl, S.J., Westminster, Maryland, The Newman Press, 1960, pp. 61-62.

[44]Pope Paul VI, "Address of Pope Paul VI to the Thirty-Second General Congregation of the Society of Jesus, March 7, 1975," in _Documents, 32 G.C._, p. 150.

[45]Very Reverend Pedro Arrupe, S.J., "Letter of Very Reverend Father General to the Whole Society Concerning the Implementation of the Decrees of G.C. 32" Rome, General Curia of The Society of Jesus, 1975, p. 2.

[46]"The Work of Inculturation of the Faith and Promotion of Christian Life," in _Documents, 32 G.C._, p. 44.

[47]_Ibid._

[48]_Ibid._

[49]Brian Daley, "Identifying Jesuits: The 32nd General Congregation," p. 148.

[50]Very Reverend Pedro Arrupe, S.J., "Letter of Very Reverend Father General to the Whole Society Concerning the Implementation of the Decrees of G.C. 32," p. 2.

[51]Paul T. Lucey, S.J., "Spiritual Dynamics," in _S.J. News_, p. 2.

[52]John R. Sheets, S.J., "A Survey of the Thirty-Second General Congregation," p. 673.

[53]"Introductory Decree," in _Documents, 32 G.C._, p. 1.

CHAPTER THREE

NATURE OF THE OCCURRENCE AND OF THE

EVIDENCE OF MODERNIZATION IN THE SOCIETY OF JESUS

Having described changes in the Catholic
Church and the Society of Jesus, it is necessary
to examine that description to gain an understanding of the underlying dynamics. This requires an interpretation. In this case, it is a
sociological interpretation which focuses on
"conceptions of the desirable influencing selective behavior."

The interpretation is attempted in a two-
fold manner: first, to understand the Congregation and change in the Society as an object of
inquiry; second, to determine by careful analysis
of the evidence how correct that understanding of
the object of inquiry really is. This present
chapter will accomplish only the first step, to
set forth an interpretive understanding of what
happened in the changing Society of Jesus as
evidenced by the Thirty-Second General Congregation. Subsequent chapters will provide verifica-
tion of the findings.

The vantage point of this interpretation is
the Congregation in its historical perspective.
The sources drawn upon for the interpretation are
participant observation in the occurences of that
historical situation, observation of the Congregation, the documents of the Congregation and
accounts and commentary from some of the delegates to this Congregation.

The interpretation consists of four
assertions:

(1) The Society of Jesus has responded to
the mandate of Vatican II to modernize and has
generalized its culture and structures in the past

83

decade. This change of culture and structures consisted of two stages, one of experimentation, the other of implementation.

(2) This modernization crystallized through the deliberations of the Thirty-Second Congregation into a specific cultural form. This cultural form fashioned by context theologizing constitutes a shift from the identity of an elite status for Jesuits within the structures of a bounded Church to a minority status addressing itself to the whole world on behalf of the disenfranchized and the poor.

(3) This new cultural form legislated by the Congregation came about as the result of an initial institutionalization effected by elites. It was a process begun by the General, implemented by secondary elites in the field and, after a process of various reenforcements, legitimated by the General Congregation.

(4) To complete the institutionalization as Society-wide implementation, the "structuring-in" of this cultural form relies on an increased following in the rank-and-file. The feasibility of this increased following is examined in terms of its predisposing factors.

The first assertion states that the Society of Jesus has responded to the mandate of Vatican II to modernize and, in order to do so, has generalized its structures extensively in the past decade. Chapter One described some changes promulgated by the Thirty-First Congregation in response to the spirit of Vatican II. Chapter Two described many of the structural changes in the interim period between the Thirty-First and the Thirty-Second General Congregation. These structural changes include accentuation of the role of the younger Jesuits, changes in the formation program from idealized to realistic and experiential, admission of non-senior members to Provincial Congregations, new appointments of younger officials into the ranks of leadership,

development of two-way communication in the
exercise of authority, and implementation of new
modes of integration.

These changes were very novel; experimentation in search of new forms were encouraged. This
experimentation had as its first effect the over-
ruling of tradition as legitimator of past behavior. The mandate to renewal and experimentation was a turning away from customs that were
in force for generations.

The Thirty-First Congregation has striven
with all its power so to promote a renewal
that those things may be removed from our
body which could constrict its life and
hinder it...[1]

Experimentation was a process of change that
caused continual intrusion of questioning and re-
evaluation into the details of Jesuit conduct.
The reasoning behind performance was articulated;
the legitimation for performance was disembedded
from its bases in traditions ("That's how it has
always been done.") to be justified on grounds of
relevancy and effectiveness.

One way to describe the actual process of
change is to analyze the frequent occurrence of
"asking permission."

Many times - in cases large and small - conflict or formal opposition would exist in the life
of any particular Jesuit within the regime of the
Order. These conflicts or oppositions were
settled in various ways. In small matters,
deviance was often the way: for example,
"breaking silence" or keeping the carfare or
smoking or smuggling cigarettes when they were
forbidden. Deviance would not work in larger
matters, generally, because of disciplined
scrutiny by authorities. In these larger cases,
the Jesuit's only recourse was to "get permission."
But "permissions" involved a perculiar anomaly.
The conflict set before the superior was generally

a conflict of self versus collectivity. To ask permission of the superior was equivalent to asking the collectivity-representative to submit to the subject's self-interest. The permission itself must necessarily come from the collectivity and must be decided in the collectivity on grounds proper to the collectivity, not on grounds of self-interest. Yet those "proper grounds for granting permission" had to be such as to allow for the self-interested activity that was asked in the first place. Thus the superior would grant permission on the grounds of some ideological interest that justified the permission. The Thirty-First General Congregation, in fact every General Congregation, is itself the highest mechanism for "enshrining" or legislating the ideological justifications of new and previously untolerated (or unthought of) forms of behavior and orientation.

An intriguing and effective facet of the interplay of these variables is seen in this: as long as a subject unquestioningly obeyed the rules and structures of the Order (as the Post-Tridentine Church taught him to do), the subject was able to maintain a distant and formal relationship to his superior, and his superior a distant and formal relationship to him. But, when the subject had to plead for an exception, he departed the formality and distance and confided with personal appeal to his superior. When, in turn, the superior acquiesced to the request, he also departed the distant and formal and related with some degree of interpersonal familiarity to the subject.

Even though the superior in this case could decide to grant the permission on ideological grounds prevailing over structures, nonetheless, if and when he extended the permission to the subject, an entirely new social relation of closely interpersonal implication would occur. As these occurrences increased in frequency, a new social structure developed; i.e., the dialogue and two-way mechanism of authority.

The entire quality of power relations was affected by these changes. Peer relations changed as well. If various members of a large community changed relations to superiors, they found relationships with one another changing in accord with the same expectations. Familiarity replaced formality. Conformity structures were reduced. Authoritarian mandates disappeared in favor of personal responsibility and cooperative decision-making.

Another concrete instance of the changing structure of authority and administration in the Society of Jesus is evidenced in the reaction of many Jesuits, especially those in missionary territories, to an important statement issued by the General of the Society. In the Congregation of Procurators of 1970, Father General outlined four basic "apostolic priorities" of the Society of Jesus. These priorities were: theological reflection, education, social action, and the media of social communication. After this address was issued, the complaint was voiced that the Society of Jesus no longer considered "the missions" as a high priority. When Father General later explained his intention, it could be seen that his "level" of enunciating priorities was at a higher level of generalization than that of his critics. He set the role of the missionary in a larger, more generalized context to which the priorities applied.

> The reason (I made no mention of the "missions") is simple. If we take "mission" to mean "spreading the faith," then it is obviously not a "Priority" at all.... It is an end, not a means: an integral part of the end pursued by the Society.... On the other hand, if we take "mission" to mean our apostolate among "non-Christians," it seems to me that today we cannot consider it something essentially different from our apostolate in the rest of the world.[2]

This important shift in the meaning of the works of the Society of Jesus was not arbitrary. The "missionaries" were themselves experiencing an identity crisis; the questions about missions, works, priorities, and the like, were disturbingly recurrent to many Jesuits.

The consequence of these intrusions of evaluative standards into behaviors formerly taken for granted, of the extensive rationalization of performance, and of the justification of new behaviors on grounds of recourse to higher values comprises a generalization of norms and abstraction of their influence on myriad behaviors and activities of the Jesuits. But rather than weakening the influence of values on behavior, this evaluation, rationalization and generalization of norms was a means of "reaching into" the behaviors and "coming to grips with" them in order to implement greater relevant guidance and direction. The experimentation stage was necessary to grant leeway for the change from older ascriptive bases of legitimation. The generalized norms developed as a new legitimation, the implementation of values in new form.

The second assertion is that the updating of the Society of Jesus crystallized through the Thirty-Second General Congregation into a legitimated cultural form which constitutes a shift from an elite status within a bounded church to a minority status in the world. In order to describe the understanding of this assertion, the following must be considered: what the transition to be incurred by modernization entails, what part of that transition and that which it entails was actually proceeded upon, and how that proceeding or movement can be evidenced.

First to the question of what the transition to be incurred by modernization entails for the Society of Jesus in this historical time. The transition is a shift from the mood of the Post-Tridentine period prior to the Second Vatican Council to that of the Post-Conciliar period beginning with the latest Council. But what is entailed by such a shift for the Society of Jesus?

The Post-Tridentine Church was characterized by the structures and successes of the Jesuit Order who largely directed and remained on the front lines of the Counter-Reformation. The Counter-Reformation Catholic Church was a Church-on-its-own, well bounded and defined, existing largely in preserving itself from the heresy of Protestantism and declaring its doctrine and distinctiveness by firm reaction to such heresy. A defensive institution builds firm boundaries and these constitute, often enough, the definition of the religious group.

This is not to confuse the definition of sectarianism with that of Church as Troeltsch employs the dichotomy.[3] It was not as if Catholicism after Trent wanted to reject the world and define itself in that rejection, but rather that in all things Catholicism wanted to assert its own claim as Church in the world in the face of contending groups. The Church would accommodate to the world but content in this accommodation with rival expressions of the Christian faith. Much of the twentieth century however has seen a dismantling of the bulwark mentality. At the Second Vatican Council, the ecumenical spirit prevailed and accommodation was extended to other religious groups.

The Post-Conciliar Church has all of the world and all of the Churches to accommodate itself to but presently it has few, if any, explicit groups against which to legitimately contend.

With the Post-Tridentine Church, the Post-Tridentine Society of Jesus was well defined. It was the front line or the light-cavalry of the Church for the defense of the faith. It was considered the elite religious group of the Catholic Church. Its principle service to the Church in this latest century has been to fashion

89

a learned laity to comprise an elite of the Church in the world. Its identification of itself was founded on the prospering of a successful Catholic clique in pluralist countries or a learned and practicing Catholic cadre in the "Catholic" nations.

However, given the change in the boundaries of the Church, the most relevant and required service is no longer to fashion high contenders who are Catholic, but to facilitate the reconciliation of a common humanity and to contend with the ravages of inhumanity.

The Society today would strive:

> To form Christians who...are able to stand back from the spurious absolutes of competing ideologies, and because of this detachment able to play a constructive part in the reform of social and cultural structures.[4]

Thus the General Congregation was faced with the shift in culture from one thought-world to another, and with the consequences of this shift in terms of Jesuit effectiveness. What this entails is a shift of the Society of Jesus' proper assertion of its strength from within a bounded Catholicism to within the unbounded environment of the whole world.

To say this another way: The boundaries of Catholicism are largely its identifiable structures. But these structures are becoming less and less suited or suitable to dealing with the issues of modern man. The structures by which the values of Catholicism have long been transmitted no longer transmit those values, can no longer be recognized as communicative of the values of Catholicism by an audience who do not live the greater part of their lives predominantly in the Catholic Church. Thus the effectiveness of the values revered in Catholicism must be achieved by their embodiment and transmission in structures

and social relations existent and viable in
cultures-at-large instead of in culture-within-
the Church. But cultures-at-large form a vast
expanse of humanity. Jesuits form only a tiny
and insignificant proportion of that unbounded
group as compared to a highly visible, ascribed,
and predominant proportion of the bounded group
within the Catholic structure. Thus, the Society
of Jesus, in effect, must abrogate its elite
status (in the Church) to take up instead a
minority status (in the world).

It is precisely this transformation from an
elite status within a bounded Church to a minority
status in the world that the modernization of the
Society of Jesus in our day and age entails. The
demand for updating and renewal in the Society of
Jesus is equivalently the shift from being a big
fish in a small pond to that of becoming a small
fish in a big pond.

Such a transformation could easily result in
oblivion for a group even 29,000 strong. For
along with the transfer of contexts comes the
loss of legitimacy. Catholicism formally and
materially legitimates the Society of Jesus as a
religious order within its ranks, "a religious
apostolic and priestly order bound to the Roman
Pontiff by a special bond of love and service."[5]
But the world does not legitimate the Society of
Jesus in that way. In some places at some times,
some Jesuits attain to legitimacy by gaining
renown in some endeavour or another, but the
legitimacy of the entire Order is not expected to
come from that. Something which is charismatic
and central to the world condition must be
deliberately sought out and assiduously pursued
as a legitimizing feature of a transformed Jesuit
life-style and occupation. Only if legitimate,
could a minority stance make sense. And given
the "signs of the times" and the emphatic posture
of altruistic movements in many parts of the
developing world, such a feature is to be found
in solidarity with the poor and a minority battle
for the rights of the disenfranchized. As the

Thirty-Second General Congregation developed, it became apparent that what the transition of modernization would entail for the Society of Jesus was a shift from elite service legitimated by a bounded Church to minority status legitimated by solidarity with the poor.

Such a step, if drastically taken, would illegitimate most of the existing Jesuit Order. The majority of Jesuit structures, particularly in the apostolic works of the Society - e.g., colleges, universities, research facilities, theological faculties - existed prior to the Second Vatican Council. To simply shift from one status to the other as described above would be structurally impossible and sociologically inane. Nevertheless, the consequences of modernization in the Society of Jesus would fit the parameters described above, if the Society chooses to transform its style and its goals as radically as the times and the insights of many Jesuits and its own Congregation suggest.

In light of what the shift of Jesuit culture and structures could entail, what actual shift or transition was made by the Thirty-Second General Congregation? The shift that was accomplished is equivalent to a "development of dogma."

As Thomas O'Dea explains:

Ideas which are at least in potential conflict are often presented together as though the possibilities of conflict did not exist.... This method of development of ideas may be called "context theology" or "setting theology" ....it does not really change any traditional positions of the Church by redefining them or explicitly qualifying or "correcting" them. Rather it presents them in a new context, in a changed setting.... But put in a different total setting, it may be understood in a new way.[6]

92

In this way, a new concept was presented by this General Congregation as an accompaniment to a very long-standing and revered concept: "The Mission of the Society of Jesus today is the service of faith, of which the promotion of justice is an absolute requirement."[7] These two concepts are given as fully complementary, although for many, only the newer concept of justice is attended to. For most, the two serve to illuminate and highlight features of one another and enrich the pursuit of both. For some few, the addition of the new element is an adulteration. More than one delegate considered the decree on these two elements "a disaster."

The document "Our Mission Today: The Service of Faith and the Promotion of Justice" is what developed from the selection of a "priority of priorities." It affects and influences all of the major documents. It is defined and referred to repeatedly as the Society's "basic choice" today. It links together the other emphases of the Congregation and consolidates real, active, and far-reaching activities that have existed in innovative sections of the Society for several years. The document and the norms of poverty insist on solidarity with the poor and the rationale is drawn from this social justice emphasis. Some of the norms on poverty are apparatus to enforce that solidarity with the poor.

The third assertion is that this new shift came about as a result of initial institutionalization effected by elites, begun with the innovations of the Superior General, implemented by secondary elites, (i.e., innovators who work "in the field,") and after various reenforcements, legitimated by the Congregation. There are several steps in this process of institutionalization.

The process can be understood analytically as beginning with Father General, a leader who took a clear and unambiguous stand on the issue of social justice. He stated in 1966:

> I have decided to begin by taking a stand
> internally, within the Society. And from
> this moment on I want this "taking of a
> stand" to be effective among the members
> of the Society. It is gravely distressing
> that still today there are those within the
> Society, even among those who hold posi-
> tions of great responsibility, who have not
> understood the urgency and the primary
> importance of the problem of social
> justice.[8]

The clear statement which was repeated and
enunciated in various ways at various times met
with the resounding acceptance of some Jesuits
"in the field." Among these were the early members of CIAS (Centro de Investigacion y de Accion
Social). With their continued activity in the
field, accompanied by strong approbation of the
General, the "doctrine" of the "primary importance
of the problem of social justice" moved from
theory to innovative praxis. Thereafter, the
General could situate the "problematic" in a
dialogic frame of reference. He influenced others
"in the field" by reference to and reenforcement
of the innovators, who would otherwise have been
stifled by structures or, at least, have remained
privatized and unknown. With this reenforcement,
the innovators and early joiners became recognized
as a ground swell. They conducted numerous international meetings. One such meeting was supported
jointly by every Province in the world and was
attended by selected Jesuits from every Province.
The General allowed and encouraged this ground
swell. As a consequence, a "movement" became
evident within the Society. Official sanction
was indirectly given to the movement. The
Secretariat for Socio-Economic Affairs was set up
as an integral part of the General's staff.
After the spiraling of reenforcements, the
General Congregation was held. The movement and
its "official" Secretariat lobbied and distributed
the General's statements on the matter. The

priority of priorities was accepted by vote. The discussions were heard, the document written and revised, then passed into law by a huge majority. Through this document the movement evoked the sanction of the Jesuit legislature. At the same time, it serves as an authoritative articulation of a rationale or working philosophy.

From the legitimation of the Congregation, there could be projected a "pervasive reordering of social behavior." The burden of proof would seem to be on those who are unaffiliated with the concerns of social justice. In this shift of the burden of proof, the concern for social justice and the minority status in solidarity with the poor should begin to attract adherents from loyal followers throughout the Society. Their adherence would cause revisions of existing structures and some new structures as well.

The movement from elite to minority as a reinstitutionalization occurring in the Society of Jesus has many implications. It evidences a change in value orientation, a retranslation of associated fundamental truths, and a necessary option of group solidarity at a corporate rather than self-interest level. Each of these implications give evidence of the higher order of generality.

In a discussion of change in value orientation, Williams lists ten possible modes of transformation. They are creation, relatively sudden destruction, attenuation, extension, elaboration, specification, limitation, explication, consistency, and intensity.[9] The process of institutionalization described above operates in the modes of creation, extension and elaboration at this early period of its prominence. The mode of intensity is also applicable throughout the process and particularly after legitimation.

Another element of the shift in the culture of the Jesuits that actually occurred is the retranslation of associated fundamental truths in

95

new contexts. It has always been a proud trait of the Jesuits that their founder was the first to break with the structures of the monastery for singing the "office" in choir. He innovated a new kind of religious order. Thus structural reform is a basic value to the Society. So too, the founder expected the Order to do anything or go anywhere for the "magis," the greater good. This, it could be said, establishes a precedent to move from bounded Church to unbounded world. The unbounded is, in a way, a Jesuit trade-mark.

An important dynamic underlies the eventual shift from elite to minority that is introduced to the culture of the Jesuits. The move into the minority status in a large secularized context is for the sake of speaking out and assisting the disenfranchized. It is, however, also a movement of survival as vital, relevant, attractive to recruits, etc. But there is no automatic leverage at the minority level except the posture itself of authentic solidarity with and sharing the lot of the poor (witness the success of Mother Theresa in India, for example). The solidarity with the poor, however, has "nothing to offer" at the level of self-interest. It is a demeaning or, at least, unambitious personal gesture. Solidarity exists only at a higher order, that of the corporate body. The "cause" of solidarity with the poor is thus also an occasion of solidarity with the organization, and this at a higher order of organization than formerly (presuming that self-interest was well served in the former state). As Martindale says: "modern man finds, to an ever increasing degree, his point of personal integration in the formal organization of human conduct."[10]

What is very apparent in each feature of this accomplishment of transition in culture is the fact that it represents a pervasive reordering of value orientation, a reordering which definitely raises the orientation to a new level of generality.

96

The very process of "context theology" is a process of generalizing the setting to accommodate the new element, and with the introduction of the new element, the amalgam exists as a more generalized doctrine. Certainly this is the case of faith and justice combined in the Mission document of the Congregation. The construction and consensus-forming process of institutionalization is a process of drawing in adherents and finding "room" for their particular advocacy in a larger rubric. This creates a more generalized form in the process. It is part, too, of the development occurring in the move from doctrine to praxis. Extension and elaboration as modes of value transformation are modes of greater generalization. Furthermore, the inclusion of associated values, such as "structure-breaking" and "unboundedness" evidences the generalizing quality of the new institutionalization. The development of value-orientations that forcefully transcend the self-interest to reach corporate, higher-order consolidation also evidences the generalization of values.

The fourth assertion in understanding the underlying dynamics of this General Congregation is that the "structuring-in" of this shift provided in culture by the Congregation relies upon an increased following in the rank-and-file Jesuit membership for its actual occurrence and implementation. The feasibility of this occurrence must be examined in terms of its predisposing factors.

To what extent is the shift implied by the documents of the Congregation too radical? If the change called for is seen as asking too much, what has the Society to fall back on?

The Thirty-First and Thirty-Second General Congregations seem to be a complete departure from what prevailed prior to Vatican II. One example of this is seen in legislation on the "Common Rules." The "Common Rules" were approved by the Fourth General Congregation in 1573. Since

97

then every Jesuit was instructed to read them monthly. In every major community of the Jesuit Order for almost four hundred years, these rules were read at table twice a year. They are a matter of thoroughgoing Jesuit socialization. The Thirty-Second General Congregation abrogated the Common Rules. In their place a recommendation is given:

> This Congregation recommends to Father General that at his discretion he publish a <u>summary</u> of the decrees of the 31st and 32nd General Congregations, together with a summary of the letters he has written to the Society since the 31st General Congregation. This summary can serve as an index of principal features of our religious life.[11]

The Thirty-First General Congregation opened the way to vast experimentation, but in its fifty-three decrees it accounted for all of the vested interests, naming them and urging their consideration. The Thirty-Second issued only sixteen documents. In these it avoided all emphasis on established institutions. What is radical in this is what is left unsaid. The established apostolates, hallowed by generations who considered them proper Jesuit works, are not re-enforced in the documents. Rather the force of the documents insists:

> We must undertake a thoroughgoing re-assessment of our traditional apostolic methods, attitudes and institutions with a view to adapting them to the changed conditions of the times and to a world in process of rapid change.... For our own sakes, just as much as for the sake of our contemporaries, we must find a new language, a new set of symbols, that will enable us to leave our fallen idols behind us and rediscover the true God...[12]

Thus every institution operated by the

Society comes under scrutiny as to how it will promote justice and serve faith jointly. What was formerly an evangelical aspiration and a laudable pursuit for some is now a requirement for all:

> Moreover, the service of faith and the promotion of justice cannot be for us simply one ministry among others. It must be the integrating factor of all our ministries; and not only of our ministries but of our inner life as individuals, as communities, and as a world-wide brotherhood. This is what our Congregation means by a basic choice.[13]

The apostolates that foster and accomplish that basic choice will continue to attract adherents and the life-lines of Jesuit values and leadership will be marshalled in those directions; apostolates that do not reform to meet these criteria will lose Jesuit support and terminate.

The very process of implementation may hasten the demise of some. As a first stage of implementation, every community is asked to accept practical norms given in the decrees, such as living from a budget approved by the Provincial and turning all excess revenues over to the Provincial. The very matter of implementing this practical norm may distinguish the viable from the non-viable institutions. Because of the radical nature of the overall expectation of change in the documents, the Provinces will begin slowly. But the leadership is determined to implement and enforce its own legislation.

The efforts to implement come at a point in time in which most sentiments, so stirred and anxious in the sixties, are quiet. This relative quiet - into which the efforts to implement must intrude - may mean one of several things. The quiet may be only the lull before the storm. Although the number of defections has decreased

99

and the number of new recruits has gained, still
the numbers of men available in the early sixties
are not available in or for the foreseeable
future. The present quiet might not be a turn-
around and the intrusion of change might be a
"last straw" for many, either because too much is
asked for or too little is done. In that case
the defections may again increase and the recruits
diminish. If so, the vision of moving to a
minority facing the world in solidarity with the
poor will be stifled by the lethargy of the
hanger-ons or accomplished in a heroic, prophetic
way by a Society easily decimated from its present
size. Or the quiet may be the expression of a
willingness to bear the experimentation of the
past decade and a readiness to accept the consolidation of the present. A third possibility
could be a failure of nerve on the part of the
existing leadership such that nothing much
changes.

From all the foregoing, the question to be
raised is as follows: The Jesuit General is a
highly charismatic leader; his plans and the
content of his policy statements are of a highly
charismatic, innovative and radical nature; yet,
if implemented, they would have the deeply
practical impact of changing the life style and
orientations of whatever share of 29,000 men
accept the leadership offered; a General Congregation, legislator of the Jesuit Order, established by strong acquiescence and in formal
documents a great deal of Father General's
vision; this legislation formally governs the
expectations as to life style and work of the
29,000 Jesuits throughout the world. The question
is: can a Congregation so accepting of the
charismatic aptly legislate for the effective
implementation of changes in the Jesuit Order?

The problem of implementation may be the
opposite of what is was two or three decades ago.
The staunch Tridentine Society of Jesus was com-
posed of what might be called loyal leaders and
innovative followers. The fame of the Society of

Jesus came from great men who were eminent and individual. Because these great men were important in the apostolate, the Society seldom earmarked them for Jesuit administrative posts. Those who were named as administrators of the Society were more often the ones who "could be spared" from apostolic works. With the revolution of the Second Vatican Council it became apparent that the leadership roles in the Society could not be handled by lesser men because the demands upon all of the Jesuit structures were increasing and the pressures had to be met by strong enough leaders to keep the disintegration at a minimum. It also became apparent that the Jesuits were engaged in the less innovative structures of society-at-large. The Jesuits, as has been said, were the bulwark of the Church's structures. But given the shifts in secular culture, the Church's structures were as a whole becoming conservative and non-innovative. Thus the quality of positions open to Jesuits in the apostolate began to dull. Reciprocal to the dulling of apostolic options, the lines of mobility for the ambitious at the juncture of Vatican II became the structures of leadership within the administrative structure of the Order. Therefore the innovators took positions of Jesuit leadership. This trend has seemed to characterize much of the Society in the important decade of readjustment and experimentation since the Thirty-First General Congregation. Thus the shift in Jesuit leadership has been from a pattern of loyal leaders and innovative followers to a pattern of innovative leaders and loyal followers.

The accomplishments of the Thirty-Second General Congregation have been the product of innovative leadership. But the task of implementation is to convince the uninnovative to accept innovative programs and policies in new structures that are democratic and corporate.

The stress on democratic and corporate structures is a definite shift in the Society of Jesus which has, heretofore, been a composite of especially individualistic persons.

> All this (implementation of the decrees
> of the 32nd Congregation) should be
> worked out in a communitarian context,
> for the individual cannot attain without
> the collaboration and support of his
> community what is demanded of him.[14]

This impact of the communitarian context as
the prerequisite of integration and solidarity
for the membership of the Society of Jesus is
noted throughout the documents and evidences the
higher order integration that is attempted by
the Congregation for the Society.

The decree on the central government mandates that the consultors to the General are to:
"form a council which in its manner of working
goes beyond the consultation of the individual
counsellors...(and) examine together what matters
ought to be treated, especially in the light of
the varied perspectives of the different
members."[15] In the mission document, it is said:
"It is this stress on the apostolic dimension of
our communities that this 32nd General Congregation wishes to add to what the 31st General Congregation has already set forth...regarding
community life."[16] The document on "Union of
Minds and Hearts" legislates that "all Jesuits,
even those who must live apart...should take an
active part in the life of some community."[17]
And the document on Jesuit Identity says: "It is
in companionship that the Jesuit fulfills his
mission. He belongs to a community of friends
in the Lord who, like him, have asked to be received under the standard of Christ, the King."[18]

The revolutionary aspect of this higher
order of integration is not the insistence of
community per se but the introduction on a corporate, collective level of a mechanism which
heretofore had been considered mainly a private
mechanism of Jesuit religious life, that is "the
discernment of spirits."

The discernment of spirits is integral to
Jesuit values. It comes from instructions of
Saint Ignatius, the Jesuit founder, in the
Spiritual Exercises. It is mainly a procedure
for testing one's affective responses in subtle
ways to perceive God's will. As the Spiritual
Exercises were originally administered to individuals, this practice of the discernment of
spirits was a form of individual discernment.
Saint Ignatius and his original followers, however, employed the practice when they were together trying to decide what to do with their
lives. Out of this "Deliberation of the First
Fathers" the impetus has recently been revived
for the use of discernment in common. The Congregation has proceeded in the documents to
enforce the importance of this mechanism of communal discernment. Sociologically this is a
development in the decision-making and problem-
solving spheres at a more generalized level of
corporate management. It places the burden of
legitimate decisions concerning the life of
individual Jesuits on the level of the collectivity, especially the decentralized collectivity.

Evidence in Support of the Interpretation
of a Shift in the Jesuit Culture and
the Advantage to be Gained

What evidence supports the assertion about
what is entailed for the Jesuit Order if it
actually implements the legislation of its
General Congregation?

The clearest evidence of this assertion is
to be found in the document itself. It was exhibited also in the delegates to the Congregation,
and the meaning of the document is best seen in
the light of the delegates' remarks. The document "Our Mission Today: The Service of Faith
and the Promotion of Justice" begins by an-
nouncing three challenges to which the document

and the Society of Jesus must respond.

> There is a new challenge to our apostolic
> mission in the fact without precedent in
> the history of mankind: Today, more than
> two billion human beings have no knowledge
> of God the Father and Jesus Christ whom
> he has sent, yet feel an increasing hun-
> ger for the God they already adore in the
> secret of their hearts without knowing
> him explicitly.

> There is a new challenge to our apostolic
> mission in that many of our contemporaries,
> dazzled and even dominated by the achieve-
> ments of the human mind, have either for-
> gotten or rejected the mystery of man's
> ultimate meaning, and thus have lost the
> sense of God.

> There is a new challenge to our apostolic
> mission in a world increasingly inter-
> dependent, yet tragically divided by
> injustice; injustice not only personal
> but institutionalized; built into economic,
> social and political structures that
> dominate the life of nations and the
> international community.[19]

Textual analysis serves to heighten the im-
port of this "preamble" to the description of our
"Mission." What is spoken of is that which is
considered to be our characteristic work for this
day and age. Yet Catholicism is not the context
given to that; "billions who do not know God,"
"contemporaries who have forgotten or rejected
God," "structures that dominate the life of
nations," these form the context of "the service
of faith of which the promotion of justice is an
absolute requirement."

The document is filled with similar insistence: "we must undertake a thoroughgoing reassessment of our traditional apostolic methods,
attitudes, and institutions with a view to

adapting them to the changed conditions of the times and to a world in process of rapid change." God "looks down on the...circuit of the globe so full of men." Our mission "demands a life in which the justice of the Gospel shines out in a willingness not only to recognize and respect the rights of all, especially the poor and the power- less, but also to work actively to secure these rights." "It demands an openness and generosity to one's neighbor whenever he is in need, even if he is alienated or hostile...." It is "the world which it is our mission to evangelize...." "A greater willingness to be in the world - the world that cries for justice - and thus to know it by experience will therefore be the decisive test of our faith, our hope, our charity." "Ecumenism will then become...an attitude of mind and a way of life. It will be an ecumenism that embraces the whole of mankind...." "...go where there is hope of the more universal good; go to those who have been abandoned; go to those who are in greatest need." "Alterations are called for in our manner and style of living so that the poverty to which we are vowed may identify us with Christ poor, and thus with the poor to whom he preached the Gospel." "If we have the humility and courage to walk with the poor, we will learn from what they have to teach us what we can do to help them. Otherwise, anything we do simply for the poor will not achieve its object, which is to help the poor help themselves...." "Is it only to the converted that we know how to preach Jesus Christ? Are we making any effort to speak the language, reach the minds and hearts of the un- converted?" Concerning professions not ordinarily engaged in by priests, two conditions among others are: "Their aim should be clearly apostolic." "Preference should be given to work in an area which is de-Christianized or under-privileged."[20]

Very many delegates recognized the insistent and radical quality of this document. One dele- gate, a noted historian, said: "If the decrees of this Congregation and the last one are ever carried out seriously, the Jesuits will probably be the first order in the Church's history to have reformed itself without being permanently split in the process."[21] One delegate saw a strength of the Congregation as "the need to witness to a counter-culture both to the world and to the Society itself as it has lived in recent years." Another complained, "We seem to have accepted the presuppositions of the 'radical left'." Another boasted, "The Congregation's option for union and solidarity with the poor sets a challenging new direction for the Society as a whole. Heretofore, we have had solidarity with the well-off."[22] Another delegate wrote: "The suffering humanity is all around us in the poor, the exploited, the starving, and the powerless. If the contemplative grasp of the passion of Christ in all things calls to the contemporary Jesuit, he will be called to the struggles of disbelief and of injustice."[23] Another wrote: "The important point for Jesuits is to recognize for structures what we have long recognized for ideas, that they do make a difference. If we do see that, we shall be as eager today to influence structures as we have been in the past to influence ideas."[24] Such comments by delegates could be multiplied.

Statements by Father Arrupe made at the time of the selection of this matter as the priority of priorities also underlines his awareness of the historical significance of the issue and all that it entails.

Often when we work for justice, as "that certain evangelical Ignatian radicalism" demands of us, we will find the cross at hand. For "despite our prudence and fidelity to our priestly and religious charism," we will find those "...who do injustice, and who...frequently may be among our benefactors or friends or even our relatives, (and) will accuse us of Marxism or subversion, will withdraw their friendship from us and,

106

consequently, their previous trust
and economic support."[25]

The transition stands in the culture of the
Society of Jesus, legitimated by its highest
legislature. The task remains to accomplish its
implementation.

Because of the weighty nature of so fundamental a change made by the delegates of the
Congregation, there must have been similarly
weighty value orientations involved in the
decision to do so. There must be seen some
historical "trade-off" between existing structures and the present Jesuit modus vivendi and
those of the projected future such that there is
advantage to the Jesuits to embark on this course.
What then were some of the values exchanged in
the decision to modernize through the support of
social justice and all that that entails?

First of all, it must be pointed out that
every delegate - and to some extent even the collective Congregation - did not know "all that it
entails." Yet the evidence is in that the delegates were aware of inculturating and calling for
a radical transformation of the Society of Jesus.

Perhaps the major impact on the delegates
in this regard consisted of the stark realities
of greatly diminishing numbers in the Society of
Jesus. One of the reports provided to the delegates was a summary of the statistics from around
the world of the number of novices, or new Jesuit
recruits, that were entering the Society. Another
set of statistics showed that many other Jesuits
were leaving the Jesuits and generally leaving
the priesthood as well. These statistics are
dramatic. (See Tables One and Two). The number
of new recruits dropped from 1,336 in 1954 to 358
in 1972, although it gained to 776 by 1974. The
numbers departing rose from 591 in 1954 to 1,135
in 1969 then declined again to 698 leaving in
1973. In the period from 1964 until 1972, on the
average of 978 men left the Jesuits each year.

TABLE ONE

PROSPECTUS ON THE MOVEMENT OF JESUITS
FROM 1954 TO 1974

At the Beginning of the Year	Total	Entering	Deaths	Departing	Difference	Total at End of Year	% Leaving	% Entering
1954	32501	1336	347	591	+ 398	32899	1.81	4.11
1955	32899	1344	351	605	+ 388	33287	1.83	4.08
1956	33287	1408	363	600	+ 445	33732	1.80	4.22
1957	33732	1298	336	678	+ 284	34016	2.00	3.84
1958	34016	1299	356	666	+ 277	34293	1.95	3.81
1959	34293	1407	304	709	+ 394	34687	2.06	4.10
1960	34687	1464	352	713	+ 399	35086	2.05	4.22
1961	35086	1466	348	766	+ 352	35438	2.18	4.17
1962	35438	1448	356	742	+ 350	35788	2.09	4.08
1963	35788	1273	355	738	+ 180	35968	2.06	3.55
1964	35968	1266	326	870	+ 70	36038	2.41	3.51
1965	36038	1107	369	847	+ 109	35929	2.35	3.07
1966	35929	874	319	911	- 356	35573	2.53	2.43
1967	35573	505	366	950	- 811	34762	2.67	1.41
1968	34762	574	408	1100	- 934	33828	3.16	1.65
1969	33828	611	406	1135	- 930	32898	3.35	1.80
1970	32898	354	413	1071	- 1130	31768	3.25	1.07
1971	31768	403	370	941	- 908	30860	2.96	1.26
1972	30860	358	423	765	- 830	30030	2.47	1.16
1973	30030	466	362	698	- 594	29436	2.32	1.55
1974	29436	776						

TABLE TWO

DISPENSATION FROM CELIBACY AND FROM ALL RESPONSIBILITIES OF RELIGIOUS LIFE AND THE PRIESTHOOD GIVEN TO JESUITS FROM DECEMBER 3, 1964 TO DECEMBER 3, 1974

ante 1950	1950–1959	1960–1974	Assistancy	1964	1965	1966	1967	1968	1969	1970	1971	1972	1973	1974	Totals
5	5	41	Italian	2	7	1		8	7	5	5	2	8	6	51
12	7	129	German		13	9	5	12	10	22	32	11	13	21	148
5	5	48	French		2	6	4	6	3	11	11	3	7	5	58
4	6	194	Spanish	1	4	5	7	10	10	26	48	28	28	37	204
4	5	132	English			5	7	20	6	29	24	15	19	16	141
12	9	411	American	2	3	7	16	18	38	75	101	65	61	46	432
5	1	11	Slavic		2	1	3	3		2	2		1	3	17
3	7	161	So. Lat. Amer.		1	10	12	15	12	22	36	16	26	21	171
2	3	146	No. Lat. Amer.	1	2	4	4	12	9	12	18	22	41	26	151
2		41	Indian		1	2	1	4	3	7	5	3	10	7	43
1	2	105	Asian		2	2	5	7	7	18	23	15	18	11	108
		12	African								1	6	1	4	12
55	50	1431	Totals	6	37	52	64	115	105	229	306	186	233	203	1536
3.6%	3.2%	93.2%													

In the period from 1966 until 1971, the average number of Jesuits leaving was over one thousand. The growth of the Jesuits occurred with every year in this time until 1965. Since that time it has declined every year until the present. Each year since 1966 more members leave than new recruits join.

It is certain that these figures affected the delegates and their decisions. It would seem that the trade-off here is not "more justice for more recruits" but "more justice for fewer defections." The move of this Congregation on several fronts was to make the Society of Jesus more credible to its own members. This is in notable contrast to the strong eloquent appeal that Father Arrupe made in 1965 shortly after his election in favor of the youth of the Society. At the time of his statement the Society had been averaging 1,367 new recruits a year for the past ten years while defections were only half that many. In the next nine years those figures were almost reversed, with nearly one thousand defections a year and slightly more than 500 recruits a year. In 1970, the number of new recruits was one-third the number of defections. Consequently the concern at this Congregation was on keeping the young priests more than on attracting novices, although both are important concerns. Both these concerns are served by the Mission document. Especially the matter of credibility for those already in the Jesuits was furthered in the attempt to democratize the Jesuits, an attempt halted at the wishes of the Pope.

At the same period of time, although figures are not available, the financial situation of the Society of Jesus was fairly solvent. Only a scattering of provinces, it is reported, are operating at worrisome deficits while more provinces than not are not deficient. This information could be relevant in the light of the warning that some benefactors, contributors to the Society, might be lost if the Jesuits adopted a position fostering the underprivileged and poor. One could conclude from this that a trade-off is apparent between members and money, opting for the first at the expense of the second.

If the number of Jesuits was a high priority in various trade-offs, a second high priority was confidence in the authority of Father General. Two major elements were existent that threatened that authority: one was the malcontent and intransigent Jesuits who openly repudiated the decrees of the Thirty-First General Congregation and the authority of Father General. The second element was the clear disfavor of officers in the Vatican with the General.

This trade-off began in 1970 at the Congregation of Procurators. The Congregation of Procurators is a meeting held every alternate triennium in Rome consisting of one representative from every province. The primary purpose of the Congregation of Procurators is to make the formal decision whether or not a new general congregation should be convened. If the Procurators decide "yes," Father General must convene a General Congregation and that congregation must meet within eighteen months.

In 1970 there was already a great deal of friction and pressure being encountered by Father General. This was the year of the smallest number of recruits and the year previous had been the year of the highest number of defections encountered in recent memory. There was need for a General Congregation in the foreseeable future. But it was also evident that a decision to convene a general congregation at that time would have been interpreted by some and publicized by many to be saying that the Congregation of Procurators was dissatisfied with the administration of Father General and would be expecting the next congregation to remedy the error of his ways and possibly remove him from office. Thus the Congregation of Procurators was faced with a dilemma: on one hand there was a need in the near future to call a

111

Congregation to face the crisis of religious life at that time; on the other hand, a decision to call one at that time would seem to be a vote of no-confidence in Father General and would undermine the already disintegrating integration of the Order in many places.

The Procurators decided on the opportuneness of a long preparation as a way out of the dilemma. By deciding against a general congregation at that particularly critical juncture, they expressed a resounding vote of confidence in Father General and left him with the responsibility to call the congregation at his own appraisal of the correct timing and opportuneness. Immediately thereafter, preparations began for the next congregation.

> The Congregation opened on December 2, 1974. Its preparation, however, had been going on since 1971; in fact, it had been going on ever since the latter part of 1970, when the decision to make a beginning had been taken, and when the first steps were set in motion.[26]

What is the trade-off on the timing of the Thirty-Second General Congregation? First of all, the right to decide in favor was traded by the Procurators for the longer preparation of the Congregation. The right to decide in favor was traded for a vote of confidence in the General. Something else was traded as well. From the day a general congregation is convoked, certain restrictions apply. Mainly:

> From the day a Congregation is called (or in the case of the death of the General from the day of his death) it is prohibited that, not only the Provincials, but also major and local superiors, who by their office have the right to attend either the Province or vice-Province of mission Congregations, be changed even if their term of office is completed.[27]

112

In the interim between the Procurators' Congregation of October 1970 and the date of Father
General's convocation of the General Congregation
in September, 1973, nearly sixty provincials were
changed. These changes involve seventy-three per
cent of all Provincials and vice-Provincials and
the number is sixty per cent of all ex officio
members plus customarily elected vice-Provincials.
The balance of the Congregation could only be
altered actually by thirty-seven of these newly
appointed, because twenty-four of the outgoing
Provincials were elected by their respective
provinces to also attend. This number of thirty-
seven comprises fifteen per cent of the total
General Congregation. The Procurators therefore
exchanged the existing personnel of leadership
positions in 1970-71, for the leisure, preparation,
and opportuneness of a Congregation called by
Father General and staffed ex officio by men appointed by Father General. In actual fact, many
of the existing leadership personnel of 1970-1971
were already his appointments.

    The third high priority in the exchange and
trade-offs of value commitments pertains to the
relationships of the Thirty-Second General Congregation with the Vatican and the Pope. This
relationship comprised a complex event lasting
over several weeks (in fact over a far longer
historical period in a larger sense) in an
intense period perceived unanimously as crisis.

    The movement from elite status to minority
status, from Church legitimation to legitimation
in the world by solidarity with the poor, and the
promotion of social justice and its non-capitalist
tendencies threaten many vested interests.
Furthermore, these inclinations challenge the very
structures and life-style of the Papal entourage.
Therefore the Vatican has many issues upon which
to disagree with the Jesuit General: first a
comfortable agenda to promote instead of the
ground swell priority of priorities; then the
series of interventions by the Secretary of State
warning administrators about touchy items, items

that were foremost in the Congregation's ranking
of priorities; there was the broad denunciation
of the General's leadership when the discussion
on grades and democratization issued in a two-
thirds vote to move to abolish grades and the
restrictions to cease all discussion on the matter
and to present all documents to the Pope for prior
censorship; finally after this compliance was
given, there was the further sharp interference
of the Pope's autograph letter closing the issue
of grades "represented" to him and insisting once
again for the treatment of orthodox "essentialia"
at the Congregation.

The Mission document, the priority of
priorities, solidarity with the poor, democratization of the levels of the Society and the shift
from elite of the Church to minority of the world
- all combined to refute the a priori dogmatic
stance, the insistence on hierarchical structure,
and the use of sacred symbolism to legitimate rank
and influence which together comprise Vatican
style. These formed the trade-offs of this
relationship and brought them to a certain
integrity and completeness.

The Pope is more adhered to by the delegates;
they turned toward him in the struggle rather than
futilely moving away. Yet their respect and
adherence is geared now in a post-Conciliar
rather than a post-Tridentine context and the
results are bound to be different, more tension-
provoking, and less familiar to many.

There is a further experience of the delegates of the General Congregation amidst their
own diversity and the conflict emanating generally
from outside the Congregation. It is an aspect of
integration that marked both the experience of the
delegates and the documents about Jesuit living.
That is the issue of community, or union of hearts,
or a sharing of faith.

Above all else the Congregation was for the
delegates an experience of the reenforcement of

their Christian beliefs and their priesthood,
particularly as Jesuits. What does this imply
in terms of process and contrast with the past?
Catholic theology has generally insisted on the
enforcement of doctrine as the cement and sustaining force of faith. The universality of
pronouncements and interpretation effectively
marked the oneness of faith. Even at the Congregation this adherence to doctrine for its own
sake was apparent in a minority of delegates. A
sharp contrast in the composition and dynamics of
faith for many delegates was discovered in the
experience of solidarity in critical events expressed and symbolized jointly in sacred ritual
and sacramental participation. Numerous delegates remarked about the intensely gripping and
memorable experience of celebrating Mass with
Father General, when the General had received the
letter from the Secretary of State sternly re-
buking him for his leadership of the Congregation.
In the intensity of these critical periods, the
familiar routine and secure reenforcement of
cherished religious ritual allowed deeper access
to the interior convictions of the delegates and
consequently a firmer learning and solidarity.

What is of particular sociological interest
in this is that the solidarity in faith comes as
much from the solidarity as from the faith - in a
matter of speaking. The faith is jointly af-
firmed, its impetus is the "togetherness" of the
affirmation. The conviction resulting is a social
reality and retains these social reenforcements
even when interiorized as faith-commitment. There
is a new level of generality and a new level of
organization attained in the prominence of that
experience.

Summary and Conclusions

This chapter conveys the changes in the
Society of Jesus in terms of an understanding of
what occurred. As the main object of inquiry for

this research, the change consists of four features. These are: (1) the Society modernized and generalized its culture and structures through a decade of experimentation and eventual implementation; (2) this process is being set as the expectation of a shift from elite of the Catholic Church to a minority in the world serving the poor; (3) elite instigation, a ground swell movement in the ranks, and spiraling re-enforcement brought this expectation to the Congregation where it was legitimated; and (4) the feasibility of implementing this shift throughout the Society depends on the willingness of the rank-and-file to accept the charismatic elements of Jesuit government today and to recognize and allow the trade-offs entailed. The foundation for this transition is the condition of increased generality in the orientations, beliefs and solidarity of the Jesuit Order. This generalization was set into motion by employing the idea and practice of experimentation as a legitimating device for changes. Experimentation granted leeway and required rationalization of behaviors.

The rationale that resulted in the Congregation's faith and social justice document is an instance of context theologizing. A revered truth and feature of Jesuit tradition, defense of the faith, is associated essentially with the promotion of justice.

This context theologizing demanded a higher level of generality in order to have occurred. Once the legitimation is granted by means of this decree the burden of proof shifts to opponents of the transition. A pervasive reordering of be-havior in the Society can be expected as the legitimate movement gains adherents from various followings within the Jesuit Order. Solidarity with the poor becomes in time a requirement of solidarity within the organization if the move-ment from doctrine to practice is successful.

In many ways this transition is a radical departure in the practice of the Society of Jesus.

116

However, it is a value with roots in the traditions and ideals of the Order. The task of
implementation rests with innovative leadership
to convince loyal followers to accept the progressive policies of change in democratic and
corporate structures.

This process of implementation occurs
through increasingly frequent events that tend
to generalization and become precedent by recurrence. These recurrences may specifically
include trade-offs of keeping manpower but losing
benefactors, gaining relevance but losing ascribed
rewards, being freed from hierarchical domination
while losing tradition routines, and gaining
support for communal faith which is taken from
former practices of individual devotion.

Footnotes

[1]"The Mission of the Society of Jesus Today" in <u>Documents of the Thirty-First General Congregation</u>, pp. 7-8.

[2]Very Reverend Pedro Arrupe, S.J., "Our Apostolate in Africa and Madagascar Today" in <u>Studies in The International Apostolate of Jesuits</u>, Vol. 1, No. 2, September, 1972, p. 66.

[3]Ernst Troeltsch, <u>The Social Teaching of the Christian Churches</u>, Vol. I, translated by Olive Wyon, New York, Macmillan and Co., 1931.

[4]"Our Mission Today: The Service of Faith and the Promotion of Justice," in <u>Documents, 32 G.C.</u>, p. 35.

[5]"Jesuits Today," in <u>Documents, 32 G.C.</u>, p. 12.

[6]Thomas F. O'Dea, <u>The Catholic Crisis</u>, pp. 34-35.

[7]"Our Mission Today: The Service of Faith and the Promotion of Justice," <u>Documents, 32 G.C.</u>, p. 17.

[8]Very Reverend Pedro Arrupe, S.J., "Jesuits and Social Justice: A Common Consciousness of the Problematic," in <u>Woodstock Letters</u>, Vol. 97, No. 1, p. 76.

[9]Robin M. Williams, Jr., "Individual and Group Values," <u>The Annals</u>, 371, May, 1967, pp. 29-31, quoted in his <u>American Society: A Sociological Interpretation</u>, Third Ed., New York, Alfred A. Knopf, 1970, pp. 633-634.

[10]Don Martindale, <u>American Society</u>, Princeton, New Jersey, 1960, p. 89.

[11]"Union of Minds and Hearts" in <u>Documents, 32 G.C.</u>, p. 92.

[12]"Our Mission Today" in Documents, 32 G.C., pp. 19, 24.

[13]"Jesuits Today" in Documents, 32 G.C., p. 8.

[14]Very Reverend Pedro Arrupe, S.J., "A Letter of Very Reverend Father General to the Whole Society Concerning the Implementation of the Decrees of G.C. 32," p. 4.

[15]"Central Government" in Documents, 32 G.C., p. 127.

[16]"Our Mission Today," Ibid., p. 37.

[17]"Union of Minds and Hearts, Ibid., p. 90.

[18]"Jesuits Today" Ibid., pp. 9-10.

[19]"Our Mission Today: The Service of Faith and Promotion of Justice," Documents, 32 G.C., pp. 17-18.

[20]Ibid., passim.

[21]Brian Daley, S.J., "Identifying Jesuits: The 32nd General Congregation," p. 151.

[22]The foregoing three comments were made anonymously by ex officio delegates in a private session.

[23]Michael J. Buckley, S.J., "The Confirmation of Promise: A Letter to George Ganss," p. 184.

[24]John W. Padberg, S.J., "Continuity and Change in General Congregation XXXII," in Studies in the Spirituality of Jesuits, Vol. VII, No. 5, November, 1975, p. 207.

[25]As quoted in G.C. News, No. 6, December 20, 1974, p. 4.

[26]Jean Yves Calvez, S.J., "A Critical Appraisal of the Preparation of the Jesuits' Thirty-Second General Congregation: in Review for Religious, Vol. 34, No. 6, 1975, p. 936.

[27]"Caput IV: De probilutus personarum mutationibus in cases indictae Congregationis" in Formula Congregationis Generalis: Congregationis Generalis XXX 1 opera et anctorita retracta Rome, Curiam Praepositi Generalis, 1973, p. 9.

CHAPTER FOUR

A WORKING MODEL OF MODERNIZATION

This chapter consists of the theoretical underpinnings of the research on Jesuit values in the form of a testable model of modernization, a hypothetical tool to connect the setting of change in the Church and Jesuits (Chapters One and Two) and the understanding given of the Thirty-Second General Congregation (Chapter Three) with the actual data. Through the medium of the model given here, the understanding can be shown to be consistent with the views and voting of the Jesuit legislature.

The model is an "ideal type."[1] It is a heuristic device formed to highlight theoretical viewpoints on the phenomena of modernization to see whether the data of the Jesuits actually meet the terms attributed theoretically to the modernization process. It follows Weber's own usage:

An ideal type is formed by the one-sided accentuation of one or more points of view and by the synthesis of a great many diffuse, discrete, more or less present and occasionally absent concrete individual phenomena, which are arranged according to those one-sidedly emphasized viewpoints into a unified analytical construct. In its conceptual purity, this mental construct cannot be found anywhere in reality.[2]

As Weber devised, the ideal type forms a conjunction of concepts and observations. The conceptual arrangement of phenomena stems from what one's "imagination accepts as plausibly motivated and hence as 'objectively possible' and which appear as adequate from the nomological standpoint."[3] The present chapter contains the conceptual arrangement; the remaining chapters

121

will assess the evidence.

The sources of this theoretical material range from the highly general to the more specific. It includes Talcott Parsons' paradigm for evolutionary change,[4] Samuel Eisenstadt's theories of institutionalization and the transformation of institutions,[5] Edward Shils' work on charisma, order, and status,[6] William Kornhauser's view of the politics of mass society,[7] Philip Selznick's development of institutional leadership[8] and Richard Simpson's treatment of precarious values.[9]

The model begins with the premise that modernization within an organization is incited by changes that occur in the external environment. In response to a perceived discrepancy between the organization and the environment, performance is revised on the basis of objective, rational-purposive criteria. This entails disembedding conduct from ascriptive bases and the rationalization of procedures.

The second phase of the model is the initial crystallization of new forms of behavior. As ascription disappears in support of certain structures, they are abandoned. Cultural activity dominates in a search for new forms through experimentation and innovation. Cultural revision intrudes upon an increasing number of details of ordinary life. Tolerance for and incentives to new occurrences emerge. The energies formerly deployed in ascribed commitments are reinvested in tentative, variable, and segmented forms.

The third phase of the model is that of integration. Attempts to gain the allegiances of people to a diverse array of behaviors sharply increase the extent and level of interactions regarding values. Loyalties develop that are differentiated and interdependent. More people share a stake in the commitments that come from and ensure these loyalties. Leadership specializes in reordering and reorganizing cultural contents through new infusions of meaning and

122

symbolization.

The fourth phase of the model deals with the
articulation of more generalized values. The
infusion of charisma and investment of value
commitments establish a more generalized level of
legitimation which affords greater scope of implementation, increased assumptions of responsibility, and more wide-ranging coordination.
Anchoring various interests in the value order
is accomplished through competition, compromise,
and eventual legitimacy. Cross-cutting solidarities and associationalism with new relations to
leadership develop.

The fifth phase of the model is that of
broad-scale implementation. It is the
structuring-in of newly shaped, interrelated, and
generalized forms of conduct, organization and
value. Norms and channels of exchange solidify
by mutual agreement; effective control is established by leaders, the extent of applied norms is
reconciled with followers' involvement, and the
value order is fostered and confirmed. A fabric
of intermediating groups form. The burden of
proof shifts from innovators to intransigents in
cases of non-fulfillment of newly legitimated
demands.

Detailed Specification of the
Working Model of Modernization

The works of the sociologists cited above
support various elements of the proposed model.
To establish this support is, at the same time,
to give a detailed construction of the modernization process from which to draw relationships
and hypotheses to be employed in the attempt to
verify the process of change undergone by the
Society of Jesus.

The model is based on values and value-
orientations. Socio-cultural factors are primary

123

in explaining change "because ideas and value-
orientations cannot be reduced to lower orders
of complexity without serious loss in understanding and predictive power."[10] The evolutionary dynamic underlying the phases derives
from Parsons' scheme of evolutionary stages of
developing societies.

        In reflection of this AGIL pattern of func-
tional exigencies, the paradigm of evolutionary
change consists of a set of four processes. They
are (1) the process of differentiation that
develops more evolved systems, (2) the process of
adaptive upgrading that develops increased pro-
ductivity within participants of the system and
the system overall, (3) the process of coordination of structural units that develops an integration of various categories of operations
which are enlarged from former stages, and finally
(4) the process of generalized inclusion that
develops resources which are independent of their
original ascriptive sources and yet fully legitimated in the functioning of the social system.[11]

        The operations of these processes may be
simply illustrated. Given changes in an environment and the relationships and activities that
proceed within it, what was once undifferentiated
routine behavior can develop into differentiated
specialties (e.g. the household develops from
being both residence and locus of production into
the situation of the household being residence
with production turned out to specialized
factories). When the differentiated specialties
appear, the roles within the environment begin
to change in order to adapt to the new differentiation (e.g. the role of husband shifts from
stay-at-home to a 9 to 5 breadwinner while the
wife's role specializes as child-rearer and house-
keeper). With the adaptive change following upon
the new differentiation, new processes of coordination occur that integrate both some previous responsibilities and some newly developed
responsibilities within the changed role network
(e.g. the role of wife enlarges to sole

disciplinarian of the family, her status and influence are raised, and she achieves greater authority over management of domestic affairs). Then, as a mirror of all these changes and eventually as legitimation of them through a process of increasing value-generalization, the value patterns and expectations of a culture change and develop to encompass the increasing range of factors and forms involved in behavior (e.g. perceptions and understandings change regarding dating and courtship, the role of women, sexual standards of conduct, kinships and marriage patterns).

The direction imputed to these processes is towards the "enhancement of adaptive capacity."[12] The theoretical prime mover of Parsons' social system is the "optimization of gratification" on all levels. The enhancement of adaptive capacity is this same optimization written large on a system-wide, long-duration level.

Phase One of the model comprises a set of predisposing factors to change, most notably the separability of culture and social structure. Structures which are most coherent and characterized by autonomy and openness toward wider societal levels will be more likely to change. Protestant countries, for example, changed more easily than Catholic ones during the Reformation, because they emphasized autonomy and strengthened internal coherence on grounds of self-sufficiency.[13]

Too close an identification between the cultural and the structural or political institutions can inhibit the possibilities for innovation. A prior restrictive social order can do the same, with a close identity between specific legitimation and concrete structures. More generalized, thus more flexible, sources of legitimation at the cultural level and thriving viable implementations of these in legal, legislative and administrative fields, and other institutional spheres are more likely to permit

125

and stimulate transformation.

An understanding of this autonomy of various institutions is crucial for tracing the developments of modernization. It entails the analytical separability of culture and structure.

In primitive societies the repertoire of possible behavior and the normative enforcement of actual behavior are virtually identical. A son sees no choice except to follow his father in farming, and, in effect, is structured into the occupational role of farmer. This is what Parsons means in saying:

> The lower a system stands in socio-cultural evolution, the more co-extensive and less independent are its societal and cultural systems empirically.[14]

Some older evolved societies, namely Israel and Greece,[15] evidence this separability of culture from social structure. The evolution towards more generalized and thus more adaptive and inclusive cultural products endow them with a saliency and importance that allow them to "out-stretch" the structures in which they began and developed. Values become perceived not only for the behaviors they reenforced and specified, but in and of themselves. The religion of Jahweh and the Greek "polis" carried that quality about them which, in effect, disassociated them from the structures of ancient Israel and the city-states and granted them perpetuity.

The saliency of the cultural products is a consequence of their more deeply penetrating the social structure. What a deeper penetration of culture into structure refers to is the irreducible impact of ideas and value orientations on an increasing array of the details of ordinary activity. Elements of the modernizing societies come increasingly under the influence of thought and deliberate direction rather than traditionally revered and unbroken routines specified by

ascriptive structures. Developments that tend to
break down ascriptive bases of legitimation tend
to modernization. The rationalization of a
culture which brings objective and functional
demands to bear on behavior causes its resources
to become "disembedded or freed from kinship,
territorial and other ascriptive units."[16] This
disembeddedness frees resources for "creative
increases in the extent and level of operations."
Transformation is thereby facilitated and is
accompanied by accelerations in differentiation
and specialization.

> On the one hand, these "free-floating"
> resources pose new problems of inte-
> gration, while on the other they may
> become the basis for a more differentiated
> social order which is, potentially at
> least, better adapted to deal with a
> more varigated environment.[17]

The structural and cultural parameters of
these processes - growing differentiation, social
mobilization and the breakdown or weakening of
tradition - pose basic problems of regulating
newly emerging groups and of integrating them
within some common institutional framework. There
occurs, gradually or abruptly as the case may be,
a weakening in the normative limitations on the
contents of social symbols, a growing secularization of these contents, a growing emphasis on
"this-worldliness," on the values of human dignity
and social equality, rewards moving from ascriptive to achieved status, a larger and larger
proportion of the population who demand participation in the formulations of the society's
actual symbols and institutions, and the loss of
legitimation to symbolic values of "pastness,"
"sacredness" and tradition and the structures
embodying them. Societies undergoing these
changes are rightly called by Eisenstadt and
others, "post-traditional."[18]

Phase Two of the modernization model is
based on the initial crystallization of new forms

127

of behavior in response to the impact of change. Where the first phase evidenced a "turning away" from ascribed legitimation, the second phase inaugurates the search for new institutional forms.

An organization can be viewed as a "web of recurring social interactions in which cultural norms and values are ceaselessly being actualized, modified, eroded or contravened - and in which new norms and values are created from time to time."[19] The question of how the actualizing, modifying, etc. takes shape is fundamental.

Any social system must take care of the "basics of life" in order to survive. This involves the creation and the definition of institutional norms.

Institutional norms are: (1) widely known, accepted and applied; (2) widely enforced by strong sanctions contin- uously applied; (3) based on revered sources of authority; (4) internalized in individual personalities; (5) in- culcated and strongly reenforced early in life, and (6) objects of consistent and prevalent conformity.[20]

Recurring interaction actualizes, modifies, evades and creates values in on-going behavior. This recurrence crystallizes into norms. The norms "cluster" into sets of patterns distinctly related to the "basics of life" or major societal problems that must be met. These sets of pat- terns are the institutions.

An organization becomes institutionalized as it develops its own culture. "In what is perhaps its most significant meaning, 'to institutionalize' is to infuse with value beyond the technical requirements of the task at hand."[21]

Similar to an undifferentiated society, an organization may begin as a simple means to an

end, a "shop" with technological skills to attain
some goal. As it functions, something more than
its technology crystallizes. It serves the
persons operating in the organization psychologically and as a group. In doing so this organization takes on a value in and of itself. "As an
organization acquires a self, a distinctive
identity, it becomes an institution. This involves the taking on of values, ways of acting
and believing that are deemed important for their
own sake."[22] The structure and the value level
of an organization combine to form an institution
recognizable as such.

The longer an organization exists, the more
the value level can penetrate into its concrete
details. This is part of the institutionalizing
process.

Truly accepted values must infuse the
organization at many levels, affecting
the perspectives and attitudes of
personnel, the relative importance of
staff activities, the distribution of
authority, relations with outside
groups and many other matters...[23]

The many different levels at which value
infuses the organization show the deeper penetration of social structure by culture. Both the
value patterns (as they generalize), and the
structural implementations (as they gain autonomy
and diversity in a larger overall coordination),
take on more a life of their own. As this occurs,
the need for integration of various parts inten-
sifies. In the daily routine, issues must be
dealt with as significant not only for themselves
but also for their long-run implications for the
role and meaning of the group.

Phase Three of this model deals with the
process of integration, the incorporation of
various elements into a working solidary unit.
It is necessary "to define the ends of group
existence, to design an enterprise distinctly

adapted to these ends and to see that design become a living reality."[24] This is accomplished
especially through the circulation of value commitments and the functioning of leadership.

The "enhancement of adaptive capacity"[25] of
an organization functions through "generalized
media of interchange." These media are "influence,
political power, money and value commitments."[26]
They serve two functions, one is to "facilitate
routine interchanges among different units of a
social system," and the other is to "facilitate
creative increases in the extent and level of
operations within social systems."[27]

The integration of complex systems is served
by the societal community, i.e. "a complex network
of interpenetrating collectivities and collective
loyalties, a system characterized by both functional differentiation and segmentation."[28]

The loyalty that binds components together
is not the consciousness of kind typical of primitive societies nor the coincidence of numerous
social reenforcements as in "inner-directed
societies." Rather, it is a more abstracted sense
of loyalty stemming from the solidarity of "being
in this together," a loyalty that obtains its
effectiveness on the basis of a larger value
commitment.

Value commitments are the symbolic media of
interchange that function at the highest level of
sub-systems, the level of the pattern-maintenance
of the social system overall. Their mediation is
to relate the structures of the social system to
the culture of that system. They must "bind"
specific behaviors into the larger value order.

Commitments as medium should be defined
as generalized capacity and credible
promises to effect the implementation
of values.[29]

Various participants share a stake in the

130

commitments that are made and draw from the generalized values the specifications which determine their behavior (rather than have behavior determined on other non-shared "irresponsible" bases). These commitments must convey the consequences of their being carried out, the prospect and the legitimacy of "trusting" their exchange, and reckoning with the relationship built on that basis. Or put in the negative case:

> Here it is important that nonfulfillment of a commitment in this sense requires specific grounds of justification; an actor wishing to be relieved of a commitment carried the burden of proving that its fulfillment is in conflict with a higher-order obligation involving the same values.[30]

The highest order function on behalf of integration is to "maintain the commitment that is the central normative condition of the process of implementation."[31] Maintaining this commitment is what Parsons means by the concept of integrity.[32] The primary requisite for integrity is trust. The influence of integrity comes from the circulation of commitments.

In what does the "circulation" of value commitments as generalized symbolic media of interchange consist? Commitments take shape as implemented one way and another. That association of participants which characterizes the societal community receives commitments from participants much as a cooperative store receives dues. These commitments form the "assets" or structured rationale of behavior for the association. When this societal community is characterized by pluralism - pluralism at varying levels from the roles of individuals up through many echelons of collective organization - the offering of commitments must be balanced off within a manifold of claims for loyalty.

131

In return for loyalty offered, the collectivity demonstrates its "togetherness" and the advantage of its "togetherness," i.e., a sense of belonging, the greater impact in numbers, etc. In so doing, the collectivity strengthens its claim of integrity and its participants gain a "strength in numbers" as they implement values derived from the collectivity in accordance with their loyalty and belonging.

One's commitments and loyalty are seldom given as an "all the eggs in one basket" phenomenon. More characteristically in a differentiated society, a whole complex of organizational attachments lay claim to some part of one's commitments. Each citizen of a societal community plays many roles. For example, an American man might have family loyalties, on-the-job loyalties, loyalties to an ethnic group, the college "boys" and a religious group. In the resulting fabric - provided it is built up of compatible implementations of a suitable generalized value pattern and culture - social solidarity and stability reside.

In the case of commitments, we have tried to make clear that there is a high premium on maintaining their "liquidity," i.e., the openness of alternatives of allocation. The primary condition of this is <u>trust</u> in the integrity of the commitments.33

The manner of running an organization as governed by values and culture is evidenced in the employment of promises and value commitments.

The formation of an institution is marked by the making of value commitments, that is, choices which fix the assumptions of policy-makers as to the nature of the enterprise - its distinctive aims, methods, and role in the community. These character-defining choices are not made verbally; they may not even be made consciously. When such commitments are made, the values

132

in question are actually built into the
social system.

A wise management will readily limit its
own freedom, accepting irreversible commitments, when the basic values of the
organization and its direction are at
stake. The acceptance of irreversible
commitments is the process by which the
character of an organization is set.[34]

What occurs structurally when value commitments are made is that the direction and nature
of the various implementation of means within
the organization are thereby defined. Some forms
are outlawed as incompatible with "who we are" or
"what we are about." Other forms of accomplishing
the goals of the organization are innovated, or
fostered, or modified, or transformed, or in-
hibited according to a more ultimate determinent.
This process is "the transformation of an
engineered, technical arrangement of building
blocks into a social organism."[35] The adaptive,
goal-attainment and integrative function levels
of the social system find their anchoring in the
value-level of pattern maintenance, the identity
level of culture.

This level, in a sense, anchors itself by
the implementation of behavior, attitudes, and
direction that are consistent with itself (the
value-level), thus forming and sustaining the
institutional feature of integrity.

Integrity combines organization and
policy. It is the unity that emerges
when a particular orientation becomes
so firmly a part of group life that it
colors and directs a wide variety of
attitudes, decisions, and forms of
organization, and does so at many
levels of experience. The building
of integrity is part of what we have
called the "institutional embodiment
of purpose" and its protection is a

133

major function of leadership.[36]

The second major element constitutive of this phase is leadership. In every feature of the change of organizations, the functions of elites are implied.

> The task of building special values and a distinctive competence into the organization is a prime function of leadership. In this sense, the leader is an agent of institutionalization, offering a guiding hand to a process that would otherwise occur more haphazardly.[37]

The elite function in institutionalization is that function which invests cultural values and value patterns with the intensity that allows them a following. This is particularly true in periods of change.

> The institutionalization of a social order congruent with the new range of problems is not necessarily given in the process of differentiation.... The crucial problem is the presence or absence, in one of several institutional spheres, of an active group of special "entrepreneurs," or an elite able to offer solutions to the new range of problems.[38]

These "entrepreneurs" manifest a special capacity "to set up broad orientations, to propound new norms, and to articulate new goals."[39] This comes from an ability through unique and extraordinary qualities to touch and affect the sources of meaning and affectivity of the collectivity, "to reorder and reorganize both the symbolic and cognitive order which is potentially inherent in such orientation and goals and the institutional order in which these orientations become embedded."[40]

The contribution of elites must be felt in

both the structural and the cultural realm, but primarily in the cultural realm. To affect orientations, goals and value patterns culturally is to indirectly affect the implementation of these in the structural order. Max Weber explained that the influence on this cultural order would be accomplished particularly through special, revered and transcendent qualities, i.e., charisma. Edward Shils gives a contemporary understanding of this term:

> The charismatic quality of an individual as perceived by others, of himself, lies in what is thought to be his connection with some very central feature of man's existence and the cosmos in which he lives.... The centrality is constituted by its formative power in initiating, creating, governing, transforming, maintaining, or destroying what is vital in man's life.[41]

The awe-inspiring centrality attenuated through "unholy forms" to all institutional sectors of society is fundamental to Shils' view of modernization and institution building. In his work "Theory of Mass Society,"[42] he defines mass society as having the condition in which the mass of the populace, extending to the periphery, has a closer integration with and into the central institutional and value systems; there is a higher feasibility and incidence of the participants and value patterns being reciprocal and "in touch" one with the other. The "center" of the society extends its boundaries in a democratization of elite functions (the routinization of charisma). The legitimation of power comes from the differentiated heterogeneous interdependency of parts. Consensus develops from the shared attachment of all elements to the broad integrating central institutional system and value order (viz., the societal community).

Routinization of charisma is focused around reordering both meaning and affectivity, the cognitive and the symbolic orders of society. This is accomplished through the generalized and symbolic interchanges of value commitments by intersecting, pluralistic and competing groups within the social system.

It may, perhaps, be postulated that the ability to institutionalize any post-traditional order and political regime is influenced mainly by the respective power-relations among the groups parti-cipating in the struggle, by the internal cohesion of the major elites that become predominant in the situation of change, and by the severity of the solidary relations between the predominant elites and the broader strata.[43]

Phase Four of this model is that of value-generalization. It results from the circulation of commitments and the influence of charisma freed from ascription.

The general value patterns of a society must be specified to a great variety of situations in which action is socially structured.... When the network of socially structured situations becomes more complex, the value pattern itself must be couched at a higher level of generality in order to ensure social stability.[44]

The integration of a rationalized innovative social system has been described in terms of Parsons' concept of the societal community. Such a societal community is vulnerable to disintegra-tion if the pluralism it comprises is too intense and cleavages within it are too sharp. Since the increase in pluralism is a major feature of the differentiation processes from which modern social systems emerge, their legitimating values must be extensive and encompassing.

It is almost impossible to ensure the

136

legitimacy of association by restricting
legitimation to quite specifically defined acts, however, because actors need
scope for considerable discretion if they
are to implement their values under
varying circumstances. One major factor
in setting the breadth of this scope is
the level of generality of the legitimating
values.[45]

The entire notion of value commitments as
influencing the integration of the system by
binding it into the value order relies on the
functioning of values as generalized symbolic
media of interchange. That interchange can be
adequately realized in a differentiated and complex organization only if it is abstracted and
higher generalized.

It is the combination of this differentiated and specified complexity with the
exposure to change - much of which is
unpredictable in advance - which makes
commitments as a generalized symbolic
medium essential to the functioning of a
society . Only in a simple and highly
traditionalized society can even approximate implementation-obligations be
specified concretely in advance. To do
so, would require the complete ascription
of commitments.... The generalized
medium permits the unit to have the
freedom to make its own decisions of
legitimacy. The unit is presumed to
possess sufficient commitment at
generalized levels so that the steps
of specification for which it assumes
responsibility will on the whole proceed
in accord with the relevant value
pattern.[46]

The increased extent and level of operations
caused by generalized values must be accomplished
without sacrificing social stability. This
stability is achieved by the trust of members in

the integrity of the system.

"Maintaining the commitment that is the central normative condition of the process of implementation" and doing so in a manner of increasing generalization is the crux of stability and development in modern social systems.

Implementation, in accord with the value of maintenance of integrity, will be enhanced in proportion as the maintenance of integrity is held to be compatible with a wider scope of action areas and opportunities in which both segmented and differentiated implementative activities can be legitimized.[47]

When a system becomes more complex and differentiated, specialization and adaptive upgrading stimulate activity of diverse forms. The coordination of these forms as structural units cannot go on in some helter-skelter way if stability is to be ensured. Rather the coordination of structural units must find its own anchorage in value-patterns. Because this demand upon the value-patterns is made in the context of change and diversity, their elements become more and more impressed upon the lower sub-systems implemented this way in one, that way in another. Were the social structure and the value-patterns (or culture) isomorphic and coextensive, the diverse implementation could not be sustained. Either change would be stifled or solidarity and stability would crumble. But given the separability occasioned precisely by the diverse implementation one way and causing culture value-patterns to stand "on their own," higher levels of generality and more abstracted reaches of implementation and meaning are attained.

Phase Five of the model is that of broad-scale implementation. This is the structuring in of the values by processes of reinstitutionalization throughout the organization.

138

All policy initiatives take a shape different than their pure form when they are implemented, for they are modified in various ways by
the structures they infuse. Transformation occurs
through echelons of elites and followers,
especially through cohesive groups that are
centered upon but not too closely aligned with
the central authority. Too close of an identity
between structures and culture inhibits transformation; the disembeddedness of values from
structure fosters it.

A fundamental element of the broad-scale
implementation of innovative forms of value,
organization, and conduct consists in how genuine-
ly the rank-and-file are bound into the value
level, the policy-making level of the organization. To what extent has something crystallized
for the rank-and-file that makes the collective
identity "worth saving," or something to be
protected. Furthermore, to what extent is the
innovation closely enough allied to that collective identity that preservation of one is
united to the preservation of the other.

Policy is operative culture. This culture
is concretely "built into the structure" when it
reaches the point throughout the organization that
it is spontaneously protected or advanced. This
is the point where: "The aspiration of individuals and groups are so stimulated and controlled,
and so ordered in their mutual relations, as to
produce the desired balance of forces."[48]

Gains of modernization occur at the cost of
tradition, to some extent. Some of the costs to
tradition are the weakening of normative limits,
the secularization of contents, a growing im-
mediacy and "this-worldliness" and a disaffection
with the past. The removal of ascriptions as
legitimation is, for some, a violent move, a
wasting of all that is valuable.

Clearly, the facile premise that change is
its own justification and that modernization is

unobstructed "progress" is unreal. It is too
often presumed that change is always "for the
better" and that the developments of modernization occur automatically as a direct and inevitable consequence of differentiation and
specialization in a social system. To the contrary, drastic changes and far-reaching cleavages
would ordinarily bring disintegration of any
social system unless forceful and well-directed
integrative forces "reverse the tide" and reorder
the thrust of the system to one of working
harmony.

Resistance to change inhibits the transformation of institutions. In the face of waning
tradition, a counter-movement of "traditionalism"
can develop. This often consists of an ideology
oriented against the new symbolization; "it
espouses certain parts of the older tradition as
the only legitimate symbols of the traditional
order and upholds them against 'new' trends."[49]
Such counter-movements are often characterized by
ritualism and formalism.

> The transition to modernity poses, even
> more than in other situations of change,
> the question of whether the old or the
> new traditions represent the true tradition
> of the new social, political or religious
> community. It must be determined how far
> any of given existing traditions can be-
> come incorporated into the new central
> patterns of culture and "tradition" and
> the extent to which it is possible to
> legitimate this order in terms of those
> existing traditions.[50]

To facilitate integration, change must occur
in continuity with tradition. Characteristics
that facilitate continuity include some precedent
for self-transformation or transcendence, allegiance to an adaptable center of authority,
accomplishment of the transfer of loyalties from
one source of legitimacy to another, and the
capacity for the innovating sector to further

collective interests. Furthering collective interests minimizes the need for justification and
can more easily obtain some conferral of the
loyalty and resources of those collectivities.[51]

The alternative of developing a new form
of organization must be viewed as attractive in terms of a cost-benefit analysis;
that is, the social and economic costs associated with starting a new organization
must be less than the benefits that are
expected to be derived.[52]

What is true of forming new organizations
is likely to be true, as well, of organizations
that undergo drastic changes. Besides the cost-
benefit advantage, it is also important that
innovators, in the perception of their followers,
have sufficient resources to effect the changes
and adequate power to offset the intransigent
members who are interested in maintaining the
older system.[53]

If the innovation and process of development
can be associated with the "true tradition," its
broad-scale implementation is greatly facilitated.
When that occurs, the burden of proof shifts to
the opposition.

Undoubtedly the most comprehensive kind
of socio-cultural change is a shift in
a major pattern of values or value-
orientations. There is a sense in which
this is true by definition: if values
are generalized criteria of desirability,
a basically different set of values (or
of emphases and relationships within a
given set) necessarily represents a pervasive reordering of social behavior.
However, the important non-truistic proposition is that once a new value pattern
has come to be accepted as so fully
legitimate that the burden of proof is
simply assumed to be on the advocate of
an opposing pattern, then the dominant

141

pattern continues to attract additional adherents and to extend its coverage into more and more activities across all institutional sectors.[54]

A complex, modern organization will not be stable and integrated due to conformity, but rather due to interdependent tensions and trade-offs. The role of elites and their imposition of the value-order require legitimacy to the extent that the burden of proof rests with the opposition. But this is not to expect unanimity.

Complex organizations specialize, in fact, in the diversity of sub-groups. The infusion of generalized value allows each of the sub-systems and associative groups to operate as autonomous centers of power.

As autonomy increases, inclusivity decreases. Differentiated organizations, therefore, evidence a greater number of centers of autonomous decision-making, but each center can claim less control over the lives of its membership.

This increase in centers of control and decrease in their inclusivity results in a growing interdependency of groups or sub-systems. Further differentiations intensify the set of alternatives controlled by autonomous units. As more alternatives develop, participants lay claim to an increasingly large array of proximate relations, i.e., attachments to near-at-hand objects of concern. As the number of proximate relations increase, more intermediate groups form as channels of these attachments. These same intermediate groups consolidate the social interest and activity of participants in regard to larger universalistic matters. This dual phenomenon is what was described as the circulation of commitments in function of the attainment of societal community.

This phenomenon effects the integration of the overall system:

A plurality of independent groups also helps to regulate participation by integrating people into a wide range of proximate concerns. Where people possess multiple interests and commitments, attachments and remote objects, such as loyalty to nation-state, are mediated by proximate relations. Therefore, people in pluralist society engage in relatively little _direct_ participation in national decisions, not because elites prevent them from doing so, but because they can influence decisions more effectively through their own group. Furthermore, people tend to be _selective_ in this participation, limiting their direct involvement in the larger society to matters that appear to them of particular concern in light of their values and interests.[55]

The results of this pluralism are numerous. It promotes an increased cohesion of members with their respective groups, the solidarity of cross-cutting memberships, and the counteracting influence of groups to increase protections for both freedom and consensus.[56]

Social pluralism engenders diversity in culture and politics. At the same time, contact between diverse sub-cultures produces a high rate of change in standards, as people from different cultural worlds are constantly exposed to one another, and, therefore, to diverse and often conflicting standards.[57]

The variety of expectations and demands communicated in complex organizations are vast. They include relations of leaders and followers, and both echelons within themselves. In many instances, they reveal tensions and sources of conflict and of change existent in any organization. They help to incite transformation even in the routine functioning of the organization.

143

The sharing of and "traffic" in loyalties and value-commitments, therefore, must go beyond the minimal extent of this sharing and infusion of value necessary to implement the policies and orientations in diverse performance. More than that is required. Some degree of socialization and social control is exerted upon the membership over and above structuring the necessary working alliances. This "further" interchange also accomplishes a working harmony between segments of the organization and between elites and the respective sub-groups.

This phenomenon is part of the cause for goal-displacement in the organization.

Any bureaucratic organization is oriented, or evolved, as a means of implementing a specific goal or set of goals. But the very conditions responsible for its development, the multiplicity of its internal sub-groups, and the numerous pressures to which it is subjected facilitate or perhaps even necessitate continuous change of at least some of its goals.[58]

In a modern differentiated system there are very many values to be served. A number of these are "precarious values." Precarious values are those values that only a part of the overall system has a direct stake in preserving, and yet they are important for the stability of the group as a whole. The preservation of precarious values is often carried out through conflict and struggle between various sub-groups.

As long as the struggle is carried out under the control of the elite ruling structure, it can strengthen the ties of both sides of the struggle to the value system as well as the ties of the elites to the various sub-groups. This is Simpson's main thesis in treating this subject:

For a social system to provide a full

144

measure of free individual participation
through associationalism, and for its
imperative control structures to be effective without being oppressive, the
precarious values of the larger collectivity must be linked to the norms
and values of its associational sub-
groupings.[59]

This entails a necessary balance of the
influences of various sub-groups. If one group
or the other gained hegemony and could circumvent
the elite structure, their defense of value could
"run away" and foresake any binding relationship
to the values of the overall system. Such a
hegemony could endanger the survival of the organization.

Besides the defense of values, the importance of intersecting and mediating groups is also
to protect each group's self-interest. In contrast to a "mass society" in which both elites
and followers are "directly accessible to one
another by virtue of the weakness of groups
capable of mediating between them,"[60] a more
effective structuring occurs when the elites are
accessible by reason of restrained but counteracting groups. The non-elites are also strengthened in that these same groups protect them from
unnecessary mobilization or misuses by the leadership. The intermediate groups serve an important
function of providing a "buffer zone" for both
the leaders and followers; this buffer zone allows freedom for followers and autonomy for the
leaders. This autonomy is part of the protection
for the elite function necessary to preserve the
integrity of the value order.[61]

Summary and Conclusions

What does it mean for an organization to
modernize? A catalogue of changes over time does
not ensure that a group adapts more to modern

145

times. And modernization does not necessarily mean "getting better." Modernization could mean many things. But for this study, modernization simply means an approximation of empirical events to each of the five stages in the hypothetical model detailed above.

The five stages of modernization according to this model are (1) rationalization of activities and disembeddedness from ascriptive resources, (2) crystallization of new forms of behavior, (3) integration of cultural contents through new infusions of meaning and symbolization, (4) value generalization, and (5) broad-scale implementation of innovative behavior, integration and values.

Rationalization of activities and disembeddedness from ascriptive resources means that an organization does more things deliberately and with a sense of efficiency and effectiveness instead of following tradition and past routines. Ideas, thinking, planning, policy all intrude more consciously on a greater array of daily activities. There is a certain "freeing" of resources, greater flexibility and openness to change, and an increase in the extent and level of operations throughout the organization.

Crystallization of new forms of behavior comes from the predictable increase in "experimental" and unprecedented behaviors that arise when formal rules and ascribed routines no longer specify the activities of an organization. Out of all the varied attempts to meet situations and demands of the organization in new ways, some behaviors take lasting shape and efficacy. In the process the "web of recurring social interactions" begins to become recognizable and predictable once again. Guidelines and formulas and plans become normative and a "modus vivendi" crystallizes.

The increasing array of behaviors that develop must do more than take shape in themselves. They must also "fit in." Therefore, there must be an integration of the expectations, guidelines, plans, norms, etc. through new infusions of meaning and symbolization. The worth of new behaviors must be seen to make sense and be esteemed above and beyond the "technical requirements of the task at hand." There must develop a fabric of many such behaviors along with people's investments of themselves in such behaviors. This fabric must be built up of compatible elements.

In order for the fabric of social norms and interactions to be compatibly and interdependently constructed, there must be an overarching framework of agreed upon values. Given an innovative and diverse arrangement of elements, these values must meet a great variety of demands in order to serve the condition of lasting integration. To meet the variety of demands for a highly diverse arrangement of elements, the values must operate in the social system and among its members at a generalized level.

The most important feature of a social system experiencing drastic change without disintegrating altogether is that the value level actually holds the allegiances of the members of the organization. This allegiance must be maintained in the midst of experimentation and innovation. It must be an attraction of loyalty such that the members of the organization are free to do things differently than past behaviors and differently than other members of the organization yet still feel a part of the same organization.

Given a level of value generalization that allows this latitude and maintains allegiance, the entire manifold of differences that has arisen through the modernization process must gradually become identified and accepted as legitimate by a predominance of the organization. This requires the broad-scale implementation of the innovative behavior, integration and values. The rank-and-file must eventually find the organization "worth saving" despite and including the changes.

147

Changes are really implemented only when they are spontaneously protected and interdependent in such a way that they serve the purposes of various segments of the organization.

The occurrence of extensive modernization raises many dilemmas for the survival of an organization. Seen according to this model of modernization, some of these dilemmas are as follows: Great differentiation and segmentation of resources will develop from rationalization and disembeddedness from ascription; interdependency must develop as well for the unification of the different parts. The emergence of many new options of behavior allow for a far greater selectivity of participation. Selective participation means a lessening of all-inclusive attachment. Therefore, the participation that does occur must be identifiable participation in the organization as well as in particular segments of the organization; there must be a binding-in of parts to an overall identification. There must be the cultivation and acceptance of innovation and yet the innovators must not gain total hegemony of the organization and roots and traditions important to the survival of the group must be preserved and protected. Finally, there must be generalization of values but this is not to imply laxity or shallowness or dissolution of values. The modernizing organization must retain and intensify the "pull" of belonging and close association between center and periphery of the organization. Charismatic and value-laden elements are crucial to its well-being.

The modernizing organization must be characterized by free-floating resources, extensive circulation of loyalties, a compatible trust between diverse, interdependent elements, and an abiding sense of the "high stakes" or deep values that the continuance of the organization represents. Continuity of such an arrangement is supported by precedent for transformation, allegiance to authority, the transfer of loyalties from one course of legitimacy to another, and

the capacity of the innovating sector to further
collective interests.

This preceding treatment is intended to
present, detail, and substantiate a model of
modernization. It is drawn from social theory
and empirical study of social organizations. Its
usefulness must be measured by how well it medi-
ates between the inductive understanding that was
gathered from changes in the Jesuit Order and its
Thirty-Second General Congregation on the one
hand and the deductive process of verifying
hypotheses from objective data representative of
the same group and Congregation on the other.
In employing this model to compare the inductive
understanding and deductive hypotheses, "one
compared two...actual sets of affairs." In doing
so, "the function of (an) ideal type is to
isolate the factors on which the comparison
becomes critical."[62] If this model serves this
purpose well, it is testimony to a certain
relevance of the discipline from which the model
was drawn.

Footnotes

[1] Max Weber, "Objectivity in Social Science and Social Policy," in The Methodology of the Social Sciences, translated and edited by Edward A. Shils and Henry A. Finch, New York, The Free Press, 1949, p. 90.

[2] Max Weber, The Methodology of the Social Sciences, translated by Edward A. Shils and Henry A. Finch, Glencoe, Illinois, The Free Press, 1949, p. 89.

[3] Ibid., p. 92.

[4] Talcott Parsons, Societies: Evolutionary and Comparative Perspectives, Englewood Cliffs, Prentice-Hall, Inc., 1966, and Talcott Parsons, The System of Modern Societies, Englewood Cliffs, Prentice-Hall, Inc., 1971.

[5] S.N. Eisenstadt, Essays on Comparative Institutions, New York, John Wiley and Sons, 1965; and Max Weber, On Charisma and Institution Building, edited with an introduction by S.N. Eisenstadt, Chicago, University of Chicago Press, 1968; and entries by S.N. Eisenstadt, "Sociological Thought" and "Social Institutions" in the International Encyclopedia of the Social Sciences, New York, Macmillan Company and The Free Press, 1968.

[6] Edward Shils, "Theory of Mass Society," originally in Diogenes, number 39, (Fall, 1962), revised and reprinted in Bernhard Rosenberg and David White, editors, Mass Culture, Glencoe, The Free Press, 1957, pp. 30-47; also Edward Shils, "Charisma, Order and Status," in American Sociological Review, vol. 39, number 2 (April, 1965), pp. 199-213, and Edward Shils, "Mass Society and Its Culture," in Culture for the Millions, Norman Jacobs, editor, New York, Van Nostrand, Co., 1961, reprinted as Bobbs-Merrill Reprint #S-510, Indianapolis, Bobbs-Merrill Co., pp. 1-62.

[7]William Kornhauser, The Politics of Mass Society, Glencoe, The Free Press, 1959.

[8]Philip Selznick, Leadership in Administration: A Sociological Interpretation, New York, Harper and Row, 1957.

[9]Richard L. Simpson, "Imperative Control, Associationalism, and the Moral Order," in Herman Turk and Richard L. Simpson, editors, Institutions and Social Exchange: The Sociologies of Talcott Parsons and George G. Homans, Indianapolis, Bobbs-Merrill, Co., 1971, pp. 253-271.

[10]Robin M. Williams, Jr., American Society: A Sociological Interpretation, Third Edition, New York, Alfred A. Knopf, 1970, p. 622.

[11]Originally presented in Talcott Parsons, "Evolutionary Universals in Society," in American Sociological Review, Vol. 29, number 3, (June, 1964), pp. 339-357.

[12]Parsons, Societies, p. 21ff.

[13]S.N. Eisenstadt, "Transformation of Social, Political, and Cultural Orders in Modernization," in American Sociological Review, Vol. 30, number 5 (October, 1965), pp. 672-673.

[14]Parsons, Societies, p. 95.

[15]Parsons refers to these as "seed-bed cultures," cf. Societies, Chapter 6, pp. 96-108.

[16]S.N. Eisenstadt, Social Change, Differentiation and Evolution, in American Sociological Review, Vol. 29, Number 3 (June, 1964), p. 376.

[17]Ibid., p. 377.

[18]S.N. Eisenstadt, "Post-Traditional Societies and the Continuity and Reconstruction of Traditions," Daedalus 102 (Winter, 1973): p. 6.

151

[19]Robin M. Williams, Jr., _American Society: A Sociological Interpretation_, Third Edition, New York, Alfred A. Knopf, 1970, p. 505.

[20]_Ibid._, p. 37.

[21]Philip Selznick, _Leadership in Administration: A Sociological Interpretation_, p. 17.

[22]_Ibid._, p. 10.

[23]_Ibid._, p. 26.

[24]_Ibid._, p. 37.

[25]Parsons, _Societies_, p. 21.

[26]_Ibid._, p. 27.

[27]_Ibid._

[28]Parsons, _System of Modern Societies_, p. 13.

[29]Parsons, "On the Concept of Value Commitments," in _Sociological Inquiry_ 38 (Spring, 1968), p. 148.

[30]_Ibid._

[31]_Ibid._, p. 140.

[32]_Ibid._

[33]_Ibid._, p. 155.

[34]Selznick, p. 55, 40.

[35]_Ibid._, p. 139.

[36]_Ibid._, p. 138.

[37]_Ibid._, p. 26.

[38]Eisenstadt, "Social Change, Differentiation

and Evolution," p. 384.

[39]Eisenstadt, "Introduction: Charisma and Institution Building," p. xxxix.

[40]Ibid., p. xl.

[41]Edward Shils, "Charisma, Order, and Status," p. 201.

[42]Edward Shils, "Theory of Mass Society," pp. 30-47.

[43]Eisenstadt, "Post-Traditional Societies and the Continuity and Reconstruction of Tradition," p. 25.

[44]Talcott Parsons, The System of Modern Societies, p. 27.

[45]Ibid., p. 15.

[46]Talcott Parsons, "On the Concept of Value Commitments," pp. 147-148.

[47]Ibid.

[48]Selznick, Leadership in Administration: A Sociological Interpretation, p. 100.

[49]Eisenstadt, "Post-Traditional Societies and the Continuity and Reconstruction of Tradition," p. 22.

[50]Ibid.

[51]Eisenstadt, "Transformation of Social, Political, and Cultural Orders in Modernization," p. 666.

[52]Arthur L. Stinchcombe, "Social Structure and Organizations," in James G. March, editor, Handbook of Organizations, Chicago, Rand McNally and Co., 1965, as cited in Richard H. Hall, Organizations: Structures and Process, Englewood

153

Cliffs, New Jersey, Prentice Hall, Inc., 1972,
p. 307.

[53]Ibid.

[54]Robin M. Williams, Jr., American Society,
pp. 632-633.

[55]William Kornhauser, The Politics of Mass
Society, p. 82.

[56]Cf. Ibid., p. 80 passim.

[57]Ibid., p. 104.

[58]S.N. Eisenstadt, "Bureaucracy and
Bureaucratization," in Essays on Comparative
Institutions, p. 191.

[59]Richard L. Simpson, "Imperative Control,
Associationalism, and the Moral Order," p. 270.

[60]William Kornhauser, The Politics of Mass
Society, p. 228.

[61]Selznick, p. 120.

[62]Don Martindale, "Sociological Theory and
the Ideal Type" in Symposium on Sociological
Theory edited by Llewellyn Gross, New York,
Harper and Row, 1959, p. 88.

154

CHAPTER FIVE

PLAN OF ANALYSIS FOR THE STUDY OF THE THIRTY-SECOND

GENERAL CONGREGATION AND JESUIT VALUES

The event of the Thirty-Second General Congregation provided a unique, significant and real occasion to study the modernization of the Society of Jesus. The Congregation was called to assist that modernization; the entire membership would be affected by its decision. The modern era, the Catholic Church since Vatican II, and the Society of Jesus itself since the previous Congregation nine years earlier, all gave the imperative to struggle with the necessary adaptation and integration.

The first two chapters of this work sketched the setting in which such modernization must occur. The efforts through the last century in Catholicism, the Vatican Council, the Thirty-First General Congregation, the interim of the past decade for both the Church and the Jesuits, and the Thirty-Second General Congregation, in all this consists the groundwork for analysis. From that background, and based on interpretation of "what actually happened," four assertions were set forth in Chapter Three to form the basis for the research design. These four assertions are: (1) The Society of Jesus did modernize in response to the mandate of Vatican II; it did so by means of greater generalization. (2) This change entailed a shift in the culture of the Society from a disposition as elite Catholics serving a bounded Church to that of a minority status serving all the world especially the disenfranchised and the poor from a position of solidarity with them. (3) This shift in culture was effected mainly through the innovations of elites, specifically the initiatives of the General, the activities of a secondary elite in the field, and, after spiraling reenforcement of a grass-root movement, the sanction and legitimation given by the Thirty-Second General Congregation. (4) The broad-scale implementation of this shift in culture of the Society must be accomplished through an increased following among the rank-and-file Jesuits throughout the world. The feasibility of this following must be judged on the basis of predisposing factors.

These four assertions should be demonstrated to be consistent with objective empirical data from the Congregation. The analytical tool intended to highlight the crucial elements in comparison of the event by induction and by data collected by questionnaires and records of voting behavior consists of a theoretical model, a working model of modernization, which is presented and substantiated by literature in Chapter Four. This model is made up of five phases; they are (1) rationalization, (2) crystallization of new behaviors, (3) integration, (4) value generalization, and (5) broad-scale implementation.

This chapter sets forth the plan of analysis. That is to say, it describes how the analysis of this research proceeds to combine the setting, the assertions, and the theoretical model in such a way as to "allow the data to speak for itself" to either confirm or deny the hypothetical modernization attributed to the Society of Jesus.

This plan of analysis is three-fold. It evaluates the data on the bases of (1) an historical rendering of the events since the Thirty-First General Congregation; (2) an argument from the predominance of "modernized Jesuits" affecting legislation for the Society of Jesus by their majority votes at the Thirty-Second General Congregation; and (3) an argument from the values of the delegates and the leadership of the Society and a projection on the basis of that regarding the feasibility of the non-delegate sample and rank-and-file Jesuits accepting the same values.

The rationale of this three-fold plan of

156

analysis is as follows: the object of inquiry is the Thirty-Second General Congregation. The thesis is one of modernization, a change over time in the values and organization of the Jesuit Order. But the Congregation is one point in time; the process of modernization is a change throughout many points of time. Therefore the General Congregation must be convincingly and verifiably understood as an indicator at one point of time of which process preceded its occurrence and what further process could be projected for the future on the basis of what it indicates. To establish this scheme, it is first exhibited that the composition of delegates to the Congregation have experienced a decade of changes in the Jesuit Order. Secondly, the hypothesis is tested that the delegates who emerged from that experience are predominantly of a "modernized" type. This hypothesis will rely on a typology of "modernized" versus "non-modernized" traits as registered on the questionnaire completed before the Congregation. The effect of this predominance is judged by determining its influence upon the legislation of this Congregation by majority votes on basic issues. By showing that more "modernized" delegates cast majority votes at the Congregation, it is argued that modernization thereby affects the entire Society of Jesus through a legislated shift in its culture. Thirdly, it is argued that the shift in culture must be implemented in the Society of Jesus at-large. The feasibility of this occurrence must be projected on the basis of evidence at the Congregation. Thus, an analysis of the change of values from "before" to "after" is made to examine this feasibility. If it can be shown that the leaders of the Congregation were predominantly of a "modernized type" and that their values were seen as the values towards which non-leaders of the Congregation changed or are more readily disposed, and if those who changed predominate over "intransigents" who evidenced no change or are disposed to the contrary, then it is hypothesized that such change is feasible for the Society of Jesus at-large. To further this hypothesis, the values of the non-delegates will be compared to those of the delegates to determine to what extent non-delegates already resemble the "modernized type," or to what extent they resemble the type that changed in the direction of modernization or to what extent they resemble the "intransigent" type delegates who did not change their values.

The entire structure of this three-fold methodology is hypothetical. That is, it is a construction that can be evidenced as consistent with the data. The ideal type was formed from induction, the construction of reality it represents must be judged according to how well it fits with actual behavioral indicators from the Congregation.

> In forming an ideal type,...(one) has abstracted, sharpened, and extended relations actually perceived. Objective possibility as a guiding criteria of such conceptualization requires that the conceptual form so produced represent an empirically possible state of affairs.[1]

Logically, the hypotheses presented here are tested by means of their reciprocal null-hypotheses which state that only a random relationship exists between the dependent and the independent variables.

The dependent variables are associated with the three-fold methodology. For the historical demonstration the dependent variable is the state of the Society of Jesus at the beginning of the Thirty-Second General Congregation. For the demonstration from the predominance of "modernized" delegates, the dependent variable is the record of votes cast and recorded at the Congregation. For the demonstration from the feasibility of implementation, the dependent variable consists of the value rank-ordering of the delegates and change in that rank-ordering after the

158

Congregation.

There are many independent and explanatory variables that will be employed in the course of analysis. The three major structural variables are age, region, and office. The variable relating to the shift of culture from elite to minority is the discrimination between delegates who are representative of a post-Tridentine bulwark Catholicism style of Jesuit life and those of a post-Conciliar humanistic style. This measure includes an indication of the theological stance of the delegates; the alternative stances are pre-Vatican II, orthodox Vatican II, or avant garde. The various value measures derived from Rokeach's Value Survey[2] are also employed as independent and explanatory variables. Numerous other indices and variables are employed. (See Table One)

The Data Collection

The data for this research comes from observation, respondent self-report on two questionnaires, and records of a sampling of voting behavior on all issues voted upon after the observor was granted access to the Congregation. These components will be described to indicate the nature of the data.

The first questionnaire consists of 103 questions. These questions include demographics (age, region, social class and work), orientation to task or person, expectations of the Congregation, and three questions for assessing which functional exigencies seem to operate in the Society as perceived by the delegate. There are thirty-seven Likert-scale questions that attempt to identify orientations of static behavior or change, universalistic value or self-interest,[3] vows[4] and religious life,[5] and the range of involvement in Jesuit apostolates. The respondents are asked to identify likely leaders at the

159

TABLE ONE

Various Indices from Value Studies Data

From Questionnaire:

    Age
    Region
    Occupation
    Social Class
    Change orientation
    Value orientation
    Task/person orientation
    Church/world orientation
    Theological position
    View of culture
    Professionalism
    Jesuit extensiveness
    Perceived leadership

From Biographical File:

    Province
    Age at entering
    Date of final vows
    Ph.D. degree or not
    Studies engaged in
    Areas of expertise
    Gregorian graduate or not
    Jesuit administration or not
    Languages spoken and understood
    Offices granted by 32 G.C.
    Editorial Commissions or not

From Issue and Voting Files:

    Non-consensual votes on -
        justice
        poverty
        formation
        spiritual life and community
        Jesuit identity
        fourth vow and formed
         members
        tertianship
        fidelity to the Magesterium
        introductory decree
        inculturation

        permanent deaconate
        conscientious objection
        central government
        general congregations
        province congregations
        procedures
        indicative voting
        definitive voting
        amendments
        intercessions

Index of all non-consensual votes

Factor-score index of Bulwark-Catholic/Conciliar-Humanist polarity

Congregation. Rokeach's <u>Value Survey</u>[6] is incorporated into the questionnaire requiring a
ranking of eighteen ultimate and eighteen instrumental values. A series of thirteen items
assesses the theological orientation of the
respondents according to representative answers
given by pre-Vatican II theology, Vatican II
orthodox theology, and post-Vatican II <u>avant
garde</u> theology. Finally there is a five element
scale to gauge the perceived professionalism of
Jesuits. (See sample questionnaires in Appendix
One).

These questionnaires were sent out to two
different groups. The first group was the entire
population of all delegates to the General Congregation. The second group was a one percent
non-delegate sample of all Jesuits throughout the
world drawn by use of a table of random numbers
and a set of all Province Catalogues. The second
questionnaire was sent only to those respondents
who completed the first questionnaire.

The response rate to the questionnaires was
very good. (See Table Two). In total, 202
delegates out of a possible 236 returned usable
questionnaires. This is an 85.5 percent response
rate. Out of 324 non-delegates in the sample,
211 returned usable questionnaires for a response
rate of sixty-five percent. However, of the 324,
eighteen questionnaires were returned either
through incorrect addresses, embargo on mail
(this occurred to a letter mailed to Viet Nam at
the time of the conquest by North Vietnamese
forces), the death of the respondent, the respondent left the Society of Jesus, or the respondent
requested it in a different language to which I
could not comply since I was in Rome attending
the Congregation. With these eighteen considered
out of the sample, the response rate of non-
delegates is sixty-nine percent. The response
rates for the questionnaires sent out after the
Congregation were sixty-six percent for the
delegate questionnaire and sixty-nine percent
for the non-delegate.

161

TABLE TWO

QUESTIONNAIRE RESPONSE RATE

Delegate Questionnaire

Total:	236	sent	First Questionnaire
	202	returned	
			85.5% response rate
	202	sent	Second Questionnaire
	134	returned	
			66.3% response rate

Non-Delegate Questionnaire

Total:	324	sent	First Questionnaire
	_18	disallowed by non-delivery	
	306	possible	
	211	returned	
			68.9% response rate
	211	sent	Second Questionnaire
	146	returned	
			69% response rate

Concerning the delegate response rate, a total of 158 (66.9 percent) delegates had responded by the time the Congregation began or shortly thereafter. On January 16th, almost seven weeks into the Congregation, a second copy of the questionnaire was provided at Rome to all of the delegates who had not responded. Forty-four more responses were received and designated for analysis as "late responses." In at least one-half of these forty-four cases, the late respondents had not received the original questionnaire because they had departed their native countries before the questionnaires reached them.

The questionnaires were sent out in one of five different language versions to each delegate. The languages were English, French, German, Italian and Spanish. Two Jesuits, a native French Canadian and a native Columbian, translated the French and Spanish versions (except for the theology scale, Rokeach's Value Survey, and some of the Likert scaled questions, which had already been administered in those languages, the translations of which were used with permission). The German language version was accomplished by a professor-emeritus of the University of Toronto German Department (Professor Victoria Muller Carson) who worked with a graduate student-native German to provide an excellent translation. The Italian version was completed by an Italian priest and a learned Italian woman who extensively revised, refined and corrected an earlier translation.

The observation of the Congregation did not begin as early as desirable, but it witnessed the greater part of all that went on and provides valid and extensive data. The Congregation convened on the evening of December 1, 1974, and adjourned on March 7, 1975. On January 22, 1975, the entire Congregation voted admission to observe their sessions. (155 in favor 76 against). The delay was due to the red tape of a crowded agenda, Christmas vacation, and need to have a Committee rewrite the original request. The Congregation

163

had run for fifty-one calendar days before admission to observe. There were forty-five calendar days from admission to final adjournment. However, I was admitted at the 22nd plenary session and there were eighty-three plenary sessions in all so I was present at seventy-three percent of all plenary sessions. The vote that admitted me was the 104th and there were over 1,200 votes in all. Thus, over ninety percent of the voting was observed and samples of that voting were recorded.

Votes were cast by turning on lights (green for "placet," yes, and red for "non placet," no) at the delegates' places. These lights were replicated on a large tally board at the front of the hall, with every light uniquely conveying the vote of one individual delegate. Thus by recording the illuminated lights on facsimile "score sheets", a record could be kept of an individual delegate's votes. The large tally board would not remain illuminated for very long on any one vote, so usually a record was taken of only one-eighth of the board. Which section would be recorded was determined ahead of time by randomizing the "score sheets" that the observations were recorded on.

The above mentioned data is supplemented by the full text of all the minutes from the Congregation (the Latin "Acta"), the preliminary postulata or "bills" submitted to the Congregation from all the Provinces and individual Jesuits, over thirty "Varia" which were important announcements or studies presented to the delegates in their work of preparing legislation, many of the intermediate texts of eventual decrees, and the final decrees of the Congregation.

The following information is computer coded and employed in the analysis of data for this research.

> 202   completed delegate questionnaires
>   before the Congregation

134 completed delegate questionnaires
    after the Congregation

211 completed non-delegate questionnaires
    before the Congregation

146 completed non-delegate questionnaires
    after the Congregation

1215 issues on which votes were taken
    coded for kind, content, subject
    and importance

959 records of voting on 1/8 or more
    sample of all the delegates of the
    Congregation

236 demographic and biographic profiles
    on all the delegates including
    occupational and academic credentials

Specification of the
Three-Fold Methodology

The first component of the plan of analysis
provides evidence of a descriptive-interpretive
nature to show the changes that have occurred in
the Society of Jesus in the decade from the start
of the Thirty-First General Congregation to the
start of the Thirty-Second. This is done with
the five phases of the model of modernization as
a "guide" to the crucial elements.

It is shown that the Society of Jesus did
update and reform its structures, at the instigation of the external environment in the form of
the Second Vatican Council. The initial evaluation was clearly the Thirty-First General Congregation. Specific evidence exists that the process
of rationalization and the disembeddedness from
ascriptive sources of legitimation occurred. The
new behaviors and their recurrence and crystallization are described. The methods and means

employed for integration of the Order are given.
Evidence of a more generalized system of values
can be seen as occurring in the Society prior to
the Thirty-Second General Congregation.
Finally, evidence for the implementation of these
changes is given.

This descriptive-interpretive component of
the methodology will be tested by each of the
following hypotheses:

(1) If there is evidence of greater
    rationalization and disembeddedness
    from ascriptive sources operative
    in 1974 than in 1965, then the
    Society of Jesus tends to be more
    modern.

(2) If various new behaviors have been
    initiated and crystallized into re-
    current patterns of behavior in the
    interim period between the Thirty-
    First General Congregation and the
    Thirty-Second and if these patterns
    of behavior are more representative
    of the stage toward which moderni-
    zation is said to develop than from
    which it is said to emerge, then the
    thesis of modernization is supported.

(3) If the Society of Jesus inaugurated
    various mechanisms for the co-
    ordination and integration of newly
    emerged behaviors and if these
    mechanisms and the leadership that
    inaugurated them were accepted as
    suitable and useful, then the process
    of modernization is being fostered
    in the Society as predicted.

(4) If pronouncements and operations of
    the period near the Thirty-Second General
    Congregation evidences a higher level
    of abstraction and a level of greater
    generalization in the values and

166

value-orientations of the entire
organization than did pronouncements
and operations of the Thirty-First,
then the process of modernization
proceeds in the Society as predicted.

(5) If some degree of wide acceptance and
broad-scale implementation of the new
behaviors, inaugurated mechanisms of
integration, and generalized values
can be evidenced in the Society of
Jesus immediately prior to the Thirty-
Second General Congregation, then the
working model of modernization is substantiated.

If these five hypotheses can all be established
as evidenced, it is possible to infer that many
members of the Society of Jesus would have felt,
and to some extent have been changed by, the
modernization process.

Further support of the historical hypothesis
consists in a brief content analysis of selected
documents of the Thirty-First and the Thirty-
Second General Congregations. This measure is an
examination of the frequency with which embedded-
ascriptive traits appear in the documents of each
Congregation and the frequency with which
generalized values appear in the documents of each
Congregation. It is predicted that the earlier
Congregation will have more embedded traits and
the later Congregation more generalized values.

The hypotheses for this secondary measure
of the historical component are as follows:

(6) If the selected documents of the
Thirty-First General Congregation
evidences a greater frequency of
embedded traits than the associated
documents of the Thirty-Second
General Congregation, then the model
of modernization is upheld.

167

(7) If the selected documents of the
Thirty-First General Congregation
evidences a lesser frequency of
generalized values than the associated documents of the Thirty-
Second General Congregation, then
the model of modernization is
further supported.

The second component of the analysis plan
is formed by quantified measures of the outcomes
of voting as determined by each of two styles of
Jesuit orientation. The styles are likenesses
to a post-Tridentine bulwark Catholicism and a
post-Conciliar humanism.

The first step in this determination is to
construct a scale of the two Jesuit styles. The
scales of style discriminate the delegates into
two groups. These two groups are compared on the
basis of their votes. The overall votes are
compared for the two groups under controls for
age, region, and office. A further control is
set for those delegates who were named on the
questionnaires as being perceived leaders of the
Congregation. Other indices will also be used
for controls. The groups are compared on various
issues of the Congregation and on the types of
voting.

The comparison of the two groups on various
issues is intended to judge the effect that the
different styles have on different elements of
the Congregation's legislation. It is expected
that in some areas more than others the two
groups will diverge.

The hypotheses for testing the outcomes of
voting by styles of Jesuit orientation are as
follows:

(8) If major factors are discriminated
according to differences of style
of orientation, then two relatively
coherent groups will be formed

168

characterized as bulwark catholicism
and conciliar humanism (hereafter
B-C and C-H respectively.)

(9) If B-C and C-H groups are discriminated
one from the other among the delegates,
then the C-H will comprise the larger
of the two groups.

(10) If the delegates of the two styles
diverge in their votes on a composite
measure of all votes taken together,
then the majority of votes cast will
be in favor of the C-H style position
on the issues.

To some extent the "control" hypotheses are
diagnostic. It is expected that the B-C style
will predominate in some categories of age, region and office. Tests of the hypotheses will
reveal this.

(11) If these two styles are discriminated
when controlling for age, C-H style
will predominate over B-C style in a
majority of age-categories.

(12) If the two styles diverge in their
votes on issues when controlling for
age, the majority of votes cast will
be in favor of the C-H style position
in a majority of age categories.

(13) If these two styles are discriminated
when controlling for region, then C-H
style will predominate over B-C style
in a majority of regions.

(14) If the two styles diverge in their
votes on issues when controlling for
region, then the majority of votes
cast will be in favor of the C-H
style position in a majority of
regions.

169

(15) If these two styles are discriminated
when controlling for office, then
C-H style will predominate over B-C
style in a majority of Jesuit administrative offices.

(16) If the two styles diverge in their
votes on issues when controlling for
for office, then the majority of votes
cast will be in favor of the C-H
style position for a majority of Jesuit
administrative offices.

(17) If these two styles are discriminated
when controlling for ascertained leadership by questionnaire response, then
C-H style will predominate over B-C
style for a majority of ascertained
leaders.

(18) If the two styles diverge in their
votes on issues when controlling for
ascertained leadership by questionnaire response, then the majority of
votes cast will be in favor of the
C-H style position for a majority of
ascertained leaders.

(19) If the two styles diverge in their
votes on individual issues, then the
majority of votes cast will favor
the C-H position in a majority of
issues.

(20) If the delegates are discriminated
according to these two styles, then
they will also be discriminated with
a high positive correlation according
to measures of theological position
and value-ranking.

The third component of the analyses plan is
the quantified analysis of value orientations and
change in values from before the Congregation to
after the Congregation as measured by Rokeach's

Value Survey. The object of this measure is partially to judge the consensus between leaders and followers at the Congregation. The non-delegate respondents are compared with the delegate respondents in respect to their orientations and change of values.

The relative size and position of differences between these groups will be analytically significant in arguing the feasibility or unfeasibility of implementing the changes of the Congregation.

The hypotheses for testing the changes in the values of the respondents are as follows:

(21) If the value-rankings of the delegates are compared, then certain coherent "profiles" of value-ranking will be evidenced from among the delegates.

(22) If the "profiles" of value-rankings of delegates are compared, then certain profiles will be evidenced as more modernized than other profiles according to criteria consonant with the model of modernization.

(23) If delegates are compared according to the extent of resemblance to the modernized profile of value-rankings, then the leadership of the Congregation will tend to resemble that profile more frequently than the non-leadership.

(24) If all delegates are measured for change of value profiles from "Before" to "After" the Congregation, the direction of that change will be towards the modernized profile more often than in other directions.

171

Summary of Analysis Plan

This chapter has outlined the plan of analysis for the study of the Thirty-Second General Congregation and Jesuit values. The plan is to show that the delegates witnessed a decade of modernizing developments before the Congregation. Enough of them bear the influence of that to form a majority of modernized members. Through these modernized members casting a predominance of majority votes, the modern developments are translated into legislation. The feasibility of implementing that legislation among the rank-and-file is suggested by comparing the delegates with a non-delegate sample. Where values of these two groups converge, the likelihood of implementation is predicted.

The decade of modernizing is portrayed from historical evidence corresponding to the model of modernization. The distribution of modernized members is determined from questionnaire data which forms a Bulwark-Catholic/Conciliar-Humanist polarity. The predominance of majority voting is counted from a sampling of nearly one thousand votes taken at the Congregation.

The overall scheme for studying the modernization of the Jesuits consists in answering the following questions: Do events in the Society of Jesus during the last ten years approximate the states of modernization set forth in the model? Do the members of the Congregation evidence differences in the effects of that modernization as indicated in questionnaire items of static orientation or change, value orientation or self-interest, theological position, and views on the relationship of the Church and the world? Do those differences translate into differences in the voting on issues in the Congregation and, if so, which style predominates in the definitive legislation? In what way do the values of the delegates and those of the non-delegates resemble one another and in what way are they very different?

172

The description of changes in the Jesuit Order, the assertions stemming from an understanding of the changes and the Thirty-Second General Congregation, and the theoretical model of modernization are combined in the analysis to "allow the data to speak for itself" and either confirm or deny the modernization which is here hypothesized of the Society of Jesus.

Footnotes

[1]Don Martindale, "Sociological Theory and the Ideal Type," in Llewellyn Gross, editor, Symposium on Sociological Theory, New York, Harper and Row, 1959, pp. 69-70.

[2]The Value Survey is explained and discussed in Milton Rokeach, The Nature of Human Values, New York, The Free Press, 1973.

[3]Sister Marie Augusta Neal, S.N.D., Values and Interests in Social Change, Englewood Cliffs, New Jersey, Prentice-Hall, 1965. In this research, developed at Harvard University's Department of Social Relations, a sample of 259 diocesan priests of the Boston diocese were surveyed for values and attitudes. The scales partially employed here are those which discriminate static-oriented from change-oriented responses and universalistic values from self-interest.

[4]National Opinion Research Center (directed by Reverend Andrew M. Greeley), (with Richard A. Schoenherr as "co-principal Investigator, (who) directed the overall project.") The Catholic Priest in the United States: Sociological Investigations, Washington, D.C., United States Catholic Conference, 1972. In this research, Andrew Greeley and Richard Schoenherr surveyed 5,110 active priests with a forty-six page attitudinal survey. The present research uses numerous questions from their section for Religious Priests concerning the vows of poverty, chastity, and obedience, and attitudes toward religious life and changes in the Church.

[5]Society of the Divine Word Self Study, Washington, D.C. (1969-1972). In this research coordinated by Reverend Richard Rashke, S.V.D., with the Sociology Department of the Catholic University of America, 3,529 priests, brothers, and seminarians were surveyed for attitudes toward the Church and religious life. Questions on changes in the church, "speaking out" and

relating to customs locally and in foreign countries, and on the theological positions were
taken from this study. These questions were
available in French, English and German.

[6]Milton Rokeach, The Nature of Human Values.
Besides the English version of the Value Survey,
translations of this survey in German, French
and Spanish were also available. The German version was translated by Dr. Hartmut Guenther, the
French version by Ms. Shirley Edwards, and the
Spanish version by Ms. Sharon Staples. These
translations were authorized by Professor Rokeach
and their use in this research was authorized by
each of the translators.

CHAPTER SIX

A DECADE OF MODERNIZING IN THE JESUIT ORDER

Much changed in the Jesuit Order from 1964 to 1974. Describing the state of affairs both early and late in the decade gives evidence of this change that corresponds with the model of modernization. The sources for this evidence are participant observation, content-analysis of documents from the beginning and end of the period, and questionnaire responses from the delegates to the Thirty-Second General Congregation.

The rationalization of many activities and the disembeddedness of evaluation from ascriptive bases occurred in administrative structures, procedures, and the course of studies.

The structures of many provinces have changed. Formerly the provincials alone governed the provinces. Various areas of province government are now administered by assistants or Vice-Provincials. These offices of specialized vice-provincial or roles of director in specialized areas have been inaugurated since the Thirty-First General Congregation.

In many Jesuit works, the major administrative offices which formerly were held exclusively by Jesuits, are frequently held by trained lay specialists. Many principals of high schools and vice-presidents of universities and colleges are determined by training and expertise rather than affiliation to the Society of Jesus. Governing boards in many Jesuit universities have become secularized. In the United States, for instance, control of most of the colleges and universities has been given over by the Jesuits to boards of trustees made up of Jesuits and non-Jesuits. These boards are officially freed from obligations of a religious nature.

177

Supervision of the Order and the operations and effectiveness of Jesuit works have been submitted to the scrutiny of management consultants and social scientists. In 1966, a three-year sociological survey of every Province of the Society of Jesus was begun. It was a recommendation of the Thirty-Second General Congregation that the administration of the Jesuit headquarters be submitted to the same sort of scrutiny and that consultation is presently underway.

Throughout the world, the course of studies has been freed from the prescriptions of Roman curricula and has incorporated modern philosophy and the physical and humane sciences. The pedagogy of most Jesuit training institutions has changed from formal seminary methods to those of academic departments elsewhere. Jesuit training institutions have combined with institutions of higher learning both Catholic and secular and many courses are no longer exclusively religious or exclusively Jesuit.

The most dramatic array of changes in the last decade are, perhaps, those changes that evidence the disembeddedness of activities and attitudes from ascriptive resources and traditional legitimation. Legitimacy is today assigned on the basis of more objective or rational criteria.

Formerly, many provincials were appointed from a "route" of administration beginning with a superior's role to rector of the Novitiate or president of a prestigious secondary school to provincial. These "automatic" channels to higher office have disappeared. Seniority itself is no longer as important in appointment to higher office within the Jesuit Order. An increasing number of young men are being assigned administrative offices including the office of provincial.

A decade ago the various "levels" or grades of membership in the Society were segregated by

178

the custom of "separation." In the dining-room and in the chapel, seating was hierarchically prescribed. Each grade of membership ordinarily inhabited determined sections of a building and recreated in segregated groups. Customs of segregation have formally diminished in all but extremely rare cases.

Formation through fifteen years of study was segregated into "long course" and "short course." An oral examination each year determined one's eligibility for the "long course." If one failed that examination, he was thereafter trained less theoretically in the "short course." Finally an examination "ad gradum" (to one's grade) was taken to establish eligibility for profession of the four vows. The distinction between long and short course no longer exists. Criteria for profession have been broadened. Various odious distinctions between the professed and the non-professed have disappeared. There are new career opportunities for the non-professed. Menial tasks are no longer characteristic of the brothers vocation and many administrative offices have opened to them.

Other signs of disembeddedness from ascription include the gradual disuse of clerical attire (the black suit and roman collar) in favor of suits and ties, the private celebration of daily Mass replaced by increased concelebration of many priests together or priests attending Mass said by another, the removal of "cloister" from many Jesuit residences such that visitors are allowed into areas formerly segregated by religious custom, the disappearance of the Latin language as a privileged "language of record," and the more general sense of "taking Father off of his pedestal" which has come from demythologizing the role and authority of the priesthood.

New patterns of behavior which have crystallized since Vatican II affect a Jesuit's life in his daily order, prayer, living arrangements, relationship to authority, financial dependence,

occupational latitude, forms of liturgy and old
age.

The "daily order" of a decade ago specified
rising at five in the morning, spending one full
hour in meditation, then spending thirty minutes
saying Mass, usually in the privacy of a basement
chapel designed for private Mass. Two periods of
a quarter hour of examination of conscience, once
at noon and once at retiring, was mandatory.
Meals were served at a set time and taken in
silence while one person read aloud some selection from a spiritually edifying book for the
relaxed thoughtfulness of the assembled community.

Today, rising time is completely variable.
Private prayer is set at each person's discretion.
The Thirty-Second General Congregation repeated
the injunction of the Thirty-First General Congregation that "our rule of an hour's prayer is
to be adapted, so that each Jesuit, guided by his
superiors, takes into account his particular
circumstances and needs, in the light of that
discerning love which St. Ignatius clearly pre-
supposed in the Constitution."[1] Some brief common prayer is recommended. This replaced the
mandatory "litanies of the Saints of the Society
of Jesus" which were said daily before the evening
meal. The Thirty-Second General Congregation,
instead, recommended occasional recourse to "a
longer period for prayer and prayerful discussion
(including) shared prayer, days of recollection,
and the Spiritual Exercises in common."[2] These
means have become recognized as alternatives to
former customs.

Living patterns have changed and broadened
much in the past decade. Many large residences
have varied their life styles. This has occurred
in various ways. "Satellite communities" have
formed in smaller family-size residences. In
other large residences, certain corridors or
wings of the building have become autonomous communities, sometimes having separate superiors,
schedules and dining arrangements. In some cases,

these houses are financially independent and in others they are not. A trend exists to have a more frugal life-style and closer identification with the poor in this emerging form of small communities.

Another pattern that has crystallized and reverses the trend of a decade ago is the movement from rural and secluded settings for Jesuit formation of its "scholastics" to diffuse, busy urban settings. In the United States, the Jesuits transferred from large estates in the country to Berkeley, Saint Louis, Chicago, New York City and Cambridge.

The relationship of authority in the Jesuit Order changed within the decade from formal guardianship on the part of the superior and diffidence on the part of the subject to a more mutual relationship. The model of a pyramid portrayed the former relationship; the model of periphery sharing increasingly in the legitimacy of the center portrays the present relationship. The process of dialogue is institutionalized in the Thirty-Second General Congregation documents by their repeated reference to communal discernment of spirits.

Another crystallization of an alternate pattern is the drastic change in dependency for financial needs. In most large communities of a decade ago, the administration provided a common store for articles of clothing, supplies, and ordinary necessities. Money for other items was given upon request for the specific item. This pattern has been replaced by the pattern of regulated "budgets" for all members of communities. Rather than "asking permission" for specific items, one sees to their acquisition individually. Money is given in lump sums to cover several months at a time. Individual checking accounts, considered sinful a decade ago, are common practice today.

Another pattern of this decade consists of

extensive Jesuit engagement in non-institutionally aligned activities. Passive resistance, community organizing, protests and mass rallies are included among these activities. The nature and variety of these engagements was unheard of twenty years ago.

There is a close relationship between financial independence and non-aligned apostolates. A stringent form of social control was exerted by superiors when subjects were required to request expenses in specific detail. Granting funds was also granting permission. Freeing the person from requesting funds was also freeing him for detailed governance. The following item is an interesting example of this change in structure:

> The FBI recently looked into the whereabouts of Joe O'Rourke, S.J. and his friends on the night when documents were stolen from the Bureau's office in Media, Pennsylvania. Catholic FBI agents, once familiar with Jesuit ways at schools like Fordham and Georgetown, went to the minister at 98th Street and asked whether the students had left New York or had funds for travel. When Father Curry (the minister) answered to all these questions that he did not know, the agents looked puzzled and not entirely convinced.[3]

Other newly crystallized patterns concern the retraining of older Jesuits, new relations to marginal groups of civil society and experiments with new forms of liturgy and prayer. Due to the drastic and rapid changes in society generally, many middle-aged Jesuits find teaching youth to be overly demanding. With increased frequency these men are retiring from the schools and are being retrained for tasks such as hospital chaplaincy, giving directed retreats, or parish responsibilities. Jesuits holding various offices of social work and civil administration has become more frequent. These offices include management of federal or regional housing programs, welfare

182

offices, specialized technical posts in government, and running for political election. New patterns of sharing functions of worship, praying in the fashion of evangelical communities, celebrating Mass in intimate "home masses," and making retreats in a one-to-one relation with a director instead of listening to preached sermons are forms of liturgy and prayer that have gained ascendancy in this modern era.

Many integrative mechanisms have developed and successfully accomplish the coordination and integration of newly emerged behaviors into suitable, useful, and legitimate processes in the Jesuit Order.

At the beginning of this era the assignment of Jesuits to various tasks was a one-sided decision. The provincial and the heads of the various institutional enterprises met to discuss needs and manpower and draw up a "Status." The "Status" would then be published on July 31st of every year. It declared all transfers of personnel for the following year. Usually this was the first notice that the newly assigned personnel received. The transfers were mandatory and complied with by virtue of one's vow of obedience. The "Status" no longer exists in most provinces of the Society of Jesus. Dialogue and negotiations determine the transfer of manpower.

Since many of the institutional affiliations have seen a secularization of control, the Jesuit superiors can no longer command the acceptance of personnel to various occupational positions. For example, a Jesuit provincial cannot insist that a university or its respective departments hire a particular Jesuit to a teaching position. This change of personnel policy was legitimated in some assistancies by agreement on a "Principle of Attraction." No Jesuit personnel is assigned to particular posts or places. Rather, it is incumbent upon the personnel to choose the position of their preference. On the other hand, no institution can have personnel forced upon them

183

and these institutions have the right under this
principle to refuse personnel as they choose to.

Originally many more traditionally-minded
Jesuits saw the emergence of this principle of
attraction as a concession to the young Jesuits.
They complained that obedience would be lost and
the institutions undermined. To some extent this
proved accurate, especially regarding the under-
mining of some institutions. Numerous Jesuit
works were forced to close because Jesuit personnel could not be attracted to them. On the other
hand, the experience of nearly a decade of the
Principle of Attraction has evidenced the greater
advantage to the institutions which gain their
personnel through competitive allocations instead
of by Jesuit mandate. This has strengthened
the requirement for Jesuits to gain necessary
credentials in order to successfully apply for
various positions. It has also left other Jesuits
free to pursue non-institutional occupations by
reason of their not seeking attraction to the
various institutions.

Another integrative process is the development of various voluntary associations within the
Order. These groups form along varying lines;
some are occupations, some are centered on various
causes, others are incentive programs that attract membership. One example of an occupational
kind of association is the Jesuit Institute of
the Arts. A brief history of this institute is
illustrative of this kind of movement in the
Society.

> After several years of preliminary
> meetings, its members met for summer
> workshops at Holy Cross College in
> the summer of 1970, at the University
> of Santa Clara in 1971, and at Mondragone,
> Frascati, near Rome, in 1972. The purpose
> of the Institute is to enable Jesuits
> who are professionally engaged in the
> fine arts to spend time together while
> reflecting, praying, and creating in an

atmosphere of brotherly help and criticism.
Membership is quite informal and open to
anyone concerned. The Institute, while
American in origin and practical membership, has become increasingly international.

At several of its performances last summer
the Institute was graced and encouraged
by the presence of Very Reverend Father
General Pedro Arrupe, Father Assistant
Harold O. Small, and other members of the
Society's curia. On one of these occasions Father General thoughtfully
surprised the assembly by reading a paper
of his own which manifestly captivated
his audience.[4]

Various causes have been responsible for the
emergence of other Jesuit agencies. The Centro de
Investigacion y de Accion Social is a Latin
American social action group. The Center of
Concern is another social action agency founded
and staffed by Jesuits. It is located in
Washington, D.C. and is financed in part by the
American Bishops. The Jesuit headquarters in
Rome also has developed a secretariat for social
action. Some older organizations within the
Society have been restructured to serve more ex-
tensive and more specialized integrative tasks.
Among these are groups of Jesuit University ad-
ministrators, secondary school administrators and
missionary supervisors and fund raisers. In the
United States, both the Jesuit Secondary Education
Association and Jesuit Missions Incorporated have
been restructured to serve more effectively and
with new purpose.

Another form that newly developed Jesuit
agencies serve is that of providing incentives for
attention to prominent values. The Jesuit Council
for Theological Reflection was inaugurated in 1973
to promote indisciplinary research and publishing
of a theologically reflective nature. It operates
as a funding agency for Jesuits by screening

185

proposals and awarding support to selected projects. In turn, the Council is funded by the entire American Assistancy.

Various provinces have individually employed this financial form of coordination by the recent practice of earmarking for specified apostolic and social welfare purposes all funds that derive from the liquidation of property and capital holdings of apostolates or institutions that are forced to close. The most recent funding agency to be established is the Charitable and Apostolic Fund of the Society of Jesus. The Jesuit General promulgated its statutes in March, 1976 in fulfillment of legislation of the Thirty-Second General Congregation. This fund will receive its support from "voluntary" taxes of the Jesuit provinces throughout the world. "It's main purpose is to foster our solidarity and unity, and a greater awareness of an openness to the many and urgent needs in our world today, within our Society and outside it."[5]

The provincials in various Assistancies have coalesced into working agencies. The Jesuit Conference is a fully-developed center in service to the ten American Provincials. The Near-East Superiors Conference is a similar organization.

An instance of the work of these specialized agencies in replacing the activities of otherwise unspecialized institutions is the publication of the English translation of the documents of the Thirty-Second General Congregation in comparison to the publication in English of those of the Thirty-First General Congregation. The documents of the Thirty-First General Congregation were published and distributed to North American Jesuits by Woodstock College, an historic Jesuit institution, a seminary for training Jesuits in theology, and a center for theological research. It published a monthly journal, Woodstock Letters, which is an historical record of much Jesuit memorabilia. Woodstock College disbanded two years ago. The English translation of the

186

documents of the Thirty-Second General Congregation was the joint effort of the Jesuit Conference and the American Assistancy Seminar on Jesuit Spirituality.

A vast array of other integrative mechanisms has developed within the Society of Jesus. Among these could be listed the numerous periodicals and "in-house" publications that have become serious endeavors of various sectors of the Society. Special institutes, seminars, theological updating sessions and retreats organized for improved sharing and communication have all flourished and served as integrative of elements of the Jesuit Order.

The generalization of values is seen occurring in the Society of Jesus through pronouncements of Father General, individuality in formation, changes in forms of piety and tradition, and in the use of guidelines instead of prescriptions for governance of the Society.

The most authoritative evidence of the attainment to a higher level of abstraction and greater generalization was the pronouncement at the Congregation of Procurators meeting in 1970 in which Father General outlined four basic "apostolic priorities of the Society of Jesus." As has been reported earlier in this study, these are the priorities of theological reflection, education, social action, and the media of social communication. Father General has stressed these as values that are generally applicable across the range of various apostolic tasks.

Greater value generalization is found in the legitimation of many changes on the grounds of "following the spirit of the law if not the letter." Appeal to the higher authority of the "spirit" has become a clear channel of legitimacy. Even in the parlance of the updated Church, the role of the Holy Spirit, third person of the Triune Godhead, is more prominent since the Second Vatican Council. This is itself evidence of greater generalization. It can be argued that God the Father represents order and authority; Christ, the Son of God, represents the incarnational and cultural forms of Christianity; whereas the Holy Spirit represents appeal to the unprecedented and more broadly innovative and charismatic elements in the Church.

Another appeal to value generalization is found in the stress within the programs of Jesuit training on "formation fitted to the individual." In a way that sharply contrasts with the regimentation of earlier forms of training, the promotion of individual differences, personal strengths and discoveries, and pluralist tendencies rely on coordination under the rubrics and rationales of greater value generalization.

Value generalization is seen in the attenuation and diminution of emphasis on specific forms of piety. Prior to the Second Vatican Council every Catholic parochial sector emphasized various pious religious practices. Among these were various devotions to the Blessed Virgin Mary, and many saints of the Church; novenas, i.e. special prayers of honor and petition usually said over a period of nine days, were widespread and popular; paraliturgical ceremonies such as Benediction, May devotions, special "mission" and family religious practices all flourished. Some of these devotions were part of Jesuit piety and Jesuit promotion, for example, Sacred Heart devotion, the Apostleship of Prayer, Sodalities of the Blessed Virgin Mary, and preached group retreats. The Novena of Grace in honor of Saint Francis Xavier was also a prominent Jesuit pious practice. Today, these pious practices, except for the preached retreats, are almost nonexistent. Special mention of any of these devotions is absent from the documents of the Thirty-Second General Congregation.

In place of pious practices, emphasis on the person of Christ, participation in the Eucharist and promotion of the Spiritual Exercises permeates the documents. These are all emphases of a more generalized and more broadly applicable nature.

Another evidence of value generalization can be traced through a series of developments during the time since the Thirty-First General Congregation. There has been a transition from the particular to the general in the way that various ecclesiastical topics and concerns are presented and discussed. Among these topics could be included liturgical reform, style of preaching, role of authority and obedience, forms of life-style and poverty, relationships between religious and laity, or relations of Jesuits to persons of the opposite sex. In the manner of discussing these and other topics, the period of the 1960's saw a proliferation of specific modes of practice in each case. Talk of particularities flourished, books on types and fashions of practice proliferated; fads rose and fell. The period of the 1970's has seen a great lessening of the particular treatments of all these matters. The attention has turned to deeper analyses of principles and underlying schemes of interpretation and meaning.

Consequently the divisiveness of particular differences has lessened. People can practice their piety, e.g., say the rosary daily, or fight for liberal causes, e.g., promote an urban tenants union, without formal sanction one way or the other. Superiors have been freed from granting permissions in such a way as to prescribe customs for a community that would be applicable to everyone alike. Instead, superiors deal with guidelines that are not published as law or regulation. This allows greater flexibility in the administration of an increasingly pluralist group. At the time of the Thirty-Second General Congregation, all the provincials were summoned by Father General to compile guidelines for their administration, but they did so outside of the sessions of the Congregation to forestall this being thought of as legislation of the Congregation.

189

Another occurrence of value generalization
is found in modern developments in theology. The
task of theologians is being seen increasingly as
the creation and refinement of methods of theologizing rather than the elaboration and updating
of traditional doctrine. This is, in large measure, to "catch up" with Protestant theology of
the past seventy-five years especially in the
area of Scripture study.

Innovations in the manner of directing the
Spiritual Exercises is another instance of value
generalization. The Spiritual Exercises had become stylized and formalized and were employed as
preached retreats of traditional content and
specific form. The modern Society legitimately
encourages numerous forms of the Exercises. The
most prominent is a return to individual direction, the one-to-one relationship between a
retreatant and a director. There is no preaching
or formal exposition but rather a daily in-depth
dialogue of unique movements of the experience
of the retreatant. The content varies limitlessly.
The Exercises form the generalized value orientation as focused on the unique content of the
everyday life and special dispositions of the
retreatant. Other forms of the Exercises also
flourish; "Annotation Nineteen"[6] retreats, for
instance, go on indefinitely with a retreatant
conferring with the director at set intervals.

The broad-scale implementation and acceptance of modernizing procedures is evidenced by
the hegemony of reform, the reordering of values
in formation, the acceptance of younger superiors
and effective service agencies, and a wide-spread
sense of increased solidarity.

The greatest evidence of rank-and-file
implementation is the cultural hegemony of
aggiornamento in the modern Church. From the
impetus of Pope John XXIII and the Second Vatican
Council, the legitimation for change was so strong
that even the tendencies emanating from the Vatican under his successor, Pope Paul, could not

reverse the movement. Through a full-scale experience of crisis, the activity of updating
prevailed as legitimate.

Secondly, the leverage of change in the
Society of Jesus applied through the program of
socialization and formation of young Jesuits was
broad-scale and intensive. This change was
clearly a pervasive reordering of social behavior
on the basis of changed values. What had been
formerly socialization by means of the ideal and
exemplary yielded to socialization by means of
the experiential and prevalent.

Another evidence of implementation was the
fact that the membership of the Society granted
legitimacy to youthful superiors when they were
appointed. Legitimacy was not claimed as the
right of seniority but as the right of higher
authorities to appoint. Obedience then legitimated the incumbent in actual practice.

Another evidence of successful implementation was the effectiveness of many agencies formed
to integrate sectors of the Society. The service
agencies were actually called upon by the rank-
and-file and their services were accepted, useful,
and effective in the desired directions. The
organs of communication and the services offered,
the decisions as to priorities, the opening of
new apostolates and closing of former institutions
were accepted as based upon the decisions of
competent specialists.

One instance of this is the work of a program in the United States entitled "Project One."
Project One is an evaluation and revision of the
educational apostolate of American Jesuits under
the supervision of the Jesuit Conference. It
developed a two-way communication through panels,
meetings, and correspondence throughout the
Assistancy. On the basis of its findings and
apparatus, the provincials are making firm
decisions about the future of various institutions and the uses of manpower. These decisions

191

have the apparent following of the rank-and-file.

Another evidence of implementation is less easily documented yet widely experienced throughout the Society. It is a sense of solidarity within the present day Society of Jesus. This seems to be based in part on the sense that "we have made it through an ordeal, together!" This is a subtle though real evidence of implementation. It exhibits itself in a renewed respect, appreciation, affection and sharing of many Jesuits. A way and intensity of "being together" which did not exist formerly is now being taken for granted. This new solidarity alleviates the "generation gap." The older Jesuits place a trust in the younger men who have remained in the Jesuit Order when many of their friends departed. The younger Jesuits experience belonging with the older Society by reason of that same decision.

Evidence has been given above for five stages of modernization in the Jesuit Order. (See Table One) From the presence of these conditions, it can be inferred that many members of the Jesuit Order have experienced and, to some extent, been changed by this modernization. If the inference is correct, then some delegates to the Thirty-Second General Congregation shall also have become more modern. If so, the documents of the Congregation and the legislation they contain must be given evidence consistent with the outcomes described in the model of modernization. Indication of modernizing developments should be seen in the results of the Thirty-Second General Congregation that were not witnessed in the results of the Thirty-First.

Content Analysis of Selected Documents of the Thirty-First and the Thirty-Second General Congregations

The documents of the past two General

TABLE ONE

SUMMARY OF DESCRIPTIVE EVIDENCE OR STAGES
OF MODERNIZATION IN THE SOCIETY OF JESUS

STAGE ONE: Greater Rationalization and Disembeddedness from Ascription	STAGE TWO: Crystallization of New Recurrent Forms of Behavior
Restructuring Provincial Administration by Specialization	Informalized Relationship of Superior and Subject in Authority Structure
Employment of Lay Experts in Former Jesuit Offices	Sharing of Legitimacy between Center and Periphery
Jesuit Universities Yield Control to Lay Boards of Trustees	Elimination of Practice of Asking Detailed Permission
Course of Studies Freed from Roman Prescriptions	Dialogue between Administration and Rank-and-File on Personnel Assignment and Major Decisions
Merger of Schools and Faculties with Non-Jesuit Institutions	Emergence of Unstructured Daily Orders as Normative
Evaluation of Works by Management Consultants and Social Scientists	Alternative Forms of Common Prayer and Introduction of Prayerful Dialogue as Community Exercise
Legitimacy granted to Authority by Reason of Objective Criteria	Proliferation of Small Communities as Satellite or Alternative to Large Residences
Disappearance of Automatic Channels to Authority	Financial Autonomy and Budgetary Self-Determination for Rank-and-File
Lessening of the Authoritative Influence of Seniority	Extensive Engagement in Non-Institutionally Aligned Activities
Disappearance of Hierarchical Arrangements in Living, Dining and Recreation Facilities	Movement from Secluded Rural Locations for Houses of Formation to Active Urban Locations
Abandonment of Two Track System of Studies	Experimental Forms of Liturgy and Prayer become regularized and accepted
Enlargement of Criteria for Grade of Profession of Four Vows	Retraining of Middle-Aged Jesuits to "Second Vocations"
Strong Impetus to Democratize and to Abandon Distinction by Grades	New Relationships of Jesuit Personnel and Institutions to Marginal Groups of Civil Society
New Career Opportunities for Brothers	
Lessening Use of Clerical Attire	
Deprivatization of Clerical Forms of Worship	
Removal of Custom of Cloister from many Residences	
Disappearance of Latin Language as Privileged	
Demythologizing the Role and Authority of Priesthood	

Table One - continued

STAGE THREE: Emergence of Mechanisms for Coordination and Integration of Newly Crystallized Patterns of Behavior

Principle of Attraction and Democratic Procedures for Allocating Manpower

Development of Solidary Groupings of Members who share Common Apostolates and Interests

Development of Specialized Agencies to Administer Services to Jesuit Personnel

Development of Special Interest Groups to Foster Particular Apostolates

Institution and Support of Funding Agencies as Incentive to Jesuit Value Promotion

Proliferation of New Publications and "In House" Organs of Communication as Integrating of Jesuit Personnel

Special Institutes, Seminars, Theological Updating Sessions, and Retreats inaugurated for Sharing and Community Development

STAGE FOUR: Generalization of Value Order and Orientations in the Society of Jesus

Pronouncement of Generalized Priorities as Criteria of Apostolic Endeavours

Legitimation of Charasmatic Elements and Spirit in Acceptance of Innovation

Emphasis in Formation upon Individual Differences, Personal Strengths, and Pluralist Tendencies

Attenuation and Diminution of Specific Forms of Religious Devotion

Trend Away from Particular Solutions to Current Problems Enforced for All toward Analysis of Perspective and Underlying Principles

Flexibility Granted to Both Superiors and Rank-and-File Through Deregulation and Development of Non-binding Guidelines

Shift in Theological Investigation from Elaboration of Traditional Doctrine to Refinement of Methodology

Generalization of Methods for Use and Promotion of the Spiritual Exercises of Saint Ignatius

STAGE FIVE: Acceptance and Implementation of Modernized Procedures in Society of Jesus at Large

Legitimated Cultural Hegemony of Aggiornamento in the Modern Church

Leverage of Change Applied Through Drastic Transformation of Programs of Jesuit Socialization

Legitimacy Granted to Youthful Superiors and Acceptance of the Diminution of Rights of Seniority

Utility and Acceptance of Integrative Agencies by Rank-and-File

Solidarity effected by Shared Experience of Having "Lived Through" Crisis and Revolution in Church and Society of Jesus

Congregations, the Thirty-First which occurred at the beginning of this period under study and the Thirty-Second which occurred at the end of this period, should exhibit differences consistent with the model of modernization. A brief content analysis of selected documents of these two Congregations reveal such differences.

The texts that were selected for comparison are those which concern the Society's mission, apostolates, and formation. These documents reflect areas of perennial concern, lengthy discussions, central importance and comparable subject matter. The comparison of the documents was made in terms of two qualities consistent with the model of modernization, the qualities of embeddedness of ascriptive sources and value generalization.

Embeddedness in ascriptive sources of legitimation is the first criterion for analysis. This quality is measured by the frequency of the explicit mention of particular works or apostolates and specific institutions that promote these particular works. For example, "university education" as an apostolate, or mention of "our retreat houses," or direct reference to "The Gregorian University" are all instances of appeal to time-honored resources of the Society of Jesus which reflect its history and traditions. The second indicator of embeddedness is the frequency of explicit mention of particular "structured-in" traditions or customs of the Society. Mention of "Sacred Heart devotion," the Spiritual Exercises of Saint Ignatius, and celebration of specific feast days are examples of this indicator.

The criterion of value generalization is measured by the frequency of explicit mention of concepts that are necessarily generalized and supra-institutional. Some examples of these indicators include mention of ecumenism, atheism, or "struggle against structures." A second indicator of value generalization is the frequency of

mention of intrinsically non-constrictive concepts.
Illustrative of the non-constrictive concepts are
mention of such terms as autonomy, liberation, and
transcendence.

The documents that were compared are the
following: the introductory decrees from both
the Thirty-First and the Thirty-Second General
Congregations, two documents on the formation of
Jesuits from the Thirty-First General Congregation and one from the Thirty-Second, and eighteen
separate decrees on apostolates from the Thirty-
First General Congregation and two documents on
apostolates from the Thirty-Second General Congregation.

Before reporting the frequency of indicators, something should be said about contrasts
in style of the two sets of documents. In the
case of the introductory decrees, both congregations take a similar approach, that of situating the Society in its present historical perspective. The introductory decree of the Thirty-
First Congregation is entitled "The Mission of
the Society of Jesus Today" and sets as a key-note
of the document "this new age in which the human
race finds itself."[7] It places the Society of
Jesus in the perspective set by the Second Vatican
Council. The introductory decree of the Thirty-
Second General Congregation is simply entitled
"Introductory Decree." It likewise places itself
in historical perspective, namely "The past
decade in the life of the Society." This latter
decree addresses itself mainly to the successes
and failures of implementing the decrees of the
former Congregation "which aimed at adapting our
life to the directives of the Second Vatican
Council."[8]

The latter Congregation's document is more
sober in its confession of failures in implementation of the former Congregation by the two
extremes of resistance to change and excessive
change, both of which threatened the unity of the
Society of Jesus. The Thirty-Second General

196

Congregation deliberately places itself in direct
continuity with the Thirty-First General Congregation by stating:

> The 32nd General Congregation makes its
> own and confirms all of the declarations
> and dispositions of the 31st General
> Congregation unless they are explicitly
> changed in the present decrees. The
> documents of the preceding Congregation
> accurately and faithfully express the
> genuine spirit and tradition of the
> Society.[9]

The approaches taken to formation by the
two General Congregations are complementary.
Both encourage opening up to a pluralism and
striving for integration. However, the former
Congregation anticipates the "opening up" and
prepares the way for it while the latter Congregation reviews the "opening up" and calls for
integration in the face of the resulting pluralism.

The greatest difference in approach is that
found in the treatment of the apostolates of the
Society. The Thirty-First General Congregation
issued eighteen distinct decrees in this area.
One decree is a general statement of the Society's
task to struggle against atheism, and the other
seventeen all deal with particular and specific
apostolates. The Thirty-Second General Congregation deals with the area of the apostolate in two
documents. Both of these documents are more
generalized than the treatment of particular
apostolates. One discusses the Jesuit apostolic
mission as the service of faith and the promotion
of justice, and the other sets the groundwork for
the work of inculturation and culturally diverse
promotion of Christian life.

The frequency of terms of embeddedness and
value generalization in the selected documents of
both Congregations totals 1,500. Terms of
embeddedness comprise sixty-five percent of all
indicators recorded; terms of value generalization

comprise thirty-five percent of all indicators. Terms of embeddedness comprise ten percent more of the Thirty-First General Congregation's recorded terms than the Thirty-Second General Congregation's. Value generalization indicators comprise ten percent less of the Thirty-First General Congregation's terms than of the Thirty-Second's.

The largest share of the difference between terms of embeddedness and appeal to tradition in the two congregations is the frequency of the use of names bearing sacred meaning. The Thirty-First General Congregation used twice as many references to sacred names per page of text as did the Thirty-Second.

There is an interesting contrast comparing the use of terms in each of three areas. In the area of introductory decree, the Thirty-Second General Congregation exhibits a reverse tendency and employs embedded terms more than three times as often as value generalization terms and more often than the Thirty-First General Congregation. These are brief decrees in both cases, but notice should be taken of the fact that the Introductory Decree of the Thirty-Second General Congregation was the product of intense struggle and earnest effort to placate the Vatican which had displayed grave displeasure with the work of the Congregation. In the remaining two areas of formation and apostolate, the Thirty-Second General Congregation used a higher percentage of the terms recorded as indicators of value generalization than did the Thirty-First General Congregation. (See Table Two)

The content analysis of these documents suggests a modernized Society at the time of the Thirty-Second General Congregation. The nature of the approach taken and the terminology used both indicate a greater degree of value generalization in the Thirty-Second General Congregation than in the Thirty-First. The appeal to embedded terms represents a higher frequency in both the

TABLE TWO

USE OF TERMS OF EMBEDDEDNESS AND VALUE
GENERALIZATION IN SELECTED DOCUMENTS OF
THE THIRTY-FIRST AND THIRTY-SECOND GENERAL CONGREGATIONS

	EMBEDDEDNESS		GENERALIZATION	
	Raw Score	% of E + VG	Raw Score	% of E + VG
Total Use of Terms (Use of terms per Page)				
Thirty-First G.C. (57.5 pages)	642 (11.17)	69	290 (5.04)	31
Thirty-Second G.C. (46.5 pages)	337 (7.25)	59	231 (4.97)	41
Use of Terms in Introductory Decree				
Thirty-First G.C. (3.5 pages)	40 (11.42)	59	28 (8.00)	41
Thirty-Second G.C. (2.5 pages)	43 (17.20)	77	13 (5.20)	23
Use of Terms in Formation Documents				
Thirty-First G.C. (16 pages)	167 (10.44)	80	42 (2.63)	20
Thirty-Second G.C. (19 pages)	57 (3.35)	46	66 (3.88)	54
Use of Terms in Apostolate Documents				
Thirty-First G.C. (38 pages)	435 (11.45)	66	220 (5.79)	34
Thirty-Second G.C. (27 pages)	237 (8.77)	61	152 (5.63)	39

former and the latter. This is, perhaps, predictable for socio-emotional organizations.

Closer scrutiny of the content suggests that even the indicators of embeddedness in the later Congregation are of a less "devout" or particularistic style than the indicators of embeddedness in the former. In the latter Congregation, reference to the Spiritual Exercises and scripture are often made whereas references to specific forms of piety are nearly absent and mention of specific apostolates are rare. Specific forms of piety and mention of specific apostolates are more frequent in the earlier congregation.

The findings of the content analysis of terms of embeddedness and value generalization are consistent with the hypotheses. These findings support the model of modernization as applicable to the past decade of development in the Society of Jesus.

Analysis of Modernization as
Represented by Delegates to the
Thirty-Second General Congregation

If the Society has undergone modernization during the past decade, then the delegates who arrived at Rome for the Thirty-Second General Congregation would presumably have experienced such changes and have been marked by modernization as a consequence. It would be inconsistent with the hypotheses of modernization if the majority of delegates evidenced a more traditional than modernized position on various issues. On the other hand, it would be consistent with and supportive of the model of modernization if the majority of delegates evidenced a more modernized than traditional position on these issues.

From an analysis of items of the questionnaire responses of eighty-five percent of the delegates, it can be shown that a majority of

200

delegates consistently evidence a more modernized than traditional position on the issues surveyed. The items used for this analysis explicitly refer to aspects of change or alliance with particular modern ideas and stated preference for theological viewpoints that represent traditional, moderate, or avant garde positions.

Sixteen of the thirty-seven Likert-type items on the questionnaire administered before the Congregation indicate aspects of change or modern trends. Of these sixteen, ten items refer to change, three others reflect a modern approach to social action, one refers to a modern sense of autonomy, another to the trend toward renewed poverty, and the sixth refers to the current acceptance of Protestant theology in Catholic circles.

In fifteen out of sixteen items the mean score for all delegates is in the direction consistent with modernization. In ten of the sixteen items, responses in support of change or modernity is indicated by agreement with the item, a Likert score of 1 or 2. In six items, support of change or modernity is indicated by disagreement, a Likert score of 4 or 5. The mean for all items in agreement is 2.14; the mean for all items in disagreement is 3.54. The mean for items in agreement relating only to change is 1.74; for items in disagreement, it is 3.53. (See Table Three)

An important indicator of the values of a religious organization is a survey of its members' theological positions. The questionnaire administered to the delegates before the Congregation included thirteen questions that allowed answers of varying theological orientations. In content, the orientations ranged from traditional to avant garde. A prior empirical survey and analysis employing eleven of the thirteen items found that the differences ranged from prior Vatican II, through Vatican II, to post-Vatican II. The principle author of this prior study characterizes

201

TABLE THREE

AGREEMENT AND DISAGREEMENT ON ITEMS OF CHANGE AND MODERNITY BY DELEGATES

Items Indicating Modernity by Agreement*	Mean	Standard Deviation
C** The creative ferment in the Church today is bringing about a deepening of my Christian faith.	1.58	.79
There are times when a person has to put his personal conscience above the Church's teachings.	2.97	1.42
The spirit of poverty is meaningless without poverty in fact.	2.19	1.22
C Any organizational structure becomes a deadening weight in time and needs to be revitalized.	1.73	.87
When I think of social reform, I think of things I believe in so deeply I could dedicate all my efforts to them.	2.46	1.19
A priest can hardly call himself a shepherd if he is not as deeply involved in the social welfare of people as he is in giving spiritual service to his parishioners.	2.49	1.28
When I am dealing with the problems of my own job, I find myself constantly trying to make decisions that will help solve the bigger issues of justice, etc., for all mankind. The world's problems are very much my problems.	2.27	1.13
C The current situation in the Church calls for change. We must respond at once.	1.77	.84
C Every great step forward in world history has been accomplished through the inspiration of reformers and creative men.	1.89	.88
C During the past ten years many religious have changed some of the basic principles and values which they formerly believed in.	2.14	.99

Items Indicating Modernity by Disagreement	Mean	Standard Deviation
C The future is in God's hands. I will await what He sends and accept what comes as His will for me.	2.19	1.32
C The problem with the Church after Vatican II is that many of the certainties we used to have have been taken away.	3.19	1.36
C The turmoil following Vatican II is resulting in a gradual weakening of my own religious beliefs.	4.59	.88
One's faith may be jeopardized by studying Protestant theologians.	3.59	1.23
C By continuing its traditional approach to its teaching role, the Church will better accomplish its mission than by experimenting with new methods.	4.10	.98
C In the final analyses, the strongest basis for planning for the future is to trust to the experience of the past and base the decision-making on the facts, the historical facts.	3.60	1.13

*All responses based on a five point scale from: "Strongly Agree" to "Strongly Disagree"; Value 3 indicates "Uncertain."

**"C" represents item which is directly in reference to change.

the three theological orientations:

> After reviewing the responses of three
> orientations to more than 300 ques-
> tionnaire items (by 3,529 respondents),
> the following description of each pat-
> tern emerged. "C" can be characterized
> by the great emphasis it gives to pro-
> gress and evolution on all levels....
> It emphasizes human values more...a human-
> istic orientation, and a thrust which can
> be historically defined as post-Vatican
> II in general.... "B" can be characterized
> by its understanding of tradition in the
> light of a biblical revelation which is
> open to progress and development in all
> areas of religious and human life....
> "B"'s approach to theology, work and
> life is a revelation and synthesis orien-
> tation as well as a thrust which can be
> historically identified as Vatican II.
> "A" can be characterized by the strong
> influence of biblical revelation, tradition,
> and the standards of Christian inheritance....
> Its attitudes and way of living reflect a
> conscious fidelity to tradition. The
> thrust of "A"'s approach to theology,
> work and life is decidedly pre-Vatican
> II.[10]

A pre-Vatican II orientation is predicated
on a lowest possible score of thirteen (mean of
1.0). A post-Vatican II orientation is predicated
on a highest possible score of forty-five (mean
of 3.46). A moderate score of twenty-nine (mean
of 2.23) would indicate a slightly modernized
position, since a Vatican II orientation is an
already updated version of theology.

In the case of one item, that of the question on the meaning of authority, the mean is
below the moderate score. In twelve of the
thirteen items, the mean is closer to the post-
Vatican II score than the pre-Vatican II score.
(See Table Four) The questionnaire items of

(See Appendix One for Complete Listing of Alternatives)

	Mean	Standard Deviation
Each of the following statements describes an aspect of GOD. By God I mean: (3 options)	2.30	.47
Each of the following statements describes an aspect of the HOLY SPIRIT. (3 options)	2.43	.65
The purpose of MISSIONARY ACTIVITY is: (3 options plus 1 scored as missing value)	2.27	.47
Each of the following Statements describing an aspect of CHURCH. (5 options)	3.24	1.00
*Each of the following statements describes some aspects of the relation of the CHURCH TO THE WORLD. By this relationship I mean: (2 options coded 1 and 3)	2.04	1.00
Each of the following statements describes an aspect of the WORLD. (3 options)	2.23	.58
Each of the following statements describes an aspect of MINISTRY. A Christian minister is: (3 options)	2.55	.53
Each of the following statements describes an aspect of FAITH. By Faith I mean: (6 options)	4.40	.82
*Each of the following statements describes some aspects of CULTURE. By Culture I mean: (2 options)	1.89	.30
Each of the following statements describes an aspect of PRAYER. (3 options plus 1 scored as missing value)	2.55	.71
Each of the following statements describes an aspect of AUTHORITY. (3 options)	1.78	.71
Each of the following statements describes an aspect of SALVATION. (4 options)	2.50	1.08

*Indicates Question and alternatives not included in the original SVD Self-Study.

change and modernity and the stated preferences
for theological view-points indicate that the
delegates were already modernized to some extent
when they arrived in Rome for the Thirty-Second
General Congregation.

Summary and Conclusions

The decade preceding the Thirty-Second
General Congregation was a period in which old
forms passed away and new forms struggled to
emerge. It was a tumultuous time. There were
excesses of change as well as resistance to
change. This suggests that modernization could
not occur without crisis and a sundering of
attachments to what "has been." Nevertheless,
modernization did occur during this time.

The events and changes reported here as
evidence in support of the model of modernization
comprise only a partial account. The account is
necessarily descriptive; it is based on the lived
experience of participant observation. Ample
evidence exists to show changes in the Jesuit
Order for every stage of the model of modernization. The impact of these many changes is shown
in the fact that the delegates arrived in Rome
already modernized. The differences in style and
in various terms of embeddedness and value-
generalization of the documents of the Thirty-
First and Thirty-Second General Congregations
bear this out.

The delegates, therefore, came to the
Thirty-Second General Congregation as individuals
who had become modernized. The climate of the
Congregation favored making that individual
modernization a corporate reality. It remains to
be demonstrated that the Congregation was a
vehicle for that corporate change and modernization. The following chapters report this further
analysis.

Footnotes

[1]"B. Guidelines" from "Union of Minds and Hearts," <u>Documents, 32 G.C.</u>, p. 88, citing an earlier document, "14. Prayer" in <u>Documents of the Thirty-First General Congregation</u>, p. 44.

[2]"B. Guidelines" from Union of Minds and Hearts," <u>Documents, 32 G.C.</u>, p. 88.

[3]Garry Wills, "The New Jesuits vs. The Unheavenly City," in <u>New York Magazine</u>, June 1971, p. 26.

[4]George Ganss, S.J., "Editors Foreword" in "The Place of Art in Jesuit Life" in <u>Studies in the Spirituality of Jesuits</u>, Vol. V, No. 3, (April, 1973), p. v.

[5]Letter of Very Reverend Father Pedro Arrupe, General of the Society of Jesus on the <u>New Charitable and Apostolic Fund of the Society of Jesus</u>, Rome, March 19, 1976, p. 1.

[6]"Annotation Nineteen" retreats are named after the nineteenth annotation in the book of the Spiritual Exercises written by Saint Ignatius in which he specifies the possibility of a person spending one and one-half hours daily on the matter of the Spiritual Exercises when "engaged in public affairs or necessary business." See Saint Ignatius of Loyola, <u>The Spiritual Exercises of Saint Ignatius</u>, A New Translation by Louis J. Puhl, Westminster, Maryland, the Newman Press, 1960, "Introductory Observations," pp. 8-9.

[7]"The Mission of The Society of Jesus Today" in <u>Documents of the Thirty-First General Congregation</u>, p. 5.

[8]"Introductory Decree" in <u>Documents, 32 G.C.</u>, p. 1.

[9]<u>Ibid</u>.

[10] "Pluralism and Pluriformity in Religious Life: A Case Study" in PRO MUNDI VITA - CENTRUM INFORMATIONIS, Publication 47, 1973, pp. 8-9. (Although the author is not listed with this publication, the article was written by Reverend Richard Rashke, S.V.D., Director of The Society of the Divine World Self-Study. The theological items were taken from this Self-Study).

CHAPTER SEVEN

BULWARK-CATHOLICISM AND CONCILIAR-HUMANISM

IN THE MODERN-DAY SOCIETY OF JESUS

The decade since Vatican II has seen fundamental social change in the Society of Jesus.
This change entails greater rationalization and
disembeddedness from ascription, the crystallization and integration of new patterns of behavior,
the generalization of values, and broad-scale
implementation. These stages which form the model
of modernization for this research, correspond to
real differences between the Society of Jesus of
a decade ago and the Society today.

This process of change can be specified
further. It entails a shift in Jesuit culture
from the style of an elite group functioning
within and for a bounded Catholic Church towards
the new style of a minority group functioning
within and for all of the world. This new style
would seek legitimacy by solidarity with the
world's poor and disenfranchized.

A transition like this does not happen by
decree. Even the beginnings of such a change
throughout an organization comes from individual
changes that have already occurred to some of its
members.[1] When the change has occurred to some
of the members, there is the condition of the
changed style and the unchanged style existing
side by side.

The unchanged style is referred to here as
Bulwark-Catholicism. This is the style of the
proud tradition of the Jesuit as defender of the
faith. It reflects the strong hierarchical and
doctrinal structures of Catholicism in the mode
of the Council of Trent and the Counter-
Reformation.

209

The changed style is referred to here as Conciliar-Humanism. This is the style of the new wave of Catholic and Christian thought and activity. It reflects the modern humanist tradition in the mode of the Second Vatican Council and the vast experimentation and dissolution of structures that have occurred since that Council.

It has already been shown that changes are occurring throughout the Jesuits and that some members reflect a more modern style. It remains to be shown that these changes entail a shift in culture and that the members who reflect the changed style characterize the shift in their way. To do this it must be demonstrated that there is a predominance of influence exerted at the Thirty-Second General Congregation which is Conciliar-Humanist instead of Bulwark-Catholic.

This predominance consists of two things; a predominance of delegates and a predominance of majority votes. First it will be determined whether or not a predominant number of delegates are Conciliar-Humanist rather than Bulwark-Catholic. Secondly, it will be determined whether or not the Conciliar-Humanists were able to translate their preferences into legislation of the General Congregation by a predominance of votes in favor of their positions or opposed to those of the Bulwark-Catholics.

Further analysis must be presented to determine whether or not the shift in culture and predominance of Conciliar-Humanists rests mainly with those delegates who were considered leaders of the Congregation by the delegates themselves.

All the delegates who responded to the original questionnaire of this research were classified according to a polarity of Bulwark-Catholic and Conciliar-Humanist. The index to measure their position in regard to this polarity came from responses to twelve items of the "Before" questionnaire. (See Table One)

210

TABLE ONE

VARIABLES COMPRISING THE INDEX OF POLARITY BETWEEN

BULWARK-CATHOLICISM AND CONCILIAR-HUMANISM

CONSOVER   There are times when a person has to put his
                 personal conscience above the Church's teaching.

                 (Responses 1-5 : (1) Agree strongly;
                 (2) Agree somewhat; (3) Uncertain; (4) Dis-
                 agree somewhat; (5) Disagree strongly)

REFORMSO   When I think of social reform, I think of
                 things I believe in so deeply I could dedicate
                 all my efforts to them.

                 (Responses 1-5, as above)

SHEPHRDA   A priest can hardly call himself a shepherd
                 if he is not as deeply involved in the social
                 welfare of people as he is in giving spiritual
                 service to his parishioners.

                 (Responses 1-5, as above)

BIGISSUA   When I am dealing with the problems of my own
                 job, I find myself constantly trying to make
                 decisions that will help solve the bigger
                 issues of justice, etc. for all mankind.
                 The world's problems are very much my problems.

                 (Responses 1-5, as above)

CHCGONCA   The current situation in the Church calls for
                 change.   We must respond at once.

                 (Responses 1-5, as above)

HOMAVODA   Even when working in their native countries,
                 Jesuits should generally avoid taking strong
                 public positions on religious or social issues.

                 (Responses 1-5, as above)

TRADAPRA

By continuing its traditional approach
to its teaching role, the Church will
better accomplish its mission than by
experimenting with new methods.

(Responses 1-5, as above)

HOSPMEAN

Each of the following statements describes
an aspect of the HOLY SPIRIT.   (Choose the
one you find most appealing)

* 1. The Holy Spirit, who proceeds from
the Father and the Son, distributes
God's grace to men.

2. The Holy Spirit guides the Church to
a better understanding of Christ's
message and to internal unity by
speaking through the entire people of
God.

3. The Holy Spirit speaks to all men of
good-will in different ways and under
different circumstances throughout
history.

MISSMEAN

The purpose of missionary activity is (Choose
the one you find most appealing)

* 1. to convert people to the Catholic
Church through preaching, teaching
catechetics, administering the sacraments, etc.

2. to be a witness of God's love, preach
the Gospel and form the Church among
people who do not yet know about
Christ.

3. to help man develop his own resources
to fulfill total human needs, i.e.,
religious, economic, educational,
political.

0. not clear to me.

TABLE ONE (continued

CHCHMEAN

Each of the following describes an aspect
of Church. (Choose the one you find most
appealing)

* 1. As mediator of God's truth and grace
       to men, the Church is the only true
       way to salvation.

   2. The Church is a perfect, religious
       society organized under the Pope and the
       Bishops.

   3. As the People of God intimately related
       with Christ, the Church is a sacrament
       or sign of man's union with God and
       with each other.

   4. The Church, as a pilgrim in this world,
       is a servant of mankind's total needs,
       i.e., religious, economic, educational
       and political.

   5. The Church is the prophetic critic of
       society and culture.

CHWDMEAN

Each of the following statements describes
some aspects of the relation of the
Church to the World. By this relationship I mean: (Choose the one you find
most appealing)

* 1. The Church is the sacrament of Salvation
       which comes from above. Radically
       different from the world, she must draw
       men and bring them in the community of
       the Baptized. Hence, priorities must
       be accorded to spiritual and sacer-
       dotal ministries. Reforming itself
       from within, the Church must work in
       the total content of its pastoral
       services and maintain its concern for
       an integral humanism developing in
       the light of faith.

TABLE ONE (continued)

CHWDMEAN (continued)

3. The Church, in the depths of
human existence, is the place from
which she is the witness in
answer to questions which she
herself has not raised.   The
Church would do well to go the
limit of deinstitutionalizing
her own works and endeavouring
to collaborate closely with priests,
laity, and secular interests to
give rise to this witness.   First
priority must be with the poor,
sharing their life to the full.

MINIMEAN

Each of the following statements
describes an aspect of Ministry.   A
Christian Minister is (Choose the
one you find most appealing)

* 1. someone ordained to the priesthood
and thereby authorized to celebrate
the Eucharist and administer the
sacraments of Penance and Anointing
the Sick.

2. someone whose fundamental obligation is to spread Christ's Gospel
and to administer the sacraments
to the faithful.

3. someone who has been authorized
by the people of God to build
Christian community, lead it in
its celebration of God's grace,
and inspire it to share actively
in the world's concerns.

* The responses to these questions are reordered to reflect the
recoding of values from more traditional to more avant garde
responses.   The letters of the original statements are converted
here to numbers.

The twelve items forming the Bulwark-Catholic/Conciliar-Humanism polarity were selected through a factor analysis of items on the questionnaire that relate to changes in the Church and alternative points of view within the Church on social change and theology. Twenty-nine different items were analyzed. Various combinations yielded similar patterns of factor loadings. In all cases the predominant factor accounted for approximately three times more variance than the second highest factor. This indicates the strength of the underlying factor. The twelve items selected to form the index were consistently the highest factor loadings on various trials.

The Bulwark-Catholic/Conciliar-Humanist index is a factor score combining distinct coefficients derived from the factor loadings of the twelve questionnaire items. The method employed was principal factoring with iteration.[2] This provides a derivation "such that the correlation between the composite factor-score variable and the respective factor is maximized."[3]

Factoring the twelve items, the strongest factor accounts for four times the variance of the second factor and over seven times the variance of the third. This warranted use of the option to draw a factor analytic solution with only one factor and to compose the factor score from this single factor without rotation.[4] "The first unrotated factor delimits the most comprehensive classification, the widest net of linkages or the greatest order in the data."[5]

While a strong relationship of the twelve variables to the underlying polarity of Bulwark-Catholicism and Conciliar-Humanism is indicated, unidirectionality is not indicated. Attempts to compose a Guttman-type scale yielded weak coefficients of reproducibility (.71 to .83) and scalability (.10 to .26) for varying dichotomies of each variable.

The correlation of the twelve variables to

215

one another is low while the relation to the underlying factor is high. Most correlation coefficients between the twelve items are under .30. Most of the factor loadings are over .48. (See Table Two)

The index employs a spectrum of twelve different elements instead of closely correlated items. It also forms a continuous set of scores instead of a dichotomization. All the analysis is based on this continuous set. It gauges social reform, welfare, justice, tradition, change, theology, the Church, its missionary activity and its relation to the world. Consequently, the polarity this index represents captures effective nuance and dissimilarity. When Jesuits around the world were given the forced choice dichotomization regarding the relation of the Church and the world in a prior questionnaire, "a very large number found that they were presented with an impossible choice in this caricature of two aspects that seemed to be complementary rather than in opposition."[6] The polarity index for this analysis provides a far broader measure of the Bulwark-Catholic and Conciliar-Humanist styles.

Delegate Representation in Bulwark-Catholic and Conciliar-Humanist Styles

Having assigned every delegate a factor score based on the polarity between Bulwark-Catholic and Conciliar-Humanist, it is possible to examine the predominance of one class or the other according to a frequency distribution. However, a factor score is a standardized score with the mean lying near zero. Therefore, any predominance shown in the frequency distribution is a function mainly of the extreme cases. Since the extreme Bulwark-Catholics are slightly more numerous than the Conciliar-Humanists, there are six more delegates in the Conciliar-Humanist classification than in the Bulwark-Catholic. This is the case whether the mean or zero is chosen as

TABLE TWO

CORRELATION COEFFICIENT AND FACTOR ANALYSIS
SCORES FOR VARIABLES COMPRISING
THE BULWARK-CATHOLICISM / CONCILIAR-HUMANISM INDEX

2A   Correlation Coefficients Between the Variables

	consover	reformso	shephrda	bigissua	chngonca	homavoda
consover	1.0000	.1896	.1078	.0826	.3445	− .2212
reformso	.1896	1.0000	.4473	.4445	.3262	− .2669
shephrda	.1078	.4474	1.0000	.3857	.2237	− .2796
bigissua	.0826	.4445	.3857	1.0000	.3120	− .2384
chngonca	.3445	.3262	.2237	.3120	1.0000	− .1563
honavoda	− .2212	− .2669	− .2796	− .2384	− .1563	1.0000
tradopra	− .2652	− .1570	− .1258	− .1020	− .3193	.0970
hospmean	− .1442	− .570	− .1080	− .1245	− .2104	.2973
missmean	− .1985	− .2087	− .2002	− .2757	− .2148	.2071
chchmean	− .1130	− .2815	− .3005	− .2520	− .2292	.1563
chedmean	− .3163	− .2389	− .2842	− .1550	− .2617	.2562
minimean	− .2906	− .1162	− .2861	− .486	− .2124	.1193

	tradapra	hospmean	missmean	chchmean	chwdmean	minimean
consover	− .2652	− .1422	− .1985	− .1130	− .3163	− .2906
reformso	− .1570	− .1570	− .2087	− .2815	− .2389	− .1162
shephrda	− .1258	− .1080	− .2002	− .3006	− .2842	− .2861
bigissua	− .1020	− .1245	− .2757	− .2520	− .1550	− .1486
chnconca	− .3193	− .2104	− .2148	− .2292	− .2617	− .2124
homavoda	.0970	.2973	.2071	.1563	.2562	.1193
tradapra	1.0000	.2729	.1382	.2593	.2196	.2765
hospmean	.2729	1.0000	.2272	.1635	.2983	.3232
missmean	.1382	.2272	1.0000	.3932	.2398	.2606
chchmean	.2593	.1635	.3932	1.0000	.2785	.2553
chwdmean	.2196	.2983	.2398	.2785	1.0000	.3520
minimean	.2765	.3232	.2606	.2553	.3520	1.0000

2B Factor Analysis Scores for Variables

Variable	Principal Factor Matrix	Communality	Factor Score Coefficients
Consover	− 0.41958	0.17604	− 0.10507
Reformso	− 0.54523	0.29728	− 0.16271
Shephrda	− 0.53217	0.23820	− 0.15143
Bigissua	− 0.48609	0.23628	− 0.21826
Chcgonca	− 0.52753	0.27829	− 0.15567
Homavoda	0.42600	0.18148	0.11026
Tradapra	0.41045	0.16847	0.10397
Hospmean	0.42497	0.18060	0.11039
Missmean	0.48132	0.23167	0.13281
Chchmean	0.51054	0.26065	0.14328
Chwdmean	0.54594	0.29805	0.16543
Minimean	0.49049	0.24058	0.13841

Eigen Value   2.83260

the dividing point. In total, there are ninety-five delegates scoring below the mean, warranting the designation Bulwark-Catholic, and 101 delegates above the mean, warranting the designation Conciliar-Humanist.[7] From the fact of this standardized score, it would be inconclusive to argue for a predominance of delegates in one classification or the other.

If one considers all cases within one standard deviation above or below the mean as neutral, and only those more than one standard deviation above or below the mean as representative of the polarity, a similarly inconclusive comparison results. In this case, thirty-nine delegates are more than one standard deviation below the mean, and thirty-seven delegates are more than one standard deviation above. The delegates are thus rather evenly distributed across the range of possible scores. (See Table Three)

The same kind of frequency distribution obtains if the standardized factor score is abandoned and an additive scale score approximating a Linkert scale index is employed. Linkert scaling allows items to be added together to express extent of agreement or disagreement across a series of items.[8] In the additive scale of these same twelve items, seventy-nine of 159 valid cases are below the mean and eighty cases are above the mean. Twenty-nine cases are at least one standard deviation below the mean and twenty-seven cases are at least one standard deviation above the mean. (See Table Four) The Pearson Product Moment Correlation between the factor score index and the additive scale index is .98.

The margin between groups is very slight and attributable to chance as easily as to an underlying factor. Therefore, the predominance of either the Bulwark-Catholic or the Conciliar-Humanist is not established by numbers of delegates.

219

TABLE THREE

DISTRIBUTION OF BULWARK-CONCILIAR COMPARISON

ACCORDING TO TWELVE ITEM FACTOR SCORE INDEX

Mean	0.004		Std. Dev.	0.874
Mode	-1.038		Variance	0.765
Median	0.048		Range	4.328
Minimum	-2.549		Maximum	1.779
Kurtosis	-0.140		Skewness	-0.322

Valid Cases 196   Missing Cases 41

TABLE FOUR

DISTRIBUTION OF BULWARK-CONCILIAR COMPARISON

ACCORDING TO TWELVE ITEM ADDITIVE LIKERT SCALING INDEX

Mean	38.74		Std. Dev.	0.504
Mode	42.00		Variance	40.458
Median	39.45		Range	31.00
Minimum	20.00		Maximum	51.00
Kurtosis	-0.104		Skewness	-0.403

Valid Cases 159   Missing Cases 78

Voting Patterns in Bulwark-Catholic
and Conciliar-Humanist Styles

Since the measurement of classes of Bulwark-
Catholics and Conciliar-Humanists does not significantly discriminate as regards numbers of delegates comprising one group and the other, it
remains to determine whether or not the actual
voting of issues evidences the predominance of
one or the other classification of Jesuit style.

For this measure, predominance consists of
the greater number of outcomes of the voting on
various issues decided by the delegates. As explained earlier, a full tally of all votes on a
particular issue was rarely obtained. A sampling
of one-eighth of all votes in randomly selected
banks of delegates provided the record of
minority votes.[9]

In order to determine the outcomes of the
voting, it is necessary first to characterize
whether the issues that were voted upon were
favored by the Bulwark-Catholic style or the
Conciliar-Humanist style voters. In order to do
this empirically, the direction of each issue
was determined by the difference between the mean
index score of the recorded minority votes and
the mean index score of the recorded majority
votes. If the mean index score of the minority
votes on an issue which passed was below that of
the majority votes, the issue was considered a
Conciliar-Humanist issue. If the mean score of
the minority votes on an issue which passed was
above that of the majority votes, the issue was
considered a Bulwark-Catholic issue. On the
other hand, if the mean score of the minority
votes on an issue which was rejected was below
that of the majority, the issue was considered a
Bulwark-Catholic issue because a Bulwark-Catholic
minority was voting in favor of an issue but was
overruled by a non-Bulwark-Catholic majority.
Likewise, if the mean score of the minority votes
on an issue which was rejected was above that of
the majority, the issue was considered a

221

Conciliar-Humanist issue. (See Table Five) In cases where the recorded votes do not indicate any difference between majority and minority, the issue is considered blank for purposes of analysis.

The Thirty-Second General Congregation voted on a total of 1,215 issues. This research collected voting records on 959 or 78.9 percent of these issues. The difference in Bulwark-Catholic/ Conciliar-Humanist scores between the minority and the majority was ascertained from the voting records for 880 issues.

The differences in scores indicated the direction of the issues. For 475 issues, the indicated direction was representative of the Conciliar-Humanist position; for 405 issues, the indicated direction was representative of the Bulwark-Catholic position.

Outcomes of the voting on these issues show that Conciliar-Humanists were in the predominance in influencing the documents and legislation of the Thirty-Second General Congregation. In total, there were 464 outcomes favorable to the Conciliar-Humanists. These consist of 322 C-H direction issues that were accepted and 142 B-C issues that were successfully rejected. There were 416 outcomes favorable to the Bulwark-Catholics. These consist of 263 B-C issues that were accepted and 153 C-H issues that were successfully rejected. The Conciliar-Humanists received favorable outcomes on 52.7 percent of all issues; the Bulwark-Catholics, 47.2 percent. This difference falls slightly short of rejecting the null-hypothesis at a significance level of .05 percent probability.[10]

Definitive votes directly formed the Congregation documents. These were votes on the actual working of the documents after all proposed changes and amendments had been made. The Conciliar-Humanists had 161 C-H direction definitive issues accepted and overturned four B-C direction definitive issues. The Bulwark-Catholics

TABLE FIVE

DETERMINATION OF THE DIRECTION OF ISSUES

AND OUTCOME OF VOTES AS EITHER

BULWARK-CATHOLIC OR CONCILIAR-HUMANIST

A. DIRECTION OF ISSUES

If issue was rejected and minority was Conciliar-Humanist voting in favor, issue is Conciliar-Humanist direction	If issue was accepted and minority was Bulwark-Catholic voting against, issue is Conciliar-Humanist direction
If issue was rejected and minority was Bulwark-Catholic voting in favor, issue is Bulwark-Catholic direction	If issue was accepted and minority was Conciliar-Humanist voting against, issue is Bulwark-Catholic direction

B. OUTCOME OF VOTES

An outcome favorable to Conciliar-Humanists can be either a Conciliar-Humanist direction issue that is accepted or a Bulwark-Catholic issue that is rejected. Conversely, an outcome favorable to Bulwark-Catholics can be either a Bulwark-Catholic issue that is accepted or a Conciliar-Humanist issue that is rejected.

	Issue Rejected	Issue Accepted
Conciliar Humanist Direction	CH for BC against BC outcome	CH for BC against CH outcome
Bulwark Catholic Direction	BC for CH against CH outcome	BC for CH against BC outcome

had 110 B-C direction definitive issues accepted and overturned three C-H direction definitive issues. In effect, this evidence indicates that 59.4 percent of all paragraphs of the Congregation documents warranted the support of the Conciliar-Humanist delegates whereas 40.6 percent warranted the support of the Bulwark-Catholic delegates.

A view of the contention involved in the passage and rejection of legislation is seen in the voting on amendments. The Conciliar-Humanists had eighty C-H direction amendments passed but 120 C-H direction amendments rejected; the Bulwark-Catholics had seventy-nine B-C direction amendments passed and 103 B-C amendments rejected. Since suggestions that met with the approval of the editorial committees of the various commissions did not have to be voted on, all amendments were in opposition to the mind of the editorial committee. Won and lost amendments, therefore, highlight the role of the Bulwark-Catholics in restraining the influence of the Conciliar-Humanists by rejecting sixty percent of all C-H amendments and of the Conciliar-Humanists in restraining the influence of the Bulwark-Catholics by rejecting fifty-six percent of all B-C amendments. (See Table Six)

In summary of the overall voting, the predominance of legislation and content of the General Congregation can be attributed to the Conciliar-Humanists. But, the total production of the General Congregation is clearly the collaboration of both segments of the Jesuit organization.

The difference between the Bulwark-Catholic and the Conciliar-Humanist outcomes is significantly large in two areas, the documents on social justice and on spiritual life and community. For these documents, the predominance of the C-H outcomes over the B-C outcomes is significant at .05 percent probability. The C-H outcomes predominate in ten documents. The B-C outcomes predominate in

TABLE SIX

SUMMARY OF TOTALS OF RECORDED VOTES ACCORDING TO BULWARK-CATHOLIC AND CONCILIAR-HUMANIST SCORES

	C-H	B-C	Total
Total # Issues	C-H 475	B-C 405	Total 880
Issues C-H Direction	Won 322	Lost 153	475
Issues B-C Direction	Won 263	Lost 142	405
C-H Position Favored	C-H Win 322	B-C Loss 142	464
B-C Position Favored	B-C Win 263	C-H Loss 153	416
% Favored Position	C-H 52.7	B-C 47.3	
% Voters Favoring C-H	C-H Win 82.7	B-C Loss 70.0	
% Voters Favoring B-C	B-C Win 80.5	C-H Loss 68.6	
Definitive Votes C-H	Won 161	Lost 4	165
Definitive Votes B-C	Won 110	Lost 3	113
% Definitive Votes	C-H Won 57.9	B-C Won 39.5	
Amendments C-H	Won 80	Lost 120	200
Amendments B-C	Won 79	Lost 103	182
% Amendments C-H	Won 40.0	Lost 60.0	
% Amendments B-C	Won 44.0	Lost 56.0	

four documents. There is equal ratio of C-H and
B-C in one document. The pattern of predominance
in each of these areas is treated separately.
(See Table Seven)

The major document of the Thirty-Second
General Congregation is "Our Mission Today: The
Service of Faith and Promotion of Justice."
This document required a greater length of discussion and more votes (196) than any other document. It resulted from the crucial decision to
establish a priority of priorities. It was the
product of three commissions operating together.
The outcomes of voting on this document, more
than on any other, indicates the role of the
Conciliar-Humanists in producing a transition in
the culture of the Society of Jesus from an elite
to a minority style of life. This document could
be considered the charter for that transition.

The direction of 175 issues was ascertained
for the Justice document voting. Of these,
ninety-four (53.4 percent) were outcomes favorable to the Conciliar-Humanist style and eighty-
two (46.6 percent) were outcomes favorable to the
Bulwark-Catholics. Twice as many C-H direction
issues were accepted than were rejected and
nearly the same number of B-C direction issues
were rejected as were accepted. There were
thirty-two definitive C-H direction issues accepted compared to fourteen definitive B-C
direction issues. Nearly seventy percent of the
document on social justice is particularly favored
by the Conciliar-Humanists.

A document allied to the Justice document
in terms of its affinity for the spirit and momen-
tum of developments in the Church since the Second
Vatican Council is the smallest document of the
Congregation. Yet is is considered by many to be
the greatest milestone for its innovative implica-
tions. This is the document on Inculturation.
Here again, the Conciliar-Humanists predominate.
Five C-H direction issues are accepted to only one
B-C direction issue while three C-H direction

226

TABLE SEVEN

SUMMARY OF TOTALS OF RECORDED VOTES ACCORDING TO B-C AND C-H SCORES FOR VARIOUS DOCUMENTS

Issue	Accept C-H Issue	Reject B-C Issue	Favorable C-H Outcomes	Accept B-C Issue	Reject C-H Issue	Favorable B-C Outcomes	Difference of CH - BC Outcomes	Ratio of BC/CH Outcomes
1. Justice	63	31	94	42	40	82	12	.87
2. Poverty	33	44	79	28	45	71	8	.89
3. Formation	40	6	46	41	5	46	0	1.00
4. Spiritual Life Community	44	13	57	29	21	50	7	.81
5. Jesuit Identity	25	9	34	14	7	21	13	.61
6. 4th Vow Formed Members	3	4	7	8	3	11	- 4	1.57
7. Tertianship	7	4	11	4	3	7	4	.63
8. Fidelity to Magesterium	6	5	11	9	4	13	- 2	1.18
9. Introductory Decree	11	4	15	7	3	10	5	.66
10. Inculturation	5	1	6	1	3	4	2	.66
11. Permanent Deaconate	1	2	3	5	0	5	- 2	1.66
12. Conscientious Objection	2	0	2	7	0	7	- 5	3.50
13. Central Government	17	8	25	12	10	22	3	.88
14. General Congregations	24	4	28	15	8	23	5	.82
15. Province Congregations	20	4	24	19	1	20	4	.83
16. Agenda and Procedures	7	3	10	8	2	10	0	1.00
17. Procedures re Departures	12	0	12	14	0	14	- 2	1.16

issues are rejected compared to one B-C direction
issue.

Perhaps the most symbolic indicator that the
style of the Jesuits is changing is the predominance of the Conciliar-Humanists in the document,
"Jesuits Today." This document is the product of
a five-man intercommission which was set up during
the Congregation. The purpose of this commission
was to draw from the deliberations and experience
of the Congregation a sense of the contemporary
Jesuit identity. This was in response to the
fact that a poll of Jesuits taken prior to the
Congregation ranked Jesuit identity as the most
important subject to be treated at the Congregation.

The outcomes of voting on this document were
one-sided. The Conciliar-Humanists predominated
overwhelmingly, particularly in definitive votes.
There were seventeen C-H direction definitive
votes accepted compared to one B-C direction
definitive vote. The Bulwark-Catholics instituted
thirteen amendments (eight passed, five were
rejected) to nine of the Conciliar-Humanists (six
passed, three were rejected). Overall, the
Conciliar-Humanists were favored with twenty-five
C-H direction issues accepted and nine B-C
direction issues rejected. The Bulwark-Catholics
had fourteen B-C direction issues accepted and
seven C-H direction issues rejected.

In the documents on the Spiritual Life and
Community, sixty percent of all issues accepted
were C-H direction issues. At the same time,
sixty-two percent of all rejected issues were also
C-H direction issues. Bulwark-Catholics blocked
sixteen of the twenty-five C-H direction amendments. In similar fashion, the Conciliar-Humanists blocked more than three times as many B-C
direction amendments as it permitted acceptance
(ten blocked, three accepted).

From these results, which are significant
at the .05 percent probability level, a view of

the contention in a particularly guarded area
can be recognized. Only in regard to Spiritual
Life and Poverty do the rejected amendments far
outnumber the accepted amendments. Both areas
reflect themselves as battlegrounds of the differing conceptions of the Society of Jesus.

The issue of Poverty is a more evenly
matched contention. Seventy-eight C-H direction
issues were submitted compared to seventy-two B-C
direction issues. Of these, a B-C following
blocked forty-four of the seventy-eight while C-H
following blocked forty-three of the seventy-two.
In the end, the Conciliar-Humanists predominated
in total issues 52.7 percent to 47.3 percent of
the Bulwark-Catholics, and 57.5 percent of the
accepted definitive issues to 42.4 percent respectively.

The government of the Society was an issue
close to the experience of over one-half of all
the delegates. Forty-nine percent of the delegates are presently involved in Jesuit administration. In the cases of legislation on central
government, Province Congregations, and future
General Congregations, the ratio of outcomes
favorable to the Conciliar-Humanists compared to
those favorable to Bulwark-Catholics measured
twenty-five to twenty-two, twenty-four to twenty,
and twenty-eight to twenty-three issues respectively. Bulwark-Catholics submitted eleven amendments
and Conciliar-Humanists submitted thirteen amendments, but B-C favorable amendment outcomes were
twice those favorable to C-H (eighteen to nine).
This is a further indication of the function of
restraint that is served by the B-C following in
the General Congregation. Thirty-two C-H
definitive votes were passed to twenty B-C
definitive votes passed.

Two more documents that were marked by predominance in favor of Conciliar-Humanists were
those on tertianship and the Introductory Decree.
In the former, C-H outcomes predominated eleven
to seven; in the latter, C-H outcomes predominated

fifteen to ten.

The Introductory Decree had a particularly stormy development. It was the product of a special intercommission which was formed to reconcile the work of the General Congregation with the instructions and wishes of the Holy See. This commission wielded strong pressure because of the intense difficulty the Congregation was experiencing with the Vatican interventions. As a result, the commission made several changes in various documents that were exempted from voting. They were exempted because the editorial committes accepted the changes or deletions as "friendly amendments."

Two entirely different versions of the Introductory Decree were found unacceptable to the delegates. In the document that finally passed, the Conciliar-Humanists had three times as many definitive issues accepted as the Bulwark-Catholics (six to two).

The recorded votes for four documents show predominance of the Bulwark-Catholic style. The nature of these documents or events surrounding their passage supports the characterization of change in the Society of Jesus as favorable to the Conciliar-Humanist direction.

The clearest testimony to the Bulwark-Catholic position at the General Congregation was the intervention of the Vatican in the affairs of the Jesuit Order. This intervention prompted three documents. The first was the Introductory Decree already discussed. The second settled the issue of grades according to the mind of the Pope at his insistence. The third was a statement of fidelity to the Vatican and to the Papacy. The documents on Grades and on Fidelity to the Papacy are two of the four documents in which the Bulwark-Catholic style voting predominates. For the documents on Grades, outcomes favorable to Bulwark-Catholics outnumber those favorable to Conciliar-Humanists, eleven to seven issues.

230

An especially noteworthy element is associated with the indicative voting on the matter of Grades. This indicative voting gave a clear predominance of seven votes to four to the Bulwark-Catholic following. Sixty-three percent of the outcomes favor the B-C position and seventy-one percent of the accepted indicative issues are B-C direction issues. This series of a dozen issues precipitated the main contention with the Vatican. Two days after this "straw vote" was taken, the Vatican sent a sharp rebuke to the Congregation. This suggests that even the Bulwark-Catholic style within the Society of Jesus is not as firm a bulwark as the Vatican would desire.

Juridical concerns of the Jesuit headquarters prompted the two remaining documents that register a predominance of Bulwark-Catholicism. One concerns the Permanent Deaconate and the other concerns Conscientious Objection.

The matter of the Permanent Deaconate was unpopular and incidental to the concerns of most delegates. Not more than a handful of Jesuits anywhere in the world would be affected. But the Vatican Congregation of Religious demanded a clarification on the matter and therefore this document was submitted. Of a total of eight issues, seven issues registered as Bulwark-Catholic and one as Conciliar-Humanist. Five of the seven were accepted.

A curious anomaly exists in regard to the document on Conscientious Objection. This document attempted a clarification of the matter of a subject's right in cases of the possible conflict between the command of a Superior and the conscience of a Jesuit. The document expresses a concern more akin to the Conciliar-Humanists than Bulwark-Catholics. Nevertheless this is the most one-sided document of the Congregation with all five definitive votes registered as B-C and seven outcomes favorable to B-C compared to two outcomes favorable to C-H. This is an instance of an overwhelmingly Bulwark-Catholic predominance determining an issue more congenial to Conciliar-Humanist interests.

The anomaly is explained by events surrounding its passage. The document on Conscientious Objection was unpopular from the beginning. It was a tangled and vague treatment which was earlier removed from the Spiritual Life document and forwarded at a later, tired time to be an appendix to that document. Common feeling among the delegates would have suggested its quick defeat. Only a slim sounding of delegates fostered the concern. But shortly before voting, an official of the Jesuit headquarters simply asserted from the floor of the assembly that "Father General needs this document." Very clearly in response to that remark, the issues were raised, voted and passed. Not a single issue on this document was rejected and the majority in every case except one amendment and one procedural vote registered as Bulwark-Catholic. The acquiescence to the needs of Jesuit headquarters brought a Bulwark-Catholic direction response that predominated in the passage of the Conscientious Objection document.

Analysis which examined the influence of the factors of region, age, office, and leadership shows further detail of the followings for both the B-C and the C-H styles. More regions favor the C-H following than the B-C (seven assistancies to five). The Northern Latin American, French, and African assistancies are the most strongly Conciliar-Humanist; the Italian, Slavic and German are the most strongly Bulwark-Catholic.

Delegates who are under fifty largely favor the Conciliar-Humanist style, although the delegates under forty taken as a group (nine delegates) have a polarity index score that favors the Bulwark-Catholic style. Comparisons of both administrative office and acknowledged leadership reveal no strong following for either the B-C or the C-H styles. Other measures of leadership

232

likewise result in negligible differences. (See Appendix Two, Tables One to Four). Overall, the influence of these variables does nothing to lessen the findings of a predominance of Conciliar-Humanists at the Thirty-Second General Congregation.

Summary and Conclusions

The votes cast by the delegates are the most important indicators of this research. They are behavioral and decisive. They translate intrinsically into the Congregation's expectations for the proximate future of the Jesuit Order.

The validity of measuring the votes relies on the validity of the Bulwark-Catholic/Conciliar-Humanist polarity index. This index capsulizes the major thesis of this research in two styles of Jesuit life and outlook. These styles characterize the transition which is predicated here of the Society of Jesus.

The index is a continuous variable which avoids condensing all delegates into some strict dichotomy. It discriminates among the delegates more strongly than any other variable except the language group they belong to.

The thesis of the Thirty-Second General Congregation bringing about a shift in the culture of the Society of Jesus from an elite status to a minority group is supported by the evidence. First of all, it is conclusive that both the changed and the unchanged styles can be found among the delegates. Secondly, a predominance of the legislation is particularly favored by the changed style, that of the Conciliar-Humanists. Three-fifths of all definitive voting on final content of the Congregations documents is attributable to a Conciliar-Humanist following.

To find a predominance of the legislation

attributable to a C-H following is not to
evidence an absolute opposition between the two
styles. The two styles have blended their support
in the final legislation. Yet, the production of
that legislation was, as is evidenced here, a
rivalry of styles, a rivalry between tradition and
modernity. The modernity that prevailed resembles
the adaptive nature and impetus of the contemporary revolutionary spearhead of Catholicism,
the Second Vatican Council.

Footnotes

[1]Cf: Williams, <u>American Society</u>, "Chapter XV, Social and Cultural Change," esp. pp. 630-633.

[2]"PA2 (i.e. principal factoring with iteration performed in SPSS factor analysis sub-program) automatically replaces the main diagonal elements of the correlation matrix with communality elements.... (It) employs the iteration process for improving the estimates of communality. First the program determines the number of factors to be extracted from the original or unreduced correlation matrix. The program then replaces the main diagonal elements of the correlation matrix with initial estimates of communalities, the R^2 estimates. Next, it extracts the same number of factors from this reduced matrix, and the variances accounted for by these factors become new communality estimates. The diagonal elements are then replaced with these new communalities." Jae-On Kim, "Chapter 24, Factor Analysis," in Norman H. Nie <u>et al</u>, <u>Statistical Package for the Social Sciences: Second Edition</u>, New York, McGraw-Hill Book Company, 1975, p. 480.

[3]<u>Ibid</u>., p. 488.

[4]"To uncover the first pattern, a factor is fitted to the data to account for the greatest regularity; each successive factor is fitted to define the remaining regularity. The result of this is that the first unrotated factor may be located between independent clusters of inter-related variables." R.J. Rummel, "Understanding the Factor Analysis" in <u>Conflict Resolution</u>, Vol. XI, No. 4, (1967), p. 472.

[5]<u>Ibid</u>., p. 473.

[6]Jean Yves Calvez, S.J., "A Critical Appraisal of the Preparation of the Jesuits' Thirty-Second General Congregation," p. 944.

[7]The total number of delegates for whom a factor score was available is 196. Of the forty-one missing cases, thirty-five of these cases were non-respondents and six were cases for which at least three of the twelve variables constitutive of the index were missing.

[8]Cf: Rensis Likert, "A Technique for the Measurement of Attitudes," in Archives of Psychology, 140 (1932), pp. 1-55, as cited in John B. Lansing and James N. Morgan, Economic Survey Methods, Ann Arbor, Michigan, Institute for Social Research, 1971, p. 280. A Likert scale is only approximated because five of the twelve items do not have the identical number and range of categories.

[9]The majority votes are assumed to be all of the votes that are not recorded as minority votes. This introduces a small bias of considering all abstentions and absences as if they were votes for the majority.

[10]The Chi-Square of the difference between B-C and C-H outcomes is 3.754. The Chi-Square associated with .05 level of significance is 3.841.

CHAPTER EIGHT

VALUE-RANKINGS OF THE DELEGATES

AND THE RELATION OF THESE VALUES TO THE

THIRTY-SECOND GENERAL CONGREGATION

The background for the Thirty-Second General Congregation was one of great change in the Church and the Jesuit Order. The Jesuits saw the Congregation as an instrument of consolidation and of transformation, both in its planning phases and in its legislative sessions.

Consolidation would seem to draw ideas and orderliness together while transformation requires some latitude between them. Too close an identification of culture and structure stifles innovation. A prior restrictive social order does the same.

In the revolutionary decade preceding this Congregation, culture superseded the existing structures. The range of new behaviors and patterns of integration was great and varied. Values generalized to encompass the greater array of possibilities. And the prior restrictive order of the Post-Tridentine Church crumbled under the impetus of aggiornamento.

As a result of this background, the level of inquiry for understanding this Congregation is predictably the level of values. Neither blind obedience to commands from on high nor schemes of recurrence and routine can provide the most accurate characterization of the Congregation. The repertoire of expectations and the hierarchies of values must give indication of the dispositions and influences underlying its legislation.

A ranking of values is thus integral to researching the Thirty-Second General Congregation.

Three elements are called for from an analysis of the value-ranking: a description of the values and priorities of different styles of Jesuit life, an assessment of the differences between them, and an account of the direction the differing values take in a time of change.

The understanding to be gained from these elements fits in with the following considerations. (1) If there are different styles comprising the delegation to this Congregation, and if one style predominates in constituting Jesuit legislation, and if this predominance marks a shift in Jesuit culture, then an examination of the kind and priority of values that can be associated to this prevalent style is germane to the status of the Society of Jesus. (2) Since two styles exist simultaneously in the Society, the similarities and the differences in their values and priorities says something of the relationship between them as a climate for the organization overall. (3) Because the emergence of a changing style constitutes an entry into culture of that style for the future of the organization, an examination of the emerging values and priorities associated with that style can determine to what extent such values and priorities harmonize with the presumed direction of change.

The source of the value-rankings is the Value Survey developed by Milton Rokeach.[1] Eighteen terminal and eighteen instrumental values are ranked in the order of their importance to the respondent. (See Table One) Not all the respondents filled in the rankings completely. Of the 202 respondents, 174 responses were able to be used for the overall analysis of the "Before" questionnaire. This consists of eighty-six percent of all respondents and seventy-four percent of all delegates.

The delegates ranked salvation as the first and highest ranked value. Of all responses to the questionnaire, sixty-five percent ranked

238

TABLE ONE

LISTING OF VALUES RANKED
IN ROKEACH'S VALUE SURVEY

I TERMINAL VALUES

A COMFORTABLE LIFE (a prosperous life)

AN EXCITING LIFE (a stimulating, active life)

A SENSE OF ACCOMPLISHMENT (lasting contribution)

A WORLD AT PEACE (free of war and conflict)

A WORLD OF BEAUTY (beauty of nature and the arts)

EQUALITY (brotherhood, equal opportunity for all)

FAMILY SECURITY (taking care of loved ones)

FREEDOM (independence, free choice)

HAPPINESS (contentedness)

INNER HARMONY (freedom fron inner conflict)

MATURE LOVE (sexual and spiritual intimacy)

NATIONAL SECURITY (protection from attack)

PLEASURE (an enjoyable, leisurely life)

SALVATION (saved, eternal life)

SELF-RESPECT (self-esteem)

SOCIAL RECOGNITION (respect, admiration)

TRUE FRIENDSHIP (close companionship)

WISDOM (a mature understanding of life)

Table One – continued

II INSTRUMENTAL VALUES

AMBITIOUS (hard-working, aspiring)

BROADMINDED (open-minded)

CAPABLE (competent, effective)

CHEERFUL (lighthearted, joyful)

CLEAN (neat, tidy)

COURAGEOUS (standing up for your beliefs)

FORGIVING (willing to pardon others)

HELPFUL (working for the welfare of others)

HONEST (sincere, truthful)

IMAGINATIVE (daring, creative)

INDEPENDENT (self-reliant, self-sufficient)

INTELLECTUAL (intelligent, reflective)

LOGICAL (consistent, rational)

LOVING (affectionate, tender)

OBEDIENT (dutiful, respectful)

POLITE (courteous, well-mannered)

RESPONSIBLE (dependable, reliable)

SELF-CONTROLLED (restrained, self-disciplined)

salvation first and seventy-eight percent ranked
it in the top three. Ten percent ranked wisdom
first and five percent ranked equality first.
Consistently, wisdom ranked second highest.
Forty-six percent of all delegate-respondents
placed this in the top three. Equality was
ranked third highest with thirty-two percent of
all delegate-respondents placing this in the top
three. The next values ranked in order of top
priority were true friendship, inner harmony,
freedom and a world at peace. National security,
a comfortable life and pleasure were consistently
the three values ranked at the end of the scale.
(See Table Two)

In terms of instrumental values, there was
strong convergence around three values as uppermost in importance. Loving (22 percent), helpful
(21 percent) and honest (20 percent) were ranked
first in importance. In overall accumulated
rankings, honest was highest, helpful second,
responsible third, and loving fourth. Forgiving,
broadminded, and courageous followed these in
priority. Jesuits valued "clean" least of all
the listed values. (See Table Three)

Difference of Value-Rankings According to
Bulwark-Catholic/Conciliar-Humanist Polarity

Comparing the delegates according to their
scores on the polarity index reveals significant
differences in the value-rankings of these two
styles. When the delegates are analyzed in four
groups, from extreme Bulwark-Catholic to extreme
Conciliar-Humanist, twenty-five percent of the
value-rankings differ significantly (beyond .05)
in a measure of Chi-Square.

The highest ranked value is salvation. This
value is ranked differently across the four groups.
The difference is significant at the level of
more than .001. Three of the four groups rank
salvation first; the extreme C-H group ranks it

TABLE TWO

OVERALL RANKINGS OF TERMINAL VALUES BY DELEGATES

N = 174

Value	Rank	Composite Score
SALVATION	1	1.30
WISDOM	2	3.86
EQUALITY	3	5.29
TRUE FRIENDSHIP	4	5.44
INNER HARMONY	5	5.94
FREEDOM	6	6.11
WORLD AT PEACE	7	6.90
HAPPINESS	8	8.65
SENSE OF ACCOMPLISHMENT	9	9.76
MATURE LOVE	10	10.29
SELF-RESPECT	11	10.35
FAMILY SECURITY	12	11.54
WORLD OF BEAUTY	13	12.43
EXCITING LIFE	14	12.50
SOCIAL RECOGNITION	15	13.36
NATIONAL SECURITY	16	14.10
COMFORTABLE LIFE	17	17.03
PLEASURE	18	17.39

TABLE THREE

OVERALL RANKINGS OF INSTRUMENTAL VALUES BY DELEGATES

N = 174

Value	Rank	Composite Score
HONEST	1	3.63
HELPFUL	2	3.71
RESPONSIBLE	3	4.17
LOVING	4	4.28
FORGIVING	5	6.00
BROADMINDED	6	7.12
COURAGEOUS	7	7.45
CAPABLE	8	9.55
IMAGINATIVE	9	9.67
SELF-CONTROLLED	10	9.95
INTELLECTUAL	11	10.14
CHEERFUL	12	10.50
OBEDIENT	13	12.83
LOGICAL	14	12.92
INDEPENDENT	15	13.17
POLITE	16	13.81
AMBITIOUS	17	14.36
CLEAN	18	16.66

seventh. The composite score for this value
lessens in priority from its uppermost ranking
(1.02) by the extreme B-C group to its lowest
priority (6.83) by the extreme C-H group.

The extreme B-C style ranking of the top
five terminal values is (1) salvation, (2)
wisdom, (3) equality, (4) world peace, and (5)
inner harmony. The extreme C-H style ranking is
(1) equality, (2) true friendship, (3) freedom,
(4) wisdom, and (5) inner harmony. The differences in ranking of equality, an exciting life,
and national security are also significant beyond
.05.

Five instrumental values differ significantly across the four categories of B-C/C-H polarity
at a level of at least .02. The instrumental
value ranked highest by Bulwark-Catholics is
honest; that ranked highest by Conciliar-Humanists
is loving. Whereas the B-C rank broadminded
tenth of eighteen, the C-H rank it fifth and,
conversely, forgiving is ranked second by B-C
followers and seventh by C-H followers. The B-C
rank ambitious last and C-H rank it thirteenth.

The B-C style ranking of the top five
instrumental values is (1) honest, (2) forgiving,
(3) helpful, (4) responsible, and (5) loving. The
C-H style ranking is (1) loving, (2) honest, (3)
responsible, (4) helpful, and (5) broadminded.

An examination of the value-ranking composite scores for all other values show a clear
consistent movement from lower to higher or higher
to lower across the four categories. For seven
of the eighteen terminal values and five of the
eighteen instrumental values, the four categories
are aligned in unbroken ascending-descending order.
In all but one instrumental value, the remaining
values are aligned across three of the four
categories in ascending-descending order. (See
Table Four)

Considering only the top five terminal and

244

TABLE FOUR

DISCRIMINATION OF VALUE-RANKINGS
ACCORDING TO B-C/C-H POLARITY INDEX

I TERMINAL	Extr. B-C Rank	B-C Score	Mod. B-C Rank	Mod. B-C Score	Mod. C-H Rank	Mod. C-H Score	Extr. C-H Rank	Extr. C-H Score	Probability
A Comfortable Life	17	16.95	17	16.93	17	17.13	18	17.08	.902
An Exciting Life	15	14.42	15	14.00	12	10.60	9	8.83	.005**
A Sense of Accomplishment	9	9.00	10	10.58	10	9.38	11	9.83	.655
A World at Peace	4	5.00	7	9.71	7	7.00	6	6.50	.584
A World of Beauty	12	11.43	13	12.86	14	12.75	12	11.25	.378
Equality	3	5.00	6	6.64	3	5.14	1	2.70	.013*
Family Security	10	10.67	12	11.25	13	11.89	14	12.17	.517
Freedom	6	6.40	5	6.40	5	6.00	3	5.00	.568
Happiness	8	8.00	8	8.33	9	9.00	10	9.17	.881
Inner Harmony	5	6.00	4	5.42	6	6.20	5	6.50	.687
Mature Love	14	13.25	11	11.25	8	8.75	8	8.00	.157
National Security	13	12.13	16	14.06	16	14.13	16	15.50	.030*
Pleasure	18	17.61	18	17.40	18	17.52	17	16.67	.270
Salvation	1	1.02	1	1.20	1	1.43	7	6.83	.001***
Self-Respect	11	10.75	9	9.25	11	10.38	13	12.00	.148
Social Recognition	16	14.63	14	13.00	15	13.31	15	13.70	.534
True Friendship	7	6.58	3	5.22	4	5.33	2	5.00	.533
Wisdom	2	3.63	2	2.92	2	4.15	4	5.50	.070

Table Four - Continued

II INSTRUMENTAL	Extr. B-C Rank	B-C Score	Mod. B-C Rank	Mod. B-C Score	Mod. C-H Rank	Mod. C-H Score	Extr. C-H Rank	Extr. C-H Score	Probability
Ambitious	18	17.13	17	15.63	17	14.00	13	12.50	.060
Broadminded	10	10.38	6	6.86	5	6.31	5	6.50	.022*
Capable	11	11.20	8	8.88	9	9.64	9	8.00	.222
Cheerful	7	7.75	15	12.86	11	10.00	10	10.00	.012*
Clean	17	15.63	18	16.69	18	16.89	18	16.83	.292
Courageous	6	7.67	7	8.38	6	6.92	8	7.00	.532
Forgiving	2	3.33	5	5.92	7	7.67	7	7.00	.062
Helpful	3	3.60	3	3.80	1	3.29	4	4.50	.849
Honest	1	3.13	1	3.43	3	4.14	2	3.83	.688
Imaginative	13	12.67	11	11.00	8	9.20	6	6.83	.002**
Independent	16	14.38	12	11.88	16	13.60	14	13.17	.056
Intellectual	9	9.38	9	9.00	12	11.14	11	10.50	.174
Logical	12	11.58	14	12.69	14	13.15	16	14.50	.003**
Loving	5	5.00	4	5.00	2	3.63	1	3.50	.770
Obedient	14	12.80	13	12.67	13	12.43	15	13.50	.543
Polite	15	13.63	16	13.44	15	13.25	17	15.63	.288
Responsible	4	5.00	2	3.56	4	4.57	3	4.17	.318
Self-Controlled	8	8.42	10	10.08	10	9.71	12	11.17	.024*

* Probability is greater than .95 significance level

** Probability is greater than .99 significance level

*** Probability is greater than .999 significance level

instrumental values, both the extreme B-C and C-H rank three of the five terminal values and four of the five instrumental values. This similarity is consistent with similarities shown throughout most discriminations. However, along all the values included in the top five, the order of priority varies.

The Bulwark-Catholics include salvation, world peace and forgiving which are not ranked in the top five rankings of the Conciliar-Humanists. The Conciliar-Humanists include true friendship, freedom and broadminded which are not in the top five rankings of the Bulwark-Catholics.

These differences are consistent with the model of modernization. Salvation and forgiving are terms rooted in the Catholic clerical tradition; both are embedded in the ascriptive role of the priest. Friendship and freedom, on the other hand, are democratized terms and generalized values. Broadminded directly implies a disembeddedness from ascription. The variation in the rankings of wisdom and equality suggests the same contrast. Wisdom is a term closer to the implications of tradition and equality, closer to the implications of contemporary humanism. Bulwark-Catholics rank wisdom (3.63) before equality (5.00); Conciliar-Humanists rank equality (2.70) before wisdom (5.50).

Among terminal values, the more traditional terms would include sense of accomplishment, family security, happiness, national security, and self-respect. In all of these the Bulwark-Catholics express a higher priority than the Conciliar-Humanists. Conversely, the more contemporary terms would include exciting life, freedom, mature love, pleasure and social recognition. In all of these, the Conciliar-Humanists express a higher priority than the Bulwark-Catholics. The same pattern associates logical, obedient, polite, and self-controlled to the B-C style and ambitious, broadminded, imaginative, and loving to the C-H style.

247

The Rokeach Value-Survey is independent of the B-C/C-H polarity index. The power of the polarity index in discriminating different groupings of value-rankings is confirmation of the consistency of findings in the preceding chapter.

The value-rankings of the delegates also differ in terms of discriminations by the structural variables of region, age, office, and leadership. These differences generally parallel the B-C/C-H differences but the extent of difference is less strong.

Comparing the various Assistancies in terms of ultimate values evidences a convergence around the values of salvation, wisdom, true friendship, equality and freedom. The diversity is greater because the rankings are spread over twelve categories. The French and the African Assistancies do not place salvation first, ten other assistancies rank it first. Seven assistancies rank wisdom second. The Spanish, French, and Northern and Southern Latin American Assistancies rank true friendship before wisdom. The French, African, English, Indian and German Assistancies rank freedom before equality; the remaining seven rank equality before freedom. The French and Germans differ strongly on ranking of exciting life (seventh and seventeenth); the Slavic differ from others in ranking a sense of accomplishment third. National security was relatively high (eleventh) and equality and freedom (eighth and ninth) were relatively low in priority for this same Assistancy. The Germans ranked a comfortable life higher in priority than an exciting life as the only region to do so.

In terms of instrumental values the greatest contrast is occasioned by the ranking of courageous. It varies in rank from third to sixteenth, with Asian Assistancy esteeming it highest and the North and Southern Latin American Assistancies esteeming it least. Honesty is esteemed by more assistancies than any other and six assistancies

rank it highest in priority. Helpful and responsible are ranked consistently high while loving
ranks first for the Spanish and Northern Latin
American Assistancies. The Italians rank loving
ninth and the Germans eleventh. Only the French
and the African Assistancies rank forgiving in
relatively low priority (tenth and fourteenth).
The African, Spanish and Italian Assistancies
rank intellectual more highly than other nations.
(See Table Five)

Except for courageous, the largest differences in ranking (i.e. exciting life, loving,
forgiving, and sense of accomplishment) differ
between the assistancies in a way that corresponds
to the assistancies differences on the polarity
index. This correspondence supports the distinctions made in Jesuit style.

In terms of age, the discriminations are
less sharp than for the polarity index. Whereas
the difference in ranking of nine values were
statistically significant when discriminated by
the polarity index, five are statistically significant when grouped for age. Some of these are
the same values at a slightly less powerful significance level than that of the polarity index.

For terminal values, salvation is ranked
first by all groups when discriminated by age.
The youngest group deviates from the others in
ranking happiness as second in importance, compared to the older groups' ranking of happiness
as eighth or ninth. The younger groups rank true
friendship, mature love, and excitement higher
in priority; the older groups rank equality,
inner-harmony, and world of beauty as higher
priorities.

For instrumental values, greater divergence
exists. No age group holds the same first
priority as any other. From youngest to oldest,
the first priorities are responsible, loving,
helpful, and honest. The largest age category
from forty-nine years rank loving first.

TABLE FIVE
DISCRIMINATION OF VALUE-RANKINGS BY ASSISTANCY

I TERMINAL	French N=14		Northern Lat.Amer. N=11		Southern Lat.Amer. N=13		Asian N=12		African N=8		English N=18		Indian N=19		American N=28		Spanish N=7		German N=18		Slavic N=6		Italian N=10	
	R	Sc	R	Sc	R	Sc	R	Sc	R	Sc	R	Sc	R	Sc	R	Sc	R	Sc	R	Sc	R	Sc	R	Sc
A Comfortable Life	18	17.17	17	17.00	17	17.11	18	17.50	17	16.90	18	17.30	17	17.19	18	17.30	17	16.67	15	13.00	17	17.00	17	17.21
An Exciting Life	7	7.00	8	8.25	13	12.00	15	13.50	10	8.50	14	12.50	12	12.00	14	13.00	12	12.00	17	16.60	13	12.50	16	15.70
A Sense of Accomplishment	10	9.00	11	10.75	10	10.75	10	10.17	6	6.50	6	6.50	10	8.67	10	9.50	11	11.00	10	10.25	3	6.00	11	11.50
A World at Peace	8	7.50	9	9.00	7	8.33	5	5.00	8	8.50	8	7.00	8	8.00	4	5.00	7	7.00	7	6.83	7	6.50	6	5.50
A World of Beauty	12	11.50	16	15.63	12	12.00	13	13.00	15	13.00	10	10.00	15	13.80	11	10.90	14	12.90	14	12.90	15	14.00	13	12.00
Equality	5	6.50	3	4.00	4	3.00	4	4.50	5	6.50	7	6.90	7	7.25	3	4.50	5	5.25	4	6.00	8	7.50	3	4.50
Family Security	15	13.50	14	12.25	9	10.00	12	12.00	14	11.50	13	12.07	14	12.88	12	11.10	13	11.50	12	11.50	12	11.50	10	10.50
Freedom	2	4.17	6	6.25	4	4.38	6	6.00	3	5.50	5	6.50	7	7.00	7	6.70	6	5.33	3	5.00	9	8.83	5	5.50
Happiness	6	7.00	7	7.00	8	10.00	9	10.00	7	7.00	9	7.50	5	6.00	9	9.50	9	9.50	9	9.83	6	6.50	8	6.00
Inner Harmony	11	10.00	5	5.75	6	5.75	3	4.50	8	8.50	4	5.17	3	5.00	5	5.10	8	7.63	8	8.00	5	6.50	7	6.00
Mature Love	3	5.17	10	10.25	15	14.00	11	11.50	12	10.00	11	11.50	11	10.13	13	11.50	3	4.00	16	13.50	16	15.00	14	12.50
National Security	16	14.17	15	14.63	16	14.67	14	13.50	13	11.17	16	13.83	16	14.60	16	15.50	16	14.25	11	11.50	11	11.50	11	11.50
Pleasure	17	16.17	18	17.13	18	17.69	18	17.17	18	17.70	17	16.88	18	17.55	17	16.64	18	17.89	18	17.75	18	17.50	18	17.67
Salvation	9	8.50	1	1.29	1	1.31	1	1.25	2	4.00	1	1.40	1	1.23	1	1.14	1	1.44	1	1.32	1	1.00	1	1.06
Self-Respect	14	13.50	12	11.00	11	11.13	8	8.50	16	14.50	12	12.00	9	8.25	8	7.36	13	12.60	13	12.11	10	11.50	12	12.00
Social Recognition	13	13.50	13	12.25	14	13.20	16	14.00	11	10.00	15	13.10	13	12.75	15	14.17	15	13.00	14	13.17	14	13.17	15	14.50
True Friendship	1	3.50	2	3.00	3	3.88	7	7.50	4	6.50	3	4.75	4	6.00	6	6.17	2	3.75	4	6.75	4	6.50	1	1.50
Wisdom	4	5.50	4	5.00	5	4.67	2	2.25	1	4.00	2	2.50	2	3.00	2	4.13	4	4.75	2	4.17	2	2.25	2	2.50

Table Five – continued

II INSTRUMENTAL	French N=14		Northern Lat.Amer. N=11		Southern Lat.Amer. N=13		Asian N=12		African N=8		English N=18		Indian N=9		American N=28		Spanish N=17		German N=18		Slavic N=6		Italian N=10	
	R	Sc	R	Sc	R	Sc	R	Sc	R	Sc	R	Sc	R	Sc	R	Sc	R	Sc	R	Sc	R	Sc	R	Sc
Ambitious	14	13.05	13	11.67	13	12.67	17	16.20	13	11.50	17	14.50	18	15.75	17	15.70	16	13.67	18	17.50	17	16.50	18	17.79
Broadminded	4	5.05	6	5.88	6	7.00	9	7.50	9	10.00	6	6.83	9	8.25	7	8.50	6	6.33	11	7.00	3	9.50	3	4.00
Capable	11	10.83	7	8.25	8	10.33	8	7.50	10	10.50	10	9.50	10	8.75	10	9.50	10	9.00	10	9.50	12	10.50	8	7.50
Cheerful	7	6.50	15	13.75	7	8.75	7	7.50	12	11.50	12	11.83	11	9.67	13	11.50	14	12.00	12	12.75	8	8.00	2	2.50
Clean	18	17.00	17	16.00	17	14.25	18	17.17	18	15.50	18	17.10	16	15.63	18	17.57	17	16.00	17	16.00	15	16.00	7	7.00
Courageous	5	5.83	16	14.25	15	13.00	3	4.00	6	5.50	7	8.00	6	7.33	5	5.75	10	10.33	4	6.83	13	16.00	1	1.50
Forgiving	10	10.00	4	5.00	3	3.00	6	5.50	14	12.00	4	5.50	5	7.00	4	4.75	5	5.33	5	5.83	5	5.00	5	6.50
Helpful	2	3.50	1	1.67	2	2.75	5	5.50	3	5.50	5	6.50	2	3.38	2	4.25	1	3.00	2	2.17	2	2.50	6	6.50
Honest	3	5.00	5	5.13	4	4.75	1	3.75	1	2.50	1	2.83	1	3.20	1	2.83	3	4.25	3	4.10	3	3.50	4	2.50
Imaginative	9	7.17	16	10.00	11	9.00	11	9.00	8	9.50	8	8.50	8	8.25	11	10.50	9	9.17	13	11.00	11	11.00	12	10.00
Independent	15	13.83	18	16.67	18	16.88	13	12.50	15	14.00	13	13.00	12	11.75	9	9.50	17	15.33	10	9.00	16	13.50	16	13.50
Intellectual	12	11.00	11	11.00	11	11.00	14	13.00	7	7.50	11	10.00	14	12.75	15	13.00	7	8.25	7	8.25	18	17.00	13	12.00
Logical	13	13.50	12	13.25	12	12.00	15	13.50	11	11.50	14	13.17	17	15.67	15	13.00	13	12.75	13	12.75	14	13.17	11	11.00
Loving	6	6.00	1	2.73	1	2.00	4	5.50	6	7.50	3	4.00	3	4.00	6	6.00	1	2.33	11	10.00	9	2.00	9	7.83
Obedient	17	15.90	9	9.00	9	10.75	12	10.50	16	14.50	16	14.50	15	14.25	14	12.83	9	9.33	9	9.33	8	8.50	14	12.50
Polite	16	15.00	4	11.33	14	13.00	16	15.00	17	15.00	15	14.50	13	12.67	16	15.38	11	12.00	16	14.17	15	14.00	15	14.00
Responsible	1	3.00	5	5.00	5	5.25	2	4.00	2	3.50	2	3.50	4	5.00	3	4.50	4	5.00	2	3.00	6	6.50	6	7.00
Self-Controlled	8	7.00	10	10.00	10	11.00	10	9.00	5	7.00	10	9.83	7	8.00	12	11.10	14	13.00	7	9.00	10	7.50	10	10.00

Generally the younger rank broadminded, capable and imaginative higher, while the older group choose to rank honest, intellectual and courageous higher. In some instances (accomplishment, self-respect, capable, forgiving) the small category of under forty years of age resembles the oldest group more than the middle groups; although this is more than offset by values the youngest rank differently than the older. (See Table Six)

In terms of the control for office, a pattern recurs that was found in voting behavior. The administrators are not different from the whole group overall. The mean of administrators is generally close to the mean of the entire population.

Administrator respondents represented 50.5 percent of the completed returns for the Value-Survey analysis (eighty-eight out of 174 returns). With all thirty-six rankings considered, the administrators vary on the average of .35 from the overall value-ranking. They vary most on a higher appraisal of a sense of accomplishment, happiness, and an exciting life and lesser appraisal of a world at peace. The respondents working in parish work or secondary schooling are generally more distinctive, but there are more similarities than differences between all groups. Parish workers rank happiness at a relatively low priority (tenth) and national security at a relatively high priority (eleventh). Secondary school personnel rank a world at peace relatively high (third) and a world of beauty and mature love relatively low (sixteenth and fourteenth). Formation personnel seem the most personalistic, ranking true friendship, inner-harmony, happiness, and mature love more highly than all other occupations. (See Table Seven)

Administrators and non-administrators are matched in their value-rankings on eleven of eighteen terminal values and on eleven of eighteen instrumental values. This is consistent with the

252

TABLE SIX

VALUE-RANKINGS DISCRIMINATED BY AGE

Value	Under 40 N=8 Rank Score		40-49 N=89 R Sc		50-59 N=62 R Sc		60 or Over N=15 R Sc		Probab-ility
I: TERMINAL									
A Comfortable Life	18	17.50	17	17.04	17	17.04	17	16.86	.501
An Exciting Life	10	10.00	13	11.92	14	12.61	16	14.75	.222
A Sense of Accomplish-ment	11	10.50	10	9.69	9	9.00	11	11.00	.563
A World at Peace	9	8.00	7	7.00	6	6.36	7	7.25	.785
A World of Beauty	16	14.00	15	13.00	12	11.83	12	11.67	.252
Equality	6	7.00	4	5.13	3	5.50	4	5.00	.778
Family Security	13	11.83	12	11.82	11	11.17	10	10.75	.534
Freedom	4	5.00	5	6.25	5	6.00	6	6.60	.558
Happiness	2	3.50	9	8.75	8	8.70	8	10.25	.100
Inner Harmony	8	8.00	5	6.14	4	6.00	3	4.67	.243
Mature Love	12	11.00	8	8.67	13	12.21	14	12.25	.009**
National Security	15	14.00	16	14.29	16	14.00	13	12.00	.823
Pleasure	17	17.00	18	17.47	8	17.29	18	17.67	.381
Salvation	1	1.17	1	1.49	1	1.20	1	1.04	.003**
Self-Respect	7	8.00	11	10.31	10	10.50	9	10.75	.902
Social Recognition	14	14.00	14	12.96	15	13.68	15	14.25	.298
True Friendship	5	5.50	3	4.29	7	6.50	5	5.88	.022*
Wisdom	3	5.00	2	4.07	2	3.68	2	2.43	.509
II:INSTRUMENTAL									
Ambitious	16	14.00	17	13.81	17	15.17	18	17.75	.296
Broadminded	6	7.00	6	6.58	7	7.36	8	8.25	.697
Capable	5	7.00	11	10.09	9	9.63	5	6.75	.025*
Cheerful	10	8.50	9	9.36	12	11.79	15	13.00	.131
Clean	18	17.50	18	16.44	18	16.81	17	16.25	.587
Courageous	7	7.25	7	8.08	6	7.30	6	6.88	.567
Forgiving	9	8.50	5	5.43	5	5.36	7	8.00	.073
Helpful	2	3.00	2	4.06	1	3.32	3	4.00	.797
Honest	3	3.83	3	4.19	2	3.50	1	2.13	.177
Imaginative	8	8.00	8	9.29	11	10.75	11	10.75	.701
Independent	15	14.00	14	13.33	15	13.00	13	12.80	.543
Intellectual	12	10.83	12	10.38	10	10.00	9	9.00	.727
Logical	14	12.50	16	13.78	14	12.39	12	11.40	.036*
Loving	4	5.50	1	3.46	4	4.83	4	6.00	.899
Obedient	17	15.50	13	13.00	13	12.25	14	13.00	.531
Polite	13	12.50	15	13.78	16	14.50	16	14.00	.865
Responsible	1	2.25	4	4.44	3	4.60	2	3.25	.030*
Self-Controlled	11	10.17	10	10.04	8	9.50	10	10.75	.530

TABLE SEVEN

VALUE-RANKINGS DISCRIMINATED ACCORDING TO OFFICE - ADMINISTRATION OR OTHER WORK

I TERMINAL	Superinstitutional Administration N=88		University Work N=35		Secondary Schooling N=9		Parish Work N=10		Writing or Research N=6		Formation N=14		Other Categories N=12		Probabilities
	R	Sc	R	Sc	R	Sc	R	Sc	R	Sc	R	Sc	R	Sc	
A Comfortable Life	17	17.03	17	17.00	17	17.00	18	18.67	18	17.50	18	16.50	18	17.00	.301
An Exciting Life	12	11.50	16	13.92	11	11.00	15	12.50	16	16.50	13	12.00	13	12.00	.369
A Sense of Accomplishment	8	7.83	8	8.75	12	11.25	16	13.50	10	10.50	11	10.50	14	12.17	.005**
A World at Peace	9	8.00	5	6.38	3	4.25	7	7.00	5	5.00	7	6.17	5	5.83	.573
A World of Beauty	14	12.36	13	12.13	16	15.25	14	12.50	12	11.50	15	13.50	10	10.50	.633
Equality	5	5.75	3	4.86	5	5.00	5	4.50	4	5.00	9	7.00	2	4.50	.835
Family Security	13	12.08	12	11.20	10	9.33	9	10.50	13	12.00	10	10.50	11	10.83	.408
Freedom	6	6.39	6	6.57	4	4.67	4	4.50	6	6.50	8	6.50	4	5.50	.235
Happiness	7	7.75	9	9.75	6	6.25	10	11.00	9	9.50	5	6.00	9	8.50	.140
Inner Harmony	4	5.50	7	7.25	9	9.25	6	5.00	7	7.00	4	5.17	8	7.50	.235
Mature Love	11	10.83	11	11.20	14	12.25	12	11.50	8	8.50	6	6.17	7	7.00	.025
National Security	16	14.32	15	13.86	13	11.33	11	11.17	15	14.50	16	15.25	16	14.25	.143
Pleasure	18	17.54	18	17.58	18	17.38	17	16.17	17	17.00	17	16.00	17	16.25	.406
Salvation	1	1.26	1	1.15	1	1.40	2	3.00	1	1.50	1	2.17	1	4.00	.126
Self-Respect	10	9.90	10	11.00	8	9.00	8	9.00	11	11.50	12	11.00	12	12.00	.885
Social Recognition	15	13.39	14	13.25	15	13.63	13	12.50	14	13.00	14	13.25	15	14.00	.974
True Friendship	3	5.50	4	6.20	7	7.75	3	4.17	2	4.17	2	3.50	6	6.00	.145
Wisdom	2	3.57	2	4.00	2	4.00	1	2.50	3	4.50	3	5.00	3	5.00	.652

Table Seven - continued

II INSTRUMENTAL	Superinstitutional Administration N=88		University Work N=35		Secondary Schooling N=9		Parish Work N=10		Writing or Research N=6		Formation N=14		Other Categories N=12		Probabilities
	R	Sc	R	Sc	R	Sc	R	Sc	R	Sc	R	Sc	R	Sc	
Ambitious	17	14.10	17	15.00	14	12.00	17	14.00	18	17.75	16	14.50	17	16.00	.693
Broadminded	6	7.17	6	7.88	7	6.75	6	6.00	7	7.00	6	6.50	6	6.50	.929
Capable	10	9.68	7	8.25	10	9.63	15	13.00	7	8.00	10	10.70	10	9.00	.536
Cheerful	12	11.00	11	10.75	9	9.25	11	11.83	10	9.50	11	10.00	9	8.50	.953
Clean	18	16.55	18	16.58	18	17.00	18	17.67	17	16.00	18	16.00	18	17.25	.592
Courageous	7	7.32	8	9.25	6	6.25	8	10.50	11	10.00	7	7.00	5	4.50	.134
Forgiving	5	6.39	5	4.94	2	4.00	3	3.50	6	7.00	5	6.00	8	8.50	.519
Helpful	1	3.17	4	4.31	1	3.13	5	4.50	5	6.50	1	2.50	4	4.50	.235
Honest	2	3.50	3	3.60	5	6.00	2	3.50	1	1.50	3	4.83	2	3.83	.549
Imaginative	8	9.38	13	11.80	8	7.00	13	12.83	12	11.00	8	8.50	7	7.50	.095
Independent	13	12.75	15	13.43	17	15.67	10	11.00	15	12.50	15	13.50	15	13.50	.867
Intellectual	11	9.70	9	9.88	12	11.00	12	12.00	3	4.50	13	11.50	12	11.50	.549
Logical	15	12.92	12	11.20	16	15.00	14	13.00	13	11.50	17	15.83	14	13.17	.084
Loving	4	4.90	1	3.33	3	5.00	1	3.17	8	7.50	2	3.17	3	4.00	.388
Obedient	14	12.83	14	13.00	11	10.00	7	10.50	16	15.50	14	13.25	13	13.00	.218
Polite	16	13.67	16	14.25	15	15.00	16	14.00	14	12.50	12	11.50	16	15.50	.819
Responsible	3	4.21	2	3.45	4	6.00	4	4.50	2	3.00	4	5.83	1	3.50	.125
Self-Controlled	9	9.50	10	10.08	13	12.00	9	10.83	9	5.50	9	10.00	11	10.17	.417

pattern found in voting behavior that administrative office is a poor discriminator of differences in the Jesuit delegation to the Thirty-Second General Congregation.

The value-rankings of leaders resembles that of non-leaders. Salvation, wisdom, equality and true friendship are the most highly ranked terminal values. None differ significantly (at .05 level). Leaders and non-leaders rank the instrumental values of helpful and honest in reverse order. Leaders rank honest more highly; non-leaders rank helpful more highly. This difference is significant at a probability level of .001. These leaders value responsible, imaginative, courageous, and broadminded more highly than non-leaders. Non-leaders rank loving, forgiving, and self-controlled more highly than leaders. (See Table Eight)

Alternate measures of both administration and leadership yield results similar to these. Very few significant differences are discernible. (See Appendix Two, Tables Five and Six)

When one examines the value-rankings controlled by age, office, and leadership in terms of the future of the Jesuit Order, the assertion of the shift to a more egalitarian, less ascriptive role in the world at large seems very likely.

The younger delegates are more egalitarian in most value-rankings, (e.g. friendship, mature love, loving, broadminded). However, many of the older delegates value equality at least as highly as the young.

Administrators and formation staff have strong commitment to the future directions of the Jesuit Order and they also resemble the model of modernization more than other occupations. The values of loving and true friendship are very high among the formation staff and other occupations but not among the administrators.

DISCRIMINATION OF VALUE-RANKINGS BY DESIGNATED LEADERSHIP

	Non-Leaders N=152		Leaders Designated once N=8		Leaders Designated more than once N=14		Probability
	R	Sc	R	Sc	R	Sc	
I TERMINAL							
A Comfortable Life	17	17.03	17	16.90	18	17.17	.328
An Exciting Life	14	12.50	12	10.50	14	13.00	.681
A Sense of Accomplishment	9	9.72	9	9.83	9	10.00	.828
A World at Peace	7	6.70	5	6.50	8	8.00	.649
A World of Beauty	13	12.43	14	11.50	13	12.00	.998
Equality	3	5.38	2	5.00	3	4.50	.773
Family Security	12	11.50	11	10.50	12	11.83	.877
Freedom	5	5.91	7	8.50	6	6.90	.204
Happiness	8	8.75	8	9.50	7	7.50	.809
Inner Harmony	6	6.03	6	7.00	4	4.83	.183
Mature Love	10	10.12	13	11.50	11	11.00	.544
National Security	16	14.18	16	12.50	15	13.83	.730
Pleasure	18	17.45	18	17.50	17	16.90	.350
Salvation	1	1.29	1	3.00	1	1.20	.267
Self-Respect	11	10.32	10	10.00	10	11.00	.676
Social Recognition	15	13.30	15	12.00	16	14.70	.603
True Friendship	4	5.43	4	6.00	5	5.50	.998
Wisdom	2	3.86	3	5.50	2	2.50	.343

Table Eight - continued

	Non-Leaders N=152		Leaders Designated once N=8		Leaders Designated more than once N=14		Probability
	R	Sc	R	Sc	R	Sc	
II INSTRUMENTAL							
Ambitious	17	14.19	17	15.50	17	16.50	.578
Broadminded	6	7.20	7	6.00	4	6.83	.674
Capable	8	9.72	2	4.50	7	8.00	.362
Cheerful	11	10.35	11	8.50	14	12.25	.203
Clean	18	16.60	18	16.00	18	17.07	.104
Courageous	7	7.70	4	5.50	3	5.00	.306
Forgiving	5	5.61	10	8.00	9	8.50	.251
Helpful	1	3.18	9	8.00	8	8.50	.001***
Honest	3	3.79	3	5.50	1	1.83	.001***
Imaginative	10	10.10	6	6.00	6	8.00	.613
Independent	15	13.19	15	14.00	11	10.50	.518
Intellectual	12	10.50	1	4.50	10	8.83	.248
Logical	14	13.00	13	11.50	12	11.50	.523
Loving	2	3.79	8	6.50	5	7.00	.332
Obedient	13	12.88	14	12.00	15	12.50	.941
Polite	16	13.68	16	15.00	16	14.50	.649
Responsible	4	4.17	5	6.00	2	3.50	.517
Self-Controlled	9	9.76	12	11.50	13	12.00	.225

The ranking of values among leaders lends itself to a modernized style, although the contrast with non-leaders is mixed. Leaders set high priority on imaginative and broadminded; non-leaders set high priority on freedom and being helpful.

Neither administrators nor leaders distinctively rank values similar to Conciliar-Humanists. They do not distinctively rank values similar to Bulwark-Catholics either. The absence of any particular polarity here between administrators and those who do not administer and between leaders and non-leaders is more likely to promote the transition of Jesuit styles than to inhibit it. A strong polarity in either group could serve to entrench a Bulwark-Catholic position through the sanctions and legitimation of office or leadership.

When the delegates are compared to one another according to other variables, various contrasts emerge. But no consistent or striking regularities are seen across various comparisons. These variables include social class, task or person orientation, date of final vows relative to the Second Vatican Council, the kind of a university degree, and whether or not the delegate graduated from The Gregorian University in Rome. Also differences are examined according to the number of publications authored and the number of languages spoken. Canon lawyers are compared to non-canon lawyers and professors of sacred subjects are compared to professors of secular subjects. (See Appendix Two, Tables Seven to Nine)

These various comparisons neither support nor deny the thesis of modernization in the Jesuit Order. For each of the variables compared, some elements could be drawn from one side of the comparison and others from the opposite side to suggest the strongest following of a Conciliar-Humanist style.

This combination of value rankings serves to add an important dimension to the findings. The examination of values looked at first one way and then another through intersecting planes of comparison is an analytical procedure which, in a sense, resembles the operations of values in actual experience. Values operate in a matrix of varied relationships. The influences of external conditions, phenomena of the moment, lasting dispositions and bias, other values in combination and the dynamics of social interaction all cooperate in a complex of both individual and group motivation.

If each discrimination of value-rankings exhibited differences that corresponded to the contrast of Jesuit styles, it would be necessary to conclude either that the Society of Jesus was hopelessly polarized or that the discriminations were artificial. Instead, what emerges from the crisscrossing variety of values examined according to different aspects of the population is the sense of a fabric that could withstand modern reshaping.

Discrimination of Selected Variables According to Language Groups

The questionnaires for this research were in five different language versions: English, Spanish, French, German and Italian. (See Appendix One) The delegates were compared on the basis of the language version they completed. No other variable exhibits as many differences both in respect to the value-rankings and in respect to other variables as this distinction of language.

A serious methodological concern arises in the face of these differences. The differences could reflect the actual differences in the cultures pertinent to the languages spoken or they could reflect a bias in the language translations.

As the evidence which follows demonstrates, the differences are found in demographic variables and voting behavior as well as in questionnaire items. Also, different cultures which used the same language version demonstrate differences one from another.

The first difference to take account of is the ratio of the different language versions. English is the language of 43.8 percent, Spanish 23.9 percent, French 13.4 percent, German 10.4 percent and Italian 8.5 percent of the delegate respondents. As regards age: more than three-quarters of the Italian-speaking were over fifty and one-quarter over sixty years of age. Just thirty percent of the French-speaking were over fifty and none were over sixty years. The Italians and English-speaking report being raised in a social class with a mean score lower than the French and German and lower still than the Spanish. Nearly all Spanish-speaking delegates were person-oriented as were three-quarters of the English-speaking, two-thirds of the German, half the French and one-third of the Italian.

The index measuring Bulwark-Catholic and Conciliar-Humanist polarity differs greatly among the language groups. The Spanish-speaking rank the most Conciliar-Humanist (.356) followed by the French-speaking (.341). The English are slightly below the mean (-.049). The German-speaking are more Bulwark-Catholic (-.211) and the Italian-speaking delegates are very strongly Bulwark-Catholic (-.899). A similar ranking characterizes the theological modernity of the language groups. The French are the most avant garde followed by the Spanish. The English are slightly above the mean while the German and the Italians rank lower on the theological modernity scale.

The English rank the Jesuits as the most professional followed by the Spanish, the German, and the French; the Italians rank the Jesuits as less professional than all the other language

261

groups. Considering leadership as attributed by other delegates after the Congregation, the Germans contributed the most leadership, the French and English language groups next, followed by the Italian; the Spanish-speaking contributed least leadership as attributed by the delegates. (See Table Nine)

Besides the differences in various positions taken on questionnaire responses and demographic variables, the various language groups show clear differences in voting. It must be cautioned that the voting scores are not independent of some questionnaire responses as twelve questionnaire responses shaped the index which discriminated the issues for voting as Bulwark-Catholic or Conciliar-Humanist.

In most subject matter categories, the Italian-speaking voters were most highly in the minority. The only exception to this pattern is the matter of grades and votes taken on procedures. In these two areas, the Germans were most in the minority. In all areas, the Spanish and the French were least often in the minority; the Spanish ranked most highly in the majority in six categories and the French in four categories. The English-speaking are closest to the mean overall and in all ten categories occupy the middle position of the five language groups. (See Table Ten) Similarly, the standard deviation and variance of the English is generally not at one extreme or the other.

Many differences are manifest when the value-rankings of the five language groups are compared. When the rankings of the eighteen terminal values are compared, ten differences are significant at least at the .05 level. When the rankings of the eighteen instrumental values are compared, thirteen differences are significant at the .05 level.

The most significant differences in respect to terminal values are the ranking for an exciting

TABLE NINE

DISCRIMINATION OF SELECTED VARIABLES

ACCORDING TO LANGUAGE GROUPS

A. Number of Respondents

	N	%
English version	88	43.8
Spanish translation	48	23.9
French translation	27	13.4
German translation	21	10.4
Italian translation	7	8.5

B. Age of Respondents

	30-39	40-49	50-59	60-69
English	2	42	35	9
Spanish	3	25	16	4
French	1	18	8	0
German	3	9	6	3
Italian	0	4	9	4
Percentage	4.5	48.8	36.8	10.0

C. Social Class Delegates were Raised in

	Poor Class	Unskilled Class	Middle Class	Upper-Middle Class	Upper Class	Mean Score
English	N=1	12	50	23	1	3.126
Spanish	0	3	28	17	1	3.313
French	1	5	9	12	0	3.185
German	0	2	12	6	1	3.286
Italian	0	4	9	4	0	3.000

D. Bulwark-Catholic/Conciliar-Humanist Polarity Scores

	Mean Score	Standard Dev.	N
English	- 0.049	.850	87
Spanish	0.356	.760	47
French	0.341	.808	24
German	- 0.211	.792	21
Italian	- 0.899	.917	16
Total	0.0095	.873	195

Table Nine - continued

E. Theological Modernity Index

	Mean Score	Standard Dev.	N
English	0.110	.786	87
Spanish	0.123	.774	46
French	0.200	.895	24
German	- 0.351	.927	21
Italian	- 0.730	.855	15
Totals	0.0090	.851	193

F. Professionalism Index

	Mean Score	Standard Dev.	N
English	0.115	.833	84
Spanish	0.110	.675	47
French	- 0.156	.682	21
German	- 0.136	.775	20
Italian	- 0.517	.790	14
Totals	.0084	.783	186

G. Leadership Attributed by Delegates after the Congragation

	Mean Score	Standard Dev.	N
English	9.385	15.543	13
Spanish	1.500	0.577	4
French	9.833	17.509	6
German	12.500	7.778	2
Italian	2.667	0.577	3

TABLE TEN

DISCRIMINATION OF MEAN VOTING SCORES ACCORDING

TO LANGUAGE GROUP OF THE DELEGATES

	English	Spanish	French	German	Italian
Justice	0.591	0.667	0.926	1.286	3.824
Poverty	0.284	−0.500	0.259	0.048	1.765
Formation	−0.068	−0.208	−0.148	0.381	1.412
Spiritual Life	0.432	0.375	0.593	0.714	2.529
Indentity	0.102	0.125	−0.074	0.048	1.706
Vows	−0.148	−0.333	−0.889	0.381	0.000
Vatican	0.011	−0.458	−0.333	0.095	0.941
Brief Document	−0.216	−0.083	−0.074	−0.143	0.118
Government	0.000	−0.396	0.370	0.667	1.824
Procedures	−0.273	−0.188	−0.222	0.286	0.176

A higher positive score designates a greater proportion of
minority votes in the difference between Conciliar-Humanist
and Bulwark-Catholic outcomes.

life and self-respect. The French language group
rank an exciting life fifth, the Italians rank it
sixteenth. The German and English language
groups rank self-respect eighth while the Spanish
rank it twelfth and the French rank it sixteenth.
The Spanish and French groups rank true friendship strongly while the Italian, German, and
English-speaking groups rank it less so. Those
who speak Italian rank salvation most highly,
the English and German-speaking next in order,
and the Spanish less highly, although all four
rank it in first place. The French-speaking rank
salvation in third place.

The English and the German language groups
rank inner-harmony very high relative to the
others whereas it ranks relatively low to the
French (eleventh place compared to third). A
comfortable life consistently ranks second last
or last. To the German-speaking group, however,
a comfortable life ranks seventh. The German
and the French are high in ranking a sense of
accomplishment and low in ranking a world at
peace.

Four rankings of instrumental values are
significant beyond the level of .001. Loving
ranks first with the German and Spanish language
groups but seventh with Italian and French.
Courageous ranks fourth among the French-speaking
and fifteenth among the Spanish. The English-
speaking rank independent twelfth where the
Italian, German, and Spanish rank it sixteenth,
seventeenth and eighteenth respectively.

The value of politeness ranks fifth to the
Italians and sixteenth to the French and English-
speaking. Imaginative ranks eighth to the English,
French and German and sixteenth to the Spanish.
The Spanish language group ranks forgiving third
where the French-speaking rank it eleventh. (See
Table Eleven)

Considering the vast diversity in the
language groups, a check on the influence of this

TABLE ELEVEN

DISCRIMINATION OF VALUE-RANKINGS BY
WHICH LANGUAGE VERSION QUESTIONNAIRE DELEGATE COMPLETED

I TERMINAL	English N=78		Spanish N=42		French N=24		German N=18		Italian N=12		Probability
	R	Sc	R	Sc	R	Sc	R	Sc	R	Sc	
A Comfortable Life	18	17.31	17	16.91	18	17.17	7	7.50	17	17.17	.003**
An Exciting Life	14	13.20	8	9.70	5	6.17	17	16.81	16	15.67	.001***
A Sense of Accomplishment	9	8.70	12	11.00	8	7.75	13	12.50	10	10.00	.017*
A World at Peace	5	5.70	7	7.90	9	8.00	6	7.50	6	6.50	.041*
A World of Beauty	11	11.30	15	14.17	12	12.17	15	13.00	13	12.75	.248
Equality	4	5.20	3	4.25	6	6.70	10	8.50	3	4.50	.026*
Family Security	13	11.83	11	11.00	14	13.00	12	11.50	11	10.50	.591
Freedom	7	6.50	5	5.30	4	5.83	4	6.00	6	6.50	.863
Happiness	10	8.93	10	10.25	7	6.75	9	8.50	8	8.00	.194
Inner Harmony	3	5.14	6	5.93	11	10.67	3	4.50	7	7.50	.020*
Mature Love	12	11.63	9	10.00	10	8.17	11	10.00	9	10.00	.665
National Security	16	14.30	16	14.58	15	13.67	16	13.50	14	13.50	.349
Pleasure	17	17.04	18	17.69	17	16.93	18	17.75	18	17.75	.008**
Salvation	1	1.20	1	1.38	3	5.50	1	1.25	1	1.10	.002**
Self-Respect	8	8.38	13	11.50	16	15.10	8	8.50	12	12.50	.001***
Social Recognition	15	13.83	14	12.93	13	12.70	14	13.00	15	14.17	.173
True Friendship	6	6.26	2	3.64	2	4.50	5	6.50	4	5.00	.005**
Wisdom	2	3.63	4	5.00	1	4.25	2	3.00	2	2.50	.050

Table Eleven - continued

II INSTRUMENTAL	English N=78		Spanish N=42		French N=24		German N=18		Italian N=12		Probability
	R	Sc	R	Sc	R	Sc	R	Sc	R	Sc	
Ambitious	17	15.67	13	12.39	13	13.00	18	17.50	18	17.83	.001***
Broadminded	7	8.00	6	6.06	6	7.00	9	9.00	3	4.00	.045*
Capable	9	9.17	8	9.50	12	10.50	10	9.17	9	9.50	.549
Cheerful	11	10.17	11	11.75	9	9.00	14	13.00	12	11.00	.067
Clean	18	17.06	17	15.50	18	16.50	16	15.70	17	16.83	.047*
Courageous	6	6.28	15	12.50	4	5.50	6	6.00	10	10.50	.001***
Forgiving	5	5.13	3	4.75	11	10.50	5	6.00	6	6.50	.005**
Helpful	2	4.36	2	3.40	3	4.17	3	3.00	4	5.50	.080
Honest	1	3.21	4	4.79	2	3.50	4	4.10	1	2.50	.036*
Imaginative	8	9.14	16	12.83	8	7.50	8	9.00	14	12.00	.001**
Independent	12	10.50	18	16.25	15	14.00	17	15.83	16	14.50	.001***
Intellectual	13	11.38	7	9.17	10	10.50	7	8.50	8	9.00	.018*
Logical	15	13.50	14	12.50	14	13.10	13	12.70	13	11.50	.126
Loving	4	4.83	1	2.25	7	7.17	1	2.50	7	7.50	.001***
Obedient	14	13.14	9	10.00	17	15.75	12	12.00	15	14.00	.007**
Polite	16	14.86	12	11.83	16	15.50	15	13.83	5	6.50	.001**
Responsible	3	4.41	5	5.30	1	2.90	2	3.00	2	3.00	.053
Self-Controlled	10	10.00	10	10.83	5	6.00	11	11.50	11	11.00	.004**

diversity in determining the measure of Bulwark-Catholic/Conciliar-Humanist was run. Along with various other relationships, partial correlation was performed controlling for language groups. In running partial correlations, the outcome of the controls would be to make negligible the zero-order correlation if the control variable were the "explaining" variable, that is, if the control variable explained the variance more than the original correlation. On the other hand, if the original zero-order correlation is increased when controlling for the structural variable, it can be said that the structural variables "suppress" the true strength of the relationship.[2]

Further partial correlations were run controlling for region, office, and leadership. For the majority of these correlations, some influence of an "explanatory" effect was detected. But in no instance did the relation between the correlated variables become negligible. (See Table Twelve)

Furthermore, in selecting other variables that correlate with greater statistical significance and controlling again for the major structural variables including language groups, the same findings emerge. The level of statistical significance remains virtually unchanged and the correlation only slightly changed. (See Table Thirteen)

The analysis of major structural variables, especially language groups, supports the assertions, interpretation, and previous findings of this research.

Change in Questionnaire Responses and
Value-Rankings during the Period of the
Thirty-Second General Congregation

A contrast of responses from before and after the Thirty-Second General Congregation show

269

TABLE TWELVE

PARTIAL CORRELATIONS OF FACTOR SCORES AND VOTING SCORES WITH AGE WHEN CONTROLLING FOR LANGUAGE, REGION, OFFICE AND ATTRIBUTED LEADERSHIP

Age Correlated with	Variables Correlation (Zero-Order Partial)	Controll- ing for Language	Controll- ing for Region	Controll- ing for Office	Controll- ing for Attributed Leadership
B-C/C-H Polarity Index	-0.1716	-0.1668	-0.1711	-0.1723	-0.1581
Jesuit Extensive- ness Index	0.0165	0.0067	0.0145	0.0102	0.0562
Change Index	0.0055	0.0007	0.0048	0.0022	0.0678
Values Index	0.0776	0.0745	0.0758	0.0762	0.0759
Self-Interest Index	0.0270	0.0237	0.0259	0.0248	-0.0274
Cultural Open- ness Index	-0.1020	-0.1002	-0.1050	-0.1067	-0.1241
Theological Position Index	-0.2308	-0.2275	-0.2312	-0.2310	-0.2113
Professionalism Index	0.0565	0.0673	0.0650	0.0578	0.0768
Justice Vote Score	0.1102	0.1028	0.1094	0.1114	0.1469
Poverty Vote Score	0.1190	0.1150	0.1179	0.1261	0.1108
Formation Vote Score	0.1895	0.1848	0.1903	0.1900	0.2046
Spiritual Life Vote Score	0.1700	0.1647	0.1695	0.1682	0.1984
Identity Vote Score	0.1279	0.1221	0.1269	0.1306	0.1248
Vows Vote Score	0.0983	0.0967	0.1973	0.1052	0.0979
Vatican Vote Score	0.0524	0.0470	0.0521	0.0489	-0.0820
Brief Documents Vote Score	0.1221	0.1195	0.1210	0.1176	0.1071
Government Vote Score	0.1003	0.0925	0.0990	0.0998	0.0736
Procedures Vote Score	0.0114	0.0043	0.0096	0.0180	0.0309

PARTIAL CORRELATIONS OF SELECTED VARIABLES

AND VOTE SCORES WITH SALVATION RANKING

CONTROLLING FOR LANGUAGE, REGION, OFFICE, AND LEADERSHIP

Salvation Ranking	Variables Correlation (Zero-Order Partial)	Controlling for Language	Controlling for Region	Controlling for Administrative Office	Controlling for Attributed Leadership
Age	-0.2589	-0.2577	-0.2593	-0.2639	-0.2482
Church-World Relation	0.2468	0.2454	0.2474	0.2481	0.2361
Social Class	0.1864	0.1865	0.1866	0.1883	0.1901
Year of Final Vows	0.2038	0.2024	0.2059	0.2013	0.1891
Study as Sacred or Secular	0.0778	0.0804	0.0756	0.0644	0.0591
Theological Position	0.3925	0.3958	0.4010	0.3936	0.3875
Justice Score	-0.2361	-0.2345	-0.2486	-0.2356	-0.2485
Poverty Score	-0.2009	-0.1981	-0.2041	-0.1962	-0.1980
Formation Score	-0.2508	-0.2491	-0.2612	-0.2512	-0.2544
Spiritual Life Score	-0.2466	-0.2453	-0.2527	-0.2495	-0.2551
Identity Score	-0.1557	-0.1515	-0.1612	-0.1539	-0.1540
Vows Score	-0.2019	-0.2007	-0.2041	-0.1972	-0.2015
Vatican Score	-0.1787	-0.1754	-0.1793	-0.1829	-0.1620
Brief Documents Score	-0.1417	-0.1395	-0.1449	-0.1474	-0.1366
Government Score	-0.1944	-0.1914	-0.1984	-0.1954	-0.1871
Procedures Score	-0.1105	-0.1058	-0.1135	-0.1050	-0.1169
B-C/C-H Polarity Index	0.4226	0.4231	0.4314	0.4231	0.4192
Professionalism Index	-0.1628	0.1750	-0.1647	-0.1620	-0.1693

greater similarity than difference. There is
strong stability in the answers from one version
to the next.

The original questionnaire was sent to the
delegates in early November, 1974. The Congregation was held from December through the first
week in March. The second questionnaire was sent
to the delegates in early April, 1975. Of 202
respondents to the "Before" version, 134 responded
to the "After" version five months later.

The scores for responses of twenty-four
questions that were used in both versions each
range from "(1) strongly agree" to "(5) strongly
disagree". The scores of four items varied to
the extent that the mean score changed by more
than .20. The mean of five other items changed
by .10. The difference in six items was negligible.

Three of the four items that changed more
than .20 belonged together as part of the Jesuit
extensiveness scale. These three responses
changed in the direction of greater identification with Jesuit projects at three levels: one's
own apostolate, one's local institution or team-
effort, and one's own province. Increased
solidarity seems indicated by the changes. Perhaps the relief of having arrived "home" after
the difficult task of the Congregation in Rome
affected the delegates' responses. A fourth item
of the same scale, measuring identification at
the international level also changed in the
direction of greater agreement (.149). The
remaining item of that scale, measuring identification at the national level, showed a slight
change towards disagreement (.097).

Of the other variables that changed notably,
two formed the following pair:

When working in foreign countries,
Jesuits should avoid taking strong
public positions on religious or

272

social issues.

Even when working in their native
countries, Jesuits should generally
avoid taking strong public positions
on religious or social issues.

The change in these items was in the direction of
greater agreement which indicates desire for more
circumspection in voicing and publicizing strong
social and religious issues.

It seems strange that, after a congregation
which issues the strongest document on social
justice of any Jesuit general congregation, the
items on taking a stand on social issues should
decrease in following. One surmise would be that
it indicates a backlash. More likely, the change
is attributable to the term "a strong public
position". Although the delegates might take
strong and even risky positions on social issues,
they may want to refrain from the publicity associated with it. This is plausible since many
delegates blamed the difficulties with the
Vatican during the Congregation on the fact that
news of the proceedings was forwarded to the Papal
Secretary of State daily.

Another item that changed was the following:

The members of my province are sufficiently
receptive to local values and sensitivities
in their people's liturgies.

The delegates express increased disagreement with
this item. This heightened appreciation of the
need to be receptive to local values coincides
with the support given to the issue of inculturation. It was also prompted, no doubt, by the
experience of relating closely and amiably with
other Jesuits from many other nations.

The final item that changed notably was the
following:

273

> In the final analysis, the strongest
> basis for planning the future is to
> trust to the experience of the past
> and base the decision-making on the
> facts, the historical facts.

The change in this item was towards greater agreement. There was a retrenching from strong disagreement with the statement before the Congregation. In the "Before" version only twenty-two
percent registered any agreement, but thirty
percent registered some agreement with this after
the Congregation. This retrenching may be an
indication of allegiance to the Vatican spurred
by its intervention or an increased willingness
to cooperate with Bulwark-Catholic elements
within the Society. (See Table Fourteen)

A group of 116 delegates completed the
"After" version of the Value-Survey. This amounts
to forty-nine percent of all delegates to the
Congregation.

The same conclusion can be drawn about the
value-rankings as was drawn about the Likert-type
responses. The findings as regards an analysis
of change are very slight. The measures of value-
rankings of the population are quite stable judging from 116 cases.

Across the entire listing of thirty-six
values, no "After" value-ranking differs from its
"Before" ranking counterpart at a significant
level of .05 or beyond. In fact, only three of
the thirty-six rankings have a probability greater
than .50. Twelve pairs of the eighteen terminal
values and seven pairs of the eighteen instrumental values do not change rank from the earlier to
the later questionnaire.

Only one ultimate value changes to an extent
of probability greater than .50. In the "After"
questionnaire, the ranking of the value freedom
moves from fifth place in priority to third place.
The ranking of equality reverses from third to

TABLE FOURTEEN

CONTRAST OF REPEATED QUESTIONNAIRE ITEMS BY DELEGATE
RESPONSES BEFORE AND AFTER THIRTY-SECOND GENERAL CONGREGATION

	Variable Name	Before: Mean-Score	After: Mean-Score	Difference (After-Before)
1.	ferment	1.584	1.657	.073
2.	turmoil	4.590	4.606	.016
3.	poor-need	3.015	2.963	− .052
4.	chastity	2.374	2.493	.119
5.	duty-obey	3.548	3.463	− .085
6.	SJ-national	2.166	2.263	.097
7.	SJ-international	2.061	1.912	− .149
8.	deadening	1.731	1.794	.063
9.	shepherd	2.497	2.400	− .097
10.	big-issue	2.276	2.241	− .035
11.	change-at-once	1.770	1.797	.027
12.	SJ-teamwork	1.716	1.471	− .245
13.	SJ-province	1.808	1.507	− .301
14.	avoid-at-home	3.719	3.582	− .137
15.	low-esteem	3.142	3.206	.064
16.	receptive-values	2.673	2.853	.180
17.	avoid-foreign	2.802	2.585	− .217
18.	power-on-side	3.882	3.847	− .035
19.	do-for-profit	3.543	3.485	− .058
20.	SJ-own-job	2.627	2.378	− .249
21.	traditional-approach	4.107	4.082	− .025
22.	trust-past	1.903	1.985	.169
23.	change-values	2.146	2.176	.030
24.	values-the-same	1.903	1.985	.082

Since responses are scored low for agreement and high for
disagreement a negative difference when subtracting
"Before" scores from "After" scores designates a change
toward greater agreement with the item as stated.

fifth place. It could be suggested that the experience of intervention and intense pressure from the Vatican stirred in the delegates a heightening of their valuation of freedom. Also, after the Congregation the value of inner-harmony was valued slightly less than before (from sixth to seventh place) and the value of world peace was valued slightly more (from seventh to sixth place).

The other change in terminal values was a lessening of the value of an exciting life and a heightening of the value of a world of beauty. In all other cases the ranking of terminal values remained the same.

In respect to instrumental values, the changes are slight in most cases. Two pairs of rankings differ at a probability beyond .50. The ranking of logical drops in priority from thirteenth to fifteenth place. On the other hand, the value of self-controlled is heightened in priority from tenth to eighth place. Broad-minded, imaginative and responsible are valued slightly less after the Congregation while courageous, helpful, loving and obedient are valued slightly more after the Congregation. (See Table Fifteen)

The changes from the "Before" questionnaire to the "After" questionnaire neither support nor detract from the findings of this research in any statistically significant way. Those changes that do occur, both in the Likert-type responses and in the value-rankings, serve to highlight the recent and dramatic experiences of the delegates rather than to trace "conversions" that coincide with the transition in Jesuit culture and styles.

Summary and Conclusions

The evidence and analysis shown in this

DISCRIMINATION OF VALUE-RANKINGS BY WHETHER RANKING

IS BEFORE THE CONGREGATION OR AFTER THE CONGREGATION

	Before The General Congregation N=116		After The General Congregation N=116		Probability
	R	Sc	R	Sc	
I TERMINAL					
A Comfortable Life	17	17.05	17	16.87	.592
An Exciting Life	13	11.83	14	12.77	.606
A Sense of Accom- plishment	9	9.83	9	9.32	.639
A World at Peace	7	6.67	6	6.50	1.0
A World of Beauty	14	12.70	13	12.17	.563
Equality	3	5.17	5	5.61	.606
Family Security	12	11.65	12	11.93	.788
Freedom	5	6.03	3	5.43	.293
Happiness	8	9.10	8	8.50	.518
Inner Harmony	6	6.08	7	6.60	.519
Mature Love	10	10.00	10	9.61	.696
National Security	16	14.11	16	14.30	.695
Pleasure	18	17.26	18	17.36	.788
Salvation	1	1.25	1	1.31	.591
Self-Respect	11	10.50	11	10.09	.564
Social Recognition	15	13.58	15	13.57	.891
True Friendship	4	5.25	4	5.58	.696
Wisdom	2	3.72	2	3.13	.563
II INSTRUMENTAL					
Ambitious	17	15.60	17	15.06	.606
Broadminded	6	7.40	7	7.90	.606
Capable	9	9.50	9	9.50	.891
Cheerful	12	10.23	12	10.72	.606

Table Fifteen - continued

	Before The General Congregation N=116		After the General Congregation N=116		Probability
	R	Sc	R	Sc	
II INSTRUMENTAL - cont'd					
Clean	18	16.70	18	16.83	.694
Courageous	7	7.43	6	6.67	.696
Forgiving	5	6.36	5	5.88	.696
Helpful	2	3.65	1	3.50	.891
Honest	1	3.56	2	3.56	.891
Imaginative	8	9.25	10	9.90	.606
Independent	15	13.14	14	13.17	.891
Intellectual	11	10.00	11	9.97	.788
Logical	13	12.80	15	13.57	.061
Loving	4	4.64	3	3.94	.519
Obedient	14	12.88	13	12.21	.563
Polite	16	13.90	16	14.61	.639
Responsible	3	4.03	4	4.17	.890
Self-Controlled	10	9.91	8	9.23	.186

chapter leads to four conclusions: (1) there is
a base of similarity in Jesuit values overall;
(2) Bulwark-Catholic and Conciliar-Humanist styles
differ from one another and the differences
support the thesis of modernization; (3) regional
and language differences are the largest source
of variation in Jesuits' ranking of values; (4)
there is no evidence of major change in response
patterns or value-rankings from before and after
the Thirty-Second General Congregation.

Similarity of values between the two styles
is seen in the fact that three of the top five
and eight of the top ten values for both terminal
and instrumental rankings are included in both
styles. In each ranking there are fewer significant differences than non-significant differences.

The similarity of Jesuit values is especially apparent when all Jesuits together are compared
to non-Jesuit groups. For example, if Jesuits
are compared to American males, not one terminal
value in the five highest Jesuit priorities is in
the ranks of the top five male priorities. This
same finding is true if Jesuit rankings are
compared to the value-rankings of a sample of
American Catholics.[3] The highest priority for
Jesuits is ranked twelfth for the sample of
American males and thirteenth for the American
Catholic sample. Similar divergencies characterize the rankings of other values. (See Table
Sixteen)

A solidarity arises from the crosscutting
of priorities evidenced in the various comparisons. The dispositions to tradition and the dispositions to change which are associated with
the value-rankings align themselves differently
when different aspects are discriminated. These
differences are complementary rather than
polarized. It is especially noteworthy that
administrators and leaders do not rank most
values distinctively in comparison to non-
administrators and non-leaders. This suggests
that the leadership of this Congregation for the

TABLE SIXTEEN

COMPARISON OF VALUE-RANKINGS OF JESUITS AND VARIOUS CATEGORIES OF NON-JESUITS

I TERMINAL	Jesuit Delegates N=174		American Males N=665		American Catholics N=322		Completed High School N=426		Grad. or Prof. Schooling N=61		$4000–$6000 N=217		More Than $15000 N=95		White Race N=1195		Black Race N=202	
	R	Sc	R	Sc	R	Sc	R	Sc	R	Sc	R	Sc	R	Sc	R	Sc	R	Sc
A Comfortable Life	17	17.03	4	7.77	12	9.91	12	9.50	15	13.75	6	8.33	15	13.40	12	9.60	5	6.60
An Exciting Life	14	12.50	18	14.62	18	15.30	18	15.48	14	13.42	18	15.58	16	14.25	18	15.37	18	15.26
A Sense of Accomplishment	9	9.76	7	8.29	7	8.53	9	9.05	4	5.42	9	9.09	5	6.08	8	8.81	11	10.23
A World at Peace	7	6.90	1	3.75	1	3.19	2	3.66	1	3.45	1	3.19	1	3.47	1	3.25	1	3.50
A World of Beauty	13	12.43	15	13.61	15	13.74	15	14.03	12	11.25	15	13.52	13	12.57	15	13.46	16	14.10
Equality	3	5.29	9	8.87	8	9.13	7	8.29	7	8.00	7	8.35	6	7.46	11	9.58	2	4.61
Family Security	12	11.54	2	3.86	2	3.21	1	3.27	5	6.58	2	3.60	2	4.09	2	3.63	4	5.06
Freedom	6	6.11	3	4.91	3	5.71	3	5.24	3	5.14	3	5.15	3	5.00	3	5.63	3	5.02
Happiness	8	8.65	5	7.94	4	7.14	4	7.15	10	9.69	4	7.16	8	9.19	4	7.56	7	7.60
Inner Harmony	5	5.94	13	11.08	11	9.83	13	10.31	9	9.25	13	10.79	9	9.20	13	10.36	12	10.91
Mature Love	10	10.29	14	12.57	14	12.20	14	12.12	11	10.13	14	12.26	12	11.75	14	12.09	14	13.66
National Security	16	14.10	10	9.21	6	8.50	10	9.25	13	13.00	12	9.74	11	11.33	9	9.13	13	11.42
Pleasure	18	17.39	17	14.14	17	14.83	17	14.81	18	16.04	16	14.66	18	15.20	17	14.68	17	14.33
Salvation	1	1.30	12	9.88	13	10.80	8	8.56	17	15.13	11	9.38	14	13.25	7	8.53	9	9.35
Self-Respect	11	10.35	6	8.16	5	7.42	5	7.83	6	6.80	5	7.58	7	7.75	5	7.72	6	7.50
Social Recognition	15	13.36	16	13.79	16	14.17	16	14.78	16	14.33	17	14.77	17	14.55	16	14.55	15	13.68
True Friendship	4	5.44	11	9.63	10	9.56	11	9.42	8	8.63	10	9.18	10	9.38	10	9.26	10	9.75
Wisdom	2	3.86	8	8.49	9	9.33	6	8.13	2	4.60	8	8.69	4	5.55	6	7.92	8	8.50

Table Sixteen - continued

	Jesuit Delegates N=174		American Males N=665		American Catholics N=322		Completed High School N=426		Grad. or Prof. Schooling N=61		$4000-$6000 N=217		More Than $15000 N=95		White Race N=1195		Black Race N=202	
	R	Sc	R	Sc	R	Sc	R	Sc	R	Sc	R	Sc	R	Sc	R	Sc	R	Sc
II INSTRUMENTAL																		
Ambitious	17	14.36	2	5.61	2	5.97	3	6.56	4	8.00	3	6.18	3	6.38	12	9.60	5	6.60
Broadminded	6	7.12	4	7.20	6	8.17	4	6.90	3	5.88	4	8.20	4	7.00	18	15.37	18	15.26
Capable	8	9.55	8	8.86	8	8.88	9	9.04	9	8.71	8	9.68	8	8.81	11	8.81	11	10.23
Cheerful	12	10.50	12	10.41	10	9.63	13	10.36	15	11.75	14	10.54	14	14.35	1	3.25	1	3.50
Clean	18	16.66	9	9.43	9	9.13	6	8.64	16	14.38	17	10.54	17	14.35	16	13.46	16	14.10
Courageous	7	7.45	5	7.49	5	8.06	7	8.64	5	8.00	5	8.00	11	7.20	2	9.58	2	4.61
Forgiving	5	6.00	6	8.23	4	7.69	5	7.26	6	8.25	7	7.38	12	10.69	4	3.63	4	5.06
Helpful	2	3.71	7	8.35	7	8.63	8	8.97	8	8.58	9	8.08	9	9.08	3	5.63	3	5.02
Honest	1	3.63	1	3.43	1	3.57	1	3.13	1	3.75	1	3.42	4	3.00	7	7.56	7	7.60
Imaginative	9	9.67	18	14.28	18	14.77	18	15.68	10	9.00	18	15.64	15	11.40	13	10.36	12	10.91
Independent	15	13.17	11	10.17	14	10.74	12	10.21	7	8.40	12	10.00	6	8.25	14	12.09	14	13.66
Intellectual	11	10.14	15	12.77	16	13.50	15	13.08	11	9.40	7	13.34	6	8.56	9	9.13	13	11.42
Logical	14	12.92	16	13.51	15	13.18	14	13.18	14	11.25	17	14.71	7	10.94	17	14.68	13	14.33
Loving	4	4.28	14	10.90	11	10.09	11	9.23	10	9.67	10	9.58	17	9.81	8	8.53	9	9.35
Obedient	13	12.83	17	13.51	17	13.23	16	13.35	18	16.60	18	13.26	18	15.29	5	7.22	5	7.50
Polite	16	13.81	13	10.85	13	10.62	14	10.53	17	14.69	16	10.20	16	13.19	16	14.55	15	13.68
Responsible	3	4.17	3	6.58	3	6.79	2	6.10	2	5.67	2	7.07	2	5.85	10	9.26	10	9.75
Self-Controlled	10	9.95	10	9.65	12	10.15	10	9.19	13	10.42	9	9.09	11	9.92	6	7.92	8	8.50

Source: Appendix B, Frequency Distributions for National NORC Sample, Milton Rokeach, *The Nature of Human Values*, New York, The Free Press, 1973, pp. 364-419

Society is constituted by the entire assembly.

Bulwark-Catholic and Conciliar-Humanist styles differ from one another and the differences support the thesis of modernization in the Jesuit Order by a shift from the former style to the latter. The B-C priorities of salvation, wisdom, honest and forgiving contrast with the C-H priorities of equality, friendship, loving and broadminded in the same way that unchanged elements of an organization contrast with changed elements according to the model of modernization. The first bears more qualities ascribed to the clerical state and particularly to traditional theology. The second does not; its priorities are more democratic and generalized. The B-C priorities of a world at peace, family, security and self-respect relates to the C-H priorities of freedom, mature love and an exciting life in the same correspondence.

Proximity to Rome, academic affiliation to a Pontifical University (The Gregorian) or fields of sacred study, task-orientation, and final incorporation into the Jesuit Order before the Second Vatican Council predictably correlate with the Bulwark-Catholic style and its associated priorities. Newer, developing nations, younger, more person-oriented delegates, and teachers of secular subjects correlate with the Conciliar-Humanist style and its priorities. And associated with the C-H style is an instrumentality that esteems loving, broadmindedness and imagination instead of the higher esteem for courage, self-control and logic associated with the B-C.

The change in culture implied by the two styles would align Jesuits with minority status, the poor and the underprivileged. When the differences between the B-C style and the C-H style are compared to non-Jesuit samples, the value-rankings of the C-H style does not incline to the poor and the underprivileged but does incline somewhat to one minority group.

The direction of the B-C/C-H differences in rankings on each of the thirty-six values with the direction of differences between poorer and richer, less educated and more educated and black race and white race, the C-H style is more often with the richer and more educated than the B-C style is. The C-H style departs from the B-C style in the same direction that the rich depart from the poor and the more educated depart from the less educated on twenty-four out of thirty-six values. But the direction of the C-H departure from the B-C resembles the direction of blacks departure from whites on twenty out of thirty-six values. This comparison can only be suggestive since the samples for wealth, education and race were from an entirely American sample.

The transition implied by the differences between the Bulwark-Catholic and Conciliar-Humanist styles is consistent and distinctive within the Jesuit environment. It is less so in relation to the rest of the world. But that is the very meaning of the shift from an elite of the bounded church to a minority group in the world. And since the transition is a shift, first of all, in culture, the meaning of its implementation is precisely in working out a new and different relationship between the structures of the Jesuit Order and the structures of other collectivities in the world.

Regional and language differences are the largest source of variance in Jesuits' value-ranking. Although there are many similarities among Jesuit values, it is also readily apparent that certain sectors of the Society of Jesus are very different from other sectors. For example, the Italian and Slavic provinces consistently differ from other groups by inclination to the Bulwark-Catholic style. The French do the same in the Conciliar-Humanist direction. The Northern and Southern Latin American provinces differ from the Spanish provinces within the same language group, and they differ even more from the Germans and Italians. Many differences in the directions of both styles exist in the English-speaking groups.

Variations in culture are evidenced in this diversity of Jesuit style and value-rankings. The delegates show a heightened sensitivity to variations in local areas. The concept of inculturation was established as part of the Congregation with the injunction: "this work must be pursued with even greater determination...and it deserves the progressively greater concern and attention of the whole Society."[4]

A locally sensitive and differing implementation of the Congregation in different regions is facilitated by the relative balance of Bulwark-Catholic and Conciliar-Humanist influences. At the same time, the mandate for eventual change is established by the predominance of Conciliar-Humanist outcomes.

There is no evidence of major change in response patterns or value-rankings from before and after the Congregation. This fact has three important implications: it indicates stability of the data, it confirms the measure of C-H predominance, and it makes the delegates' dispositions the important factor of comparison with the non-delegates.

The data from the "Before" version of the questionnaire remained constant over the five month period. The elements of concern to this examination of Jesuit values and the future of the Society of Jesus are settled enough in the minds of the delegates to be repeated in the later questionnaire. The differences between Bulwark-Catholic style value-rankings and Conciliar-Humanist style value-rankings remained distinct.

The differences that did appear in both responses to Likert-scale items and value-rankings were not major changes. Instead, they reflect the immediate experiences of Rome and the assembly of Jesuits. They reflect an increased sense of

284

Jesuit solidarity and a desire for mature autonomy
while respecting the tradition of allegiance to
the Vatican.

Since the values of the delegates are
manifestly stable, the measured differences which
were translated into votes and legislation are
evidenced as more deeply characteristic of the
General Congregation. Therefore, the Conciliar-
Humanist predominance in legislation associates
itself with the settled dispositions of the C-H
delegates. Also, the dispositions of the B-C
delegates underscore more firmly the effect of
balance, constraint, and complementarity that
is represented by those values in relation to the
Conciliar-Humanist trend.

Finally, a comparison of delegates and non-
delegates relies on similarity or dissimilarity
of present dispositions. If the delegates had
indicated a process of conversion or backlash, it
would be probable that such a change could affect
similar tendencies among the rank-and-file in the
months after the Congregation ended. Since stability characterizes the delegates, any similarity
of delegates and non-delegates would indicate
more likely implementation of the decrees of the
Congregation. Dissimilarity of delegates and non-
delegates would illumine problem areas in respect
to implementation.

Jesuit value-rankings strongly support the
thesis of a transition in Jesuit culture by the
distinct influence of the more modernized delegates to the Congregation. The distinctiveness
of the complementary styles and the diversity
within each of the styles combine to indicate an
amalgam that can withstand the tension of implementation.

Implementation must occur in the rank-and-
file. Therefore, a comparison of the delegates
with the sample of non-delegates comprises
Chapter Nine.

Footnotes

[1]Milton Rokeach, The Nature of Human Values, New York, The Free Press, 1973.

[2]From the treatment of Patricia L. Kendall and Paul F. Lazarsfeld, "Problems of Survey Analyses," in Robert K. Merton and Paul F. Lazarsfeld, eds., Continuities in Social Research, New York Free Press, 1950, pp. 135-167. See also James A. Davis, Elementary Survey Analysis, Englewood Cliffs, N.J., Prentice-Hall, 1971, pp. 81-103.

[3]The National Opinion Research Center administered the Value-Survey to a sample of nearly 1,500 American adults in April, 1968. This included 665 males and 322 Catholics. The frequencies of these survey results are reproduced in Milton Rokeach, The Nature of Human Values, Appendix B, pp. 364-419.

[4]"The Work of Inculturation of the Faith and Promotion of Christian Life" in Documents, 32 G.C., p. 44.

CHAPTER NINE

COMPARISON OF DELEGATES TO THE

THIRTY-SECOND GENERAL CONGREGATION

WITH A SAMPLE OF NON-DELEGATE JESUITS

The Thirty-Second General Congregation was a forum for the Society of Jesus in which changes were introduced and agreed upon. Through the predominance of Conciliar-Humanists, a shift in the culture of the Jesuits was instituted and set into legislation. But long-lasting change will only be realized when that culture and legislation filter down through the organization and the rank-and-file Jesuits implement them in their own various ways.

To gauge the probable success of this implementation, we must ask where in relation to the dispositions and changes of the delegates, the rank-and-file stand; what similarities and dissimilarities exist between the two; and what is the likelihood of change among non-delegates in the direction of the proposed transition. This is done by comparing the delegates with a one percent sample of non-delegate Jesuits.

The comparison is not between random groups of identical samples. The delegates form a population of Jesuit leadership. Non-delegates are a random sample of the rank-and-file. Analysis of the delegates has provided characteristics of the Thirty-Second General Congregation. Analysis of the non-delegates should serve to highlight which of those characteristics are representative of the Society of Jesus and which are not.

If the delegates had shown changes after the Congregation, that would be an indication from a short span of time of probable changes in other Jesuits over a longer time. But the delegates' dispositions were stable. Therefore, the similarity of non-delegates' dispositions is taken to indicate a willingness to accept the Congregation's direction. Divergence of dispositions is taken to indicate a resistance to implementation.

Since Curia Administrators and Provincials attend the Congregation ex officio one half of the delegate respondents (100) are employed in administration. One quarter (51) are in higher education or writing and research and one-tenth (18) work in the formation of Jesuits.

While fifty percent of the delegates are administrators only 1.4 percent of the non-delegates are administrators. This difference is translated into a greater variety of occupations for non-delegates. Twenty-five percent of them (54) work in parishes (compared to 3.5 percent of the delegates). Twenty percent (41) work in secondary education (compared to less than five percent of the delegates). (See Table One) All other comparisons of delegates and non-delegates must be seen in the light of this difference between administration and rank-and-file.

The average age of the delegates in the Congregation is forty-eight years old; the average age of the 211 non-delegate respondents is fifty-three years. The range of delegates' ages is thirty-six to seventy-one years; the range of non-delegates includes nine percent (19 cases) who are under thirty years old and eleven percent (24 cases) who are over seventy years old.

Three-quarters of the delegate respondents considered their work person-oriented rather than task-oriented. They were closely divided considering the Province's first concern as adaptive or goal-attaining (55%) on the one hand, and integrating or pattern-maintenance (45%) on the other. Fully ninety-five percent of the delegate respondents answered that the major decisions of their province were settled on the grounds of

288

TABLE ONE

THE KIND OF WORK DONE BY DELEGATES AND
NON-DELEGATES RESPONDING TO QUESTIONNAIRE

	Kind of Work	Delegates		Non-Delegates	
		Frequency	Percentage	Frequency	Percentage
A.	Supra-Institutions Administration (e.g. Provincial, Mission Director)	100	49.5	3	1.4
B.	Institution of Higher Learning: Administration (e.g. President or Rector of University	13	6.4	3	1.4
C.	Institution of Secondary Education: Administration (e.g. High School President or Rector or Principal)	8	4.0	18	8.5
D.	Higher Education: Teaching (and Allied Research)	31	15.3	32	15.2
E.	Secondary School: Teaching (and Allied Research)	1	0.5	23	10.9
F.	Parish Administration or Pastoral Work	7	3.5	54	25.6
G.	Writing or Research Full-time	7	3.5	7	3.3
H.	Social Apostolate, Socio-Economic Development	3	1.5	8	3.8
I.	Formation of Ours, of other Clerics, Seminary Administration	18	8.9	6	2.8
J.	Other	14	6.9	56	21.8

religious concerns or the care of personnel
rather than on political or economic grounds.

In the group of non-delegates, almost the
exact same percentage as the delegates rank their
occupation to be person-oriented rather than task-
oriented (72.5% compared to 72.3%). Fewer non-
delegates see the first concern of their province
as instrumental (39.8% compared to 55%) and yet
the non-delegates say in twenty-five percent of
the cases that the majority of decisions in the
province are based on political and economic
considerations (only 4.5% of the delegates said
this). (See Table Two)

The delegates say that they were raised in
less than middle class in only twenty-eight cases
(14%), in middle class in 108 cases (53.5%), and
in more than middle-class or in wealthy circumstances in sixty-five cases (33%). The figures
for the life-style that they presently live in
are nearly identical. The people these Jesuit
delegates serve are slightly lower in social class
than the backgrounds or life-style of the Jesuits
themselves.

Slightly more of the non-delegates than
delegates were raised in less than middle-class
surroundings, thirty-eight (19%) compared to
twenty-eight cases, and slightly fewer non-
delegates were raised in more than middle-class,
fifty-one (24%) compared to sixty-five cases.
Present life-style is identical to the class they
were raised in as it was for the delegates. (See
Table Three) Also, the category of social class
for those who the Jesuit non-delegates serve is
slightly below that of background and life-style
of the Jesuits themselves.

When the Jesuit delegates compare themselves
to other professionals in terms of skill, autonomy,
responsibility, commitment and esteem, they rate
themselves generally lower. A little over two-
fifths of all delegate respondents rank Jesuits
as lower overall, another one-fifth ranks Jesuits

290

COMPARISON OF DELEGATE AND NON-DELEGATE
RESPONDENTS ON CRITERIA FOR WORKS

Which Do You Consider Your Work to Be:	Delegates Frequency	Percentage	Non-Delegates Frequency	Percentage
1. Mainly task-oriented, geared to a job to be done	49	24	46	21.8
2. Mainly person-oriented, the care and service of people	146	73	153	72.5
Which of the following would you say is your Province's first concern:				
A. Adapting means to desired goals. Deployment of resources	74	36.6	54	25.6
B. Seeing the accomplishments of stated goals, attainment of objectives by coordination and executive management	37	18.3	30	14.2
C. Fitting the works and accomplishments of the Province into an overall pattern; helping to define the identity of the Province	65	32.2	64	30.3
D. Preserving the traditions of the Province and the Society and maintaining the religious life and well-being of its members	25	12.4	59	28.0
Broadly speaking, which of the following seem to govern the majority of decisions made by your Province and its major institutions?				
A. Religious	110	54.5	97	46.0
B. Political	4	2.0	16	7.6
C. Economic	5	2.5	38	18.0
D. _Curia Personalis_	82	40.5	55	26.1

TABLE THREE

SOCIAL CLASS THAT DELEGATE AND NON-DELEGATE
RESPONDENTS SERVE, WERE RAISED IN, AND LIVE IN NOW

Which of the categories do the people that you serve most of the time belong to?	Delegates Frequency	Percentage	Non-Delegates Frequency	Percentage
Category				
1. Poor people	7	3.5	21	10.0
2. Unskilled workers	19	9.4	39	18.5
3. Middle-class people	107	53.0	100	47.4
4. Upper-middle-class	58	28.7	38	18.0
5. Rich people	0	0	6	2.8

Which of the categories do you feel your parents belonged to when you were growing up?	Delegates Frequency	Percentage	Non-Delegates Frequency	Percentage
Category				
1. Poor people	2	1.0	6	2.8
2. Unskilled workers	26	12.9	32	15.2
3. Middle-class people	108	53.5	120	56.9
4. Upper-middle-class	62	30.7	50	23.7
5. Rich people	3	1.5	1	0.5

Which of the categories do you think the life-style that you presently have as a Jesuit fits into?	Delegates Frequency	Percentage	Non-Delegates Frequency	Percentage
Category				
1. Poor people	8	4.0	16	7.6
2. Unskilled workers	12	5.9	19	9.0
3. Middle-class people	112	55.4	118	55.9
4. Upper-middle-class	64	31.7	50	23.7
5. Rich people	3	1.5	6	2.8

as average. Forty-five percent of the delegates rate Jesuit autonomy as less than other professionals and a third of them rank responsibility and esteem lower for Jesuits than other professionals.

A greater percentage of non-delegates than delegates rank the professionalism of Jesuits lower than that of other professionals. One-half (as compared to two-fifths) of the non-delegates rank Jesuits lower overall. In each separate category, as well, the non-delegates rank the Jesuits lower. This could be explained by the fact that non-delegates are afforded less status and authority or it could be a gauge of the actual differences in professionalism between those who are given position in the Society and those who are not. (See Table Four)

Comparison of Delegates and Non-Delegates in Relation to Items of Analysis

From the questionnaires that were completed by the 211 non-delegates, they compare somewhat closely to the delegates in terms of modernity (See Chapter Six). The non-delegates show a greater range of response than the delegates.

A mean of 3.00 would indicate disagreement with change and modern ideas in ten of the sixteen items. The non-delegates register a mean score of 2.23. This is .11 points higher than the delegates. A mean of less than 3.00 would indicate agreement with non-change and non-modern ideas in the six remaining items. The non-delegates' mean score is 3.31. This is .33 lower than the delegates. For items directly relating to change, non-delegates show a mean score of 1.97 which is .23 higher than that of the delegates where lower scores reflect modernity and a mean score of 3.31 which is .22 lower than the delegates' mean where higher scores reflect modernity.

TABLE FOUR

RANKING OF PROFESSIONALISM BY DELEGATE
AND NON-DELEGATE RESPONDENTS

With some exceptions, most Jesuits in my Province...

| | Delegates | | Non-Delegates | |
	Frequency	Percentage	Frequency	Percentage
Regarding Depth of Knowledge and Skill				
1) Jesuits have more	36	17.8	41	19.4
2) have about the same	130	64.4	114	54.0
3) have less	21	10.4	25	11.8
4) have much less	1	0.5	5	2.4
5) don't know	3	1.5	18	8.5
Regarding Autonomy to make Decisions				
1) Jesuits have more	25	12.4	26	12.3
2) have about the same	71	35.1	48	22.7
3) have less	76	37.6	73	34.6
4) have much less	16	7.9	29	13.7
5) don't know	6	3.0	24	11.4
Responsibility for an Undertaking				
1) Jesuits have more	53	26.2	43	20.4
2) have about the same	73	36.1	74	35.1
3) have less	51	25.2	43	20.4
4) have much less	10	5.0	23	10.9
5) don't know	7	3.5	18	8.5
Commitment to Serving the Needs of People				
1) Jesuits have more	147	72.8	113	53.6
2) have about the same	36	17.8	54	25.6
3) have less	6	3.0	12	5.7
4) have much less	2	1.0	9	4.3
5) don't know	3	1.5	15	7.1
Satisfaction and Self-Esteem gained from one's work				
1) Jesuits have more	25	12.4	31	14.7
2) have about the same	86	42.6	74	35.1
3) have less	57	28.2	41	19.4
4) have much less	7	3.5	17	8.1
5) don't know	18	8.9	38	18.0

Non-delegates show stronger agreement with three items of modernity than delegates. The three items are those dealing with social action and pastoral activity. They disagree more strongly with one item of non-modernity concerning the study of Protestant theology. For every item, the standard deviation of non-delegate scores is higher than that of the delegates. Throughout the entire set of questionnaire items, non-delegates more often respond with both strong agreement and strong disagreement. The delegates more often respond with the milder options of agree and disagree "somewhat." (See Table Five)

The non-delegates also evidence modernity on the thirteen items indicating theological orientation. The mean score for delegates overall is 2.53. The mean score for non-delegates is 2.43. In three items the non-delegates have higher mean scores, but they are not appreciably different than the delegate scores. The standard deviations for the two groups are closer together in the theological items than the change and modernity questions suggesting less variance across this set of questions. (See Table Six)

Generally, therefore, the questions of change and modernity and those of theological orientation indicate that delegates and non-delegates alike are more modernized than tradition-al. The delegates are more modernized than the non-delegates across the set of all items. To some extent, this latter difference between delegates and non-delegates reflects the differences in age and office. Other differences also characterize the two groups.

The questionnaires administered to delegates and non-delegates were identical. (See Appendix One) Summary statistics are drawn from the questionnaire responses in the form of various indices. The delegates and non-delegates are here compared in terms of five such indices. These indices measure Jesuit extensiveness, orientation to change, orientations to value and self-interest

TABLE FIVE

AGREEMENT AND DISAGREEMENT ON ITEMS OF

CHANGE AND MODERNITY BY NON-DELEGATE SAMPLE

Items Indicating Modernity by Agreement[*]

		Mean	Standard Deviation
C[**]	The creative ferment in the Church today is bringing about a deepening of my Christian faith.	1.86	1.13
	There are times when a person has to put his personal conscience above the Church's teachings.	3.13	1.54
	The spirit of poverty is meaningless without poverty in fact.	2.31	1.34
C	Any organizational structure becomes a dedenning weight in time and needs to be revitalized.	1.79	.97
	When I think of social reform, I think of things I believe in so deeply I could dedicate all my efforts to them.	2.38	1.24
	A priest can hardly call himself a shepherd if he is not as deeply involved in the social welfare of people as he is in giving spiritual service to his parishioners.	2.48	1.38
	When I am dealing with the problems of my own job, I find myself constantly trying to make decisions that will help solve the bigger issues of justice, etc., for all mankind. The world's problems are very much my problems.	2.15	1.21
C	The current situation in the Church calls for change. We must respond at once.	2.02	1.15

Table Five   (continued)

		Mean	Standard Deviation
C	Every great step forward in world history has been accomplished through the inspiration of reform- ers and creative men.	2.06	1.05
C	During the past ten years many religious have changed some of the basic principles and values which they formerly believed in.	2.15	1.13

Items Indicating Modernity by Disagreement

C	The future is in God's hands. I will await what He sends and accept what comes as His will for me.	2.19	1.42
C	The problem with the Church after Vatican II is that many of the certainties we used to have have been taken away.	3.17	1.47
C	The turmoil following Vatican II is resulting in a gradual weaken- ing of my own religious beliefs.	4.47	1.05
	One's faith may be jeopardized by studying Protestant theolo- gians.	3.67	1.39
C	By continuing its traditional approach to its teaching role, the Church will better accomplish its mission than by experimenting with new methods.	3.62	1.33
C	In the final analyses, the strongest basis for planning for the future is to trust to the experience of the past and base the decision-making on the facts, the historical facts.	3.14	1.39

*All responses based on a five point scale from "Strongly Agree" to "Strongly Disagree"; Value 3 indicates "Uncertain."

**"C" represents item which is directly in reference to change.

TABLE SIX

NON-DELEGATE RESPONSES TO

THEOLOGICAL ORIENTATION ITEMS

(See Appendix One for Complete Alternatives)

	Mean	Standard Deviation
Each of the following statements describes an aspect of GOD. By God I mean: (Choose the One you find most appealing) (3 options)	2.35	1.59
Each of the following statements describes an aspect of the HOLY SPIRIT. (Choose the One you find most appealing) (3 options)	2.51	.67
The purpose of MISSIONARY ACTIVITY is: (Choose the one you find most appealing) (3 options plus 1 scored as Missing Value)	2.21	.54
Each of the following statements describing an aspect of CHURCH. (Choose the One you find most appealing) (5 options)	3.01	.87
* Each of the following statements describes some aspects of the relation of the CHURCH TO THE WORLD. By this relationship I mean (Choose the One you find the most appealing) (2 options coded 1 and 3 in Value)	1.94	1.00
Each of the following statements describes an aspect of the WORLD. (Choose the One you find most appealing) (3 options)	2.12	.69
Each of the following statements describes an aspect of MINISTRY. A Christian minister is: (Choose the One you find most appealing) (3 options)	2.46	.61

Table Six (continued)

	Mean	Standard Deviation
Each of the following statements describes an aspect of FAITH. By Faith I mean: (Choose the One you find most appealing) (6 options)	4.23	.96
* Each of the following statements describes some aspexts of CULTURE. By Culture I mean: (Choose the One you find most appealing) (2 options)	1.78	.41
Each of the following statements describes an aspect of CHRIST. (Choose the One you find most appealing) (4 options)	2.69	.83
Each of the following statements describes an aspect of PRAYER. (Choose the One you find most appealing) (3 options plus 1 scored as missing value)	2.16	.81
Each of the following statements describes an aspect of AUTHORITY. (Choose the One you find most appealing) (3 options)	1.87	.68
Each of the following statements describes an aspect of SALVATION. (Choose the One you find most appealing) (4 options)	2.37	1.09

*Indicates Question and alternatives not included in the original SVD Self-Study.

and Jesuit receptivity to cultural variation.
(See Table Seven)

The Congregation delegates are more directly
connected to the central bureaucracy. In terms
of Jesuit extensiveness, it is understandable
that they rank involvement at the Province,
national and international levels more highly
than the non-delegates. Conversely, non-delegates
rank one's own apostolate and local institution
and teamwork more highly. The pattern of scores
for both delegates and non-delegates show highest
agreement on teamwork and province and less agreement on other levels. All the extensiveness
scores tend towards agreement.

The delegates score higher on the inclination to change index, ranking the change items
with higher agreement and non-change items with
higher disagreement. In terms of both value-
ranking and self-interest ranking, the non-
delegates rank in higher agreement than the delegates. On the value index, the non-delegates show
higher agreement with the concern for social justice and action for social welfare than the delegates. Scores on the self-interest index designate a sober view of the importance of power and
self-interest in the outcomes of decisions,
especially among non-delegates.

The delegates score as more critical of
Jesuit openness to cultural variation and serving
the poor. This is consistent with the willingness
shown by delegates to accept criticism of the
Jesuits in the midst of their deliberations. (See
Table Eight)

Of special consequence is the comparison
between delegates and non-delegates on the index
to measure the polarity between Bulwark-Catholic
and Conciliar-Humanist. Again the delegates and
non-delegates have very similar distributions.
Of the twelve variables comprising the index, the
delegates tend more to the Conciliar-Humanist
direction in eight and the non-delegates in four.

TABLE SEVEN

LISTING OF INDICES BASED ON FACTOR

SCORES FROM QUESTIONNAIRE RESPONSES

A. JESUIT EXTENSIVENESS INDEX

Items: In a Jesuit's work, the immediate and overall needs of the
         particular apostolate he serves warrant his primary consid-
         eration and effort.

         Some concerns of an individual Jesuit's work in the apostol-
         ate are necessarily subservient to the institution or Jesuit
         team-effort of which he is a part.

         The Province has the right to expect a Jesuit to work on
         Province-wide tasks even if that work interferes with the
         individual's attention to his own apostolate and the
         institution he belongs to.

         It is advisable for Jesuits to concern themselves with
         regional or national projects they are competent to serve
         even if the fruit of such concerns serve neither the Province
         nor the institution that the Jesuit belongs to.

         The work and purposes of the entire Society of Jesus at the
         International level deserve precedence over all other levels
         of effectiveness whenever a Jesuit has opportunity to exert
         influence at that level.

B. CHANGE INDEX (from Values and Interest in Social Change)[1]

         Any organizational structure becomes a deadening weight in
         time and needs to be revitalized.

         Every great step forward in world history has been accom-
         plished through the inspiration of reformers and creative
         men.

         In the final analysis the strongest basis for planning for
         the future is to trust to the experience of the past and
         base the decision-making on the facts, the historical facts.

         I like conservatism because it represents a stand to pre-
         serve our glorious heritage.

Table Seven - continued

C. <u>VALUES INDEX</u> (from <u>Values and Interest in Social Change</u>)[2]

>When I think of social reform, I think of things I believe
>in so deeply I could dedicate all my efforts to them.

>A priest can hardly call himself a shepherd if he is not as
>deeply involved in social welfare of people as he is in giving
>spiritual service to his parishioners.

>When I am dealing with the problems of my own job, I find my-
>self constantly trying to make decisions that will help solve
>the bigger issues of justice, etc., for all mankind. The
>world's problems are very much my problems.

D. <u>SELF-INTEREST INDEX</u> (from <u>Values and Interest in Social Change</u>)[3]

>In the last analysis, it's having the power that makes the
>difference.

>No matter how wonderful the ideals you are trying to get
>across may be, you cannot do a thing unless you have the
>powers that be on your side.

>When you come right down to it, it's human nature never to
>do anything without an eye to one's own profit.

E. <u>INDEX OF ORGANIZATIONAL OPENNESS TO CULTURAL DIFFERENCES</u> (from <u>Self-
Study of The Society of the Divine Word</u>)[4]

>The activities of my Province are sufficiently concerned with
>the poor and those held in low esteem.

>The members of my Province are sufficiently receptive to
>local values and sensitivities in their people's liturgy.

>The Society as a whole is sufficiently open to cultural
>variations in the expression of our Religious life and
>community.

TABLE EIGHT

COMPARISON OF DELEGATES AND NON-DELEGATES
ON QUESTIONNAIRE INDICES

Variable	Delegate Mean Score	% Agreement	Non-Delegate Mean Score	% Agreement
Jesuit Extensiveness Index				
SJ own job	2.627	60.1	2.054	76.4
SJ teamwork	1.716	88.3	1.597	90.8
SJ province	1.808	85.4	1.952	80.2
SJ national	2.166	70.9	2.346	65.4
SJ international	2.061	76.8	2.053	72.9
Index Mean	−0.004		−0.003	
Change Index				
deadening	1.731	88.3	1.794	86.6
step-forward	1.899	81.4	2.062	77.0
trust-past	3.601	22.7	3.140	41.1
conservatism	4.563	2.0	4.134	15.8
Index Mean	−0.000		0.010	
Value Index				
think-of-reform	2.460	58.6	2.380	62.4
shepherd	2.497	62.9	2.483	62.3
big-issue	2.276	66.3	2.155	70.9
Index Mean	0.013		0.012	
Interest Index				
Power-difference	3.523	26.9	3.422	28.6
Side-of-Power	3.882	19.0	3.537	29.3
Do-for-Profit	3.543	27.4	3.296	41.3
Index Mean	0.014		−0.010	
Cultural Openness Index				
low-esteem	3.142	37.6	2.923	44.0
receptive-values	2.673	54.6	2.599	55.1
variation-of-expression	2.663	55.8	2.449	58.0
Index Mean	0.001		−0.000	

Delegates rank in higher agreement with autonomy, change, speaking out on social issues and being less traditional. Delegate theology is more in the <u>avant</u> <u>garde</u> direction regarding missionary activity, the Church and its relation to the world and the meaning of ministry. Non-delegates are higher in agreement on the three issues concerning social justice and on the theological meaning of the Holy Spirit.

The delegates have fewer polarity scores below and above one standard deviation from the mean (thirty-one below, twenty-seven above). The non-delegates have thirty-nine scores beyond one standard deviation below the mean and forty-five above. It is due to the extremes that the index score for the non-delegates is higher (i.e. closer to Conciliar-Humanist pole) than the delegates. However, the difference is very slight. The factor analysis accounts for greater variation in the non-delegate responses than the delegates. (See Table Nine)

Comparison of Value-Rankings of Delegates and Non-Delegates

When all delegates and non-delegates are compared in respect to their value-rankings, there are usable responses for 173 delegates and 181 non-delegates from the "Before" questionnaire. The value-rankings are very similar. Eleven of the eighteen terminal values are matched in ranking and nine of the instrumental values are matched in ranking. Two terminal values differ significantly and five instrumental values differ significantly. The two terminal values of significant difference rank at the bottom of priority in sixteenth and seventeenth place. These are the values of national security and comfortable life. In both cases the non-delegates rank these values higher in priority. Salvation is ranked first for both groups and wisdom second. Non-delegates rank true friendship and inner-harmony next while delegates

304

TABLE NINE

COMPARISON OF DELEGATES AND NON-DELEGATES

9A   ON BULWARK-CATHOLIC/CONCILIAR-HUMANIST POLARITY INDEX

Variable	Delegate Mean Score	Non-Delegate Mean Score
CONSOVER	2.979	3.139
REFORMSO	2.460	2.380
SHEPHRDA	2.497	2.483
BIGISSUA	2.276	2.155
CHCGONCA	1.770	2.024
HOMAVODA	3.719	3.541
TRADAPRA	4.107	3.627
HOSPMEAN	2.437	2.517
MISSMEAN	2.278	2.214
CHCHMEAN	3.241	2.010
CHWDMEAN	2.040	1.945
MINIMEAN	2.557	2.464
Polarity Index Mean	0.004	0.006
Standard Deviation	0.874	0.910
Median	.048	0.018
Range	4.328	3.905
Skewness	- .322	- .307

Table Nine - continued

9B   FACTOR ANALYSIS SCORES FOR VARIABLES COMPRISING

    THE NON-DELEGATE BULWARK-CATHOLICISM/CONCILIAR-HUMANIST INDEX

Variable	Principal Factor Matrix	Communality	Factor Score Coefficients
CONSOVER	− 0.48463	0.23487	− 0.08826
REFORMSO	− 0.57280	0.32810	− 0.12242
SHEPHRDA	− 0.54566	0.29774	− 0.11402
BIGISSUA	− 0.57470	0.33028	− 0.12865
CHCGONCA	− 0.60485	0.36585	− 0.12981
HOMAVODA	0.31312	0.09804	0.04748
TRADAPRA	0.61394	0.37693	0.14559
HOSPMEAN	0.55905	0.31254	0.12056
MISSMEAN	0.57024	0.32517	0.12703
CHCHMEAN	0.56428	0.31841	0.13046
CHWDMEAN	0.68472	0.46885	0.19401
MINIMEAN	0.57343	0.32882	0.11947

Eigen Value: 3.78561

rank equality and true friendship.

Delegates significantly evaluate independence (at .005 level) and imagination (at .001 level) higher than non-delegates. Non-delegates rank self-controlled (at .011 level), polite (at .011 level), and clean (at .001 level) more highly than delegates. In the five highest ranked instrumental values there is close similarity. Both groups place honest as highest, helpful second, responsible third, loving fourth and forgiving fifth. Delegates rank broadminded and capable higher while non-delegates rank cheerful and courageous more highly. (See Table Ten)

There are many differences when the two groups are discriminated according to the Bulwark-Catholic/Conciliar-Humanist polarity index, but these differences are accountable to the different styles more than they are accountable to being a delegate or not. In most cases, B-C delegates resemble B-C non-delegates more than they resemble C-H delegates. Likewise, C-H delegates resemble C-H non-delegates more than they resemble B-C delegates. It is particularly important that the differences between the two styles is greater than the differences between delegates and non-delegates of the same style.

Comparing Bulwark-Catholic delegates and non-delegates, one terminal value and five instrumental values differ significantly (.05 level). Comparing Conciliar-Humanist delegates and non-delegates, no terminal value-rankings differ significantly and two instrumental value-rankings do (.01 level). (See Table Eleven)

Comparing Bulwark-Catholic delegates and Conciliar-Humanist delegates, the rankings of four terminal values and three instrumental values differ with statistical significance (.05 level or more). Eight terminal value-rankings and four instrumental value-rankings are significantly different (.05 level or more) when B-C

307

TABLE TEN

COMPARISON OF DELEGATES' AND NON-DELEGATES' VALUE-RANKING

I TERMINAL	Delegates N=173		Non-Delegates N=181		Probability
	R	Sc	R	Sc	
A Comfortable Life	17	17.03	17	16.73	.010**
An Exciting Life	14	12.54	14	12.91	.613
A Sense of Accomplishment	9	9.78	9	9.31	.544
A World at Peace	7	6.85	8	7.55	.521
A World of Beauty	13	12.46	13	12.17	.613
Equality	3	5.31	5	5.77	.597
Family Security	12	11.56	12	11.59	.989
Freedom	6	6.08	6	6.64	.609
Happiness	8	8.62	7	7.18	.102
Inner Harmony	5	5.97	4	5.68	.583
Mature Love	10	10.25	11	11.00	.597
National Security	16	14.08	16	13.06	.023*
Pleasure	18	17.38	18	17.20	.557
Salvation	1	1.30	1	1.40	.204
Self-Respect	11	10.31	10	9.69	.518
Social Recognition	15	13.34	15	12.92	.515
True Friendship	4	5.47	3	4.95	.300
Wisdom	2	3.88	2	3.63	.557
II INSTRUMENTAL					
Ambitious	17	14.39	17	14.78	.750
Broadminded	6	7.08	8	7.91	.661
Capable	8	9.52	10	9.25	.754
Cheerful	12	10.63	9	9.04	.050
Clean	18	16.68	18	15.45	.001***
Courageous	7	7.42	6	7.29	.918
Forgiving	5	6.05	5	7.13	.167
Helpful	2	3.68	2	4.13	.642
Honest	1	3.61	1	3.96	.764
Imaginative	9	9.58	15	12.65	.001***
Independent	15	13.14	16	14.54	.005**
Intellectual	11	10.18	11	10.92	.597
Logical	14	12.94	14	12.54	.273
Loving	4	4.33	4	6.07	.067
Obedient	13	12.81	12	11.35	.088
Polite	16	13.85	13	12.42	.011*
Responsible	3	4.14	3	4.74	.283
Self-Controlled	10	9.98	7	7.67	.011*

TABLE ELEVEN

COMPARISON OF B-C DELEGATES WITH B-C NON-DELEGATES
AND C-H DELEGATES AND C-H NON-DELEGATES

I TERMINAL	B-C Delegates N=81		B-C Non-Delegates N=81		Probability	C-H Delegates N=91		C-H Non-Delegates N=98		Probability
	R	Sc	R	Sc		R	Sc	R	Sc	
A Comfortable Life	17	16.94	17	16.35	.017*	17	17.11	17	16.90	.258
An Exciting Life	16	14.33	16	14.29	.870	11	10.14	13	11.70	.522
A Sense of Accomplishment	10	10.11	10	9.69	.642	10	9.54	9	8.50	.726
A World at Peace	7	6.67	8	8.42	.271	7	6.86	6	6.30	.711
A World of Beauty	13	12.43	14	12.73	.752	14	12.43	12	11.50	.593
Equality	6	6.42	6	6.69	.870	2	4.42	2	4.64	.942
Family Security	11	11.11	11	10.75	.642	13	11.96	14	11.88	.887
Freedom	5	6.35	7	7.40	.562	5	5.69	5	5.93	.960
Happiness	8	8.13	5	6.29	.206	9	9.08	8	7.79	.278
Inner Harmony	4	5.75	3	4.56	.153	6	6.31	7	6.33	.924
Mature Love	12	11.75	15	13.78	.154	8	8.38	10	8.94	.629
National Security	15	13.55	12	11.89	.080	16	14.46	16	14.03	.631
Pleasure	18	17.48	18	17.15	.203	18	17.30	18	17.36	.795
Salvation	1	1.13	1	1.12	1.0	1	2.25	4	4.90	.515
Self-respect	9	9.57	9	8.63	.643	12	11.00	11	10.28	.515
Social Recognition	14	13.25	13	12.29	.205	15	13.46	15	13.63	.828
True Friendship	3	5.69	4	5.31	.643	4	5.20	1	4.44	.608
Wisdom	2	3.25	2	2.55	.654	3	4.55	3	4.81	.734

Table Eleven - continued

II INSTRUMENTAL	B-C Delegates N=81		B-C Non-Delegates N=81		Probability	C-H Delegates N=91		C-H Non-Delegates N=98		Probability
	R	Sc	R	Sc		R	Sc	R	Sc	
Ambitious	17	16.40	16	14.75	.206	16	13.65	17	15.17	.152
Broadminded	6	7.80	8	8.81	.562	5	6.35	6	7.10	.641
Capable	10	9.75	10	9.63	1.0	9	9.44	8	9.00	.734
Cheerful	12	12.00	9	8.88	.017*	10	10.00	9	9.07	.268
Clean	18	16.44	17	15.39	.152	18	16.88	18	15.56	.002**
Courageous	7	8.00	6	7.33	.643	6	6.95	5	7.00	.795
Forgiving	5	5.29	5	6.71	.206	7	7.38	7	7.38	.933
Helpful	2	3.65	3	5.20	.080	2	3.63	1	3.65	.951
Honest	1	3.27	1	3.57	.752	3	4.05	2	4.36	.696
Imaginative	11	11.43	15	14.25	.038*	8	8.36	12	11.50	.007**
Independent	15	12.78	18	15.42	.017*	15	13.44	16	14.17	.178
Intellectual	8	9.22	12	10.92	.153	12	10.95	11	11.07	.787
Logical	13	12.06	13	11.75	.751	14	13.41	15	13.25	.924
Loving	4	5.13	7	8.42	.012*	1	3.60	3	4.50	.600
Obedient	14	12.69	11	10.25	.080	13	12.85	14	13.10	.969
Polite	16	13.55	14	12.19	.079	17	14.54	13	12.67	.278
Responsible	3	3.96	2	3.71	.642	4	4.44	4	5.40	.230
Self-Controlled	9	9.67	4	6.33	.017*	11	10.23	10	9.61	.247

non-delegates and C-H non-delegates are compared.
(See Table Twelve)

The comparisons of delegates and non-delegates discriminated according to the polarity index gives very strong support for probable implementation. When the Bulwark-Catholics are compared, the non-delegates are more intensely B-C than the delegates. When the Conciliar-Humanists are compared, the non-delegates are more intensely C-H. The entire B-C group values national security and a comfortable life more than the C-H group. The non-delegate B-C group values these significantly more than the delegate B-C group. The entire C-H group values true friendship more and salvation less than the B-C group. The non-delegate C-H group differs strongly from the delegate C-H group in this direction.

The comparisons of Bulwark-Catholics and Conciliar-Humanists also show that the polarity is more intense and that each style is followed with closer allegiance among the non-delegates than the delegates. In a dozen rankings, the C-H non-delegates show significant differences from the B-C delegates (.05 level or more). The C-H non-delegates rank equality, mature love, an exciting life, loving and imaginative significantly higher in priority and salvation, wisdom, inner-harmony, a comfortable life, obedience, and responsibility significantly lower in priority than the B-C non-delegates. The values associated with democratization and disembeddedness from ascription are valued by the Conciliar-Humanists; the values associated with tradition and embeddedness in ascription are valued by the Bulwark-Catholics.

From every comparison it can be substantiated that the differences in the Society of Jesus between Bulwark-Catholics and Conciliar-Humanists are greater than the differences which would separate legislators from the rank-and-file. The rank-and-file evidences stronger affiliation to

311

TABLE TWELVE

COMPARISON OF B-C DELEGATES WITH C-H DELEGATES
AND COMPARISON OF B-C NON-DELEGATES WITH C-H NON-DELEGATES

I TERMINAL	B-C Delegates N=81		C-H Delegates N=91		Probability	B-C Non-Delegates N=81		C-H Non-Delegates N=98		Probability
	R	Sc	R	Sc		R	Sc	R	Sc	
A Comfortable Life	17	16.94	17	17.11	.635	17	16.35	17	16.90	.009**
An Exciting Life	16	14.33	11	10.14	.002**	16	14.29	13	11.70	.032*
A Sense of Accomplishment	10	10.11	10	9.54	.513	10	9.69	9	8.50	.620
A World At Peace	7	6.67	7	6.86	.895	8	8.42	6	6.30	.113
A World of Beauty	13	12.43	14	12.43	.880	14	12.73	12	11.50	.174
Equality	6	6.42	4	4.42	.033*	6	6.69	2	4.64	.010*
Family Security	11	11.11	13	11.96	.226	11	10.75	14	11.88	.156
Freedom	5	6.35	5	5.69	.595	7	7.40	5	5.93	.256
Happiness	8	8.13	9	9.08	.560	5	6.29	8	7.79	.232
Inner Harmony	4	5.75	6	6.31	.599	3	4.56	7	6.33	.014*
Mature Love	12	11.75	8	8.38	.094	15	13.78	10	8.94	.001***
National Security	15	13.55	16	14.46	.134	12	11.89	16	14.03	.001***
Pleasure	18	17.48	18	17.30	.682	18	17.15	18	17.36	.249
Salvation	1	1.13	1	2.25	.001***	1	1.12	4	4.90	.001***
Self-Respect	9	9.57	12	11.00	.157	9	8.63	11	10.28	.165
Social Recognition	14	13.25	15	13.46	.852	13	12.29	15	13.63	.140
True Friendship	3	5.69	4	5.20	.758	4	5.31	1	4.44	.081
Wisdom	2	3.25	3	4.55	.037*	2	2.55	3	4.81	.002**

Table Twelve -- continued

II INSTRUMENTAL	B-C Delegates N=81		C-H Delegates N=91		Probability	B-C Non-Delegates N=81		C-H Non-Delegates N=98		Probability
	R	Sc	R	Sc		R	Sc	R	Sc	
Ambitious	17	16.40	16	13.65	.021*	16	14.75	15	15.17	.896
Broadminded	6	7.80	5	6.35	.305	8	8.81	6	7.10	.100
Capable	10	9.75	9	9.44	.866	10	9.63	8	9.00	.640
Cheerful	12	12.00	10	10.00	.123	9	8.88	9	9.07	.878
Clean	18	16.44	18	16.88	.609	17	15.39	15	15.56	.811
Courageous	7	8.00	6	6.95	.226	6	7.33	5	7.00	.967
Forgiving	5	5.29	7	7.38	.080	3	5.20	7	7.38	.543
Helpful	2	3.65	2	3.63	.983	3	5.20	1	3.65	.051
Honest	1	3.27	3	4.05	.297	1	3.57	2	4.36	.566
Imaginative	11	11.43	8	8.36	.006**	15	14.25	12	11.50	.012*
Independent	15	12.78	15	13.44	.587	18	15.42	16	14.17	.148
Intellectual	8	9.22	12	10.95	.084	12	10.92	11	11.07	.983
Logical	13	12.06	14	13.41	.008**	13	11.75	15	13.25	.156
Loving	4	5.13	1	3.60	.628	7	8.42	3	4.50	.002**
Obedient	14	12.69	13	12.85	.910	11	10.25	14	13.10	.019*
Polite	16	13.55	17	14.54	.783	14	12.19	13	12.67	.694
Responsible	3	3.96	4	4.44	.587	2	3.71	4	5.40	.045*
Self-Controlled	9	9.67	11	10.23	.582	4	6.33	10	9.61	.058

each of the two styles than the members of the
Thirty-Second General Congregation who impressed
those styles on Jesuit legislation.

The evidence in support of successful implementation is further supported by the differences in the number of representatives of each
style. When the sample of non-delegates is discriminated according to the Bulwark-Catholic/
Conciliar-Humanist polarity, the Conciliar-
Humanists have predominance of numbers. There
are ninety-eight non-delegates with a C-H polarity
index score and eighty-one non-delegates with a
B-C polarity index score. This difference of
54.7 percent compared to 45.3 percent is a larger
ratio of predominance in favor of the Conciliar-
Humanist style than that existing at the Congregation.

The non-delegate value-rankings also show
similarity to the delegates when they are discriminated according to region, age, and office.
One notable change does occur when delegates and
non-delegates are compared with respect to age
groups. The tendency among the small number of
young delegates at the Congregation to favor the
Bulwark-Catholic style is not representative of
younger Jesuits generally. Younger non-delegates
tend to favor the Conciliar-Humanist style.

Although there are mixed differences in one
discrimination or another, the direction of the
differences varies in such a way that no discernible pattern emerges. Overall, non-delegate
rankings are seldom more than two or three ranks
different than delegates. (See Appendix Two,
Tables Ten to Twelve)

Similarity is also found when delegates and
non-delegates are compared on other control
variables. Fewer differences emerge from non-
delegate rankings than from delegate rankings in
respect to social class. Only one of thirty-six
rankings is significantly different when non-
delegates are discriminated according to task and

314

person-orientation.

Non-delegates' value-rankings differ according to the language group they belong to in a
pattern similar to the differences between delegates. These consistently show the greatest
variation in the data. This confirms the conclusion that geographical differences and variations
in culture must be accommodated in implementing
the Thirty-Second General Congregation. (See
Appendix Two, Tables Thirteen and Fourteen)

Reasoning from the findings (1) that there
is a predominance of Conciliar-Humanists in both
delegate and non-delegate groups, and (2) there
is greater similarity between delegates and non-
delegates than between Bulwark-Catholics and
Conciliar-Humanists, it is probable that the
dynamics and decrees of the General Congregation
could be accepted by the rank-and-file. And
since the Conciliar-Humanist following is in predominance among both delegates and non-delegates,
it is possible, on the basis of findings presented here, to project that the transition inaugurated by the delegates would be accepted and
implemented by the rank-and-file to a similar
extent and with a similar predominance.

Summary and Conclusions

This comparison of delegates to the Thirty-
Second General Congregation and non-delegates
randomly selected from the rank-and-file of the
Jesuit Order is both illuminating and hopeful. It
is illuminating of the many similarities within
the Jesuit Order and it is hopeful of implementation on the evidence of the dispositions and
styles of the non-delegates in relation to the
Congregation.

The non-delegates are a more varied group
than the delegates. There are younger and older
Jesuits in this group, many more directly pastoral

315

and school-oriented men. It is a sample of less
influential Jesuits, but at the same time, it is
a sample of the kind of men who will be affected
as the Congregation documents filter down through
the many communities and apostolates of the Jesuit
Order.

Although somewhat less inclined to change
and less inclined to theological modernity, the
non-delegates are closer to post-Vatican II ideas
than pre-Vatican II ideas. They are more concerned with self-interest, but they are also more
concerned with social action and the bigger issues
of welfare and justice. They rank Jesuit professionalism lower than the delegates but remain
staunchly identified to their own works and institutions.

The expectations of successfully implementing the decrees of the Congregation can be
grounded in the strong contrasts revealed in this
non-delegate sample. Because of these contrasts,
the polarity index shows stronger discrimination
and the value-rankings exhibit greater divergence
in the contrast of Jesuit styles.

The most important conclusion of comparing
these men with the legislators is that the differences in style represented by the delegates
are also found between the non-delegates and the
contrasts are stronger among the non-delegates.
The predispositions of both the Bulwark-Catholic
style and the Conciliar-Humanist style are
clearly present in the Jesuit rank-and-file and,
judging from the non-delegate sample, the
Conciliar-Humanists predominate in numbers and in
support for modernized ideas and values.

To the extent that modernization and the
Thirty-Second General Congregation is asking for
identification with the poor and underprivileged,
the non-delegate sample is nearer to these social
classes in both their backgrounds and in their
work than the delegates. They hold more firmly
to the concerns of welfare and social action than

the delegates. The Conciliar-Humanists among them rank the modernized values more highly than the delegates.

The shift in culture for the Society of Jesus will be realized only when the rank-and-file Jesuits claim it as their own. The predisposition for this change is there and the complementary tradition and reserve in defense of the organization is there as well. The mandate for change is given in the decrees and the climate awaits implementation. So the possibility of the Thirty-Second General Congregation having definite impact is promising and inevitable. The schedule for change is necessarily flexible and unhurried. But the trends of modernization, the sustaining authority and initiative of its members, and the unfolding of Congregation legislation will shape the course of the next decade in the Society of Jesus.

[1]This Change Index employs items originally constructed and published by Sister Marie Augusta Neal, S.N.D., in Values and Interests in Social Change, Englewood Cliffs, N.J., Prentice Hall, Inc., 1965, p. 45 ff.

[2]Ibid.

[3]Ibid.

[4]Society of the Divine Word Self-Study, Washington, D.C. (1969-1972) under the coordination of Reverend Richard Rashke, S.V.D.

CHAPTER TEN

RESUME AND PROSPECT OF

JESUIT MODERNIZATION

This research study has compiled accounts of background, observation, interpretation, evidence and analysis concerning the values of the Society of Jesus and changes these values have undergone in the past decade. Its point of focus has been an actual engagement of these values in the Thirty-Second General Congregation. This final chapter forms a resume of distinctive aspects of the research and a prospect of likely outcomes. Conclusions drawn from the research form the final segment of this report.

The methodology for the research is intensively and extensively distinctive. It has searched out the complex area of Jesuit values, giving predominance to cultural forms and expressions of selective importance instead of to structural components. It has pursued the investigation of values through several lines of evidence gathered from the highest ranking legislative body of the Jesuit Order.

The access to and the cooperation of the General Congregation was unique in itself and unprecedented. A vast majority of delegates (eighty-five percent) responded to a mail questionnaire. Systematic observations within the meetings of the Congregation and record taking of reports, discussion and voting were allowed for the first time in history for sociological analysis.

The lines of evidence marshalled for this value study included testimony, choices, directions of interest, content analysis, and corporate sanctions. The setting upon which the values were brought to bear was an assembly of

319

the Jesuit Order called to treat "long-lasting and important matters...pertaining to the whole body of the Society or its manner of proceeding."[1]

The Congregation engaged Jesuit values not only in the three months of its deliberations, but in a period of nearly four years preparation as well. It was clearly and deliberately a forum for reflecting on these values. "This 32nd General Congregation should be...the final, juridical expression of all the work of the provinces and of the communal reflection of all their members on the best means of assuring our spiritual and apostolic renewal."[2]

The time in which the assembly met was a time of continuing, religious revolution and reinstitutionalization for the entire Catholic Church. This assembly can be seen in conjunction with its immediate predecessor ten years earlier, thus giving a unique portrait of social change in a world-wide organization through the entire period of Catholicism's most tumultuous decade since the Reformation.

The Jesuits inevitably play a very important part in the Church's renewal. It is the largest religious order in the Church. Its teachings and structures have been mirrored in the Church's teachings and structures since the Reformation. It is entrusted with many select responsibilities and apostolates and is able to marshall varied and powerful intellectual forces for its self-examination and renewal. By reason of its charter and constitutions, it stands in unique relationship to the Holy See.

> Wherever in the Church, even in the most difficult and extreme fields, in the crossroads of ideologies, in the front line of social conflict, there has been and there is confrontation between the deepest desires of man and the perennial message of the Gospel, here also there have been, and there

are, Jesuits. Your Society is in
accord with and blends with the
society of the Church in the multiple
works which you direct, also taking
account of the necessity that all
should be unified by a single aim,
that of God's glory and the sancti-
fication of men, without dissipating
its energies in the pursuit of lesser
goals.[3]

Assessment of the values of the present-day
Jesuit Order, therefore, has fundamental ramifi-
cations for an understanding of contemporary
Catholicism and the sociology of religious institutions generally. It serves the Jesuit Order
as well in providing a touchstone of where it is
and where it is going.

Summary and Salience of this Account
of Modernization and its Evidence

This study combines a sociohistorical case
study of the Jesuits with a documented analysis
of social change within a segment of the religious institution and a generalized model of
modernization of formal organizations. In a
manner of methodological triangulation,[4] these
elements are substantiated by different and
complementary data.

From the description of changes since
Vatican II, it is asserted that the Jesuits
responded to aggiornamento by generalizing their
culture and changing their structures through
experimentation and new implementation. In the
Thirty-Second General Congregation this implementation crystallized in the specific cultural form
of a shift from an elite status within the bounded
Church to a minority status in the world seeking
solidarity with the poor. This cultural form
resulted from the efforts of elites, spiralling
reenforcements, and eventual legislation. The

feasibility of broad-scale implementation is projected on the basis of the predisposing factors of similar values between officials and elected delegates and between delegates and non-delegates.

The process of social change is evidenced by two novel and distinctive procedures. These are experimentation-as-legitimation and context-theologizing.

Changes in the Church and Jesuit Order disrupt revered traditions. They are changes which originated with a mandate from the Second Vatican Council. However, the process of change was problematic. If tradition ruled predominantly, what would legitimate disrupting that tradition? The evidence indicates a two stage process of "breaking down" and "building up." The first of these was accomplished by a "carte blanche" kind of rubric. This rubric was labelled "experimentation" and it became its own legitimator once the mandate for change was given.

The process of experimentation gave leeway for youthful innovation, heightened rationalization, the entry of thought, intention, and deliberation into formerly sacred routines, the disembeddedness of conduct from ascription and an inevitable pluralism and division. Through all this, culture came to "stand on its own." The predominance of former structures crumbled.

The second notable process is the integrative technique of context-theologizing. Revered traditions form the central normative content for the Church and the religious practice of Jesuits. When the routines that these traditions supported give way to reinstitutionalization, they must be incorporated into the new routines in a way that provides continuity. Put the other way around, the new behaviors must "piggy-back" on the revered traditions. This occurs as a development of doctrine by context-theologizing. The meaning and content of traditional doctrine is changed by situating it in a context that changes the emphasis and attention to aspects of the doctrine. It is an intellectual, ideational device to harmonize change with continuity.

This process is clearly evidenced in the Jesuit response to the Pope's mandate to combat atheism at the Thirty-First General Congregation and in the central document on faith and justice at the Thirty-Second General Congregation. In both cases the revered content was generalized to allow a far broader array of elements as legitimate and expected; e.g. "The mission of the Society of Jesus today is the service of faith, of which the promotion of justice is an absolute requirement."[5]

The most important and original development of this research is the assessment of the change in Jesuit values in terms of the cultural shift from elite status in the Church to minority status in the world. Evidence throughout this study supports the assertion of the change as consistent with these terms and directions. There is evidence, furthermore, that both Jesuit delegates and non-delegates manifest these styles of elite status and minority status. They exist simultaneously in the Society at this period of transition.

The shift mainly entails a change of legitimation. The Church legitimates the Society of Jesus as "a religious, apostolic and priestly order bound to the Roman Pontiff."[6] The world offers no such legitimation. Its terms of legitimation are functional and achieved.

The process of updating the Jesuit Order over the past decade has inculcated functional and achieved terms in its own frames of reference. It is readied, therefore, to seek out legitimation on these terms. The area chosen to seek legitimation is on behalf of the poor and disenfranchized. This combines a "Gospel" apostolate and a world movement, individuals souls and

323

institutional references, faith and justice, poverty and work, and exemplarity and service. Loyalties to Jesuit traditions and modern social activism are merged in this shift in culture.

Support for the existence of these two styles and the predominance of the more modernized style comes from questionnaire data, voting, and value-rankings by the delegates and by questionnaire data and value-rankings by the non-delegates. The balance of styles is pervasive in both groups; neither group shows a significant majority in numbers. However, both groups reveal themselves as more to the side of the modernized and <u>avant garde</u> theology than to the side of the unchanging and pre-Vatican II theology.

Sixty percent of all definitive votes cast at the Congregation to legislate the final documents bear a predominant following of the Conciliar-Humanist modernized style. Many more of the final documents show a majority of voting outcomes favorable to Conciliar-Humanists (ten to four) and the modernizing position. On the other hand, the influence of Bulwark-Catholics was constantly shown as strong and effective. The evidence indicates a complementarity of influences.

The value-rankings of the delegates and nondelegates vary significantly with their belonging to one style or the other. These rankings provide forceful, independent support for the presence of both styles and they detail something of the differences. Values which are rooted in the Catholic clerical tradition and embedded in the ascriptive role of the priest are favored by Bulwark-Catholics. Values which indicate inclinations to democratization and generalized values are favored by Conciliar-Humanists. The French, the Latin American, the Asian and the African nations favor modernization and modernized values while the Spanish, German, Slavic, and Italian nations favor the more "Catholic" and traditional values. The English, Indian, and American nations group together in a middle position.

324

The contrast of these two styles marks a balance and complementarity between change and continuity in the Jesuits. This balance and complementarity, however, takes place in a changing environment. The Congregation's task was continuing renewal and modernization. The Conciliar-Humanist delegates predominated in defining the legislation; they also prevailed in setting the context of deliberations and future movement. They set the cultural shift from elite to minority into motion for the Jesuit Order over-all.

A shift in culture is not a transformation of the entire organization. At first, it is a shift merely in ideal-types. Beyond that, it is a shift in administrative support, not by relinquishing the older status but by making room for the newer. Subsequently, it is a shift in generalized values. The General Congregation has gone "on record" in support of this. "Our mission...demands a life in which the justice of the Gospel shines out in a willingness not only to recognize and respect the rights of all, especially the poor and the powerless, but also to work actively to secure these rights."[7]

Besides evidencing the change in ideal-types, this research has shown the change in administrative support towards the positions most favorable to this shift. This process of social change is effected by strong and highly publicized statements of Father General. Secondary elites in the field took these pronouncements as sanction and encouragement of their work in social action, service to the poor, and combatting social injustice. The General and his central staff reenforced the work of the secondary elites, and they in turn took steps to increase and gain following for their efforts. A groundswell developed and further reenforcements stirred it into a movement. This entire following clearly represented the concerns of these elites. Through effective lobbying in every province congregation by a group of young Jesuits and information and statements of

Father General furnished by his secretariat on socioeconomic development, the Thirty-Second General Congregation accepted the issue of faith and justice as a priority of priorities and passed its formulation into Jesuit legislation. What had comprised a two-page mention of one particular apostolate in the Thirtieth General Congregation had become as an outcome of the Thirty-Second General Congregation: "the integrating factor of all our ministries; and not only of our ministries but of our inner life as individuals, as communities, and as a world-wide brotherhood."[8]

The second most important and original development of this research is the formulation and substantiation of a theoretical model of modernization. From treatments of modernization and institutionalization of social systems, a model of five stages of change in formal organizations was constructed for this study. The stages are (1) rationalization and disembeddedness from ascription, (2) crystallization of new forms of behavior, (3) integration of new forms with old in more diverse coordination, (4) the generalization of values and value orientations and (5) broad-scale implementation of the changes among the rank-and-file.

This model of modernization is supported by a descriptive account of changes in the Jesuit Order, by content-analysis of the documents of the Thirty-First and Thirty-Second General Congregations, by questionnaire responses, voting, and value-rankings. These are all consistent with stages of the model.

But more than being supported in itself, the model of modernization offers a theoretical "mapping," or rationale for the changes that have occurred in the Jesuits. Three elements of that rationale are emphasized here as particularly salient in understanding the changes and directions of Jesuit values. These elements are the importance of the shift from ascription to achievement, the increase in the level and extent of operations prompted by value-generalization, and the reconciliation of continuity and change on the basis of disposing factors in the Society of Jesus.

During the decade preceding the Thirty-Second General Congregation, _aggiornamento_ became an established fact. The Congregation was clearly aware that the Society of Jesus had endured great changes and, though expensive in resources, must continue to do so. The job hereafter would not be "to set things back in order," but to find a method for constant change and updating. There had been a qualitative change; the frame of reference had shifted from static to dynamic.

An effect of the mandate from the Jesuit major environment, the Church speaking in the Second Vatican Council, and of the changes that ensued through experimentation and new implementation, was to remove the mystery from revered routines. Things were seen as inadequate that had been accepted unquestioningly. The entire correspondence of superior to subject changed, whether that meant priest to laity, Jesuit supervisor to worker, Jesuit provincial to institution, older Jesuit to younger, General's headquarters to provinces, or the Holy See to the Society of Jesus. The sources of solidarity and interaction came gradually to emanate from self-generated or self-aligned forces much as thought and decision do instead of being based on submission and recurrence. And they came to do so legitimately. This was the result and the immense significance of the shift from ascription to achievement.

Given this increased rationalization and relativity, and more diverse and generalized points of view, there developed in turn the need for expanding horizons and the possibility of "fitting in" to new environments. The very process of change seemed to "stand on its own" as the "jumping off" point for further renewal.

The value-generalization that can result

when there exists the condition of culture
"standing on its own" is a phenomenon in the social realm analogous to the formation of an idea
in the cognitive realm. One might think of the
moment Helen Keller first abstracted the meaning
of water.[9] That power of abstraction projected
to an organization or social system resembles
value-generalization in its effects.

From the generalization of values comes an
increase in the extent and level of interactions
as tied in to the central normative sphere of the
organization. Center and periphery are enabled
to relate more compatibly; diverse and contrary
elements can come to terms.

As diversity and pluralism emerged and were
coped with in the Society of Jesus, its experiences of modernization seem to have combined in a
workable potential for relating to and within the
larger, varied sphere of the world. The Jesuit
Order was thus readied for the transformation
from the Tridentine to the post-Conciliar. The
Thirty-Second General Congregation occasioned
that shift in the culture of the Jesuit Order.

The document "Our Mission Today: The
Service of Faith and the Promotion of Justice" is
the central vehicle for translating that potential
into legislation. However, it is not only due to
the fact that the document deals with social
justice. It is more to the point that the document employs generalized values aimed towards
broadening the horizons of Jesuits world-wide.
The level of exposition forms a rubric containing
many more concerns as legitimate. This indicates
modernization in the Society of Jesus and ushers
the Jesuits into a functional, non-ascribed setting for its apostolates.

Generalization such as this could be fatal
dissipation unless it were integrated properly
with the thrust of the overall organization. As
is cited in the model of modernization: "Maintaining the commitment that is the central

normative condition of the process of implementation, and doing so in a manner of increasing generalization is the crux of stability and development in modern social systems."[10]

This development is complex. It relies on the two-fold process of "breaking down" and "building up." The "breaking down" demands an inner core that can endure purification; the "building up" demands predisposing characteristics that facilitate continuity during a time of transformation.

The "breaking down" arrives at the core of religious practice. The core of religion is a sense of the holy or acknowledgment of faith. Thus it is always an ascribed rather than an achieved resource. The history of religions shows repeated instances of that core ascription being extended to a multitude of mundane vested interests. The "breaking down" of ascription to these mundane interests can be seen as a purification, a return to the core of one's religious adherence. O'Dea speaks of this as a desired outcome of Vatican II:

> The sociological demythologization of the Church involves the dismantling of this vast superstructure, the disentangling of its essential, timeless elements from their historically and culturally conditioned expressions, and their new institutionalization. It is a process fraught with conflict, danger, and suffering, but it is the price of vitality and relevance.[11]

The "building up" or new implementation phase of this development relies on characteristics which facilitate continuity during a time of transformation. The Jesuit Order shows evidence of having these characteristics. They include some precedent for self-transformation or transcendence (e.g. the Gospel itself, the 'revolutionary' character of Saint Ignatius in founding the

Jesuits), allegiance to an adaptable center of
authority (e.g. tradition of obedience and continuing, though modified, hierarchical structures),
an accomplishment of the transfer of loyalties
(e.g. context-theologizing, balance of B-C and
C-H styles), and capacity for the innovating sector to further collective interests (e.g. relevance, wider agendas and greater opportunity).[12]
The normative commitments of the Society allow
for that change or, at least, can be allied to it.

The move from ascription to achievement, the
generalization of values, and setting transformation in line with tradition are particular aspects
of the model of modernization. They highlight
actual dispositions and occurrences in the Jesuit
Order. Other aspects that do the same are detailed in the earlier analysis. The Congregation's shift in culture from elite to minority
status is consistent with the model, and both are
supported by the data. Together they comprise
the major developments of this research.

            Findings of the Research as
            Prospect of Future Outcomes

After long, involved analysis of many lines
of evidence, it is practical to ask: what do we
learn from this research that will be useful for
the future? Empirical findings and theoretical
development provide answers to that question.

The empirical data issue most importantly in
three allied conclusions. These conclusions concern similarity and dissimilarity, the amalgam of
differing styles, and the shaping of a climate.

The delegates to the Thirty-Second General
Congregation have much in common. They value
the Spiritual Exercises of Saint Ignatius as the
common character of Jesuit life. They give primary importance to sincere service in the apostolate. They acknowledge the increased importance

                    330

of solidarity and simplicity in community life.
They differ most markedly in regard to Bulwark-
Catholic and Conciliar-Humanist styles and
national-cultural characteristics.

Ex officio delegates to the Congregation are
similar to elected delegates, and delegates are
similar to non-delegates. Those delegates who
favor the Bulwark-Catholic styles are more dis-
similar from Conciliar-Humanist delegates than
they are from non-delegates who favor the B-C
style. The same holds for Conciliar-Humanist
delegates and non-delegates. This finding suggests that the leadership which this General
Congregation experienced as a whole is less a
function of explicit innovation and more a
function of mirroring the demands and needs of
the rank-and-file.

The amalgam of differences is the most intriguing part of this research. The B-C and C-H
styles created legislation and established future
expectations for the Society of Jesus as a blend
of these styles. The priority of priorities as
a governing horizon, the faith and justice document, and all major documents and discussions
gives evidence of this blending and complementarity. It was enacted by context-theologizing.

Context-theologizing, in this case, changes
the meaning of "defense of the faith" and "combat
with atheism" by setting the context for that
doctrine. The context for "service of faith" becomes "two billion human beings who have no
knowledge of God," "our dazzled contemporaries
who have...lost the sense of God," and "a world
increasingly interdependent, yet tragically
divided by injustice...built into economic, social,
and political structures."[13] Enlarging the context generalizes the values embodied in the new
context and changes the thrust and direction of
its doctrine.

The outstanding feature of this methodology
is this: what the delegates did to the document,

they also did to the entire character of the
Society of Jesus. Context-theology in reference
to the document is in perfect correspondence to
the shift in culture in reference to Jesuit life.
The context-theology enlarged the context of faith
to include social justice. The shift in culture
enlarged the context of Jesuit apostolates to
include all mankind. Enlarging the context of
apostolates generalizes the values embodied in
the new context and changes the thrust and direction of the Jesuit Order.

Shaping the climate for Jesuit expectations
emerges from this General Congregation as a prevailing and potent form of leadership for a time
of reinstitutionalization based on cultural innovation and the inadequacy of former structures.
Instead of leadership by domination and the
enactment of binding, enforceable rules and regulations, leadership - by shaping the climate of
expectations - employs a form of manipulation,[14]
the subtle steering of a constituency towards
resources and experiences which will, in turn,
influence them in favor of the desired responses
and directions. The form of legislation in the
Thirty-Second General Congregation served far
more to set a tone and engender new expectations
than it did to radically change structures.

Further important findings that bear on
future outcomes are derived from the theoretical
model of modernization. In each case they are
reenforced by developments in the Jesuit Order
and the Thirty-Second General Congregation. These
findings deal with the role of questioning in cultural innovation, the role of generalization and
interchange in increased pluralism, the role of
generalization and pluralism in an increase of
solidary groupings, the defense of precarious
values, the increased integration at formal levels
of organization, and the utility of the model of
modernization for formal organizations.

The greater the amount of cultural questioning and reassessment that goes on in a condition

of leeway from structural constraints, the more useful that culture will be in fostering innovation, provided the central normative values are not lost sight of. The "building up" of new behaviors, integration and generalized values in the Jesuit Order only occurred after a period of the "breaking down" of constraints. Recovery from the "breaking down" took the form of an intensive "return to culture" and tradition as the source of rationalization for many experimental projects.

> To go this far was possible only for a general congregation of a rather exceptional character, one intended to transact its business at a particularly crucial moment in the life of the Church.

> This advantage, however, remains: there was broad consultation, there was the opportunity for free discussion and discernment prior to the taking of decisions. In the spirit of the Society, this should strengthen, rather than weaken, the decisions taken - on condition, of course, of true spiritual discernment.[15]

Increased interchange in the midst of a condition of more generalized value commitments is likely to result in greater diversity and pluralism. Given the breaking down of structural constraints and ascribed routines, the array of behaviors submitted by Jesuits for "permission," legitimation and integration in the Society escalated enormously. Many such behaviors were short lived; many others entered the fabric of reformed Jesuit life. These latter "permissions" made more personal many encounters with authority, stretched or eliminated many rules and regulations, and revamped the acceptance of, criteria for and engagement in Jesuit ministries.

Increased pluralism in the midst of a condition of more generalized values is likely to result in an increase of distinct solidary groupings. If adequately coordinated in terms of

the generalized values, these groupings can increase the collective solidarity. During this
time of change, many fashions of behavior and
interests gathered Jesuit followings. Integration of these followings had to result from the
mediation between the value commitments of the
entire collectivity and the interests of the new
following. To the extent that these were not all-
inclusive so that various group members could
adhere to different elements of Jesuit life in
interdependent ways, collective solidarity could
result.

The possibility of this collective solidarity is evidenced in documents of the Congregation.
They call for the equivalent of what Parsons means
by "societal community." This consists of interpenetrating collectivities, functional differentiation, and loyalty that obtains its effectiveness on the basis of larger value commitments.[16]
This same emphasis combines what Simpson calls
associationalism and imperative control. The
tendency of the Congregation in reference to
communities is to increase the number of semi-
autonomous decision making centers, to strengthen
the role of local superiors, and to promote the
cohesion of cross-cutting relations. Three
communal elements emphasized by the Congregation
stand in tension one with another. These are
service to a wide "family of man," familiarity
and solidarity with the Jesuits one lives with,
and close collaboration with a further group of
Jesuits and non-Jesuits that one works with. The
thrust of the documents is to integrate but not
to merge these three elements. As a result,
interpenetrating collectivities and functional
differentiation could obtain.

The function of leadership in the midst of
extended legitimation and increased solidary
groupings is the defense of precarious values.
If any particular group or faction gained hegemony
over the direction of changes in the Society,
tensions and rebellion would erupt. Leaders
function to intensify the compatibility and

interdependence of various groups and to increase the "traffic" between the center and the periphery. In preparation for the Thirty-Second General Congregation, all communities were instructed to corporately discuss important thematic issues. Surveys from Jesuit headquarters in Rome, broad consultation, and free exchange of views proved to be self-correcting and reasonable. The very extensive similarity between the values of ex officio and elected delegates and between delegates and non-delegates uncovered by this research implies continuity of "precarious values" in different echelons and groupings of the Society.

In a period of drastic change, new solidarities, extended legitimacies and generalized values, personnel who choose to remain in the organization are prompted to form closer alliances with the organization and its value-system. "Modern man finds, to an ever increasing degree, his point of personal integration in the formal organization of human conduct."[17] This movement of the personal integration of Jesuits changing from a highly individualistic basis to that of the Jesuit community is evidenced by two emphases of the Congregation, the stress on communal discernment and on poverty.

Communal discernment is a structure to allow the fundamental value level of Jesuit life to penetrate the ordinary daily routines. This emphasis replaces a pragmatic or political decision-making process with a spiritual, communal process. It intends the promotion of group loyalty in a climate of support for value-level concerns. It also shifts the emphasis of consultation with superiors from formal declarations made to the Provincial once a year, to an increased openness with local superiors on a more recurrent and informal basis.

The document on poverty asks for greater solidarity with the poor and sets up structures to curtail abuses too far removed from that ideal. Since solidarity with the poor is not socially

335

aspired to, the poverty document effectively sets
before the individual Jesuit the dilemma of
choosing solidarity with the poor and gaining
Jesuit support or forsaking solidarity with the
poor and losing Jesuit support as well.

> Those who are unwilling to observe this
> double law of common life (i.e. contri-
> bute to the community everything he
> receives; receive from the community
> everything he needs) separate themselves
> from the fraternity of the Society in
> spirit if not in law.[18]

Finally, a wide ranging consistency between
the model of modernization and the findings of
this research suggests that the model is useful
for this kind of organizational analysis generally. It supports the belief that a Parsons-
Eisenstadt type of perspective on societies can
be brought down to a "middle-range" as a theory
of organizational development. In the experience
of the Jesuit Order, changes in the environment
induced changes in the Order in such a way that
experimentation and questioning led to disembeddedness from ascription and rationalization of behavior. This led in turn to the pluralism of
new behaviors and new forms of integration. This
increased activity resulted in the eventual
generalization of values. Implementation of the
changes rely on the strength of predisposing
factors and the adherence to a central normative
core of values in the Society of Jesus. This
development could serve as a paradigm of organizational activity and evaluation for other organizations as well.

Conclusions from the Research

In a study of as many small details and
large generalizations as this one, the matter of
forming conclusions is complex. Many particular
conclusions from specific accounts of evidence

occur frequently throughout the text. The
findings already summarized in this chapter provide further conclusions. Nevertheless, four
major, overall conclusions are given here as the
closing contribution of this research. They
regard the radical nature of fully implemented
transition, the problematic of leadership in this
time, a proposition on the change of environments,
and the role of nations in implementing the Congregation.

First, the Thirty-Second General Congregation effected a change in culture which represents
for the Jesuit Order a shift from an elite status
in the Catholic Church to a minority status in
the world seeking legitimation from the poor and
the disenfranchized. This is a radical shift in
the life of the Society of Jesus. Many aspects
and influences must converge, amidst real difficulties, before it comes to be fully implemented.
The General of the Jesuits stated this when
writing to the whole Society regarding the implementation of the Congregation's decrees:

> The implementation of the decrees will
> pose special difficulty, for it demands
> of us before everything else a deep and
> clear affirmation of faith - a faith that
> is lived, a manifest faith in Jesus Christ
> and His Church. It asks of us, moreover,
> a change of attitudes, of criteria, of
> ways of thinking, and of the standard
> and style of life. It calls for a radical
> revision of our objectives and apostolic
> priorities and of the means used for their
> attainment. It demands a more resolute
> insertion in the world and a more intimate
> contact with the human realities of our
> times. In many cases it requires a change
> not only in the individuals but also in
> the institutions and structures.

> It is evident that so complete a trans-
> formation cannot be brought about without
> conviction in and enthusiasm for our

vocation so that the difficulties may
be faced with joy and fortitude (Cfr.
allocution of Pope Paul VI on 7th of
March). To be effective, we have to
proceed positively, gradually, organically. Otherwise a chain of reactions
and traumas may be let loose, blocking
all possibility of change. We need a
"pedagogy" to avoid the danger of falling
into the extremes of unrealizable utopian
radicalism or pusillanimous fear which
presents those new attitudes as impossible
for us. All this should be worked out in
a communitarian context, for the individual
cannot attain without the collaboration
and support of his community what is demanded
of him.[19]

Implementation of so pervasive a change is
problematic. This research has shown that few
Jesuit respondents were raised in less than
middle-class surroundings. Their values were
seldom those of the poor and the uneducated.
Their present clientele are seldom less than
middle-class. Their life-style presently is at
least middle-class. The institutions they staff
were often formed to create a Catholic elite;
these cannot be converted easily to serve the
poor. The Jesuits cannot be converted easily
from one world to another.

The Society of Jesus is unprepared to cope
with the innumerable details of changing its life-
style and legitimacy. Although its culture is
more functional, its values now generalized and
its normative commitments in support of the
change, the fabric of men and means cannot be
refashioned all of a sudden. Despite individual
reenforcements for sacrifice and solidarity and
community innovations of decision-making and subsidiarity, inertia is strong and resistance inate.

Legislation can only initiate this kind of
social change. Time and the ardent employment of
many resources are required to make the difference.

338

And the difference which is made is necessarily a
difference worked out in relation to the vast
complex of influences which comprise the environment surrounding the Jesuit Order.

Secondly, the role of leadership in implementing the Congregation is also problematic. A
majority of the delegates are administrators and
leaders in their respective provinces and apostolates. They enacted the Congregation's legislation in firm solidarity. They overwhelmingly
passed the final version of all documents. They
support the cause of implementation.

At the same time, the type of leadership
that is evidenced is what has been called above
"shaping the climate" of the Society. Rigid enforcement and domination is wholly unsuited for
the kind of legislation these leaders enacted.

The terms of the problematic must be rightly
defined. They are not the terms of suddenly
changing all Jesuits into apostles of the poor.
Rather, they are the terms of positively,
gradually, and organically "bridging the gap" by
shaping a climate that is conducive to the shift
in culture envisioned and enacted by the Congregation.

The character of the Jesuit organization
evidenced in this study manifests capacities for
change and an aptitude for modernization. Given
the climate in which further changes are required
and congenial, Jesuits could be expected to adapt
accordingly. At the same time, the character of
the organization must retain the defense of its
traditions and commitments. Both the adaptability
and the defense of values is necessary for survival.

Thirdly, the manner of meeting this problematic, of bringing about both adaptation and the
defense of core values is described in a proposition of changing environments. This proposition
is as follows: The Jesuit Order has changed in

339

the past dozen years by means of a response to
demands and changes in the surrounding environment. It was an environment with which the Jesuit
Order was very familiar and effectively in touch.
The prospect for future change in the directions
decreed by the Thirty-Second General Congregation
rely on the same capacities for change. These
new directions likewise intend a response to
demands and changes in a surrounding environment.
However, the environment is one with which the
Jesuit Order is far less familiar and far less in
touch. Therefore, implementation relies not only
on the dynamics and directions laid out by the
Congregation but also it relies intrinsically on
how closely and effectively the Society of Jesus
moves into that new surrounding environment.

Jesuits are, by and large, intelligent sensitive men engaged in the care and service of
other people. Through their history of such care
and service, they have responded somewhat ap-
propriately to the conditions of "their people."
Jesuits also have a tradition of and capacity for
mobility and change in apostolates. Since the
time of Saint Ignatius of Loyola, the "unbounded"
has been a hallmark of the works they undertook
for "the greater glory of God."

In the light of these qualities, it could be
predicted that the Thirty-Second General Congregation's designs will be realized as Jesuits
effectively change from one environment to another.
Just as they so often adapted themselves to (and
recruited from the ranks of) the middle classes
of the Church when forming a Catholic intelligentia, Jesuits could be expected to adapt accordingly if and when they are exposed to, actively encounter, learn from and come to care for, live
with, and serve people who are poor and disenfranchized.

The process of implementation of the Congregation, then, is the process of positively,
gradually, and organically "bridging the gap" between an elite past and minority future for an

340

increasing number of Jesuits. This is already being accomplished in some ways by changes in formation programs, in the residences and life-styles of some Jesuits, and in a growing apostolate of social action and promotion of justice. The phenomenon of naming "missionaries" who are more accustomed to arduous surroundings as pro-vincials and major superiors is another incentive in "bridging the gap."

Fourthly, the role of various nations is important in accomplishing the implementation of this Congregation. Changes in social structures occur each in their own cultural environment. This research has shown that the Jesuits reflect various cultural environments. The language groups and nationalities represented accounted for the greatest variance. The Jesuits in these environments must be prompted to change in a manner suited to each.

In some cultures that change has already occurred and is likely to advance further to the broad advocacy of social justice in secular do-mains. In other cultures, it has hardly begun. But the Congregation documents apply to the uni-versal Jesuit Order. Therefore the shift in major value-orientations represented by its de-crees is generally legitimated. On the basis of solidarity within the Congregation and its similarity to non-delegate characteristics, this legitimation can be expected to gradually obtain throughout the Society.

> Once a new value-pattern has come to be accepted as so fully legitimate that the burden of proof is simply assumed to be on the advocate of the opposing pattern, then the dominant pattern con-tinues to attract additional adherents and to extend its coverage into more and more activities across all institu-tional sectors.[20]

There is a further difficulty in the Jesuit

Order's extending the coverage of this transition into various cultural sectors. The Congregation impressed a dominant character on this shift in culture. Its implementation relies on adaptation to the local and national environments that various Jesuits move into. But some cultures will be distinctly hostile and alien to the direction and character of the new Jesuit thrust. In many instances, Jesuits will be stifled in their attempts to influence structures on behalf of the poor and disenfranchized. In other instances, the difficulties will be such that the attempt will not even be made.

In the face of conditions that are alien to the thrust of Jesuit modernization, perhaps the most telling accent of the Congregation will prove to be its concern for inculturation. Judging from the Bulwark-Catholic/Conciliar-Humanist scores for various national groups, it is apparent that the developing nations are more inclined to relate to their respective cultures in terms of the Congregation's mind than the developed nations. Rather than insisting that Jesuits from developing nations strictly conform to expectations of those from prosperous North-Atlantic countries, the Congregation gives leeway for local initiatives. From such initiatives might develop the pedagogy required to prepare more dominant sectors of the Society to accept the non-elitist role.

In conclusion, the Thirty-Second General Congregation of the Society of Jesus is highly significant. It attempted to give the Jesuits direction, sanctions, solidarity, and elan in an intense time of transformation. And it was a sign of where they are and where they are going. Like all social realities, the Jesuit organization is a complicated blend of many forces. These forces do not take shape singly or in isolation. They become recognizable as signs of what Jesuits value only in the intersection of different people, interests, behaviors, alignments, styles and beliefs. The Congregation was an occasion for

this, and it developed harmony and direction. The
entire Society of Jesus in its many apostolates
must also be an occasion for this, and do the
same. This must be done among people and their
concerns, and among structures and all their
entanglements. Through the costs and changes
this entails for the Jesuits, they must sustain
a central, quickening spirit.

Footnotes

[1] Saint Ignatius of Loyola, *The Constitutions of the Society of Jesus*, translated by George F. Ganss, S.J., p. 295.

[2] Very Reverend Pedro Arrupe, S.J., General of the Society of Jesus, quoted in Calvez, "A Critical Appraisal of the Preparation of the Jesuits' Thirty-Second General Congregation," p. 939.

[3] Pope Paul VI, "Address of Pope Paul VI to the Thirty-Second General Congregation of the Society of Jesus: December 3, 1974" in *Documents, 32 G.C.*, p. 140.

[4] Donald T. Campbell, "Leadership and Its Effects upon the Group," p. 73-74.

[5] "Our Mission Today: The Service of Faith and the Promotion of Justice," in *Documents, 32 G.C.*, p. 17.

[6] "Jesuits Today," in *Documents, 32 G.C.*, p. 12.

[7] "Our Mission Today," p. 21.

[8] "Jesuits Today," p. 8.

[9] Helen Keller, *My Religion*, New York, Swedenborg Foundation, 1927 (1962), p. 201.

[10] Cf: Parsons, "On the Concept of Value Commitments," p. 148 and Chapter Four above.

[11] Thomas F. O'Dea, *The Catholic Crisis*, p. 166.

[12] Cf: S.N. Eisenstadt, "Transformation of Social, Political and Cultural Orders in Modernization," p. 660.

[13] "Our Mission Today," p. 17.

[14]The terms of domination and manipulation
are taken from Morris Janowitz, "Changing Patterns
of Organizational Authority: The Military Estab-
lishment," <u>Administrative Science Quarterly</u>, Vol.
3, March, 1959, pp. 473-493.

[15]Jean Yves Calvez, S.J., "A Critical Appraisal of the Preparation for the Jesuits' Thirty-
Second General Congregation," p. 944.

[16]Talcott Parsons, <u>System of Modern Socie-
ties</u>, p. 13.

[17]Don Martindale, <u>American Society</u>, p. 89.

[18]"Poverty" in <u>Documents, 32 G.C.</u>, p. 99.

[19]Very Reverend Pedro Arrupe, S.J., "To
the Whole Society: Concerning the Implementation
of the Decrees of G.C. 32," p. 3-4.

[20]Robin M. Williams, Jr., <u>American Society</u>,
p. 633.

BIBLIOGRAPHY

I. Cited Works

Abbott, Walter M., S.J. (ed.)
   1966 The Documents of Vatican II. New York:
       Guild Press.

Arrupe, Very Reverend Pedro, S.J.
   1965 "A Letter of Very Reverend Father
       General to the Whole Society on the
       Thirty-First General Congregation."
       (July 31). Rome: General's Curia of
       The Society of Jesus.

   1968 "Jesuits and Social Justice: A Common
       Consciousness of the Problematic,"
       Woodstock Letters 97 (Winter): 67-79.

   1971a "Father General's Statement on the Oc-
       casion of His Meeting with the Secretary-
       General of the United Nations, New York,
       May 4, 1971." Visit of Father General
       to the American Assistancy. Washington,
       D.C.: The Jesuit Conference.

   1971b "The Society of Jesus in the World of
       Today" in visit of Father General to the
       American Assistancy - 1971: Talks and
       Writings, Washington, D.C.: The Jesuit
       Conference.

   1972 "Our Apostolate in Africa and Madagascar
       Today." Studies in the International
       Apostolate of Jesuits I (September):
       65-89.

   1973a Men for Others: An Address delivered to
       the Tenth International Congress of
       Jesuit Alumni of Europe, July 31, 1973 in
       Valencia, Spain. Washington, D.C.:
       Jesuit Secondary Educational Association.

   1973b "Letter of Very Reverend Father General
       convoking the Thirty-Second General

Congregation." (September 8). Rome:
General's Curia of The Society of Jesus.

1975 "Letter of Very Reverend Father General
to the Whole Society concerning the
Implementation of the Decrees of G.C.
32." Rome: General's Curia of The
Society of Jesus.

1976 A Letter of Very Reverend Father General
concerning the new Charitable and Apostolic Fund of The Society of Jesus
(March 19). Rome: General's Curia of
The Society of Jesus.

Biever, Bruce F. and Thomas M. Gannon, S.J. (eds.)
1969 General Survey of The Society of Jesus:
North American Assistancy, Volumes I-V.
Oak Park, Illinois, National Office of
Pastoral Research.

Buckley, Michael J., S.J.
1975 "The Confirmation of Promise: A Letter
to George Ganss." Studies in the
Spirituality of Jesuits VII (November):
175-195.

Calvez, Jean-Yves
1975 "A Critical Appraisal of the Preparation
for the Jesuits' Thirty-Second General
Congregation." Review for Religious 34
(November): 936-948.

Campion, Donald, S.J.
1974-75 G.C. News, English Edition. Nos. 1-21,
(December-March). Rome: Society of
Jesus Press and Information Office.

Caporale, Rock, S.J.
1964 Vatican II: Last of the Councils.
Baltimore: Helicon Press.

Daley, Brian, S.J.
1975 "Identifying Jesuits: The 32nd General
Congregation." The Month CCXXXVI (May):

146-151.

Davis, James A.
    1971   Elementary Survey Analysis.   Englewood
            Cliffs: Prentice-Hall.

Eisenstadt, S.N.
    1964   "Social Change, Differentiation and
            Evolution." American Sociological
            Review 29 (June):   375-386.

    1965a   Essays on Comparative Institutions.   New
            York: John Wiley and Sons.

    1965b   "Transformation of Social, Political,
            and Cultural Orders in Modernization."
            American Sociological Review 30
            (October):   659-673.

    1968a   "Social Institutions" in International
            Encyclopedia of the Social Sciences.
            New York: Macmillan and The Free Press.

    1968b   "Sociological Thought" in International
            Encyclopedia of the Social Sciences.
            New York: Macmillan and The Free Press.

    1973   "Post-Traditional Societies and the
            Continuity and Reconstruction of
            Tradition." Daedalus 102 (Winter):
            1-27.

Ganss, George E.
    1965   "Impressions of the 31st General Congre-
            gation." Woodstock Letters 94 (Fall):
            372-395.

    1973   "Editor's Foreword" in "The Place of
            Art in Jesuit Life." Studies in the
            Spirituality of Jesuits V (April): v-vi.

General's Curia of The Society of Jesus
    1973   Formula Congregationis Generalis:
            Congregationis Generales XXXI Opera et
            Auctorita Retracta.   Rome: General's

Curia of The Society of Jesus.

1974   Thirty-Second General Congregation
        Society of Jesus Press Pack. Rome:
        Society of Jesus Press and Information
        Office.

1975   Supplementum Catalogorum Societatis
        Jesu: 1976. Rome: General's Curia of
        The Society of Jesus.

Greeley, Andrew M.
1970   "Myths, Meaning and Vatican II."
        America (December 19): 538-542.

Guindon, William G., S.J.
1975   "Overview." S.J. News 5 (April): 2.

Hall, Richard H.
1972   Organizations: Structures and Process.
        Englewood Cliffs: Prentice-Hall.

Haring, Bernard, C.S.S.R.
1966   "Marriage and the Family" in John H.
        Nuller, (ed.), Vatican II: An Interfaith
        Appraisal, International Theological
        Conference, University of Notre Dame,
        March 20-26, 1966. Notre Dame, Indiana:
        University of Notre Dame Press.

Hoyt, Robert C. (ed.)
1968   The Birth Control Debate: Interim His-
        tory from the Pages of National Catholic
        Reporter. Kansas City: National
        Catholic Reporter.

Ivern, Francis, S.J.
1974   "The Society's Commitment to the Promo-
        tion of Justice: Analysis of the
        Postulata Submitted to the 32nd General
        Congregation." Unpublished paper. Rome.

Jurich, James P., S.J. (ed.)
1966   "Thirty-First General Congregation: The
        First Session." Woodstock Letters 95

(Winter): 5-79.

1968 "The 31st General Congregation: Letters from the Second Session." Woodstock Letters 97 (Winter): 5-31.

Jesuit Conference, The
1975 Documents of the Thirty-Second General Congregation of the Society of Jesus: An English Translation. Washington, D.C.: The Jesuit Conference.

Kim, Jae-On
1975 "Factor Analysis." Pp. 468-514 of Norman H. Nile et al, Statistical Package for the Social Sciences: Second Edition. New York: McGraw-Hill.

Kornhauser, William
1959 The Politics of Mass Society. Glencoe: The Free Press.

Lansing, John B. and James N. Morgan
1971 Economic Survey Methods. Ann Arbor, Michigan: Institute for Social Research.

Lewin, Kurt
1935 "The Conflict Between Aristotelian and Galileian Modes of Thought in Contemporary Psychology." Pp. 1-42 in his A Dynamic Theory of Personality. New York: McGraw-Hill.

Lonergan, Bernard, S.J.
1967 "Dimensions of Meaning." Pp. 252-267 in F.E. Crowe, S.J. (ed.), Collection: Papers by Bernard Lonergan, S.J. New York: Herder and Herder.

1970 "The Response of the Jesuit, as Priest and Apostle, in the Modern World." Studies in the Spirituality of Jesuits II (September): 89-110.

Lucey, Paul R., S.J.

1975 "Spiritual Dynamics." S.J. News 5 (April): 2-3.

Martindale, Don
1959 "Sociological Theory and the Ideal Type." Pp. 57-91 of Llewellyn Gross (ed.) Symposium on Sociological Theory. New York: Harper and Row.

1972 American Society. Huntington, N.Y., R.E. Krieger Publishing Company.

National Opinion Research Center
1972 The Catholic Priest in the United States: Sociological Investigations. Washington, D.C.: The United States Catholic Conference.

Neal, Sister Marie Augusta, S.V.D.
1965 Values and Interests in Social Change. Englewood Cliffs: Prentice-Hall.

O'Dea, Thomas F.
1968 The Catholic Crisis. Boston: Beacon Press.

Padberg, John W., S.J.
1974 "The General Congregations of The Society of Jesus: A Brief Survey of their History." Studies in the Spirituality of Jesuits VI (January and March): 1-126.

1975 "Continuity and Change in General Congregation XXXII." Studies in the Spirituality of Jesuits. VII. (November): 197-215.

Parsons, Talcott
1964 "Evolutionary Universals in Society." American Sociological Review 29 (June): 339-357.

1966 Societies: Evolutionary and Comparative Perspectives. Englewood Cliffs: Prentice-Hall.

352

1968   "On the Concept of Value-Commitments."
Sociological Inquiry 38 (Spring):
135-160.

1971   The System of Modern Societies. Englewood Cliffs: Prentice-Hall.

Paul VI, Pope
1966   "Papal Brief Declaring the Council
Completed." Pp. 738-739 in Walter M.
Abbott, S.J., The Documents of Vatican
II. New York: Guild Press.

1973   "Letter of the Holy Father on the Convo-
cation of the 32nd General Congregation."
(October 4). Rome: General's Curia of
The Society of Jesus.

1974   "Address of Pope Paul VI to the Thirty-
Second General Congregation of The
Society of Jesus." (December 3). Rome:
General's Curia of The Society of Jesus.

1975   "Address of Pope Paul VI to the Thirty-
Second General Congregation of The
Society of Jesus." (March 7). Rome:
General's curia of The Society of Jesus.

Rahner, Karl
1966   The Church After The Council. New York:
Herder and Herder.

Rashke, Richard, S.V.D.
1973   "Pluralism and Pluriformity in Religious
Life: A Case Study." Pro Mundi Vita-
Centrum Informationis 47. Brussels:
Pro Mundi Vita International Research
and Information Center.

Reese, Thomas J., S.J.
1973   "The General Congregation: A Study in
the Legislative Process." Unpublished
paper submitted to Department of
Political Science, University of
California at Berkeley.

Rippee, Loretta J. and Theodore Greenstein
    1973 "User's Guide to Program Valutest: A
          Fortran Program for Analysis of Inter-
          group Difference or Rank-Ordered Scales."
          Mimeographed article. Pullman, Washing-
          ton, Sociological Data Processing
          Center - Washington State University.

Roche, Douglas J.
    1968 The Catholic Revolution. New York:
          David McKay Company.

Rokeach, Milton
    1973 The Nature of Human Values. New York:
          The Free Press.

Rummel, R.J.
    1967 "Understanding Factor Analysis."
          Journal of Conflict Resolution XI
          (December): 444-480.

Saint Ignatius of Loyola
    1960 The Spiritual Exercises of Saint Ignatius:
          A New Translation by Louis J. Puhl, S.J.
          Westminster, Maryland: Newman Press.

    1970 The Constitutions of the Society of
          Jesus, translated by George E. Ganss.
          Saint Louis: The Institute of Jesuit
          Sources.

Selznick, Philip
    1957 Leadership in Administration: A Socio-
          logical Interpretation. New York:
          Harper and Row.

Sheets, John R., S.J.
    1975 "A Survey of the Thirty-Second General
          Congregation." Review for Religious 34
          (September): 672-689.

Shils, Edward
    1961 "Mass Society and Its Culture" in Norman
          Jacobs (ed.), Culture for the Millions.
          New York: Van Nostrand.

354

1965 "Charisma, Order and Status." American Sociological Review 30 (April): 199-213.

1967 "Theory of Mass Society." Pp. 30-47 in Bernhard Rosenberg and David White, (eds.), Mass Culture. Glencoe: The Free Press.

Simpson, Richard L.
  1971 "Imperative Control, Associationalism, and the Moral Order," in Herman Turk and Richard L. Simpson, (eds.) Institutions and Social Exchange: The Sociologies of Talcott Parsons and George G. Homans. Indianapolis: Bobbs-Merrill, Co.

Sponga, Edward J., S.J.
  1965 "The General Congregation: Its Atmosphere and Hopes." Woodstock Letters 94 (Fall): 396-406.

  1967 "Jesuits Face the Future." America (February 11): 208-214.

Stinchcombe, Arthur L.
  1965 "Social Structure and Organizations," in James G. March (ed.) Handbook of Organizations. Chicago: Rand McNally and Co.

Thorman, Donald J.
  1967 "Today's Layman: An Uncertain Catholic." America (January 14): 39-41.

Walsh, Maurice, B., S.J.
  1975 "Highlights." S.J. News 5 (April): 3.

Weber, Max
  1949 The Methodology of the Social Sciences, translated by Edward Shils and Henry A. Finch. Glencoe, Illinois: The Free Press.

  1968 On Charisma and Institution Building, edited with introduction by S.N. Eisenstadt. Chicago: University of Chicago

355

Press.

Williams, Robin M., Jr.
　1967　"Individual and Group Values." The
　　　　Annals of the American Academy of Poli-
　　　　tical and Social Science, 371. (May).

　1970　American Society: A Sociological Inter-
　　　　pretation, Third Edition. New York,
　　　　Alfred A. Knopf.

Wills, Garry
　1971　"The New Jesuits vs. The Unheavenly
　　　　City." New York Magazine (June 14).

　1972　Bare Ruined Choirs: Doubt, Prophecy and
　　　　Radical Religion. Garden City, N.Y.:
　　　　Doubleday Company.

Woodstock College
　1967　Documents of the Thirty-First General
　　　　Congregation. Woodstock, Md.: Woodstock
　　　　College.

'Editor'
　1965a The Official Catholic Directory: Anno
　　　　Domini, 1965. New York: P.J. Kennedy
　　　　and Sons.

　1965b "The Jesuits in the Post-Conciliar Era:
　　　　The Thirty-First General Congregation
　　　　and the New General." Herder Correspon-
　　　　dence, (November): 351-356.

　1966　"Editorials - Pope and Jesuits: Invi-
　　　　tation and Response." America (December
　　　　3): 729.

　1975a The Official Catholic Directory: Anno
　　　　Domini 1975. New York: P.J. Kennedy
　　　　and Sons.

　1975b "Extending the Vow." Time Magazine:
　　　　Europe edition (February 10): 32-33.

356

II. Background and Reference Works

Aberle, David
    1950 "Shared Values in Couplex Societies."
          American Sociological Review 15.
          (August): 495-502.

Albert, Ethel M.
    1968 "Value Systems" in International Ency-
          clopedia of the Social Sciences. New
          York: Macmillan and The Free Press.

American Assistancy of The Society of Jesus
    1969 Santa Clara II. Santa Clara, California:
          University of Santa Clara.

Arrupe, Very Reverend Pedro, S.J.
    1972 "Witnessing to Justice." Justice in the
          World: Synod of Bishops. Vatican City:
          Pontifical Commission on Justice and
          Peace.

Bales, Robert F.
    1951 Interaction Process Analysis. Reading,
          Massachusetts: Addison-Wesley Publish-
          ing Company.

                   , and Arthur S. Couch
    1969 "The Value Profile: A Factor Analytic
          Study of Value Statements." Sociologi-
          cal Inquiry 39 (Winter): 3-17.

Bauer, Raymond A. (ed.)
    1966 Social Indicators. Cambridge,
          Massachusetts: Massachusetts Institute
          of Technology Press.

Bellah, Robert N.
    1967 "Civil Religion in America.: Daedalus
          96 (Winter): 1-21.

    1970 Beyond Belief: Essays on Religion in a
          Post-Traditional World. New York:
          Harper and Row.

Berelson, Bernard and Gary A. Steiner
   1964   Human Behavior: An Inventory of Scienti-
          fic Findings. New York: Harcourt, Brace
          and World.

Berger, Peter L., and Thomas Luckmann
   1966   The Social Construction of Reality: A
          Treatise in the Sociology of Knowledge.
          Garden City, N.Y.: Doubleday and
          Company.

Berger, Peter L.
   1969   The Sacred Canopy: Elements of a Socio-
          logical Theory of Religion. Garden
          City, N.Y.: Doubleday and Company.

   1970   A Rumor of Angels: Modern Society and
          the Rediscovery of the Supernatural.
          Garden City, N.Y.: Doubleday and
          Company.

Blalock, Hubert M., Jr.
   1969   Theory Construction: From Verbal to
          Mathematical Formulations. Englewood
          Cliffs: Prentice-Hall.

   1970   An Introduction to Social Research.
          Englewood Cliffs: Prentice-Hall.

   1972   Social Statistics, Second Edition. New
          York: McGraw-Hill.

Blau, Peter M. and Richard A. Schoenherr
   1971   The Structure of Organizations. New
          York: Basic Books.

Boguslaw, Robert
   1965   The New Utopians: A Study of System
          Design and Social Change. Englewood
          Cliffs: Prentice-Hall.

Breese, Gerald
   1966   Urbanization in Newly Developing Coun-
          tries. Englewood Cliffs: Prentice-Hall.

Buckley, Walter
 1967 Sociology and Modern Systems Theory.
   Englewood Cliffs: Prentice-Hall

Callahan, Daniel
 1967 "The Quest for Social Relevance."
   Daedalus 96 (Winter): 151-179.

Campbell, Donald T. and Julian C. Stanley
 1966 Experimental and Quasi-Experimental
   Designs for Research. Chicago: Rand
   McNally and Company.

Campion, Donald R.
 1967 "Jesuit Grass-Roots Renewal." America
   (February 25): 286.

Cantrel, Hadley
 1965 The Pattern of Human Concerns. New
   Brunswick, N.J.: Rutgers University
   Press.

Casey, Rick et al
 1974 "A Gospel as Varied as the World Itself:
   A Presentation of the Meeting on the
   International Dimensions of Our Jesuit
   Apostolates, Saint Paul, Minnesota,
   August 11-16, 1974." Studies in the
   International Apostolate of Jesuits III.
   (November): 1-100.

Chapin, F. Stuart
 1935 Contemporary American Institutions: A
   Sociological Analysis. New York:
   Harper and Bros.

Clarke, Thomas E., S.J.
 1975 "Ignatian Spirituality and Societal
   Consciousness." Studies in The
   Spirituality of Jesuits VII. (September):
   127-150.

Cogley, John
 1969 Religion in a Secular Age! The Search
   for Final Meaning. New York: The New

American Library.

Cook, Stuart W. (ed.)
    1962   "Review of Recent Research Bearing on
           Religious and Character Formation."
           Research Supplement to Religious Educa-
           tion LVII (July-August).

Cox, Harvey G.
    1965   The Secular City: A Celebration of Its
           Liberties and an Invitation to its
           Discipline. New York: Macmillan
           Company.

    1967   "The 'New Breed' in American Churches:
           Sources of Social Activism in American
           Religion." Daedalus 96 (Winter): 135-
           150.

Dommeyer, Frederick C. (ed.)
    1963   In Quest of Value: Readings in Philoso-
           phy and Personal Values. San Francisco:
           Chandler Publishing Company.

Dougherty, Philip L., C.F.X.
    1976   "Religious Life and The 'Signs of the
           Times'." America (February 28): 156-
           158.

Eisenstadt, S.N.
    1963   The Political Systems of Empires: The
           Rise and Fall of the Historical Bureau-
           cratic Societies. New York: The Free
           Press.

    1966   Modernization: Protest and Change.
           Englewood Cliffs: Prentice-Hall.

    1971   Social Differentiation and Stratification.
           Glenview, Illinois: Scott, Foresman and
           Company.

Ellis, John Tracy (ed.)
    1971   The Catholic Priest in The United States:
           Historical Investigations. Collegeville,

Minnesota: Saint John's University Press.

Etzioni, Amitai
1961 A Comparative Analysis of Complex Organizations: On Power, Involvement and Their Correlates. New York: The Free Press.

_____ and Eva Etzioni-Halevy (eds.)
1973 Social Change: Sources, Patterns and Consequences, Second Edition. New York: Basic Books.

Festinger, Leon and Daniel Katz (eds.)
1953 Research Methods in The Behavioral Sciences. New York: Holt, Rinehart and Winston.

Fichter, Joseph H., S.J.
1951 Southern Parish, Volume I: Dynamics of a City Church. Chicago, Illinois: University of Chicago Press.

1954 Social Relations in the Urban Parish. Chicago, Illinois: University of Chicago Press.

Foss, Michael
1969 The Founding of The Jesuits: 1540. London, Hamish Hamilton.

Fromm, Erich
1968 The Revolution of Hope: Toward a Humanized Technology. New York: Harper and Row.

Gamson, William A.
1968 Power and Discontent. Homewood, Illinois: The Dorsey Press.

Ganss, George E. et al
1972 "On Continuity and Change: A Symposium." Studies in the Spirituality of Jesuits IV. (October): 115-154.

General's Curia of The Society of Jesus
    1961 Collectio Decretorum Congregationum
          Generalium Societatis Iesu. Rome:
          General's Curia of The Society of Jesus.

    1967 Decreta: Congregationis Generalis
          XXXI: A Restituta Societate XII - Annis
          1965-1966. Rome: General's Curia of
          The Society of Jesus.

    1969 Praxis: Congregationis Provinciae.
          Rome: General's Curia of The Society
          of Jesus.

    1973a Formula Congregationis Generales:
          Congregationis Generalis XXXI Opera et
          Auctoritate Retructata. Rome: General's
          Curia of The Society of Jesus.

    1973b The Jesuits: Year-Book of The Society
          of Jesus 1973-1974, English Edition.
          Rome: General's Curia of The Society of
          Jesus.

    1975 The Jesuits: Year-Book of The Society of
          Jesus 1975-1976, English Edition. Rome:
          General's Curia of The Society of Jesus.

Glock, Charles Y. and Rodney Stark
    1965 Religion and Society in Tension. Chicago,
          Illinois: Rand McNally and Company.

                    Benjamin B. Ringer, and Earl R.
                    Babbie
    1967 To Comfort and to Challenge: A Dilemma
          of the Contemporary Church. Berkeley:
          University of California Press.

Greeley, Andrew M.
    1967 The Catholic Experience: An Interpre-
          tation of the History of American
          Catholicism. Garden City, N.Y.: Double-
          day and Company.

    1972a Priests in The United States: Reflections

       on a Survey. Garden City, N.Y.:
       Doubleday and Company.

  1972b The Denominational Society: A Socio-
       logical Approach to Religion in America.
       Glenview, Illinois: Scott, Foresman
       and Company.

Habermas, Jurgen
  1971 Toward a Rational Society: Student Pro-
       test, Science and Politics, translated
       by Jeremy Shapiro. Boston: Beacon Press.

  1973 Legitimation Crisis, translated by
       Thomas McCarthy. Boston: Beacon Press.

Henle, Robert J., S.J. (ed.)
  1967 Santa Clara Conference: Total Develop-
       ment of The Jesuit Priest Volumes I-IV.
       Santa Clara, California: University of
       Santa Clara.

Hennelly, Alfred T., S.J.
  1976 "'Church and World' and Theological
       Developments." America (February 28):
       153-156.

Jesuit Conference
  1974-1975 Project I: The Jesuit Apostolate
       of Education in The United States,
       Numbers 1-6. Washington, D.C. Jesuit
       Conference.

Kaplan, Abraham
  1964 The Conduct of Inquiry: Methodology for
       Behavioral Science. San Francisco:
       Chandler Publishing Company.

Katz, Daniel and Robert L. Kahn
  1966 The Social Psychology of Organizations.
       New York: John Wiley and Sons.

Kennedy, Eugene C. and Victor J. Heckler
  1972 The Catholic Priest in The United States:
       Psychological Investigations. Washington,

D.C.: United States Catholic Conference.

Kerlin, Michael J.
1973 "A New Modernist Crisis? Hardly."
America (October 6): 239-242.

King, Morton B. and Richard A. Hunt
1972 Measuring Religious Dimensions: Studies
of Congregational Involvement. Dallas:
Southern Methodist Press.

Kluckhohn, Clyde
1951 "Values and Value Orientations." Pp.
305-433 of Talcott Parsons and Edward A.
Shils, (eds.) Toward a General Theory
of Action. New York: Harper and Row.

1963 Mirror for Man. Greenwich, Conn.:
Fawcett Publications.

Kluckhohn, Florence
1950 "Dominant and Substitute Profiles of
Cultural Orientations: Their Significance for the Analysis of Social Strati-
fication." Social Forces 28 (May): 376-
393.

Lenski, Gerhard
1961 The Religious Factor. Garden City, N.Y.:
Doubleday and Company.

Lerner, Daniel (ed.)

1962 The Human Meaning of the Social Sciences.
Cleveland: Meridian Books.

L'Heureux, John
1969 "The New American Jesuits." The Atlantic
Monthly. (February)" 59-64.

Lonergan, Bernard J.F., S.J.
1957 Insight: A Study of Human Understanding.
New York: Longman, Green and Company.

1971   Docrinal Pluralism: The 1971 Pere
        Marquette Theology Lecture. Milwaukee:
        Marquette University Press.

1972   Method in Theology. New York: Herder
        and Herder.

Lundberg, George
    1948   "Semantics and the Value Problems."
            Social Forces 27 (October): 114-117.

    1952   "Science, Scientists, and Values."
            Social Forces 30 (May): 373-379.

Martin, David
    1969   The Religious and the Secular: Studies
            in Secularization. New York: Schocken
            Books.

Marty, Martin
    1967   "The Spirit's Holy Errand: The Search
            for a Spiritual Style in Secular America."
            Daedalus 96 (Winter): 99-115.

Maslow, Abraham H. (ed.)
    1959   New Knowledge in Human Values. New
            York: Harper and Row.

Meehan, Eugene J.
    1969   Value Judgment and Social Science.
            Homewood, Illinois: Dorsey Press.

Miller, Randolph C. (ed.)
    1974   "The Open Society: Shaping Religion and
            Values." Religious Education LXIX
            (March-April) 117-276.

Missouri Province of The Society of Jesus
    1969a General Resources: Some Informational
            Resources on History, Manpower and
            Finances. Saint Louis: Missouri Pro-
            vince Center for Jesuit Resources.

    1969b Attitudinal Resources: Santa Clara
            Survey: Jesuit Work, Community Life and

Comments. Saint Louis: Missouri Province Center for Jesuit Resources.

1969c Pastoral Resources: Some Informational Resources for the Pastoral Apostolate. Saint Louis: Missouri Province Center for Jesuit Resources.

1969d Secondary Educational Resources: Some Informational Resources for the High School Apostolate. Saint Louis: Missouri Province Center for Jesuit Resources.

1969e High Educational Resources: Some Informational Resources for the College and University Apostolate. Saint Louis: Missouri Province Center for Jesuit Resources.

Moberg, David O.
1962 The Church as a Social Institution: The Sociology of American Religion. Englewood Cliffs: Prentice-Hall.

Moore, Wilbert E.
1963 Social Change. Englewood Cliffs: Prentice-Hall.

Morris, Charles
1956 Varieties of Human Value. Chicago, Illinois: The University of Chicago Press.

Moser, C.A. and G. Kalton
1958 Survey Methods in Social Investigation. New York: Basic Books.

Nisbet, Robert A.
1969a Social Change and History: Aspects of the Western Theory of Development. London: Oxford University Press.

1969b The Quest for Community. London: Oxford University Press.

Nottingham, Elizabeth K.
    1971 Religion: A Sociological View. New
          York: Random House.

Novak, Michael
    1967 "Christianity: Renewed or Slowly
          Abandoned?" Daedalus 96 (Winter): 237-
          266.

O'Dea, Thomas F.
    1958 American Catholic Dilemma: An Inquiry
          into the Intellectual Life. New York:
          Sheed and Ward.

    1966 The Sociology of Religion. Englewood
          Cliffs: Prentice-Hall.

    1967 "The Crisis of Contemporary Conscious-
          ness." Daedalus 96 (Winter): 116-134.

O'Flaherty, Vincent J., S.J.
    1971 "Some Reflections on The Jesuit Commit-
          ment." Studies in the Spirituality of
          Jesuits III. (April): 33-67.

O'Hare, Joseph A., S.J.
    1972 "The Summer of '72." America (September
          30): 228-232.

Orsy, Ladislas, S.J.
    1973 "Toward a Theological Evaluation of
          Communal Discernment." Studies in the
          Spirituality of Jesuits V. (October):
          139-188.

    1975 "Faith and Justice: Some Reflections."
          Studies in the Spirituality of Jesuits
          VII. (September): 151-172.

Parsons, Talcott
    1951 The Social System. New York: The Free
          Press.

                   , Robert Bales and Edward Shils
    1953 Working Papers in The Theory of Action.

          Glencoe, Illinois: The Free Press.

Rahner, Karl
    1967 The Christian of the Future. Montreal:
          Palm Publishers.

    1972 The Shape of the Church to Come, trans-
          lated by Edward Quinn. London: SPCK.

Rashke, Richard, S.V.D.
    1972 "A Report on Phase Two of the Self-
          Study: Preliminary Descriptive Analysis
          of the Attitudinal Survey." Verbum
          Supplementum (9): Dialogi De Constitu-
          tionibus Nostris (5). Washington, D.C.:
          Society of the Divine Word Self-Study.

Rokeach, Milton
    1960 The Open and Closed Mind: Investigations
          into the Nature of Belief Systems and
          Personality Systems. New York: Basic
          Books.

    1964 The Three Christs of Ypsilanti: A
          Psychological Study. New York: Random
          House.

    1968 Beliefs, Attitudes, and Values: A
          Theory of Organization and Change. San
          Francisco: Jossey-Bass Inc., Publishers.

Rosenberg, Morris
    1968 The Logic of Survey Analysis. New York:
          Basic Books.

Schuyler, Joseph B., S.J.
    1960 Northern Parish: A Sociological and
          Pastoral Study. Chicago: Loyola Uni-
          versity Press.

Stark, Rodney and Charles Y. Glock
    1968 American Piety: The Nature of Religious
          Commitment. Berkeley: University of
          California Press.

Toner, Jules, J., S.J.
    1971 "A Method for Communal Discernment of
          God's Will." Studies in the Spirituality
          of Jesuits III. (September): 121-152.

Troeltsch, Ernst
    1931 The Social Teaching of the Christian
          Churches, translated by Olive Wyon.
          New York: Macmillan and Co.

Tyrrell, George
    1903 The Church and the Future. Edinburgh:
          Turnbull and Spears.

Washburne, Norman F.
    1954 Interpreting Social Change in America.
          New York: Random House.

Weber, Max
    1958 The Protestant Ethic and the Spirit of
          Capitalism, translated by Talcott Parsons
          with Foreword by R.H. Tawney. New York:
          Charles Scribner's Sons.

    1971 The Interpretation of Social Reality,
          edited by J.E.T. Eldridge. London:
          Michael Joseph.

Weick, Karl
    1969 The Social Psychology of Organizing.
          Reading, Massachusetts: Addison-Wesley
          Publishing Company.

Wendling, Ronald C.
    1973 "The Modern Catholic as Parricide."
          America (November 17): 375-377.

Williams, Robin M., Jr.
    1968 "The Concept of Values" in International
          Encyclopedia of The Social Sciences. New
          York: Macmillan and The Free Press.

    1973 "Continuity and Change in Recent Research
          on Social Institutions." The Annals of
          The American Academy of Political and

Social Science 406 (March).

Winter, Gibson
    1963   The New Creation as Metropolis: A
            Design for the Church's Task in an Urban
            World. New York: Macmillan Company.

    1968   Religious Identity: A Study of Religious
            Organization. New York: Macmillan
            Company.

Woodward, Kenneth L.
    1976   "The Birth-Control Factor (A Review of
            Andrew Greeley et al, Catholic Schools
            in a Declining Church)." Newsweek
            (April 5): 57.

Yinger, J. Milton
    1961   Sociology Looks At Religion. New York:
            The Macmillan Company.

APPENDIX ONE

DATA COLLECTION INSTRUMENTS

The following pages contain facsimiles of the questionnaires that were sent to all of the delegates of the Thirty-Second General Congregation of the Society of Jesus and to a one percent random sample of non-delegates who were also members of the Society of Jesus.

Two questionnaires were mailed out. The first was administered in the month preceding the Congregation (October-November, 1974) and the second was administered a month after the Congregation adjourned (April, 1975).

The initial questionnaire had been preceded by a personal mailing to every potential respondent. This mailing included a letter of introduction and recommendation of the researcher by Father John Swain, S.J. of Guelph, Ontario. Father Swain is known of by virtually every Jesuit in the world. He was Vicar General of the Society of Jesus under the preceding General. It was Father Swain who convoked the Thirty-First General Congregation. The mailing also included a letter of introduction and explanation of the project written by the researcher. A follow-up letter was sent one month after the questionnaire was mailed to remind the respondents and to ask them again to complete the questionnaire.

Since the second questionnaire was mailed only to the respondents who completed the first questionnaire, no introductory or reminder letters were sent.

The contents of this appendix are as follows:

"Before" Questionnaire

- English Version

- Spanish Version

- French Version

- German Version

- Italian Version

"After" Questionnaire

- English Version

- Spanish Version

- French Version

- German Version

- Italian Version

Jesuit   Organizational   Analysis

Dear Delegate, P.C.

The questions contained here provide a vital part of an organizational analysis of the values of the Society of Jesus. As a delegate
to the Thirty-Second General Congregation, your generous efforts will
help guide us for years to come. This survey is part of a reverent
and grateful reflection on this guidance.

Please answer the questions on the following pages by simply
encircling the number or letter next to what you consider to be the
most appropriate response. Because the delegates to the Congregation
comprise a small number of Jesuits, it is very important to have your
responses. I deeply ask and pray, therefore, that you will return
the completed survey in the enclosed envelope. If you attend to this
in the next day or two, it is less apt to interfere with the many
concerns you must have in preparing to travel to Rome.

You have my fullest assurance that all information gathered
in this survey will remain in my very strictest confidence. No one
else will have access to identification of this data; no superiors
or other Jesuits or any one else will be provided any specific
information about who answered what question in what way. No report
whatsoever will be made of this information before the Thirty-Second
General Congregation has completed its work and come to final adjournment.

I apologize for not providing postage for the return mailing.
The numerous nations involved in this survey make it impossible to
provide postage proper to each nation.

Thank you very much for your attention to this survey. You
will receive a resume of all findings from this study in return for
your kind and significant assistance.

God bless you and your efforts on behalf of all Jesuits.
My prayers and Masses will ask His Grace for you daily.

Sincerely,

(Rev.) Thomas P. Faase, S.J.

Code # _____

This number is for identification
of the data and will not be associated with the respondent in any
other way. No names are required
on this survey.

Please answer the questions below according to the following choice of responses.

1. Agree strongly.
2. Agree some what.
3. Uncertain.
4. Disagree somewhat.
5. Disagree strongly.

(PLEASE CIRCLE ONE CODE ON EACH LINE)

The future is in God's hands. I will await what He sends and accept what comes as His will for me.   1 2 3 4 5

The creative ferment in the Church today is bringing about a deepening of my Christian faith.   1 2 3 4 5

The problem with the Church after Vatican II is that many of the certainties we used to have have been taken away.   1 2 3 4 5

The turmoil following Vatican II is resulting in a gradual weakening of my own religious beliefs.   1 2 3 4 5

There are times when a person has to put his personal conscience above the Church's teaching.   1 2 3 4 5

One's faith may be jeopardized by studying Protestant theologians.   1 2 3 4 5

The spirit of poverty is meaningless without poverty in fact.   1 2 3 4 5

Poverty means dependence on the community for all one's material needs.   1 2 3 4 5

The traditional way of presenting the vow of chastity in religious formation has often allowed for the development of impersonalism and false spirituality.   1 2 3 4 5

The duty of the subject is to obey; it is the responsability of the superior to discern God's will and declare it.   1 2 3 4 5

It is advisable for Jesuits to concern themselves with regional or national projects they are competent to serve even if the fruit of such concerns serve neither the Province nor the institution that the Jesuit belongs to.   1 2 3 4 5

The work and purposes of the entire Society of Jesus at the International level deserve precedence over all other levels of effectiveness whenever a Jesuit has opportunity to exert influence at that level.   1 2 3 4 5

Any organizational structure becomes a deadening weight in time and needs to be revitalized.   1 2 3 4 5

I would rather be called an idealist than a practical man.   1 2 3 4 5

When I think of social reform, I think of things I believe in so deeply I could dedicate all my efforts to them.   1 2 3 4 5

A priest can hardly call himself a shepherd if he is not as deeply involved in the social welfare of people as he is in giving spiritual service to his parishioners.   1 2 3 4 5

When I am dealing with the problems of my own job, I find myself constantly trying to make decisions that will help solve the bigger issues of justice, etc., for all mankind. The world's problems are very much my problems   1 2 3 4 5

The current situation in the Church calls for change. We must respond at once.   1 2 3 4 5

Liberalism is a good thing because it represents a spirit of reform. It is an optimistic outlook expecting meaningful advance. It may not always represent justice, light, and wisdom, but it always tries to.   1 2 3 4 5

Every great step forward in world history has been accomplished trough the inspiration of reformers and creative men.   1 2 3 4 5

Some concerns of an individual Jesuit's work in the apostolate are necessarily subservient to the institution or Jesuit team-effort of which he is a part.   1 2 3 4 5

The Province has the right to expect a Jesuit to work on Province-wide tasks even if that work interferes with the individual's attention to his own apostolate and the institution he belongs to.   1 2 3 4 5

Even when working in their native countries, Jesuits should generally avoid taking strong public positions on religious or social issues.   1 2 3 4 5

In my Province the Society seems to be more concerned with providing for people than teaching them how to provide for themselves.   1 2 3 4 5

The activities of my Province are sufficiently concerned with the poor and those held in low esteem.   1 2 3 4 5

Please check the **Assistancy** that you belong to:
(circle the one code, i. e. number or letter, that applies)

1.- Italian

2.- German

3.- French

4.- Spanish

5.- English

6.- American

7.- Slavic

8.- Northern Latin American

9.- Southern Latin American

10.- Indian

11.- East Asian

12.- African

Please check, in general, the kind of work you do full time :
(circle the code that applies)

A. Supra-institutions administration
(e. g. Provincial, Mission director)

B. Institution of higher learning : administration
(e. g. President or Rector of University)

C. Institution of secondary education : administration
(High school President or Rector or Principal)

D. Higher education : teaching (and allied research)

E. Secondary school : teaching (and allied research)

F. Parish administration or pastoral work

G. Writing or Research full time

H. Social Apostolate, socio-economic development

I. Formation of Ours, of other clerics; seminary administration

J. Other : (please specify) _____

What is your age :
(circle the code that applies)

A. Under 30

B. 30 – 39

C. 40 – 49

D. 50 – 59

E. 60 – 69

F. 70 or over.

Which do you consider your work to be:
(circle the code that applies)

1. Mainly task-oriented, geared to a job to be done.

2. Mainly person-oriented, the care and service of people.

Which of the following would you say is your Province's first concern :
(circle the code that applies)

A. Adapting means to its desired goals, deployment of resources.

B. Seeing the accomplishments of stated goals, attainment of objectives by coordination and executive management.

C. Fitting the works and accomplishments of the Province into an overall pattern : helping to define the identity of the Province.

D. Preserving the traditions of the Province and the Society and maintaining the religious life and well being of its members.

Which of the following would you say is your Province's second concern :
(circle the code that applies)

A. Adapting means to its desired goals, deployment of resources.

B. Seeing the accomplishments of stated goals, attainment of objectives by coordination and executive management.

C. Fitting the works and accomplishments of the Province into an overall pattern; helping to define the identity of the Province.

D. Preserving the traditions of the Province and the Society and maintaining the religious life and well being of its members.

The major thrust and concern of the Thirty - Second Congregation will probably be :
(choose the one you expect)

A. DOCTRINAL : to give definitions or explanations, to make statements about our beliefs, our goals.

B. PASTORAL : to exhort, encourage.

C. PRACTICAL : to reform structures, legislate procedures.

Broadly speaking, which of the following seem to govern the majority of decisions made by your Province and its major institutions :
(circle the code that applies)

A. Religious

B. Political

C. Economic

D. Cura Personalis

The members of my province are sufficiently receptive to local values and sensitivites in their people's liturgy.

1 2 3 4 5

The Society as a whole is sufficiently open to cultural variations in the expression of our Religious life and community.

1 2 3 4 5

When working in foreing countries, Jesuits should avoid taking strong public positions on religious or social issues.

1 2 3 4 5

In the last analysis, it's having the power that makes the difference.

1 2 3 4 5

No matter how wonderful the ideals you are trying to get across may be, you cannot do a thing unless you have the powers that be on your side.

1 2 3 4 5

When you come right down to it, it's human nature never to do anything without an eye to one's own profit.

1 2 3 4 5

In a Jesuit's work, the immediate and overall needs of the particular apostolate he serves warrant his primary consideration and effort.

1 2 3 4 5

By continuing its traditional approach to its teaching role, the Church will better accomplish its mission than by experimenting with new methods.

1 2 3 4 5

In the final analysis the strongest basis for planning for the future is to trust to the experience of the past and base the decision-making on the facts, the historical facts.

1 2 3 4 5

I like conservantism because it represents a stand to preserve our glorious heritage.

1 2 3 4 5

During the past 10 years many religious have changed some of the basic principles and values which they formerly believed in.

1 2 3 4 5

The Basic Values of the Church remain the same, but their expression is changing.

1 2 3 4 5

On the lines below, please NAME the three delegates that you expect will exert the strongest influence at this General Congregation :

_____

_____

_____

Below are five categories of social class. Please read these and answer the questions following:

1. Poor people, having no regular means of support or a standard of living below what is considered in your part of the country as the minimum necesseary for subsiding.

2. People who are not skilled workers, but have the minimun required for subsistence according to the standards in your part of the country.

3. Middle class people according to the standards of your part of the country. Usually this group will include office workers, small shopkeepers, farmers, skilled workers, school teachers, etc.

4. People who have an income permiting them to enjoy more than the usual luxuries of life relative to your part of the country. Usually this group will include landowners, managers, physicians, businessmen, teachers at 'higher educational institutions', etc.

5. Rich people. The most influential people in the part of the country in which you are working, such as big landowners, big businessmen, government officials, etc.

Which of the categories above do the people that you serve most of the time belong to?

Category 1 _____

Category 2 _____

Category 3 _____

Category 4 _____

Category 5 _____

Which of the categories above do you feel your parents belonged to when you were growing up?

Category 1 _____

Category 2 _____

Category 3 _____

Category 4 _____

Category 5 _____

Which of the categories above do you think the life style that you presently have as a Jesuit fits into?

Category 1 _____

Category 2 _____

Category 3 _____

Category 4 _____

Category 5 _____

Below is a list of 18 values in alphabetical order. We are interested in finding out the relative importance of these values to you.

Study the list carefully. Then place a 1 next to the value which is most important to you, place a 2 next to the value which is second most important, etc. The value which is least important should be ranked 18.

We realize that each of the terms is capable of many subtle differences in meaning. Nonetheless, order these values without becoming overly analytical about their meaning.

When you have completed ranking all the values, go back and check over your list. Feel free to make changes. Please take all the time you need to think about this, so that the end result truly represents yours values.

_____ A COMFORTABLE LIFE (a prosperous life)

_____ AN EXCITING LIFE (a stimulating, active life)

_____ A SENSE OF ACCOMPLISHMENT (lasting contribution)

_____ A WORLD AT PEACE (free of war and conflict)

_____ A WORLD OF BEAUTY (beauty of nature and the arts)

_____ EQUALITY (brotherhood, equal opportunity for all)

_____ FAMILY SECURITY (taking care of loved ones)

_____ FREEDOM (independence, free choice)

_____ HAPPINESS (contentedness)

_____ INNER HARMONY (freedom fron inner conflict)

_____ MATURE LOVE (sexual and spiritual intimacy)

_____ NATIONAL SECURITY (protection from attack)

_____ PLEASURE (an enjoyable, leisurely life)

_____ SALVATION (saved, eternal life)

_____ SELF - RESPECT (self-esteem)

_____ SOCIAL RECOGNITION (respect, admiration)

_____ TRUE FRINDSHIP (close companionship)

_____ WISDOM (a mature understanding of life)

Below is another list of 18 values. Arrange them in order of importance, the same as before.

_____ AMBITIOUS (hard-working, aspiring)

_____ BROADMINDED (open-minded)

_____ CAPABLE (competent, effective)

_____ CHEERFUL (lighthearted, joyful)

_____ CLEAN (neat, tidy)

_____ COURAGEOUS (standing up for your beliefs)

_____ FORGIVING (willing to pardon others)

_____ HELPFUL (working for the welfare of others)

_____ HONEST (sincere, truthful)

_____ IMAGINATIVE (daring, creative)

_____ INDEPENDENT (self-reliant, self-sufficient)

_____ INTELLECTUAL (intelligent, reflective)

_____ LOGICAL (consistent, rational)

_____ LOVING (affectionate, tender)

_____ OBEDIENT (dutiful, respectful)

_____ POLITE (courteous, well-mannered)

_____ RESPONSIBLE (dependable, reliable)

_____ SELF-CONTROLLED (restrained, self-disciplined)

Each of the following statements describes an aspect of GOD. By God I mean :
(choose the ONE you find most appealing)

a. the all-knowing and all-powerful Lord of Creation.

b. the loving Father who sent His Son to reveal the mysteries of Divine Grace.

c. the Divine Presence in this world whom I discover through people, things and events.

Each of the following statements describes an aspect of the HOLY SPIRIT.
(Choose the ONE you find most appealing)

a. The Holy Spirit guides the Church to a better understanding of Christ's message and to internal unity by speaking through the entire people of God.

b. The Holy Spirit, who proceeds from the Father and the Son, distributes God's grace to men.

c. The Holy Spirit speaks to all men of good will in different ways and under different circumstances throughout history.

The purpose of missionary activity is:
(choose the ONE you find most appealing)

a. to convert people to the Catholic Church through preaching, teaching catechetics, administering the sacraments, etc.

b. to help man develop his own resources to ful-fill total human needs, i.e. religious, economic, educational, political.

c. to be a witness of God's love, preach the Gospel and form the Church among people who do not yet know about Christ.

d. not clear to me.

Each of the following statements describes an aspect of CHURCH.
(Choose the ONE you find most appealing)

a. As mediator of God's truth and grace to men, the Church is the only true way to salvation.

b. The Church is a perfect, religious society organized under the Pope and the Bishops.

c. As the People of God intimately related with Christ, the Church is a sacrament or sign of man's union with God and with each other.

d. The Church is the prophetic critic of society and culture.

e. The Church, as a pilgrim in this world, is a servant of mankind's total needs, i.e. religious, economic, educational and political.

Each of the following statements describes some aspects of the relation of the Church to the World. By this relationship I mean:
(choose the ONE you find most appealing)

a. The Church, in the depths of human existence, is the place from which arises the Word of which she is the witness in answer to questions which she herself has not raised. The Church would do well to go the limit of deinstitutionalizing her own works and endeavoring to collaborate closely with priests, laity, and secular interests to give rise to this witness. First priority must be with the poor, sharing their life to the full.

b. The Church is the sacrament of Salvation which comes from above. Radically different from the world, She must draw men and bring them in the Community of the Baptized. Hence, priorities must be accorded to spiritual and sacerdotal ministries. Reforming itself from within, the Church must work in the total content of its pastoral services and maintain its concern for an integral humanism developing in the light of faith.

Each of the following statements describes an aspect of the WORLD.
(Choose the ONE you find most appealing)

a. The world is the arena where man proves himself for God by trusting in His Providence and following His will.

b. The world is good, and God's creative activity continues through the development of man and his culture to make it even better.

c. The world, created and sustained by God's love, became enslaved by man's sin but has been set free by the love of Christ.

Each of the following statements describes an aspect of MINISTRY. A Christian minister is:
(choose the ONE you find most appealing)

a. someone who has been authorized by the people of God to build christian community lead it in its celebration of God's grace, and inspire it to share actively in the world's concerns.

b. someone ordained to the priesthood and thereby authorized to celebrate the Eucharist and administer the sacraments of Penance and Anointing the Sick.

c. someone whose fundamental obligation is to spread Christ's Gospel and to administer the sacraments to the faithful.

Each of the following statements describes an aspect of FAITH. By Faith I mean:
(choose the ONE you find most appealing)

a. an affirmation of the ultimate goodness of man and this world.

b. an assurance of salvation.

c. a personal relationship with God.

d. an affirmation of God's Providence in my life.

e. an acceptance of the teachings of the Church

f. a total surrender of myself to God.

Each of the following statements describes some aspects of CULTURE. By Culture I mean:
(choose the ONE you find most appealing)

a. Culture is best conceived of empirically. It is the set of meanings and values informing a common way of life, and there are as many cultures as there are distinct sets of such meanings and values. Such meanings and values are to be understood relative to the contexts and cultures from which they emerge.

b. Culture is best conceived of normatively. It is a matter of acquiring and assimilating the tastes and skills, the ideals, virtues and ideas of refined upbringing and the liberal arts. It is as universalist as the immortal works of art and perennial philosophy.

Each of the following statements describes an aspect of CHRIST.
(choose the ONE you find most appealing)

a. As the Risen Lord, Christ is the liberator of all those oppressed by the forces of this world.

b. As the incarnate, suffering Son of God, Christ is our Mediator and Redeemer.

c. As the maturest and holiest man who ever was or will be, Christ is the embodiment of God in human nature and history.

d. As truly God, Christ is our Lord to whom adoration is due.

Each of the following statements describes an aspect of AUTHORITY.
(Choose the ONE you find most appealing)

a. Authority flows from the office of a superior; the response is obedience.

b. Authority flows from the able coordination and direction of activities; the response is a co-responsible implementation of directives.

c. Authority flows from a personal charism to inspire and encourage others; the response is trust in the leader's charism.

Each of the following statements describes an aspect of PRAYER.
(Choose the ONE you find most appealing)

a. Prayer is lifting up my mind and heart to God.

b. Prayer is my encounter with God by serving the needs of others.

c. Prayer is my sensitivity and response to the personal God.

d. Prayer is the work I am doing.

Each of the following statements describes an aspect of SALVATION.
(Choose the ONE you find most appealing)

a. All Christian Churches are channels of God's saving grace for men.

b. The Catholic Church is the medium of God's saving grace for men.

c. All religions are channels of God's saving grace for men.

d. God's grace of salvation is equally at work within each man.

Think of the professional men you know – for example, doctors, dentists, lawyers, scientists. How do you think Jesuit priests of your Province would generally compare to them in regard to the following attributes?

CIRCLE ONE CODE ON EACH LINE.

	With some exceptions, most Jesuits of my Province ...				
	have more	have about same	have less	have much less	don't know
Depth of knowledge and skill.	1	2	3	4	5
Autonomy to make decisions.	1	2	3	4	5
Responsibility for an undertaking.	1	2	3	4	5
Commitment to serving the needs of people.	1	2	3	4	5
Satisfaction and self-esteem gained from one's work.	1	2	3	4	5

THANK YOU VERY MUCH

Analisis

Organizacional

Jesuistico

Estimado Delegado, P. C.

Las preguntas aquí incluídas proveen una parte vital de un análisis organizacional de los valores de la Compañía de Jesús. Como un delegado a la Congregación General Treinta y Dos sus esfuerzos generosos nos guiarán a través de muchos años. Este survey por lo tanto es parte de una reflexión seria y generosa sobre ésta guía.

Por favor responda a las preguntas en las páginas siguientes encerrando en un círculo el número o la letra en frente de lo que Ud. considere sea la respuesta más apropiada. Como los delegados a la Congregación comprenden un número pequeño de Jesuítas, por lo tanto es muy importante el tener sus respuestas. Por lo tanto, sinceramente le pido, que me retorne el cuestionario una vez completado, en el sobre aquí incluído. Si Ud. presta atención a este pequeño pedido de inmediato, yo le aseguro que dejará de ser un posible obstáculo en el medio de todos los otros negocios a los cuales debe prestar atención como preparación para su viaje a Roma.

De antemano le aseguro que toda la información adquirida como resultado de este survey permanecerá en mi más estricta confidencia. Ninguna otra persona tendrá acceso a la identificación de este material; ningún superior ni otros jesuítas o cualquier otra persona podrá proveerse de alguna información específica concerniente a quien o como determinadas preguntas fueron respondidas. Además, ningún reportaje de ésta información se hará público hasta que la Congregación General haya completado su trabajo y haya llegado a la clausura final.

Le pido excusas al no poder proveer el valor adecuado para el correo de regreso. El número cuantioso de naciones que están tomando parte de este survey me hacen imposible el proveer el valor adecuado de correos para cada nación.

Desde ahora le agradezco su atención y colaboración en éste survey. Al mismo tiempo le prometo un resumen de todos los resultados de éste estudio, como apreciación por su asistencia significativa y generosa.

Que Dios bendiga todos sus esfuerzos en nombre de todos los Jesuítas. Cuente también con mis misas y oraciones diarias, pidiendo a Dios por un aumento de Su gracia.

Sinceramente,

Thomas P. Faase, SJ

(Rev.) Thomas P. Faase, S.J.

Clave _____

Este número es estrictamente para la identificación del material aquí incluído y no será asociado en ninguna forma con la persona que lo responda. Nombres de personas no son necesarios en este survey.

Por favor indique la Asistencia a que pertenece :
(Haga un círculo alrededor de la clave, i. e.
número o letra que corresponda.)

1.- Italiana

2.- Alemana

3.- Francesa

4.- Española

5.- Inglesa

6.- Americana

7.- Eslava

8.- América Latina Septentrional

9.- América Latina Meridional

10.- India

11.- Asia Oriental

12.- Africana

Por favor indique, en general, el tipo de trabajo que desempeña tiempo completo :
(Haga un círculo alrededor de la clave que corresponda.)

A. Administración Superior - Institucional
(e.g. Provincial, Director de Misiones)

B. Institución de estudios superiores : administración
(e.g. Presidente o Rector de Universidad)

C. Institución de educación secundaria : administración
(e.g. Presidente, Rector o Director Académico de Colegio)

D. Estudios superiores : Enseñanza (y campo relacionado de investigación)

E. Educación secundaria : Enseñanza (y campo relacionado de investigación)

F. Administración de Parroquia o trabajo pastoral

G. Escritor o investigador tiempo completo

H. Apostolado Social, desarrollo socio - económico

I. Formación de los nuestros, de otros clérigos, administración de seminario

J. Otro (especifique) _____

Cual es su edad :
(haga un círculo en la clave que corresponda)

A. Menos de 30

B. 30 - 39

C. 40 - 49

D. 50 - 59

E. 60 - 69

F. 70 o más.

Cual considera Ud. como su trabajo :
(Haga un círculo alrededor de la clave que corresponda)

1. Principalmente orientado al trabajo manual dirigido a un trabajo determinado.

2. Principalmente orientado a las personas, al servicio y cuidado de la gente.

Cual de los siguientes diría Ud. es la preocupación primordial de su Provincia :
(Haga un círculo alrededor de la clave que corresponda)

A. Adaptar los medios para el fin deseado, despliegue de recursos.

B. Mirar a la realización de los fines establecidos, logro de objetivos a través de coordinación y dirección ejecutiva.

C. Acomodar los trabajos y realizaciones de la Provincia dentro de un modelo general; ayudar a definir la identidad de la Provincia.

D. Preservar las tradiciones de la Provincia y de la Compañía y mantener la vida religiosa y el bienestar de sus miembros.

Cual de los siguientes diría Ud. es la preocupación secundaria de su Provincia :
(Haga un círculo alrededor de la clave que corresponda)

A. Adaptar los medios para el fin deseado, despliegue de recursos.

B. Mirar a la realización de los fines establecidos, logro de objetivos a través de coordinación y dirección ejecutiva.

C. Acomodar los trabajos y realizaciones de la Provincia dentro de un modelo general; ayudar a definir la identidad de la Provincia.

D. Preservar las tradiciones de la Provincia y de la Compañía y mantener la vida religiosa y el bienestar de sus miembros.

El mayor empuje y preocupación de la Congregación General Treinta y Dos probablemente será :
(Escoja por Ud. espera.)

A. DOCTRINAL : dar definiciones o explicaciones, hacer declaraciones acerca de nuestras creencias y nuestros fines.

B. PASTORAL : exhortar, animar.

C. PRACTICO : reformar las estructuras, legislar procedimientos.

Ampliamente hablando, cual de los siguientes parece gobernar la mayoría de las decisiones hechas por su Provincia y sus instituciones mayores:
(Haga un círculo en la clave que corresponda)

A. Religioso

B. Político

C. Económico

D. Cura Personalis

Por favor, responda las preguntas que siguen de acuerdo con las siguientes alternativas:

1. Fuertemente de acuerdo.
2. Algo de acuerdo.
3. Dudoso.
4. Un tanto en desacuerdo.
5. Fuertemente en desacuerdo.

(POR FAVOR HAGA UN CIRCULO EN UNA CLAVE DE CADA UNA DE LAS LINEAS)

El futuro está en las manos de Dios. Esperaré lo que El envíe y acepto lo que venga como Su voluntad para mí.   1 2 3 4 5

El fermento creativo de hoy en la Iglesia me lleva a una profundización de mi fe cristiana.   1 2 3 4 5

El problema con la Iglesia después del Vaticano II es que muchas de las certezas que teníamos han desaparecido.   1 2 3 4 5

La confusión que sigue al Vaticano II está resultando en un gradual debilitamiento de mis creencias religiosas.   1 2 3 4 5

Hay veces que la persona tiene que poner su conciencia personal sobre las enseñanzas de la Iglesia.   1 2 3 4 5

La fe de uno puede peligrar por el estudio de teólogos protestantes.   1 2 3 4 5

El espíritu de pobreza no tiene sentido sin pobreza de hecho.   1 2 3 4 5

Pobreza significa dependencia de la comunidad en las necesidades materiales.   1 2 3 4 5

La forma tradicional de presentar el voto de castidad en la formación religiosa ha permitido a menudo el desarrollo del impersonalismo y falsa espiritualidad.   1 2 3 4 5

El deber del sujeto es el de obedecer; la responsabilidad del superior es la de discernir la voluntad de Dios y manifestarla.   1 2 3 4 5

Es aconsejable para los jesuitas interesarse con proyectos regionales o nacionales en los cuales ellos son competentes para servir, aún si el fruto de tales intereses no sirvan ni a la Provincia ni a la Institución a que el jesuita pertenezca.   1 2 3 4 5

Los trabajos e intenciones de toda la Compañía de Jesús a nivel internacional merecen prioridad sobre todos los otros niveles de efectividad siempre y cuando un jesuita tenga la oportunidad de ejercer influencia en ese nivel.   1 2 3 4 5

Cualquiera estructura organizacional se convierte en un peso muerto con el tiempo y necesita ser revitalizada.   1 2 3 4 5

Yo preferiría ser llamado un idealista en lugar de un hombre práctico.   1 2 3 4 5

Cuando pienso en reforma social, yo pienso en cosas que creo tan profundamente que podría dedicar todos mis esfuerzos a ellas.   1 2 3 4 5

Un sacerdote difícilmente puede llamarse pastor si no está tan profundamente envuelto en el bienestar social de la gente como lo está en dar servicio espiritual a sus feligreses.   1 2 3 4 5

Cuando estoy resolviendo los problemas de mi propio negocio, me encuentro constantemente tratando de hacer decisiones que ayudarán a resolver los asuntos más importants de justicia, etc. , para todo el mundo. Los problemas del mundo son profundamente mis problemas.   1 2 3 4 5

La situación actual en la Iglesia pide de un cambio. Debemos responder de inmediato.   1 2 3 4 5

El liberalismo es una cosa buena porque éste representa un espíritu de reforma. Es una visión optimista que espera avances significativos. No representará justicia, luz y virtud, pero siempre lo trata.   1 2 3 4 5

Cada paso adelante en la historia del mundo ha sido obtenido a través de la inspiración de reformadores y hombres creadores.   1 2 3 4 5

Algunos de los intereses del trabajo individual de un jesuíta en el apostolado están necesariamente subordinados a la institución o al esfuerzo del equipo jesuístico del cual él es parte.   1 2 3 4 5

La Provincia tiene el derecho a demandar de un jesuíta el trabajar en empresas que abarquen toda la Provincia aún si este trabajo interfiere con la preocupación del individuo por su propio apostolado y de la Institución a la que pertenece.   1 2 3 4 5

Aún cuando trabajen en sus países nativos, los jesuítas deberían en general abstenerse de tomar fuertes posiciones públicas en custiones sociales o religiosas.   1 2 3 4 5

La Compañía en mi Provincia parece ocuparse más en abastecer al pueblo que en enseñarle como ayudarse a sí mismo.   1 2 3 4 5

Las actividades de mi Provincia están suficientemente comprometidas con los pobres y con los tenidos en baja estima.   1 2 3 4 5

Los miembros de mi Provincia están suficientemente abiertos a los valores locales y a la sensibilidad del pueblo en la realización de las ceremonias litúrgicas.   1 2 3 4 5

La Compañía en general está suficientemente abierta a las variaciones culturales en la expresión de la vida religiosa y de la comunidad.   1 2 3 4 5

Los jesuítas que trabajan en países extranjeros deberían abstenerse de tomar fuertes posiciones públicas en cuestiones sociales o religiosas.   1 2 3 4 5

En el último análisis, lo que hace la diferencia es tener el poder.   1 2 3 4 5

No importa que tan maravillosamente sean los ideales que tú quieras comunicar, tú no puedes hacer nada a noser que tengas el poder que sea de tu parte.   1 2 3 4 5

Cuando llegamos a la realidad de los hechos, es propio de la naturaleza humana el nunca hacer nada sin poner un ojo al provecho propio.   1 2 3 4 5

En el trabaj o propio de un jesuíta, las necesidades totales e inmediatas del apostolado particular en el que sirve merecen su esfuerzo y consideración primordial.   1 2 3 4 5

La Iglesia alcanzará mucho mejor su misión continuando su actitud tradicional de sus enseñanzas que a través de experimentaciones con nuevos métodos.   1 2 3 4 5

En última instancia las bases más fuertes para el planeamiento del futuro es el confiar en la experiencia del pasado y basar las decisiones que se hacen en los hechos, los hechos históricos.   1 2 3 4 5

Me gusta el conservadurismo porque éste representa la base para preservar nuestra gloriosa herencia.   1 2 3 4 5

Durante los pasados diez años, muchos religiosos han cambiado algunos de los principios y valores básicos en los cuales ellos creían anteriormente.   1 2 3 4 5

Los valores básicos de la Iglesia permanecen estables, pero su forma de expresión está cambiando.   1 2 3 4 5

En las líneas de abajo, por favor escriba el NOMBRE de los tres delegados que Ud. espera ejercerán la influencia más fuerte en ésta Congregación General :

_____

_____

_____

Debajo hay cinco categoría de clases sociales. Por favor, léalas y responda las preguntas siguientes.

1.   Gente pobre, los que no tienen los medios regulares de sustento o un nivel de vida por debajo de lo que es considerado en la parte de su país como el mínimo necesario para subsistir.

2.   Gente que no son peritos en un oficio determinado, pero que tienen el mínimo requerido para subsistir de acuerdo con los niveles económicos en su parte de su país.

3.   La gente de clase media de acuerdo con los niveles o standards de su región. Generalmente este grupo incluiría trabajadores de oficina, pequeños negocios, agricultores, trabajadores de oficio, maestros de escuela, etc.

4.   Gente que tiene un salario que les permite gozar más ampliamente de los lujos que son permitidos en su región de su país. Por lo general este grupo incluiría terratenientes, administradores, médicos, hombres de negocios, profesores de instituciones de educación superior, etc.

5.   Gente rica, la gente más influyente en la parte del país en la cual usted está trabajando, tales como grandes terratenientes, grandes negociantes, oficiales del gobierno, etc.

A cual de las categorías antes mencionadas cree usted que sus padres pertenecieron cuando usted era joven?

Categoría 1 _____

Categoría 2 _____

Categoría 3 _____

Categoría 4 _____

Categoría 5 _____

A cual de las categorías antes mencionadas cree usted que corresponde el estilo de vida que vive en el presente como jesuíta?

Categoría 1 _____

Categoría 2 _____

Categoría 3 _____
Categoría 4_____

Categoría 5 _____

A cual de las categorías antes mencionadas pertenece la gente que usted sirve la mayoría del tiempo?

Categoría 1 _____

Categoría 2 _____

Categoría 3 _____

Categoría 4 _____

Categoría 5 _____

A continuación se presenta una lista de 18 valores ordenados alfabéticamente. Estos valores tienen que ordenarse de acuerdo con la importancia para USTED, como principios que guían su vida.

Estudie la lista cuidadosamente; luego ponga el número 1 al valor que sea el más importante para usted, el número 2 para el valor que le sigue en importancia, etc. El valor que tenga la menor importancia, en relación con los demás, consecuentemente, deberá tener el número 18.

Nos damos cuenta que cada uno de los términos tiene diferentes matices en su significado. Sin embargo, ordene estos valores sin llegar a ser demasiado analítico con relación a su significado.

Piense con cuidado, y tome el tiempo necesario. Si usted cambia de opinión, tome la libertad de cambiar sus respuestas a las más apropiadas. Los resultados finales deberán mostrar lo que Ud. siente verdaderamente.

_____ AMISTAD SINCERA (compañerismo)

_____ AMOR MADURO (intimidad sexual y espiritual)

_____ FELICIDAD (contento)

_____ IGUALDAD (hermandad, igualdad de oportunidades para todos)

_____ LIBERTAD (independencia, libre elección)

_____ PAZ INTERNA (libre de conflictos internos)

_____ PLACER (una vida deleitable y despreocupada)

_____ RECONOCIMIENTO SOCIAL (respeto, admiración)

_____ RESPETO A SI MISMO (estimación personal)

_____ SABIDURIA (entendimiento de la vida)

_____ SALVACION (salvación del alma y vida eterna)

_____ SEGURIDAD FAMILIAR (proporcionar cuidados a los seres queridos)

_____ SEGURIDAD NACIONAL (protección contra ataques)

_____ UN MUNDO DE PAZ (libre de guerra y conflictos)

_____ UN MUNDO DE BELLEZA (belleza de la naturaleza y las artes)

_____ UN SENTIMIENTO DE LOGRO (una contribución permanente)

_____ UNA VIDA COMODA (una vida próspera)

_____ UNA VIDA DINAMICA (una vida activa y estimulante)

A continuación se presenta otra lista de valores. Ordene estos valores de acuerdo con su importancia en la misma forma como lo hizo en la lista anterior.

_____ AFECTUOSO (amor al prójimo)

_____ CAPAZ (competente, eficaz)

_____ COMPASIVO (dispuesto a perdonar a otros)

_____ CORTES (educado, fino)

_____ DISCIPLINADO (control de si mismo, moderado)

_____ HONESTO (sincero, confiable)

_____ IMAGINATIVO (arrojado, creativo)

_____ INDEPENDIENTE (bastarse a si mismo)

_____ INTELECTUAL (inteligente, reflexivo)

_____ JOVIAL (alegre)

_____ LIMPIEZA(ordenado, responsable)

_____ LOGICO (consistente, racional)

_____ MADURO (una persona moderna, tolerante, de ideas nuevas)

_____ OBEDIENTE (leal, respetuoso)

_____ PERSISTENTE (trabajador, ambicioso)

_____ RESPONSABLE (seguro, confiable)

_____ SERVICIAL (trabaja para el bienestar de otros)

_____ VALEROSO (defensor de sus creencias)

Cada una de las siguientes proposiciones describe un aspecto de DIOS. Para mi Dios es: (Elija la que le guste más)

a. el omnisciente y todopoderoso Señor de toda la Creación.

b. el Padre amoroso que envió a su Hijo para revelar los Misterios de la Gracia Divina.

c. la Presencia Divina en este mundo, la que descubro en los hombres, en las cosas y en los acontecimientos.

Cada una de las siguientes proposiciones describe un aspecto del ESPIRITU SANTO. (Elija la que le guste más)

a. El Espíritu Santo guía a la Iglesia a una mejor comprensión del mensaje de Cristo y a su unidad interna al hablar por medio de todo el pueblo de Dios.

b. El Espíritu Santo, quien procede del Padre y del Hijo, distribuye la gracia de Dios a los hombres.

c. El Espíritu Santo habla a lo largo de la historia a todos los hombres de buena voluntad de diferentes maneras y en diversas circunstancias.

La finalidad de nuestra actividad misionera es:
(Elija uno)

a. Convertir el pueblo a la Iglesia Católica por medio de la predicación, enseñanza del catecismo, administración de los sacramentos, etc.

b. ayudar al hombre a desarrollar sus propios recursos con el fin de habilitarlo a satisfacer todas sus necesidades humanas, como ser : religiosas, económicas, educativas, políticas.

c. ser testigos del amor de Dios, predicar el Evangelio y fundar la Iglesia entre los pueblos que aún no conocen a Cristo.

d. no me es del todo clara.

Cada una de las siguientes proposiciones describe un aspecto de la IGLESIA.
(Elija la que a Ud. le guste más)

a. Como mediadora de la verdad y de la gracia de Dios para los hombres, la Iglesia es el único verdadero camino de salvación.

b. La Iglesia es una sociedad religiosa perfecta, organizada y bajo la dirección del Papa y de los obispos.

c. Como pueblo de Dios íntimamente relacionado con Cristo, la Iglesia es un sacramento o signo de la unión del hombre con Dios y de los hombres entre si.

d. La Iglesia es la censora profética de la sociedad y de la cultura.

e. La Iglesia, como peregrina en este mundo, es la servidora de la humanidad en todas sus necesidades, e. d. religiosas, económicas, educacionales y políticas.

Cada una de las siguientes proposiciones describe alguno de los aspectos de la relación de la Iglesia al Mundo.

a. La Iglesia, en lo profundo de la existencia humana, es el lugar de donde nace la Palabra de la cual ella misma es testigo en respuesta a preguntas que ella misma no se ha formulado. La Iglesia haría bien en irse al extremo desinstitucionalizando sus propios trabajos y procurando el colaborar de cerca con sacerdotes, laicos e intereses seculares para así dar cabida a este tipo de testimonio. La preocupación primordial debe de ser con los pobres, compartiendo totalmente en su vida diaria.

b. La Iglesia es el sacramento de Salvación que viene de arriba. Es radicalmente diferente del mundo. Ella debe de atraer a los hombres e incorporarlos dentro de la comunidad de los bautizados. Por lo tanto, las prioridades deben de estar relacionadas a los ministerios espirituales y sacerdotales. Reformándose a si misma desde dentro, la Iglesia debe trabajar para abarcar el contenido total de sus servicios pastorales y mantener su preocupación por un humanismo integral desarrollándose a la luz de la fe.

Cada una de las siguientes proposiciones describen un aspecto del MUNDO.
(Elija la que a Ud. le guste más)

a. El mundo es el lugar de lucha en el cual el hombre demuestra estar de parte de Dios al confiar en su Providencia y al cumplir su voluntad.

b. El mundo es bueno, y la acción creadora de Dios continúa haciéndolo aún mejor por medio del desarrollo del hombre y de su cultura.

c. El mundo, creado y sostenido por el amor de Dios, fue esclavizado por el pecado del hombre, pero ha sido liberado por el amor de Cristo.

Cada una de las siguientes proposiciones describe un aspecto del MINISTERIO. Un ministro cristiano es:
(Elija la que más le guste)

a. alguien que ha sido autorizado por el pueblo de Dios a construir la comunidad cristiana, guiarla en sus celebraciones de la gracia de Dios e inspirarla a participar activamente en las preocupaciones del mundo.

b. alguien ordenado al sacerdocio y por eso mismo autorizado a celebrar la Eucaristía y a administrar los sacramentos de la penitencia y de la Unción de los enfermos.

c. alguien cuya obligación principal es difundir el Evangelio de Cristo y el administrar los sacramentos a los fieles.

Cada una de las siguientes proposiciones describe un aspecto de la FE.
(Elija la que le guste más)

a. la afirmación de la bondad radical del hombre y de este mundo.

b. una seguridad de salvación.

c. una relación personal con Dios.

d. una afirmación de la Providencia de Dios.

e. una aceptación de las enseñanzas de la Iglesia.

f. una total sumisión de mi mismo a Dios.

Cada una de las siguientes proposiciones describe un aspecto de Cultura. Para mi CULTURA es
(Elija la que a Ud. le guste más)

a. Cultura se comprende mejor de un modo empírico. Esta es la serie de valores y significados que informan una forma común de vida, y hay tantas culturas como hay series diferentes de tales valores y significados. Tales valores y significados deben de ser entendidos con relación a los contextos y culturas de los cuales se desprenden.

b. Cultura se comprende mejor de un modo normativo. Esta es la habilidad de adquirir y asimilar los gustos y las técnicas, los ideales, las virtudes y las ideas de un crecimiento refinado y de las artes liberales. Esta es tan universal como los trabajos inmortales del arte y la filosofía perenne.

Cada una de las siguientes proposiciones describe un aspecto de CRISTO.
(Elija la que le guste más)

a. Como el Señor Resucitado, Cristo es el libertador de todos aquellos que están oprimidos por las fuerzas de este mundo.

b. Como el Encarnado y Sufriente Hijo de Dios, Cristo es nuestro mediador y nuestro Redentor.

c. Como el hombre más maduro y más santo que jamás existió o existirá, Cristo es la incorporación de Dios en la naturaleza humana y en la historia.

d. Como verdadero Dios, Cristo es nuestro Señor a quien se debe adoración.

Cada una de las siguientes proposiciones describe un aspecto de la AUTORIDAD.
(Elija la que le guste más)

a. La autoridad emana del mismo oficio del superior; la respuesta a ella es: obediencia.

b. La autoridad emana de la hábil coordinación y dirección de las actividades; la respuesta a ella es : una corresponsable ejecución de las directivas.

c. La autoridad emana del carisma personal de inspirar y animar a otros; la respuesta a ella es : confianza en el carisma del líder.

Cada una de las siguientes proposiciones describe un aspecto de la ORACION.
(Elija la que le guste más)

a. La Oración es la elevación de mi mente y corazón a Dios.

b. Oración es mi encuentro con Dios cuando sirvo a las necesidades de los demás.

c. Oración es mi sentir y mi responder al Dios personal.

d. Mi oración es el trabajo que hago.

Cada una de las siguientes proposiciones describe un aspecto de la SALVACION.
(Elija la que le guste más)

a. Todas las Iglesias Cristianas son canales de la gracia salvífica de Dios para los hombres.

b. La Iglesia Católica es el instrumento de la gracia salvífica de Dios para los hombres.

c. Todas las religiones son canales de la gracia salvífica de Dios para los hombres.

d. La gracia salvífica de Dios está actuando igualmente en cada hombre.

Piense en los hombres profesionales que Ud. conoce - por ejemplo : doctores, dentistas, abogados, científicos. Como cree Ud. que los Sacerdotes Jesuítas de su Provincia se compararían en general con ellos de acuerdo con los siguientes atributos?

(ENCIERRE UNA CLAVE EN CADA LINEA)

| | Con algunas excepciones, la mayoría de los Jesuítas de mi Provincia ... | | | |
	tienen más	tienen más o menos lo mismo	tienen menos	tienen mucho menos	no se
Profundidad de conocimiento y destreza.	1	2	3	4	5
Autonomía para tomar decisiones.	1	2	3	4	5
Responsabilidad para una empresa.	1	2	3	4	5
Compromiso para servir las necesidades de la gente.	1	2	3	4	5
Satisfacción y estima propia adquiridos por su trabajo.	1	2	3	4	5

MUCHAS GRACIAS

Analyse de l'organisation jesuite

2ᵉ PARTIE: QUESTIONNAIRE AUX DELEGUES

Cher délégué,

P.C. Les questions ci-incluses forment une partie essentielle
d'une analyse des valeurs qui animent l'organisation qu'est la Com-
pagnie de Jésus. Comme délégué à la 32ᵉ Congrégation Générale, vous
allez contribuer à nous diriger pendant plusieurs années à venir.
Ce questionnaire fait partie d'une effort de réflexion sur les lignes
de force et sur les modalités de votre direction.

Auriez-vous l'amabilité de répondre aux questions que vous trou-
verez sur les pages suivantes, en encerclant le numéro ou la lettre
à côté des réponses que vous trouvez les plus exactes? Puisque les
délégués a la Congrégation forment un groupe restreint de jésuites,
il est très important de recevoir une réponse de chacun d'entre vous.
Donc je vous prie instamment de répondre au questionnaire et de me
le renvoyer par la poste dans l'enveloppe ci-incluse. J'espère que
si vous le faites d'ici quelques jours, il y aura moins de chances
que ce léger travail vous dérange dans une période de temps qui doit
être très chargée de préparatifs.

Soyez assuré que tous les renseignements que je recueillerai dans
ces questionnaires seront entourés d'ine stricte confidence. Nul autre
que moi ne pourra identifier ceux qui ont fourni les renseignements;
aucun supérieur, aucun autre jésuite, aucune autre personne ne saura
qui a répondu aux questions de telle ou de telle façon. Aucune analyse
de ces renseignements ne sera divulguée avant la toute fin de la 32ᵉ
Congrégation Générale.

Je m'excuse de ne pas vous fournir d'affranchissement pour le
retour du courrier. Trop de pays sont impliqués dans ce projet pour
que je puisse fournir l'affranchissement approprié.

Je vous remercie d'avoir prêté attention à ma demande. Moyennant
votre assistance, vous receverz un résumé complet des conclusions de
cette étude.

Que Dieu vous bénisse dans la charge que vous accepté à notre
compte. Je vous accompagne chaque jour de mes prières et du S.Sacri-
fice de la Messe.

Sincèrement

Thomas P. Faase, S.J.

Code No. _____

Ce numéro permet l'identification des
données et ne sera associé au répondant
d'aucune autre façon. Dans ce survey,
les noms ne sont pas requis.

Veuillez indiquer l'Assistance à laquelle vous appartenez: (Encercler le numéro approprié)

1. Italie
2. Allemagne
3. France
4. Espagne
5. Angleterre
6. Etats-Unis
7. Pays slaves
8. Amérique centrale
9. Amérique du Sud
10. Inde
11. Asie
12. Afrique

Parmi les items ici mentionnés, lequel est de fait priori-taire dans votre province?
(Encercler la lettre appropriée)

A. Adapter les moyens aux objectifs en vue, aux ressources à développer.

B. Promouvoir la réalisation d'objectifs clairement définis, réalisation basée sur la coordination et sur une administration efficace.

C. Adapter le travail et les oeuvres de la province à l'ensemble général; aider à définir une identité dans la province.

D. Préserver les traditions de la province et de la Com-pagnie; travailler au maintien de la vie religieuse et au bien-être de ses membres.

Veuillez indiquer le genre de travail que vous faites (emploi principal): (encercler la lettre appropriée)

A. Administration supérieure
(Provincial, directeur des missions)

B. Education supérieure (administration)
(Président, recteur d'université)

C. Education secondaire: administration
(Ecole secondaire: président, recteur, principal)

D. Education supérieure: enseignement (ou recherche)

E. Education secondaire: enseignement (ou recherche)

F. Pastorale paroissiale ou autre travail pastoral

G. Ecrivain ou recherche à temps plein

H. Apostolat social (développement socio-économique)

I. Formation des nôtres, séminaristes; administration d'un séminaire

J. Autre (veuillez indiquer) _____

Quel âge avez-vous? (Encercler la lettre appropriée)

A. 30 ans ou moins
B. 30-39
C. 40-49
D. 50-59
E. 60-69
F. 70 ans ou plus

A quelle catégorie rattachez-vous votre travail?
(Encercler le numéro approprié)

1. Projet axé sur le sens de l'organisation et sur des objectifs précis.

2. Soutien des personnes et aide aux individus.

Lequel des items suivants constitue en second lieu une priorité dans votre province? (Encercler la lettre qui correspond à votre choix)

A. Adapter les moyens aux objectifs en vue, aux ressources à développer.

B. Promouvoir la réalisation d'objectifs clairement définis, réalisation basée sur la coordination et sur une administration efficace.

C. Adapter le travail et les oeuvres de la province à l'ensemble général; aider à définir une identité dans la province.

D. Préserver les traditions de la province et de la Com-pagnie; travailler au maintien de la vie religieuse et au bien-être de ses membres.

La préoccupation majeure de la 32e Congrégation générale sera à mon avis d'ordre: (encercler la lettre appropriée)

A. DOCTRINAL: produire des définitions, faire des énoncés au sujet de nos objectifs et de nos idéaux.

B. PASTORAL: encourager, stimuler, supporter.

C. PRATIQUE: améliorer les structures, produire des textes de loi sur les procédures et sur les façons de faire.

En général, quelle préoccupation semble inspirer la majorité des décisions de votre province et de ses prin-cipales oeuvres? (Encercler la lettre appropriée)

A. Religieuse
B. Politique
C. Economique
D. Cura personalis

Veuillez répondre aux prochaines suivantes d'après
le tableau suivant:

1. Tout à fait d'accord
2. Partiellement d'accord
3. Je suis indécis.
4. En désaccord partiellement
5. Tout à fait en désaccord

VEUILLEZ N'ENCERCLER QU'UN NUMERO PAR LIGNE

Le futur dépend de Dieu. J'accepte ce
qu'il veut bien m'envoyer et je le
considère comme sa volonté.   1 2 3 4 5

L'élément créateur dans l'Eglise
m'aide à approfondir ma foi chrétienne.   1 2 3 4 5

Le problème de l'Eglise après Vatican
11 est qu'on n'a plus rien de défini
comme sûr.   1 2 3 4 5

Le désordre faisant suite à Vatican 11
affaiblit mes propres convictions religieuses.   1 2 3 4 5

Il peut arriver que quelqu'un ait à
obéir à sa conscience plutôt qu'à
l'enseignement de l'Eglise.   1 2 3 4 5

Quelqu'un expose sa foi en étudiant
des auteurs protestants.   1 2 3 4 5

La pauvreté en esprit n'a aucun sens
sans la pauvreté dans les faits.   1 2 3 4 5

Pauvreté religieuse veut dire
dépendre de la communauté pour
ses besoins personnels.   1 2 3 4 5

La façon de présenter la chasteté
au cours de la formation a souvent
favorisé l'impersonnalisme et une
fausse spiritualité.   1 2 3 4 5

Le devoir du sujet est d'obéir; il
appartient au supérieur de discerner la
volonté de Dieu et de dire ce qu'elle
est.   1 2 3 4 5

Il est sage de recommander aux jésuites de s'intéresser à des projets
d'ordre régional ou national pour
lesquels ils se sentent compétents,
même si ceux-ci n'ont rien à faire
avec les plans de la province ou de
l'institution à laquelle l'individu
appartient.   1 2 3 4 5

Les oeuvres et institutions de caractère international de la Compagnie
doivent avoir priorité sur l'influence
personnelle qu'un jésuite peut exercer
au niveau de son travail.   1 2 3 4 5

Toute organisation devient avec le
temps inefficace; seul du sang nouveau
peut la revitaliser.   1 2 3 4 5

Je préfère être accusé d'idéalisme que
d'être regardé comme un homme pratique.   1 2 3 4 5

Quand je pense "réforme sociale", je
pense à ces objectifs auxquels je me
crois sincèrement appelé à donner
mes meilleures énergies.   1 2 3 4 5

Un prêtre ne mérite pas le nom de pasteur s'il n'est pas tout autant préoccupé de pourvoir aux besoins sociaux de
ses gens qu'à leur fournir des services
d'ordre spirituel.   1 2 3 4 5

Quand j'ai à prendre des décisions
dans mon travail, j'ai le sentiment
que je dois essayer de prendre des
décisions qui aideront à solutionner
les problèmes de justice au profit
de l'humanité entière. Je considère
ces problèmes de l'humanité comme
mes problèmes.   1 2 3 4 5

La situation de l'Eglise doit changer;
un engagement actuel est impératif.   1   2   3   4   5

Le libéralisme est excellent parce
qu'il constitue un esprit de réforme.
C'est une attitude saine que d'avoir
des objectifs précis, même si ceux-ci
vont contre la justice et la prudence.
L'essentiel est d'entretenir un désir
de poursuivre ces valeurs.   1   2   3   4   5

Tout progrès significatif au cours de
l'histoire a été accompli grâce aux es-
prits réformateurs et créateurs.   1   2   3   4   5

Les préoccupations de l'apostolat individuel jésuite doivent être subordonnés
au bien de l'institution ou de l'équi-
pe dont le jésuite fait partie.   1   2   3   4   5

Une province a le droit d'exiger qu'un
jésuite travaille sur un projet d'envergure provinciale, même si cette tâche entre en conflit avec son apostolat
ou les intérêts de l'institution dont
il est membre.   1   2   3   4   5

Même chez eux les jésuites devraient
s'abstenir de se prononcer publiquement
sur des questions d'ordre religieux
ou social.   1   2   3   4   5

La tendance dans ma province est de
donner aux gens plutôt que de les aider
à se procurer ce dont ils ont besoin.   1   2   3   4   5

Il y a suffisamment de souci dans ma
province pour les pauvres, les délaissés et les peu considérés.   1   2   3   4   5

Les gens de ma province sont suffisamment soucieux de respecter les valeurs
des différentes cultures dans les liturgies de groupe.   1   2   3   4   5

La Compagnie en général est soucieuse
de respecter les différentes cultures
dans notre vie religieuse et communau-
taire.   1   2   3   4   5

Les jésuites en pays étranger s'abstenir de se prononcer publiquement sur
des questions d'ordre religieux ou
social.   1   2   3   4   5

En dernier lieu, celui qui a le pouvoir
est celui qui décide.   1   2   3   4   5

Peu importe les idéaux que vous soutenez, vous ne pouvez réaliser vos objectifs qu'à condition de mettre les pouvoirs de votre côté.   1   2   3   4   5

Quand vous y pensez, c'est la nature
humaine intéressée par le gain qui
l'emporte.   1   2   3   4   5

Les exigences de l'apostolat individuel
du jésuite justifient ce dernier de
consacrer à son travail toutes ses
énergies.   1   2   3   4   5

C'est en continuant à prêcher et à
enseigner plutôt qu'en expérimentant
avec de nouvelles méthodes que l'Egli-
se accomplira le mieux sa mission.   1   2   3   4   5

En dernier lieu, la meilleure base de
planification pour le futur est de faire confiance à l'expérience du passé
et de baser nos décisions sur des
exemples historiques.   1   2   3   4   5

J'appuie le conservatisme parce que
c'est le seul moyen de garder intact
notre glorieux héritage.   1   2   3   4   5

Au cours des 10 dernières années, bon
nombre de religieux ont évolué en ce
qui a trait aux principes de base et
aux valeurs auxquelles ils croyaient
auparavant.   1   2   3   4   5

Les valeurs de base de l'Eglise demeurent
les mêmes; seules leur expression
varient.   1   2   3   4   5

Dans l'espace réservé à cet effet, veuillez indiquer les
noms des 3 délégués qui, selon vous, exerceront le plus
d'influence à la Congrégation générale:

———————————————

———————————————

———————————————

Cinq différentes classes sociales sont ici décrites. Après avoir lu le texte, veuillez répondre aux questions qui le suivent.

1. Gens pauvres, qui ne se suffisent pas à eux-mêmes et qui ont un niveau de vie inférieur à ce qui est considéré dans votre région comme l'essentiel pour survivre.

2. Gens qui ne sont pas des ouvriers spécialisés, mais qui jouissent de ce qui est considéré dans votre région comme le minimum vital.

3. Gens de classe moyenne d'après les critères de votre région. Ce groupe comprend habituellement les employés de bureau, les petits marchands, les fermiers, les ouvriers spécialisés, les professeurs de niveau élémentaire et parfois secondaire.

4. Gens qui ont un revenu tel qu'ils peuvent se permettre plus que ce qui est considéré dans votre région comme les commodités usuelles. En général font partie de ce groupe les propriétaires de terrain, les directeurs d'entreprise, les médecins, les hommes d'affaire, les professeurs au niveau de l'éducation supérieure.

5. La classe riche. Gens qui ont le plus d'influence dans la région où vous travaillez, tels que les gros propriétaires, les directeurs de la finance, les ministres, députés et officiels du gouvernement.

A quel groupe appartiennent les gens pour lesquels vous travaillez la plupart du temps? (Ne donnez qu'une réponse)

Groupe 1 _____   Groupe 4 _____

Groupe 2 _____   Groupe 5 _____

Groupe 3 _____

Auquel de ces groupes appartenaient vos parents lors de votre enfance et adolescence?

Groupe 1 _____   Groupe 4 _____

Groupe 2 _____   Groupe 5 _____

Groupe 3 _____

Auquel de ces groupes rattacheriez-vous le style de vie que vous avez comme jésuite?

Groupe 1 _____   Groupe 4 _____

Groupe 2 _____   Groupe 5 _____

Groupe 3 _____

Vous avez ici une liste de 18 valeurs. Mettez-les en ordre d'après l'importance qu'elles ont pour vous dans votre vie.

Etudiez la liste avec soin. Ensuite, placez le chiffre 1 avant la valeur qui est la plus importante pour vous. La seconde valeur par ordre d'importance recevra le chiffre 2 et ainsi de suite, de telle sorte que la valeur la moins importante pour vous se verra attribuée le chiffre 18.

Travaillez lentement. Si vous le jugez bon, changez l'ordre de vos réponses. La classification finale devrait révéler vos sentiments les plus profonds.

Nous réalisons qu'entre les expressions il n'y a parfois qu'une subtile distinction. Toutefois, classifiez ces valeurs sans trop analyser leur sens.

_____ UNE VIE CONFORTABLE (une vie prospère)

_____ UNE VIE PASSIONNANTE (une vie stimulante et active)

_____ UN SENTIMENT DE REALISATION (sens de la contribution)

_____ UN MONDE EN PAIX (sans guerre ni conflit)

_____ UN MONDE DE BEAUTE (beauté de nature et artistique)

_____ EGALITE (fraternité, chances égales pour tous)

_____ SECURITE DE FAMILLE (prendre soin des siens)

_____ LIBERTE (indépendance, liberté de mouvement)

_____ BONHEUR (joie intérieure)

_____ HARMONIE INTERIEURE (sans conflits intérieurs)

_____ AMOUR PARFAIT (intimité sexuelle et spirituelle)

_____ SECURITE NATIONALE (protection contre l'ennemi)

_____ PLAISIR (une vie agréable, remplie de loisir)

_____ SALUT (désir d'être sauvé, vie éternelle)

_____ AMOUR PROPRE (estime de soi-même)

_____ INFLUENCE SOCIALE (respect, admiration)

_____ AMITIE PROFONDE (camaraderie, intimité)

_____ SAGESSE (compréhension du sens de la vie)

Vous avez ici une liste de 18 qualités. Classifiez-les d'après leur importance pour vous. Procédez de la même façon que pour la première liste.

_____ AMBITIEUX (travailleur laborieux)

_____ LARGE D'ESPRIT (tolérant)

_____ TALENTUEUX (compétent, efficace)

_____ JOYEUX (gai d'esprit et de coeur)

_____ PROPRE (bien rangé, de bonne apparence)

_____ COURAGEUX (capable de défendre ses convictions)

_____ CLEMENT (conciliant, capable de pardonner)

_____ SOCIABLE (désireux d'aider les autres)

_____ HONNETE (sincère, véridique)

_____ IMAGINATIF (créateur, audacieux)

_____ INDEPENDANT (confiant en soi)

_____ INTELLECTUEL (intelligent)

_____ LOGIQUE (rationel, ferme d'esprit)

_____ AFFECTUEUX (tendre, aimant)

_____ OBEISSANT (soumis, respectueux)

_____ POLI (courtois, bien élevé)

_____ RESPONSABLE (digne de confiance, fiable)

_____ MAITRE DE SOI-MEME (sens de la retenue et discipline)

Chacun des énoncés suivants décrit une facon de parler de
DIEU. Dieu pour moi signifie (indiquez l'énoncé qui vous
parle le plus)....

    a. le Seigneur de la création qui sait tout et peut
       tout.

    b. le Père qui nous aime tant qu'il envoie son Fils
       pour nous révéler les mystères de sa grâce.

    c. la présence divine que je découvre dans ce monde
       à travers les gens, les événements et la création.

Chacun des énoncés suivants représente une facon de parler
de l'ESPRIT-SAINT. (indiquez votre choix)

    a. L'Esprit-Saint aide l'Eglise à mieux comprendre
       le message du Christ et contribue à son unité en
       s'adressant au peuple de Dieu.

    b. L'Esprit-Saint qui procède du Père et du Fils et
       celui qui distribue les grâces divines aux hommes.

    c. L'Esprit-Saint s'adresse à tous les hommes de bonne
       volonté, et ce, de bien des facons et dans des
       circonstances bien variées au cours de l'histoire.

L'activité MISSIONNAIRE a pour but de (indiquez l'énoncé
qui vous semble le plus significatif) ....

    a. travailler à convertir les hommes à l'Eglise catho-
       lique et ce, par la prédication, l'enseignement de
       la catéchèse et l'administration des sacrements.

    b. Aider l'homme à développer ses propres ressources
       pour qu'il satisfasse à ses besoins d'ordre reli-
       gieux, économique, politique et éducationel.

    c. être un témoignage de l'amour de Dieu, prêcher
       l'Evangile et construire l'Eglise au milieu de gens
       qui n'ont pas encore entendu parler du Christ.

    d. aucune opinion précise sur le sujet.

Des conceptions différentes de l'EGLISE sont ici exprimées.
(Indiquez celle qui vous plaît davantage)

a. Médiatrice des vérités et des grâces divines aux hommes,
   l'Eglise est indispensable dans l'économie du salut.
b. L'Eglise est cette parfaite société religieuse, organi-
   sée autour du pape et des évêques.
c. Peuple de Dieu rattaché au Christ, l'Eglise est le sacrement ou le signe de l'union de l'homme avec Dieu et des
   hommes entre eux.
d. L'Eglise a pour mission prophétique d'évaluer les socié-
   tés et les cultures.
e. L'Eglise, pèlerine dans ce monde, est au service de l'humanité et de ses besoins d'ordre religieux, éducationel
   économique et politique.

Les affirmations qui suivent décrivent deux aspects de la
relation Eglise - Monde. (Indiquez celle qui vous paraît
la plus appropriée)

a. L'Eglise, dans son histoire humaine, est le lieu d'où
   surgit le Verbe de Dieu. Témoin de ce Verbe, il lui
   appartient de répondre aux questions qu'on lui pose.
   Il serait souhaitable pour l'Eglise de se désinstitu-
   tionaliser et d'avoir le courage de collaborer plus
   étroitement avec les prêtres, les laïcs et les intérêts
   du monde en vue d'un meilleur témoignage. Comme priorité,
   elle devrait être avec les pauvres et partager leur vie.

b. L'Eglise est le sacrement du salut qui vient d'en haut.
   Différente du monde, elle a pour mission de s'adresser
   aux hommes et de les intégrer dans la communauté des
   croyants baptisés. Ses priorités devraient aller aux
   ministères spirituels et à l'administration des sacrements. Se réformant de l'intérieur, l'Eglise doit s'in-
   terroger sur le contenu de ses services d'ordre spirituel et se préoccuper de l'édification d'un humanisme
   intégral éclairé par la foi.

Des différentes conceptions du MONDE ici énoncées, indiquez
celle qui vous plaît davantage.

    a. Le monde est le lieu où l'homme répond à Dieu en
       s'abandonnant à sa providence et en faisant sa
       volonté.

    b. Le monde est bon, et l'activité créatrice de Dieu
       continue à se manifester à travers le progrès de
       l'homme et la culture qui contribuent à l'améliorer.

    c. Le monde, surgi de l'amour de Dieu, a été corrompu
       par le péché de l'homme puis racheté par l'action
       du Christ.

Vous avez ici trois facons différentes de parler du
MINISTERE. Est en charge d'un ministère dans l'Eglise
(choisissez l'énoncé qui vous semble le meilleur) ...

a. celui qui a recu du peuple de Dieu la mission
   d'édifier la communauté chrétienne, qui guide cette
   dernière dans la célébration des bienfaits de Dieu
   et l'invite à s'intéresser aux problèmes du monde.

b. celui qui a été ordonné au sacerdoce et par le fait
   même est autorisé à célébrer l'Eucharistie et à
   administrer les sacrements du pardon et des malades.

c. celui dont le premier devoir est de répandre la
   bonne nouvelle du Christ et d'administrer les sacrements.

Vous avez ici différentes façons de décrire la FOI. (indiquez l'énoncé qui vous parle le plus) Par FOI, j'entends .....

    a. l'affirmation de la bonté infinie de l'homme et de ce monde.

    b. la certitude d'être sauvé.

    c. une relation personnelle avec Dieu.

    d. l'affirmation de la providence divine dans ma vie.

    e. la soumission à l'enseignement de l'Eglise

    f. un abandon entier de moi-même à Dieu.

Les deux paragraphes suivants représentent des conceptions différentes de la CULTURE. (Indiquez celle qui vous semble la plus appropriée)

    a. La notion de culture est matière de définition. La culture est un ensemble de valeurs qui influencent notre mode de vie. Il y a autant de cultures qu'il y a d'ensemble de valeurs. Ces valeurs sont à être analysées à l'intérieur du milieu culturel desquelles elles sont issues.

    b. La notion de culture est avant tout normative. La culture consiste à acquérir et à intégrer des goûts, des talents personnels, des idéaux et des valeurs d'art. La culture est universelle aussi bien que les travaux d'art et la philosophie qui défient le temps.

Les affirmations suivantes concernent le CHRIST. (Choisissez celle qui vous parle davantage)

    a. Seigneur ressuscité, le Christ est celui qui libère ceux qui sont opprimés par les forces de ce monde.

    b. Homme incarné et Fils de Dieu souffrant, le Christ est notre médiateur et notre sauveur.

    c. Etant parfaitement homme et infiniment saint, le Christ est l'incarnation de Dieu dans le monde et l'histoire.

    d. Etant parfaitement Dieu, le Christ est notre Seigneur à qui nous devons toute adoration.

Chacun des énoncés suivants parle de la prière. (Choisissez l'énoncé qui vous semble le plus significatif)

    a. Prier, c'est élever son esprit et son coeur vers Dieu.

    b. La prière est cette rencontre avec Dieu qui m'invite à me mettre au service des autres.

    c. Prier, c'est être sensible à la présence d'un Dieu personne et y répondre.

    d. Ma prière est le travail que j'accomplis.

Les énoncés suivants parlent de l'autorité. (Indiquez l'énoncé qui vous frappe davantage)

    a. L'autorité est celle du supérieur; collaborer avec l'autorité signifie obéir.

    b. Toute autorité se construit à partir d'une coordination et d'une planification; obéissance équivaut à une mise en pratique co-responsable des décisions.

    c. L'autorité vient d'un charisme personnel pour inspirer et encourager; la confiance dans le charisme du chef de file conditionnera la réponse des sujets.

Différentes conceptions du SALUT sont ici exprimées. (Indiquez l'énoncé qui vous parle le plus)

    a. Toutes les églises chrétiennes contribuent à dispenser aux hommes la grâce salvifique de Dieu.

    b. L'Eglise catholique est le lieu de la grace salvifique de Dieu pour les hommes.

    c. Toutes les religions contribuent à dispenser la grâce salvifique de Dieu aux hommes.

    d. La grâce divine du salut est à l'oeuvre dans chaque être humain.

En les comparant aux professionnels que vous connaissez, par example, médecins, professionnels de la santé, avocats, hommes de science, comment classifierez-vous les jésuites prêtres de votre province sous les aspects suivants? (N'ENCERCLER QU'UN CHIFFRE PAR LIGNE HORIZONTALE)

	Sauf exception, la plupart des jésuites de ma province ont				
	plus de	à peu près de également ment	moins de	beaucoup coup	Ne sais pas
Profondeur de savoir et intelligence.	1	2	3	4	5
Capacité de prendre ses propres décisions.	1	2	3	4	5
Sens de la responsabilité dans son travail.	1	2	3	4	5
Désir de rencontrer les besoins des gens.	1	2	3	4	5
Satisfaction et estime personnelle fondées sur le travail personnel.	1	2	3	4	5

MERCI BEAUCOUP

Sehr geehrter Pater, PC

Die hierin gestellten Fragen enthalten einen ueberaus wichtigen Aspekt einer organisatorischen Analyse der religioesen und sittlichen Werte der Gesellschaft Jesu. Sie als Delegierter zur 32. Generalkongregation werden durch Ihre unermuedlichen und grossherzigen Bemuehungen uns ueber Jahre hinaus helfen, den rechten Weg zu gehen. Diese Umfrage ist Teil einer umfassenderen Bemuehung, wertvolle und dankbarer Bestimmung auf eben diese Richtung und Anleitung.

Beantworten Sie bitte die Fragen auf den folgenden Seiten, indem Sie einfach die Zahl oder den Buchstaben neben dem Text ankreuzen, den Sie fuer die passendste Antwort halten. Da unter den Delegierten zur Kongregation nur eine kleine Anzahl von Jesuiten sind, sind Ihre Antworten auf diese Umfrage besonders wichtig. Deshalb bitte ich Sie von ganzem Herzen, dass Sie die beantworteten Fragebogen im beiliegenden Briefumschlag zuruecksenden wollen. Wenn Sie innerhalb der naechsten Tage dieser Sache

Organisatorische

Analyse

der Gesellschaft Jesu

sich annehmen, dann wird sie weniger danach angetan sein, mit den vielen Dingen, die Ihnen bei der Vorbereitung Ihrer Reise Sorge machen muessen, in Konflikt zu geraten.

Teil II - Delegierten-Umfrage

Ich moechte Sie nachdruecklich versichern, dass alle durch diese Umfrage eingeholten Auskuenfte von mir streng vertraulich behandelt werden. Niemand anderer als ich wird Zugang zur Identifikation dieser Daten haben; weder Obern, noch andere Jesuiten, noch irgendwer sonst wird irgendeine bestimmte Auskunft darueber erhalten, wer welche Frage auf welche Weise auch immer beantwortet habe. Kein Bericht, in welcher Form auch immer, wird aus diesen Auskuenften zusammengestellt werden, ehe die 32. Generalkongregation ihr Werk zu Ende gefuehrt und sich endgueltig vertagt hat.

Leider ist es mir, bei der Anzahl und Verschiedenheit der Laender, die an dieser Umfrage beteiligt sind, nicht moeglich, das jeweils angemessene Porto fuer die Ruecksendung Ihrer Antworten beizulegen. Bitte, entschuldigen Sie diesen Umstand.

Fuer die Beachtung und Aufmerksamkeit, die Sie dieser Umfrage schenken, danke ich Ihnen vielmals. Ein Resumé aller Ergebnisse dieser Untersuchung wird Ihnen zugehen; verstehen Sie das bitte als einen Ausdruck meiner Dankbarkeit fuer Ihre freundliche und wichtige Unterstuetzung und Mitarbeit.

Moege Gott Sie und Ihre Bemuehungen um die allen Jesuiten gemeinsamen Anliegen segnen. Meine Gebete und Messen werden tagelich um Seine Gnade fuer Sie bitten.

Ihr Ihnen sehr ergebener

[Unterschrift]

(Rev.) Thomas P. Faase, S.J.

Geben Sie bitte die Assistenten an, der Sie angehoeren:
(Kreuzen Sie den entsprechenden Code an, i.e. Ziffer oder Buchstabe))

1 Italienische Assisten
2 Deutsche
3 Franzoesische
4 Spanische
5 Englische
6 Amerikanische

7 Slawische Assisten
8 Nord-lateinamerikanische
9 Sued-lateinamerikanische
10 Indianische
11 Ostasiatische
12 Afrikanische

Geben Sie bitte, allgemein ausgedrueckt, Ihre hauptberufliche Taetigkeit an.
(Kreuzen sie den entsprechenden Code an)

A Supra-Institutionen: Verwaltung
  (z.B. Provinzial, Missionsdirektor)
B Hoehere Bildungsanstalten: Verwaltung
  (z.B. Rektor einer Universitaet)
C Gymnasien und Oberschulen: Verwaltung
  (z.B. Rektor solcher Bildungsanstalten)
D Universitaeten und Hochschulen: Unterrichten (und damit zusammenhaengende Forschung)
E Gymnasien und Oberschulen: Unterrichten (und damit zusammenhaengende Forschung)
F Verwaltung einer Pfarrei oder pastorale Taetigkeit
G Schriftstellerei oder Forschung als hauptberufliche Taetigkeit.
H Sozialapostolat: sozio-oekonomische Entwicklung
I Priesterausbildung: sowohl von SJ als auch von anderen Priestern;
J Andere Taetigkeit: (Bitte naeher bestimmen) ....

Was ist Ihr Alter: (Kreuzen Sie den entsprechenden Code an)

A Juenger als 30
B 30-39
C 40-49
D 50-59
E 60-69
F 70 und aelter.

Welcher Art ist Ihre Ansicht nach Ihre Arbeit: (Kreuzen Sie den entsprechenden Code an)

1 Hauptsaechlich Aufgabe-orientiert: auf die Erledigung eines Arbeitsauftrags ausgerichtet.
2 Hauptsaechlich Personen-Orientiert: Fuersorge und Dienst zum Wohl der Leute.

Welche der folgenden Aussagen beschreibt Ihrer Ansicht nach das wichtigste Anliegen Ihrer Provinz: (Kreuzen Sie den entsprechenden Code an)

A Anpassung der Mittel an das erwuenschte Ziel, Anwendung dieser Mittel.
B Erreichung festgesetzter Ziele; Erreichung dieser Ziele durch Koordination und zielstrebiges Management der Exekutive.
C Anpassung der Arbeit und der hieraus gewonnenen Erfolge der Provinz an ein allgemeingueltiges Verhaltensmuster; Mithilfe bei der Definierung der Identitaet der Provinz.
D Bewahrung der Traditionen der Provinz und der Gesellschaft; Aufrechterhaltung des religioesen Lebens und des Wohlergehens Ihrer Mitglieder.

Welche der folgenden Aussagen beschreibt Ihrer Ansicht nach das zweitwichtigste Anliegen Ihrer Provinz: (Kreuzen Sie den entsprechenden Code an)

A Anpassung der Mittel an das erwuenschte Ziel, Anwendung dieser Mittel.
B Erreichung festgesetzter Ziele; Erreichung dieser Ziele durch Koordination und zielstrebiges Management der Exekutive.
C Anpassung der Arbeit und der hieraus gewonnenen Erfolge der Provinz an ein allgemeingueltiges Verhaltensmuster; Mithilfe bei der Definierung der Identitaet der Provinz.
D Bewahrung der Traditionen der Provinz und der Gesellschaft; Aufrechterhaltung des religioesen Lebens und des Wohlergehens Ihrer Mitglieder.

Schwerpunkt und Hauptanliegen der 32. Kongregation wird voraussichtlich sein: (Entscheiden Sie sich fuer das eine, Ihrer Erwartung nach wahrscheinliche Hauptanliegen.)

A Wissenschaftliche Anliegen: Aufstellung von Definitionen und Abgabe von Aussagen; Aussagen ueber unsere Glaubensanschauungen und Ziele.
B Pastorale Fragen: Ermahnung und Ermutigung.
C Praktische Anliegen: Reform von Strukturen; Legislierung von Verfahrensweisen.

Ganz allgemein gesprochen, welche der folgenden Richtlinien bestimmt Ihrer Ansicht nach die Mehrheit der Beschluesse, die von Ihrer Provinz und deren bedeutendsten Institutionen gefasst werden: (Kreuzen sie den entsprechenden Code an)

A Religioese Richtlinien
B Politische Richtlinien
C Oekonomische
D Cura Personalis

Wollen Sie bitte die folgenden Fragen nach der angefuehrten Skala
moeglicher Reaktionen beantworten.

1 stimme nachdruecklich zu

2 stimme bedingt zu

3 bin nicht sicher

4 bin bedingt nicht einverstanden

5 bin ueberhaupt nicht einverstanden

Bitte kreuzen Sie einen Code auf jeder Ziffernskala an.

Die Zukunft liegt in Gottes Hand. Ich werde
dem entgegengehen, was ir mir zeigt und
das als Seinen Willen akzeptieren, was auf
mich zukommt.   1 2 3 4 5

Die schoepferische Unruhe in der heutigen
Kirche bringt eine Vertiefung meines christ-
lichen Glaubens mit sich.   1 2 3 4 5

Die Kirche steht nach Vatikan II dem frohen
Gegenueber, dass viele Gewissheiten, die wir
hatten, uns weggenommen wurden.   1 2 3 4 5

Die lebhafte Unruhe, die auf Vatikan II folgte,
hat nur Folge, dass meine Glaubensueberzeugun-
gen allmaehlich schwaecher werden.   1 2 3 4 5

Es gibt Zeiten, in denen ein Mensch sein ei-
genes Gewissen ueber die Lehren der Kirche
stellen muss.   1 2 3 4 5

Unser Glaube kann durch das Studium prote-
stantischer Theologen gefaehrdet werden.   1 2 3 4 5

Armut im Geiste ist bedeutungslos ohne
Armut in facto.   1 2 3 4 5

Arm sein heisst: von der Gemeinde fuer unsere
ganzen materiellen Beduerfnisse abhaengig sein.   1 2 3 4 5

Die traditionelle Teilen, wie sie in der Priesterausbildung das Kreuschmiegelaeube praesentiert
wird, hat oft dazu gefuehrt, dass sich unser-
soeniliches Verhalten und falsche Geistigkeit
entwickeln konnten.   1 2 3 4 5

Es ist die Pflicht des Untergebenen zu gehor-
chen: die Verpflichtung des Oberen ist es,
Gottes Wille zu erkennen und ihn zu verkuen-
den.   1 2 3 4 5

Es ist fuer Jesuiten ratsam, sich mit regio-
nalen oder nationalen Projekten zu befassen,
deren Aufgabenkreis sie sich gewachsen fueh-
len. Sie sollten dies auch dann tun, wenn das
Ergebnis derartiger Unternehmen weder der Provinz noch anderen Institutionen, denen Jesuiten
angehoeren, Nutzen bringt.   1 2 3 4 5

Die Aufgaben und Ziele der gesamten Gesellschaft
Jesu auf internationaler Ebene verdienen es,
allen anderen Wirkungsbereichen immer dann vor-
gezogen zu werden, wenn ein Jesuit wirksamen
Einfluss auf internationaler Ebene geltend machen kann.   1 2 3 4 5

Jede organisatorische Struktur wird mit der Zeit
zu einer drueckenden Last und muss revitalisiert
werden.   1 2 3 4 5

Lieber moechte ich ein Idealist genannt werden
als ein praktisch veranlagter Mensch.   1 2 3 4 5

.enn ich an Sozialreform denke, dann denke ich
an Dinge, an die ich von ganzem Herzen glaube,
so dass ich ihnen alle meine Kraefte widmen
koennte.   1 2 3 4 5

Ein Priester darf sich wohl kaum Hirte nennen,
wenn er sich nicht ebenso intensiv um die so-
ziale Wohlfahrt der Leute kuemmert wie um den
geistlichen Dienst zum wohl der Gemeinde.   1 2 3 4 5

.wenn ich mich mit den Problemen meiner Arbeit
befasse, dann uebernrasche ich mich immer bei
dem Versuch, Entscheidungen zu treffen, die die
wichtigeren Fragen der Gerechtigkeit und zum
wohl der ganzen Menschheit loesen helfen. Die
Probleme der Menschheit sind im Grunde meine
Probleme.   1 2 3 4 5

Die gegenwärtige Lage der Kirche macht eine Veränderung erforderlich. Wir müssen darauf ohne Verzug reagieren.

1 2 3 4 5

Der Liberalismus ist gutzuheissen, da er den Geist der Reform repräsentiert. Er stellt eine optimistische Einstellung zur Welt dar, die auf sinnvollen Fortschritt hofft. Er mag nicht immer Gerechtigkeit, aufgeklärte Einsicht und Weisheit verkörpern, doch strebt er immer danach.

1 2 3 4 5

Jeder bedeutende Schritt vorwärts in der Weltgeschichte ist durch die Inspiration von Reformatoren und schöpferischen Menschen erzielt werden.

1 2 3 4 5

Gewisse Anliegen in Aufgabenbereich eines einzelnen Jesuiten innerhalb des Apostolats müssen der Institution oder der guten Zusammenarbeit aller Jesuiten, an der er Anteil nimmt und Anteil hat, notwendig untergeordnet werden.

1 2 3 4 5

Die Provinz hat das Recht, von einem Jesuiten Mitarbeit an den die ganze Provinz betreffenden Angelegenheiten zu verlangen, selbst dann sogar, wenn diese Tätigkeit mit den Interessen seines eigenen Apostolats und denen der Institution, der er angehört, in Konflikt geraet.

1 2 3 4 5

Selbst im Heimatland sollten die SJ-Mitglieder im Ausland leben nicht zu herausfordernd Stellung nehmen zu religiösen und sozialen Fragen.

1 2 3 4 5

Ob meiner Provinz macht die Gesellschaft den Eindruck, dass sie sich mehr damit befasst, selber für die Leute zu sorgen, statt diese anzuleiten, für sich selbst zu sorgen.

1 2 3 4 5

Die Arbeitsprogramme meiner Provinz berücksichtigen genügend die armen Leute und die niederen Klassen.

1 2 3 4 5

Die Mitbrüder in meiner Provinz haben beim Vollzug des Gottesdienstes genügend Feingespür für die Eigenwerte und Fühlweisen der Einheimischen.

1 2 3 4 5

Die Gesellschaft als ganze ist offen genug für die volkischen und kulturellen Eigenarten der Mitglieder, in der Ausprägung ihres Ordenslebens und Gemeinschaftslebens.

1 2 3 4 5

Wo SJ-Mitglieder im Ausland arbeiten, sollten sie nicht zu herausfordernd Stellung nehmen zu religiösen und sozialen Fragen.

1 2 3 4 5

Die Macht, die man hat, ist letztlich entscheidend.

1 2 3 4 5

Es spielt keine Rolle, wie grossartig die Ideale sein mögen, um deren Verbreitung man sich bemüht; man kann nichts erreichen, wenn man die ausgeglichene Beachtnahme nicht auf seiner Seite hat.

1 2 3 4 5

Wenn Dir an der Sache wirklich auf den Grund geht, dann liegt es in der menschlichen Natur, unter keinen Umstaenden etwas zu tun, ohne dabei seinen Vorteil im Auge zu haben.

1 2 3 4 5

Ein Jesuit sollte innerhalb des besonderen Apostolates, in dem er dient, den dringlichen und umfassenden Ansprüchen dieses Apostolates alles anderen voran seine wohlbedachte Bemühungen zuwenden.

1 2 3 4 5

Indem die Kirche ihre traditionelle Einstellung zu ihrer Lehrerrolle beibehaelt, wird sie ihre Mission besser erfüllen als durch Experiente mit neuen Methoden.

1 2 3 4 5

Im Grunde ist es die sicherste Grundlage einer jeden, Planung fuer die Zukunft, sein Vertrauen auf die Erfahrungen der Vergangenheit zu setzen und alle Beschluesse auf Tatsachen, auf die historischen Tatsachen zu gründen.

1 2 3 4 5

Meine Sympathien gehoeren dem Konservatismus, da er entschlossenem Eintreten dafuer repräsentiert, unser ruhmreiches Erbe zu bewahren.

1 2 3 4 5

Im Zeitraum der vergangenen 10 Jahre haben viele Ordensleute einige ihrer Grundprinzipien und zertigkeiten geaendert, an die sie zuvor geglaubt hatten.

1 2 3 4 5

Die religiösen und sittlichen Grundwerte der Kirche bleiben dieselben, doch deren Ausdrucksweise aendert sich.

1 2 3 4 5

Wollen Sie bitte die drei Delegierten nennen, die Ihrer Erwartung nach den grössten Einfluss auf dieser Generalkongregation ausuben werden!

....
....
....

Die folgenden Aussagen decken sich etwa mit 5 Kategorien von sozialen Klassen. Wollen Sie diese bitte lesen und die diesen Aussagen folgenden Fragen beantworten.

Fragen

1. Arme Leute, die keine regelmässigen Einkuenfte oder die einen Lebensstandard haben, der unter dem liegt, was in ihrem Teil des Landes fuer das notwendige Existenzminimum gehalten wird.

2. Leute, die ungelernte Arbeiter sind, die jedoch das in ihrem Teil des Landes erforderliche Mindesteinkommen haben.

3. Leute des Mittelstandes je nach den in ihrem Teil des Landes geltenden Massstaeben. Diese Gruppe wird sich gewoehnlich aus Bueroangestellten, Ladenbesitzern, Bauern, Handwerkern, Schullehrern usw. zusammensetzen.

4. Leute, die ein Einkommen haben, das es ihnen gestattet, ueber das hinaus, was man in ihrem Teil des Landes als 'normale Lebensbeduerfnisse' ansieht, sich einen aufwendigeren Luxus zu erfreuen. Diese Gruppe wird sich gewoehnlich aus Haus- und Grundbesitzern, Managern, Aerzten, Geschaeftsleuten, Universitaetsprofessoren usw. zusammensetzen.

5. Welche Leute. Die einflussreichsten Leute in dem Teil des Landes, in dem Sie taetig sind, wie z.B. Grossgrundbesitzer, Grossindustrielle, Privatbankiers usw.

Unter welche der obengenannten Kategorien fallen die Leute, deren Sie den groessten Teil Ihrer Zeit zuwenden? Kategorie 1 ..... Kategorie 2 ..... Kategorie 3.... Kategorie 4 ..... Kategorie 5.....

Zu welcher dieser Kategorien wuerden Sie Ihre Eltern zur Zeit Ihres Aufwachsens zurechnen? Kategorie 1 ..... Kategorie 2 ..... Kategorie 3 .... Kategorie 4 .... Kategorie 5 .....

Unter welcher der obengenannten Kategorien liesse sich Ihrer Meinung nach der Lebensstil beschreiben, den Sie als Jenult zur Zeit fuehren? Kategorie 1 ..... Kategorie 2 ..... Kategorie 3 .... Kategorie 4 ..... Kategorie 5 ....

Auf den folgenden Seiten finden Sie zwei Gruppen von Lebenszielen in alphabetischer Reihenfolge. Bitte bringen Sie diese Werte in die Reihenfolge, in die sie Ihrer Ansicht nach gehoeren, d.h., so wie sie fuer Ihr Leben wichtig sind.

Bitte sehen Sie sich die erste Liste auf Seite 3 sorgfältig an, und wählen Sie das Lebensziel aus, welches Ihnen am allerwichtigsten erscheint. Schreiben Sie eine "1" in das Feld links neben dem Begriff. Dann wählen Sie das Lebensziel aus, welches Ihnen als zweitwichtigstes erscheint. Schreiben Sie eine "2" in das Feld ... so ... mit den restlichen sechzehn Lebenszielen der Seite 3. Das am wenigsten wichtig erscheinende Ziel erhält dann natürlich die Nummer "18".

Bitte arbeiten Sie langsam, und denken Sie sorgfältig nach. Falls Sie Ihre Meinung korrigieren wollen, so können Sie dies leicht durch radieren oder durchstreichen machen. Wenn Sie fertig sind, sollten die Lebensziele in der Reihenfolge nummeriert sein, in der sie für Sie von Wichtigkeit sind.

Es ist uns bewusst, dass jeder dieser Begriffe viele subtile Bedeutungsnuancen zulässt. Dennoch bitten wir, Sie diese Wertbegriffe in eine Rangordnung einzustufen, ohne indessen über deren Bedeutung zu sehr analytisch zu werden.

___ DAS GEFÜHL, ETWAS ERREICHT ZU HABEN (ein dauerhafter Beitrag)

___ EIN ANGENEHMES LEBEN (ein wohlhabendes Leben)

___ EIN AUFREGENDES LEBEN (ein anregendes, tätiges Leben)

___ EINE FRIEDLICHE WELT (ohne Krieg oder Konflikte)

___ EINE SCHÖNE WELT (Schönheit der Natur und der Künste)

___ ERLÖSUNG (zum ewigen Leben) [d.h. Heilsweg]

___ FREIHEIT (Unabhängigkeit, Freiheit der Entscheidung)

___ GENUSS (ein vergnügliches, genussvolles Leben)

___ GESELLSCHAFTLICHE ANERKENNUNG (Respekt, Bewunderung)

___ GLEICHHEIT (Brüderlichkeit, gleiche Chance für jeden)

___ GLÜCK (Zufriedenheit)

___ INNERE HARMONIE (Eintracht mit sich selbst)

___ REIFE LIEBE (geistig-sexuelle Vertrautheit)

___ SELBSTACHTUNG (Respekt vor sich selbst)

___ SICHERHEIT FÜR DIE FAMILIE (für seine Lieben sorgen)

___ STAATLICHE SICHERHEIT (Sicherheit vor Angriffen)

___ WAHRE FREUNDSCHAFT (enge Kameradschaft)

___ WEISHEIT (ein tiefes Verständnis des Lebens)

Unten gibt es eine zweite Reihe von achtzehn Werten. Bitte bringen Sie diese Werte in die Reihenfolge nach deren Wichtigkeit für Sie, genauso wie Sie es schon oben getan habt.

_____ BEHERRSCHT (zurückhaltend, diszipliniert)

_____ EHRGEIZIG (fleissig, strebsam)

_____ EHRLICH (aufrichtig, wahrhaftig)

_____ FÄHIG (kompetent, wirkungsvoll)

_____ GEHORSAM (pflichtbewusst, respektvoll)

_____ HILFREICH (sich um das Wohlergehen anderer kümmern)

_____ HÖFLICH (wohlerzogen)

_____ INTELLEKTUELL (intelligent, nachdenklich)

_____ LIEBEVOLL (zärtlich, sugend)

_____ LOGISCH (übereinstimmend, rational)

_____ MUNTER (leichten Herzens, fröhlich)

_____ MUTIG (zu seiner Überzeugung stehen)

_____ NACHSICHTIG (bereit sein, anderen zu verzeihen)

_____ PHANTASIEVOLL (kühn, schöpferisch)

_____ SAUBER (ordentlich, nett)

_____ TOLERANT (aufgeschlossen)

_____ UNABHÄNGIG (selbstgenügsam, selbstvertrauend)

_____ VERANTWORTLICH (zuverlässig, verlässlich)

Jeder der folgenden Sätze beschreibt eine Sicht von GOTT.(Entscheiden Sie sich für DEN Satz, der Ihnen am meisten zusagt.) Unter Gott verstehe ich...

a. den allwissenden und allmächtigen Schöpfer aller Dinge;

b. den liebenden Vater, der seinen Sohn sandte, um die Geheimnisse göttlicher Gnade zu offenbaren;

c. die Anwesenheit Gottes in der Welt, die sich mir zeigt in den Menschen, den Dingen und Ereignissen.

Jeder der folgenden Sätze beschreibt eine Sicht von HEILIGEN GEIST. (Entscheiden Sie sich für DEN Satz, der Ihnen am meisten zusagt.)

a. Der Heilige Geist führt die Kirche zum wachsenden Verständnis der Botschaft Christi und zu ihrer inneren Einheit, indem er durch das ganze Volk Gottes spricht;

b. Der Heilige Geist, der vom Vater und vom Sohn ausgeht, teilt die Gnade Gottes an die Menschen aus.

c. Der Heilige Geist spricht im Laufe der Geschichte zu allen Menschen guten Willens auf verschiedene Weise und unter verschiedenen Umständen.

d. mir nicht klar.

(Entscheiden Sie sich für EINE der folgenden Auffassungen.) Das Ziel unserer missionarischen Arbeit ist:...

a. Leute zur katholischen Kirche zu bekehren durch: Predigen, religiöse Unterweisung, Sakramentenspendung, usw.;

b. Menschen zu helfen, ihre eigenen Hilfsquellen zu erschliessen, um alle ihre menschlichen Bedürfnisse zur erfüllen, und zwar im religiösen, wirtschaftlichen und politischen Bereich;

c. Zeuge der Liebe Gottes zu sein, das Evangelium zu verkünden und die Kirche aufzubauen unter den Menschen, die noch nichts von Christus wissen;

d. mir nicht klar.

Jeder der folgenden Sätze beschreibt eine Sicht der KIRCHE. (Entscheiden Sie sich für DEN Satz, der Ihnen am meisten zusagt.)

a. Als Verwalterin der göttlichen Wahrheit und Gnade für die Menschen, ist die Kirche der einzig wahre Weg zum Heil.

b. Die Kirche ist eine vollkommene, religiöse Gesellschaft unter der Leitung des Papstes und der Bischöfe.

c. Als Volk Gottes, in engster Verbindung mit Christus, ist die Kirche ein Sakrament oder Zeichen der Vereinigung der Menschen mit Gott und untereinander.

d. Die Kirche hat die Aufgabe prophetischer Kritik an Gesellschaft und Kultur.

e. Die Kirche bleibt in dieser Welt stets unterwegs, im Dienst an aller menschlichen Not, d.h. im Bereich von Religion, Wirtschaft, Erziehung und Politik.

Jede der folgenden Aussagen beschreibt einige Aspekte des Verhältnisses zwischen Kirche und Welt. Unter diesem Verhältnis verstehe ich (Entscheiden Sie sich fuer die Aussage, die Ihnen am meisten zusagt). .....

a. Die Kirche, in Innersten der menschlichen Existenz zuhause, ist die Staette, von der das Wort ausstrahlt, dessen Zeuge sie ist in Hinsicht auf die Antwort zu Fragen, die sie selbst nicht gestellt hat. Die Kirche wuerde gut daran tun, in der Deinstitutionalisierung ihrer eigenen Belange bis zum Aeussersten zu gehen. Sie sollte sich ersichlich um eine Zusammenarbeit mit Priestern, Laien und weltlichen Kreisen bemuehen, um diese ihre Zeugenschaft sichtbar zu machen. Ihr vordringliches Anliegen muss ihre Sorge fuer die Armen sein, deren Leben wir in allen teilen muessen.

b. Die Kirche ist das Sakrament des Ewigen Heils, das von oben kommt. Fundamental von der Welt verschieden, muss Sie die Menschen anziehen und als die Gemeinschaft der Getauften aufrichten. Deshalb muss den geistlichen und priesterlichen Aemtern Vorrang eingebilligt werden. Die Reform der Kirche muss aus ihrem eigenen Schooss kommen und ihre Arbeit sich in umfassendes Zusammenhang ihrer seelsorgischer Dienstleistungen abstecken. Sie muss ihr besorgtes Interesse fuer einen in Licht des Glaubens sich entfaltenden, allumfassenden Humanismus bewahren und pflegen.

Jeder der folgenden Sätze beschreibt eine Sicht der WELT.
(Entscheiden Sie sich für DEN Satz, der Ihnen am meisten zusagt.)

a. Die Welt ist der Kampfplatz, auf dem der Mensch sich für Gott bewährt, indem er Gottes Verehrung verbreitet und den Willen Gottes öffnet.

b. Die Welt ist gut. Gottes schöpferische Tätigkeit setzt sich in der Entwicklung der Menschheit und seiner Kulturarbeit fort, um der Welt ein besseres Geleucht zu geben.

c. Die Welt ist erschaffen und wird erhalten von der Liebe Gottes, sie wurde durch die Sünde des Menschen verschlaart, aber durch die Liebe Christi in die Freiheit geführt.

Jeder der folgenden Sätze beschreibt eine Sicht des GEISTLICHEN AMTES. (Entscheiden Sie sich für DEN Satz, der Ihnen am meisten zusagt.) Ein christlicher Geistlicher...

a. ist jemand, der vom Volk Gottes ermächtigt wurde; christliche Gemeinschaft aufzubauen, ihre Reifen der Offenbarung Gottes zu sichten und sie zu aktiver Mitarbeit an der Lösung der Probleme der Welt;

b. ist jemand, der die Priesterweihe empfangen hat und dadurch befugt ist, die Eucharistie zu feiern und das Busssakrament und die Krankensalbung zu spenden;

c. hat als Hauptaufgabe die Glaubensverkündigung und die Spendung der Sakramente an die Gläubigen.

Jeder der folgenden Sätze beschreibt eine Sicht des GLAUBENS.
(Entscheiden Sie sich für DEN Satz, der Ihnen am meisten zusagt.)

a. die Bejahung dessen, dass die Welt und die Menschen

b. die Heilsgewissheit;

c. die persönliche Beziehung zu Gott;

d. die Feststellung, dass es in meinem Leben eine Vorsehung Gottes gibt;

e. die Annahme der Lehren der Kirche;

f. meine totale Hingabe an Gott.

Jeder der folgenden Aussagen beschreibt einige Aspekte der Kultur. Unter Kultur verstehe ich (Entscheiden Sie sich fuer die Aussage, die Ihnen am meisten zusagt). ......

a. Kultur kann am besten empirisch verstanden werden. Sie besteht aus einer Reihe von Sinngehalten und Wertbegriffen, die fuer eine gemeinsame Lebensweise verbindlich sind. Es gibt ebenso viele Kulturen wie es voneinander unterschiedene Gruppen derartiger Sinngehalte und Wertbegriffe gibt. Solche Sinngehalte und Wertbegriffe muessen in ihrem Verhältnis zu den Milieus und Kulturen verstanden werden, aus denen heraus sie sich entwickeln.

b. Kultur kann am besten normativ verstanden werden. Sie besteht darin, dass man sich die Meinungen und Fertigkeiten, die Tugenden, die Ideale und die Vorstellungen, die mit einer kultivierten Erziehung und mit dem freien Kunstsein zusammengehen, erwirbt und sich zu eigen macht. Sie ist ebenso allgemeingültig wie es die unsterblichen Werke der Kunst und die alles überdauernde Philosophie sind.

Jeder der folgenden Sätze beschreibt eine Sicht von CHRISTUS.
(Entscheiden Sie sich für DEN Satz, der Ihnen am meisten zusagt.)

a. Als der auferstandene Herr ist Christus der Befreier für alle, die von den Mächten dieser Welt unterdrückt werden.

b. Als der menschgewordene und leidende Sohn Gottes ist Christus unser Mittler und Erlöser.

c. Als der reifste und heiligste Mensch, der je gelebt hat und jemals leben wird, ist Christus die Verwirklichung Gottes in menschlicher Natur und Geschichte.

d. Als wahrer Gott ist Christus unser Herr, dem Anbetung gebührt.

Jeder der folgenden Sätze beschreibt eine Sicht von GEBET.
(Entscheiden Sie sich für DEN Satz, der Ihnen am meisten zusagt.)

a. Gebet ist das Erheben von Herz und Sinn zu Gott.

b. Gebet ist meine Begegnung mit Gott im Dienst an den anderen.

c. Gebet ist mein Offensein für den persönlichen Gott und meine Antwort an ihn.

d. Gebet ist die Arbeit, die ich tue.

Jeder der folgenden Sätze beschreibt eine Sicht für AUTORITÄT.
(Entscheiden Sie sich für DEN Satz, der Ihnen am meisten zusagt.)

a. Autorität ist gegeben mit dem Amt eines Vorgesetzten; dem entspricht der Gehorsam der Untergebenen.

b. Autorität ist gegeben mit der Fähigkeit, Arbeiten systematisch durchzuplanen und auszuführen; dem entspricht die Mitverantwortung bei der Ausführung der Anweisungen.

c. Autorität ist gegeben mit der persönlichen Ausstrahlungskraft, andere anzuregen und zu ermutigen; dem entspricht Vertrauen in das persönliche Charisma des Führers.

Jeder der folgenden Sätze beschreibt eine Sicht der HEILSGNADE.
(Entscheiden Sie sich für DEN Satz, der Ihnen am meisten zusagt.)

a. Jede christliche Kirche ist nach Gottes Willen Vermittlerin der Heilsgnade an die Menschen.

b. Die katholische Kirche ist nach Gottes Willen die Vermittlerin der Heilsgnade an die Menschen.

c. Jede Religion ist nach Gottes Willen Vermittlerin der Heilsgnade an die Menschen.

d. In jedem Menschen ist die Heilsgnade Gottes in gleicher Weise am Werk.

Denken Sie an Fachleute, die Sie kennen - z.B. an Ärzte, Zahnärzte, Anwälte, Wissenschaftler. Wie waren Ihrer Ansicht nach Priester der Gesellschaft in Ihrer Provinz mit diesen Fachleuten in Bezug auf die folgenden Eigenschaften zu vergleichen? Kreuzen Sie einen Code auf jeder Vergleichsskala an.

Von einigen Ausnahmen abgesehen, haben die Jesuiten in meiner Provinz......

	mehr	ungefähr dasselbe / lass an	weniger	viel weniger	weiss nicht
Umfang von Wissen und Fähigkeit	1	2	3	4	5
Selbstständigkeit in Fassen von Entschlüssen	1	2	3	4	5
Verantwortlichkeitssinn fuer Projekte	1	2	3	4	5
Hingabe zum Dienst fuer die Wohlfahrt der Leute	1	2	3	4	5
Zufriedenheit und Selbstachtung als Resultat geleisteter Arbeit	1	2	3	4	5

VIELEN DANK

ANALISI ORGANIZZATIVA
DEI GESUITI

PARTE II --- SONDAGGIO DEI DELEGATI

Rev. Delegato, P.C.

Le domande qui accluse forniscono una parte vitale di un'analisti organizzativa dei valori della Compagnia di Gesu. Come delegato alla Trentaduesima Congregazione Generale, il Su sforzo generoso contribuira a guidarci negli anni futuri. Questo sondaggio e parte di una grata e reverente riflessione su questa guida.

La prego di rispondere alla domande poste nella pagine seguenti col disegnare un circoletto intorno al numero o la lettera che contrassegna la risposta piu appropriata. Siccome i delegati alla Congregazione includono un piccolo numero di Gesuiti e molto importante ricevere le Sue risposte. Per questo chiedo umilmente di voler rimandare l'intero questionario nella busta acclusa. Se questo verra fatto nei prossimi giorni ci sono meno probabilita che interferisca con i preparativi per il viaggio a Roma.

La assicuro che tutte le informazioni raccolte in questo sondaggio saranno da me considerate strettamente confidenziali. Nessun altro avra accesso all'identificazione di questi dati; nessun superiore o altro Gesuita o altra persona avra accesso ad informazioni specifiche riguardanti chi diede quale risposta. Nessun rapporto basato su queste informazioni verra diffuso prima che la Trentaduesima Congregazione Generale abbia concluso i suoi lavori e sia stata definitivamente aggiornata.

Mi scuso per non aver accluso francobolli per la risposta. Questo e stato impossibile a causa del numero di nazioni a cui il sondaggio e indirizzato; non mi era possibile trovare l'affrancatura appropriata a tutte.

Ringrazio infinitamente per l'attenzione concessa a questo sondaggio. In cambio del Suo gentile ed importante contributo Lei ricevera un estratto dei risultati di questo studio.

Che Dio benedica Lei ed i Suoi sforzi che beneficiamo tutti i Gesuiti. Le mie preghiere e le mie Messe invocheranno la Sua Grazia su di Lei ogni giorno.

Ossequi.

Thomas P Faase

(Rev.) Thomas P. Faase, S.J.

Codice _____

Questo numero verra usato per l'identificazione dei dati e non verra associato a chi li ha forniti in alcun mondo. Nomi non sono richiesti per questo sondaggio.

Per favore specifichi a quale tipo di regione lei appartiene:
(Per favore, faccia un cerchietto intorno al numero oppure alla lettera di sua scelta)

1.- Italiano

2.- Tedesco

3.- Francese

4.- Spagnolo

5.- Inglese

6.- Americano

7.- Slavo

8.- America Latina del Nord

9.- America Latina del Sud

10.- Indiano

11.- Asia dell'Est

12.- Africa

Per favore, specifichi il tipo di lavoro che lei fa a tempo pieno:

A. Amministrazione di super-istituzioni
(e.g. Provinciale, Direttore di Missioni)

B. Amministrazione di istituzione di cultura elevata
(e.g. Presidente oppure Rettore di Universita')

C. Amministrazione di istituzione di educazione secondaria
(e.g. Rettore, Preside di scuola liceale)

D. Educazione liceale : insegnamento (e comune ricerca)

E. Educazione secondaria : insegnamento (e comune ricerca)

F. Amministrazione parrocchiale oppure lavoro pastorale

G. Scrivere oppure ricerca a tempo pieno

H. Apostolato sociale, sviluppo socioeconomico

I. Formazione di nostri oppure di altri chierici; amministrazione di seminari

J. Altro (per favore specificare) _____

Qual'e' la sua eta'

A. Sotto 30

B. 30 - 39

C. 40 - 49

D. 50 - 59

E. 60 - 69

F. 70 ed oltre

Quale pensa sia il suo lavoro:
(Per favore segni il numero o la lettera interessata)

1.- Soprattutto un lavoro d'ufficio, conneso ad una particolare funzione da svolgere.

2.- Lavoro a contatto con la gente, servizio e cura del popolo.

Delle seguenti quali secondo lei sono le preoccupazioni della sua provincia:

A. Adattare i mezzi per gli scopi desiderati, spiegamento di risorse.

B. Vedere il compimento dei fini gia' stabiliti, ottenere gli obbiettivi per mezzo di una coordinazione ed una centrale direzione.

C. Mettere il lavoro e gli scopi che si ottengono dalla provincia in uno schema piu' generale : cercare di definire l'identita' della provincia.

D. Preservare le tradizioni della provincia e della societa' e la vita materiale e religiosa dei propri membri.

Quali dei seguenti lei direbbe che sia lo scopo secondario della sua provincia:

A. Adattare i mezzi agli scopi desiderati, spiegamenti di risorse.

B. Vedere il compimento dei fini gia' proposti, ottenere gli obbiettivi per mezzo di una coordinazione ed una centrale direzione.

C. Mettere il lavoro e gli scopi che si ottengono dalla provincia in uno schema piu' generale : cercare di definire l'identita' della provincia.

D. Preservare le tradizioni della provincia e della societa' e la vita materiale e religiosa dei propi membri.

L'impegno maggiore di questa trentaduesima Congregazione sara' molto probabilmente :
(Scelga un solo aspetto)

A. DOTTRINALE : dare definizioni oppure spiegazioni, fare dichiarazioni sulla nostra fede, sui nostri scopi.

B. PASTORALE : Esortare, incoraggiare.

C. PRATICO : riformare strutture, dettare procedure.

Parlando generalmente, secondo lei qual' é dei seguenti criteri quello piu considerato nel prendere decisioni nella sua provincia:

A. Religioso

B. Politico

C. Economico

D. Cura Personalis

(Segni solo una lettera)

Per favore risponda alle seguenti domade secondo la scelta delle risposte :

1. Molto in favore
2. Daccordo in qualche maniera
3. Incerto
4. In favore juxta modo
5. Contrario fortemente

Per favore scelga una de queste risposte.

Il futuro e' nelle mani di Dio. Aspettero' quello che Egli mi mandera' e accettero' quello che verra' da Lui come sua volonta' per me.

1 2 3 4 5

Oggi il fermento creativo nella chiesa consiste nell' approfondimento della mia fede cristiana.

1 2 3 4 5

Il problema con la Chiesa dopo il Vat. II sta' nel fatto che molte delle certezze a cui eravamo abituati sono state tolte.

1 2 3 4 5

La confusione venuta dopo il Vat. II e' il risultato di un graduale risveglio delle mie propie credenze religiose.

1 2 3 4 5

Ci sono delle occasioni in cui una persona deve porre la sua coscienza personale al di sopra dell' insegnamento della Chiesa.

1 2 3 4 5

La fede di ognuno di noi puo' essere intaccata dallo studio di teologi protestanti.

1 2 3 4 5

Lo spirito di poverta' e' senza senso se non si vince la poverta' materialmente.

1 2 3 4 5

Poverta' significa dipendenza dalla comunita' per quanto concerne i bisogni materiali di ognuno.

1 2 3 4 5

La maniera tradizionale di presentare il voto di castita' nella formazione religiosa ha dato spesso occasioni di uno sviluppo di impersonalismo e di falsa spiritualita'.

1 2 3 4 5

Il dovere del religioso e' obbedire; e' responsabilita' del superiore scoprire la volonta' di Dio e dichiararla.

1 2 3 4 5

E' consigliabile per i Gesuiti, lavorare con progetti regionali e nazionali in quei campi in cui sono competenti per servire anche se il frutto di tale impegno non da' un risultato per la provincia o per quella instituzione Gesuita a cui si appartiene.

1 2 3 4 5

Il lavoro e la finalita' della intera Compagnia di Gesu' su un piano internazionale richiedono precedenza assoluta su tutte le altre attivita', qualora un Gesuita ha l'opportunita' di influire in tal senso.

1 2 3 4 5

Ogni stuttura organizzata diventa di peso nel tempo e ha bisogno di un rinnovamento.

1 2 3 4 5

Preferisco essere chiamato un' idealista che un uomo pratico.

1 2 3 4 5

Quando penso alle riforme sociali penso a dei progetti in cui credo cosi' tanto che che vorrei dedicare tutti i miei sforzi per essi.

1 2 3 4 5

Un prete molto difficilmente puo' dirsi pastore se egli non e' impegnato profondamente nella assistenza sociale del suo popolo come nel dare il servizio spirituale ai suoi parocchiani.

1 2 3 4 5

Quando io tratto i problemi del mio lavoro cerco costantemente di prendere decisioni che siano utili a risolvere i piu' grandi problemi della giustizia sociale etc., per tutta l'umanita'. I problemi del mondo sono molto sentiti come miei problemi.

1 2 3 4 5

La situazione attuale della chiesa richiede un cambiamento. Dobbiamo dare una risposta.

1 2 3 4 5

Liberalismo e' buono perche' ha uno spirito di riforma. E' una apertura ottimistica che ha bisogno di un seguito. Non sempre rappresenta giustizia, charezza, saggezza, ma sempre tenta di arrivare a questi scopi.

1 2 3 4 5

Ogni grande passo in avanti della storia del mondo e' stato provocato dall' aspirazione di uomini creativi e riformatori.

1 2 3 4 5

Alcuni lavori espletati nell'apostolato della Compagnia di Gesu' sono necessariamente di servizio all'istituzione Gesuita di cui si fa' parte.

1 2 3 4 5

La Provincia ha il diritto che un Gesuita lavori per compiti di Congregazione anche quando questo lavoro interferisce con il desiderio dell'individuo di dedicarsi al suo propio apostolato a cui si sente portato.

1 2 3 4 5

Nella mia Provincia la Compagnia sembra piu' interessata a provedere alle persone piu' che insegnar loro come provvedere a se stessi.

1 2 3 4 5

Le attivita' della mia provincia sono sufficientemente dirette ai poveri - e alle persone meno fortunate.

1 2 3 4 5

I membri della mia provincia sono sufficentemente aperti ai valori locali come pure al gusto della liturgia del loro popolo.

1 2 3 4 5

Lo scopo dell' attivita' missionaria é :
(ne scelga una, la piu' rappresentativa)

a. Convertire gente alla Chiesa Cattolica per mezzo della predicazione, l'insegnamento del catechismo, l'amministrazione dei sacramenti, etc.

b. Aiutare l'uomo a sviluppare tutte le sue risorse per soddisfare tutti i suoi bisogni, per es. religiosi, economici, educativi, politici, etc.

c. Essere un testimone dell'amore di Dio, predicare il Vangelo e formare la Chiesa fra gente che ancora non conosce Dio.

d. Non ancora chiaro per me.

Ognuna delle seguenti affermazioni descrive un aspetto della Chiesa :
(ne scelga una, la piu' rappresentativa)

a. Come mediatrice della grazia e della verita' tra Dio e gli uomini, la Chiesa é l'unica vera via della salvezza.

b. La Chiesa é una perfetta societa' religiosa, organizzata sotto il Papa i vescovi.

c. Siccome il popolo di Dio é intimamente in relazione con Cristo, la Chiesa é un sacramento o segno dell'unione dell'uomo con Dio e con gli altri.

d. La Chiesa é la critica profetica della societa' e della cultura.

e. Come un pellegrino su questa terra é al servizio dei bisogni dell'intera umanita', nei suoi bisogni religiosi, economici, educativi e politici.

Ognuna delle seguenti affermazioni descrive alcuni aspetti della relazione della Chiesa con il mondo. Io intendo questa relazione :
(ne scelga una, la piu' rappresentativa)

a. La Chiesa, nella profondita' della sua esistenza umana é il luogo da cui viene la Parola di cui lei é testimone nel rispondere a quelle domande che le sono poste. La Chiesa farebbe bene a svestirsi delle istituzioni per collaborare piu' da vicino con sacerdoti, laici, con interessi secolari per dar maggior risalto alla sua testimonianza. Priorita' su tutto dovrebbe darla ai poveri, condividendo pienamente la loro vita.

b. La Chiesa é il sacramento della salvezza che deriva dall'alto. Radicalmente differente dal mondo, la Chiesa deve attirare e portare gli uomini nella comunita' dei battezzati. Percio', precedenza deve essere data a tutto quello che é spirituale e sacerdotale. Riformandosi dall'interno, la Chiesa deve lavorare tenendo in considerazione tutta la globalita' del suo servizio pastorale e l'umanesimo integrale che si sviluppa alla luce della fede.

Ognuna di queste affermazioni descrive un aspetto del mondo :
(ne scelga la piu' rappresentativa)

a. Il mondo é l'arena dove l'uomo prova se stesso per Dio avendo fiducia nella sua Provvidenza e seguendo la sua volonta'.

b. Il mondo é buono, e l'attivita' creativa di Dio continua attraverso lo sviluppo dell' uomo e della sua cultura nel migliorarlo.

c. Il mondo, creato e sostenuto dall'amore di Dio, divento' corrotto per il peccato dell'uomo, ma é stato risanato per l'amore di Cristo.

Ognuna delle seguenti affermazioni descrive un aspetto del Ministero . Il ministro cristiano é :
(ne scelga una, la piu' rappresentativa)

a. Qualcuno che é stato autorizzato dal popolo di Dio di costruire la comunita' cristiana, guidarla nella celebrazione della grazia di Dio, e ispirarla nel condividere le ansie del mondo.

b. Qualcuno ordinato sacerdote e percio' autorizzato a celebrare l'Eucaristia ed amministrare i sacramenti della Confessione e dell' unzione degl' infermi.

c. Qualcuno, il cui compito principale é spargere il Vangelo di Cristo ed amministrare i sacramenti ai fedeli.

Ognuna delle seguenti affermazioni descrive un aspetto della fede. Per fede intendo :
(ne scelga una, la piu' rappresentativa)

a. Un affermazione dell'ultima bonta' dell'uomo e di questo mondo.

b. Sicurezza della salvezza.

c. Una relazione personale con Dio.

d. Un' affermazione della Provvidenza di Dio nella mia vita.

e. Un' accettazione degli insegnamenti della Chiesa.

f. Donazione completa di me stesso a Dio.

Ognuna delle seguenti affermazioni descrive alcuni aspetti della cultura. Per cultura intendo :
(ne scelga una, la piu' rappresentativa)

a. Cultura é il meglio concepito empiricamente. Sono quei valori e significati che danno luce sul come vivere la vita, e ci sono cosi tante culture quanti sono i valori e significati usati per vivere. Tali valori e significati sono da considerarsi relativi ai sistemi e alle culture di vita da cui emergono.

b. Cultura é il meglio concepito normativamente. E questione di acquisizione e assimilazione di gusti, maniere, intelligenza, capacita', ideali, virtu', idee delle arti liberali e molto definite. E universale come i capolavori inmortali e le filosofie perenni.

Segue una lista di 18 valori. Siamo interessati nel trovare la relativa importanza di ognuno di questi valori per lei.

Prenda seriamente in considerazione la lista. Quindi metta 1 al valore che e' piu' importante per lei, poi ponga 2 al valore che e' secondo per importanza, etc. Il n. 18 sara', quindi, quel valore che ha meno importanza per lei.

Siamo perfettamente a conoscenza che alcuni valori sono similari nel loro significato. Tuttavia, li ponga in ordine senza diventare troppo analitico riguardo al loro significato. Quando ha finito di porli in ordine, dia uno sguardo di nuovo alla sua lista.

Sia libero di cambiare la lista. Prenda il suo tempo nel compilare la lista in modo che rappresenti i suoi valori.

_____ VITA CONFORTEVOLE (vita ricca)

_____ VITA ECCITANTE (vita stimolante, attiva)

_____ UN SENSO DI REALIZZAZIONE (una durevole collaborazione)

_____ UN MONDO IN PACE (senza guerra e conflitti)

_____ UN MONDO DI BELLEZZA (bellezza di natura e di arti)

_____ UGUAGLIANZA (fratellanza, uguali possibilita' per tutti)

_____ SICUREZZA FAMIGLIARE (cura per le persone amate)

_____ LIBERTA' (indipendenza - liberta' di scelta)

_____ GIOIA (contentezza)

_____ ARMONIA INTERIORE (niente conflitti interni)

_____ AMORE MATURO (intimita' sessuale e spirituale)

_____ SICUREZZA NAZIONALE (difesa da attacco)

_____ PIACERE (una vita goduta e vissuta facilmente)

_____ SALVEZZA (essere salvato per la vita eterna)

_____ AUTO-RISPETTO (stima di se stessi)

_____ RISPETTO DA PARTE DI ALTRI (ammirazione)

_____ AMICIZIA SINCERA (amicizia intima)

_____ SAGGEZZA (comprensione matura della vita)

Segue un' altra lista di 18 valori. Metterli in ordine di importanza come prima.

_____ AMBIZIONE (grande lavoratore - aspirante)

_____ APERTURA DI MENTE (mentalita' aperta)

_____ CAPACE (competente, efficiente)

_____ SORRIDENTE (gioioso, allegro)

_____ PULITO (ordinato, lindo)

_____ CORAGGIOSO (difendere le proprie convinzioni)

_____ UNA PERSONA CHE SA PERDONARE (perdonare altri)

_____ AIUTANTE (che lavora per il benessere degli altri)

_____ ONESTO (sincero, veritiero)

_____ IMMAGINATIVO (audace, creativo)

_____ INDIPENDENTE (fiducioso, auto- sufficiente)

_____ INTELLETTUALE (intelligente, riflessivo)

_____ LOGICO (razionale, coerente)

_____ AMABILE (affettuoso, tenero)

_____ OBBEDIENTE (sottomesso, rispettoso)

_____ GENTILE (cortese, educato)

_____ RESPONSABILE (attendibile)

_____ AUTO-CONTROLLO (misurato, autodisciplinato)

Ognuna delle seguenti affermazioni descrive un aspetto di Dio. Per Dio io intendo : (scelga una delle seguenti affermazioni per lei piu' rappresentativa)

a. L'Onnipotente e onnisciente Dio della Creazione.

b. Il Dio-Amore che ha mandato suo figlio per rivelarci i misteri della Grazia Divina.

c. La sua Divina presenza nel mondo che io scopro nella gente, cose e avvenimenti.

Ognuna delle seguenti affermazioni descrive un aspetto dello Spirito Santo : (scelga una delle seguenti affermazioni, la piu' rappresentativa)

a. Lo Spirito Santo guida la Chiesa a capir meglio il messaggio di Cristo ed ad un' unita' fra noi parlando attraverso tutto il popolo di Dio.

b. Lo Spirito Santo, che procede dal Padre e dal Figlio, distribuisce la Grazia di Dio agli uomini.

c. Lo Spirito Santo parla a tutti gli uomini di buona volonta' in differenti maniere e in circostanze differenti della storia.

La Compagnia in generale e' sufficientemente aperta a variazioni culturali nella espressione della nostra vita religiosa e comunitaria.　1　2　3　4　5

Quando si lavora all'estero i Gesuiti dovrebbero evitare di prendere degli atteggiamenti forti in pubblico riguardo ad argomenti religiosi o sociali.　1　2　3　4　5

Anche quando si lavora nel propio paese i Gesuiti dovrebbero generalmente evitare di prendere degli atteggiamenti forti in pubblico riguardo ad argomenti religiosi o sociali.　1　2　3　4　5

In ultima analisi, la differenza consiste nell' avere il potere.　1　2　3　4　5

Non importa la bellezza degli ideali che vuoi raggiungere, li puoi conseguire solo se hai le forze del potere della tua parte.　1　2　3　4　5

Nell'azione e' naturale agire anche per propio interesse.　1　2　3　4　5

Nel lavoro di un Gesuita i bisogni immediati e generali del suo particolare apostolato devono avere il primo sforzo e considerazione.　1　2　3　4　5

La Chiesa compirebbe meglio la sua missione continuando nel suo tradizionale ruolo di insegnamento, che non sperimentando sempre nuovi metodi.　1　2　3　4　5

In una analisi finale, la parte piu' forte base per un programma per il futuro sta' nel suo basarsi sull'esperienza del passato e nei fatti storici.　1　2　3　4　5

Io preferisco il conservatorismo perche' preserva la nostra gloriosa eredita'.　1　2　3　4　5

Durante i trascorsi dieci anni molti religiosi hanni cambiato alcuni dei principi e valori in cui essi precedentemente credevano.　1　2　3　4　5

I valori basilari della Chiesa rimangono gli stessi, ma la loro espressione viene cambiando.　1　2　3　4　5

Sullo spazio lasciato libero sotto, ponga i nomi di tre delegati che secondo lei influenzeranno maggiormente questa Generale Congregazione:

―――――――――――――――――

―――――――――――――――――

―――――――――――――――――

Seguano cinque categorie di classi sociali. Le legga e risponda alle domande :

1.　I poveri, che non hanno i mezzi necessari per un tenore di vita che nel suo paese è considerato come il minimo per vivere.

2.　Persone que non sono lavoratori specializzati, ma che hanno il minimo richiesto per vivere secondo il tenore di vita del suo paese.

3.　La classe media. Usualmente in questa classe si includono lavoratori, piccoli commercianti, piccoli propietari terrieri, lavoratori specializzati, insegnanti, etc.

4.　Gente avente una entrata superiore che permette loro di avere una vita considerata nel suo paese, superiore alla normale. Questa classe include medici, uomini d'affari, propietari terrieri, professori, etc.

5.　Gente ricca. La gente piu influente nel tuo paese, quali grossi propietari terrieri, grandi uomini d'affari, ufficiali governativi, etc.

A quale di queste classi lei dedica maggiormente il suo tempo?

Categoria 1 _____

Categoria 2 _____

Categoria 3 _____

Categoria 4 _____

Categoria 5 _____

A quale di queste cinque categorie appartengono i tuoi genitori mentre eri ancora in famiglia?

Categoria 1 _____

Categoria 2 _____

Categoria 3 _____

Categoria 4 _____

Categoria 5 _____

Come Gesuita, a quali di queste cinque categorie lei pensa di appartenere ora?

Categoria 1 _____

Categoria 2 _____

Categoria 3 _____

Categoria 4 _____

Categoria 5 _____

Ognuna delle seguenti affermazioni descrive
un aspetto di Cristo :
(ne scelga una, la piu' rappresentativa)

a. Siccome Cristo é Risorto, Cristo é il libe-
ratore di tutti gli oppressi dalle forze di
questo mundo.

b. Siccome Cristo si é incarnato, il Figlio sof-
ferente di Dio, il Cristo é nostro Mediatore
e Redentore.

c. Siccome Cristo é l'uomo piu' maturo e piu'
santo che fu e che ci sara', Cristo ha incarnato Dio nella natura umana e nella storia.

d. Siccome Cristo é veramente Dio, egli é il
nostro Signore, che dobbiamo adorare.

Ognuna delle seguenti affermazioni descrive
un aspetto della preghiera :
(ne scelga una, la piu' rappresentativa)

a. Preghiera é l'innalzare mente e cuore a
Dio.

b. Preghiera é il mio incontro con Dio serven-
do i bisogni degli altri.

c. Preghiera é il mio modo di sentire e rispondere al Dio personale.

d. Preghiera é il lavoro che porto avanti.

Ognuna delle seguenti affermazioni descrive
un aspetto dell'autorita'.
(ne scelga una, la piu' rappresentativa)

a. L'autorita' deriva dall'ufficio di un superiore : la risposta é l'obbedienza.

b. L'autorita' deriva da una coordinazione e
direzione delle attivita' i la risposta é cor-
responsabilita' nella concretizzazione di di-
rettive.

c. L'autorita' deriva da un carisma personale nello ispirare ed incoraggire gli altri;
la risposta é fiducia nel carisma del leader.

Ognuna delle seguenti affermazioni descrive
un aspetto della salvezza :
(ne scelga una, la piu' rappresentativa)

a. Tutte le Chiese cristiane sono mezzi usati
dalla grazia di Dio per salvare l'uomo.

b. La Chiesa Cattolica é il mezzo che Dio usa
per salvare l'uomo.

c. Tutte le religioni sono canali che Dio usa
per salvare l'uomo.

d. La grazia della salvezza di Dio é operan-
te in ogni uomo.

Pensi ad uomini professionisti che lei conosce, avvocati, dottori, den-
tisti, scienziati. Come pensa che i sacerdoti gesuiti della sua provincia si paragonerebbero a loro prendendo in considerazione gli attribu-
ti che seguono?
Segni solo un numero per linea.

Con qualche eccezione, i gesuiti
della mia provincia ...

	hanno piu'	hanno lo stesso	meno	molto meno	non so
Profonda conoscenza ed intelligenza.	1	2	3	4	5
Autonomia di prendere decisioni	1	2	3	4	5
Responsabilita' di impegno	1	2	3	4	5
Dedizione nel servizio del popolo	1	2	3	4	5
Soddisfazione e stima di se stessi guadagnata dal proprio lavoro	1	2	3	4	5

MOLTE GRAZIE

Jesuit Organizational Analysis

Please answer the questions below according to the following choice of responses.

1. Agree strongly.
2. Agree some what.
3. Uncertain.

4. Disagree somewhat.
5. Disagree strongly.

(PLEASE CIRCLE ONE CODE ON EACH LINE)

The creative ferment in the Church today is bringing about a deepening of my Christian faith.   1 2 3 4 5

The turmoil following Vatican II is resulting in a gradual weakening of my own religious beliefs.   1 2 3 4 5

Poverty means dependence on the community for all one's material needs.   1 2 3 4 5

The traditional way of presenting the vow of chastity in religious formation has often allowed for the development of impersonalism and false spirituality.   1 2 3 4 5

The duty of the subject is to obey; it is the responsability of the superior to discern God's will and declare it.   1 2 3 4 5

It is advisable for Jesuits to concern themselves with regional or national projects they are competent to serve even if the fruit of such concerns serve neither the Province nor the institution that the Jesuit belongs to.   1 2 3 4 5

The work and purposes of the entire Society of Jesus at the International level deserve precedence over all other levels of effectiveness whenever a Jesuit has opportunity to exert influence at that level.   1 2 3 4 5

Any organizational structure becomes a deadening weight in time and needs to be revitalized.   1 2 3 4 5

A priest can hardly call himself a shepherd if he is not as deeply involved in the social welfare of people as he is in giving spiritual service to his parishioners.   1 2 3 4 5

When I am dealing with the problems of my own job, I find myself constantly trying to make decisions that will help solve the bigger issues of justice, etc., for all mankind. The world's problems are very much my problems   1 2 3 4 5

The current situation in the Church calls for change. We must respond at once.   1 2 3 4 5

Some concerns of an individual Jesuit's work in the apostolate are necessarily subservient to the institution or Jesuit team-effort of which he is a part.   1 2 3 4 5

The Province has the right to expect a Jesuit to work on Province-wide tasks even if that work interferes with the individual's attention to his own apostolate and the institution he belongs to.   1 2 3 4 5

Even when working in their native countries, Jesuits should generally avoid taking strong public positions on religious or social issues.   1 2 3 4 5

The activities of my Province are sufficiently concerned with the poor and those held in low esteem.   1 2 3 4 5

The members of my province are sufficiently receptive to local values and sensitivites in their people's liturgy.   1 2 3 4 5

When working in foreing countries, Jesuits should avoid taking strong public positions on religious or social issues.   1 2 3 4 5

No matter how wonderful the ideals you are trying to get across may be, you cannot do a thing unless you have the powers that be on your side.   1 2 3 4 5

When you come right down to it, it's human nature never to do anything without an eye to one's own profit.   1 2 3 4 5

In a Jesuit's work, the inmediate and overall needs of the particular apostolate he serves warrant his primary consideration and effort.   1 2 3 4 5

By continuing its traditional approach to its teaching role, the Church will better accomplish its mission than by experimenting with new methods.   1 2 3 4 5

In the final analysis the strongest basis for planning for the future is to trust to the experience of the past and base the decision-making on the facts, the historical facts.   1 2 3 4 5

During the past 10 years many religious have changed some of the basic principles and values which they formerly believed in.   1 2 3 4 5

The Basic Values of the Church remain the same, but their expression is changing.   1 2 3 4 5

Below is a list of 18 values in alphabetical order. We are interested in finding out the relative importance of these values to you.

Study the list carefully. Then place a 1 next to the value which is most important to you, place a 2 next to the value which is second most important, etc. The value which is least important should be ranked 18.

We realize that each of the terms is capable of many subtle differences in meaning. Nonetheless, order these values without becoming overly analytical about their meaning.

When you have completed ranking all the values, go back and check over your list. Feel free to make changes. Please take all the time you need to think about this, so that the end result truly represents yours values.

_____ A COMFORTABLE LIFE (a prosperous life)

_____ AN EXCITING LIFE (a stimulating, active life)

_____ A SENSE OF ACCOMPLISHMENT (lasting contribution)

_____ A WORLD AT PEACE (free of war and conflict)

_____ A WORLD OF BEAUTY (beauty of nature and the arts)

_____ EQUALITY (brotherhood, equal opportunity for all)

_____ FAMILY SECURITY (taking care of loved ones)

_____ FREEDOM (independence, free choice)

_____ HAPPINESS (contentedness)

_____ INNER HARMONY (freedom fron inner conflict)

_____ MATURE LOVE (sexual and spiritual intimacy)

_____ NATIONAL SECURITY (protection from attack)

_____ PLEASURE (an enjoyable, leisurely life)

_____ SALVATION (saved, eternal life)

_____ SELF - RESPECT (self-esteem)

_____ SOCIAL RECOGNITION (respect, admiration)

_____ TRUE FRINDSHIP (close companionship)

_____ WISDOM (a mature understanding of life)

Below is another list of 18 values. Arrange them in order of importance, the same as before.

_____ AMBITIOUS (hard-working, aspiring)

_____ BROADMINDED (open-minded)

_____ CAPABLE (competent, effective)

_____ CHEERFUL (lighthearted, joyful)

_____ CLEAN (neat, tidy)

_____ COURAGEOUS(standing up for your beliefs)

_____ FORGIVIN((willing to pardon others)

_____ HELPFUL (working for the welfare of others)

_____ HONEST (sincere, truthful)

_____ IMAGINATIVE (daring, creative)

_____ INDEPENDENT (self-reliant, self-sufficient)

_____ INTELLECTUAL (intelligent, reflective)

_____ LOGICAL (consistent, rational)

_____ LOVING (affectionate, tender)

_____ OBEDIENT (dutiful, respectful)

_____ POLITE (courteous, well-mannered)

_____ RESPONSIBLE (dependable, reliable)

_____ SELF-CONTROLLED (restrained, self-disciplined)

On the lines below, please NAME those three delegates that you believe exerted the greatest influence at this General Congregation:

_____

_____

_____

THANK YOU VERY MUCH

Analisis Organizacional Jesuistico

Por favor, responda las preguntas que siguen de acuerdo con las siguientes alternativas:

1. Fuertemente de acuerdo.   4. Un tanto en desacuerdo.
2. Algo de acuerdo.   5. Fuertemente en desacuerdo.
3. Dudoso.

(POR FAVOR HAGA UN CIRCULO EN UNA CLAVE DE CADA UNA DE LAS LINEAS)

El fermento creativo de hoy en la Iglesia me lleva a una profundización de mi fe cristiana.   1 2 3 4 5

La confusión que sigue al Vaticano II está resultando en un gradual debilitamiento de mis creencias religiosas.   1 2 3 4 5

Pobreza significa dependencia de la comunidad en las necesidades materiales.   1 2 3 4 5

La forma tradicional de presentar el voto de castidad en la formación religiosa ha permitido a menudo el desarrollo del impersonalismo y falsa espiritualidad.   1 2 3 4 5

El deber del sujeto es el de obedecer; la responsabilidad del superior es la de discernir la voluntad de Dios y manifestarla.   1 2 3 4 5

Es aconsejable para los jesuitas interesarse con proyectos regionales o nacionales en los cuales ellos son competentes para servir, aún si el fruto de tales intereses no sirvan ni a la Provincia ni a la Institución a que el jesuíta pertenezca.   1 2 3 4 5

Los trabajos e intenciones de toda la Compañía de Jesús a nivel internacional merecen prioridad sobre todos los otros niveles de efectividad siempre y cuando un jesuíta tenga la oportunidad de ejercer influencia en ese nivel.   1 2 3 4 5

Cualquiera estructura organizacional se convierte en un peso muerto con el tiempo y necesita ser revitalizada.   1 2 3 4 5

Un sacerdote difícilmente puede llamarse pastor si no está tan profundamente envuelto en el bienestar social de la gente como lo está en dar servicio espiritual a sus feligreses.   1 2 3 4 5

Cuando estoy resolviendo los problemas de mi propio negocio, me encuentro constantemente tratando de hacer decisiones que ayudarán a resolver los asuntos más importants de justicia, etc. , para todo el mundo. Los problemas del mundo son profundamente mis problemas.   1 2 3 4 5

La situación actual en la Iglesia pide un cambio. Debemos responder de inmediato.   1 2 3 4 5

Algunos de los intereses del trabajo individual de un jesuíta en el apostolado están necesariamente subordinados a la institución o al esfuerzo del equipo jesuístico del cual él es parte.   1 2 3 4 5

La Provincia tiene el derecho a demandar de un jesuíta el trabajar en empresas que abarquen toda la Provincia aún si este trabajo interfiere con la preocupación del individuo por su propio apostolado y de la Institución a la que pertenece.   1 2 3 4 5

Aún cuando trabajen en sus países nativos, los jesuítas deberían en general abstenerse de tomar fuertes posiciones públicas en cuistiones sociales o religiosas.   1 2 3 4 5

Las actividades de mi Provincia están suficientemente comprometidas con los pobres y con los tenidos en baja estima.   1 2 3 4 5

Los miembros de mi Provincia están suficientemente abiertos a los valores locales y a la sensibilidad del pueblo en la realización de las ceremonias litúrgicas.   1 2 3 4 5

Los jesuítas que trabajan en países extranjeros deberían abstenerse de tomar fuertes posiciones públicas en cuestiones sociales o religiosas.   1 2 3 4 5

No importa que tan maravillosamente sean los ideales que tú quieras comunicar, tú no puedes hacer nada a noser que tengas el poder que sea de tu parte.   1 2 3 4 5

Cuando llegamos a la realidad de los hechos, es propio de la naturaleza humana el nunca hacer nada sin poner un ojo al provecho propio.   1 2 3 4 5

En el trabaj o propio de un jesuíta, las necesidades totales e inmediatas del apostolado particular en que sirve merecen su esfuerzo y consideración primordial.   1 2 3 4 5

La Iglesia alcanzará mucho mejor su misión continuando el enfoque tradicional de sus enseñanzas que a través de experimentaciones con nuevos métodos.   1 2 3 4 5

En última instancia las bases más fuertes para el planeamiento del futuro es el confiar en la experiencia del pasado y basar las decisiones que se hacen en los hechos, los hechos históricos.   1 2 3 4 5

Durante los pasados diez años, muchos religiosos han cambiado algunos de los principios y valores básicos en los cuales ellos creían anteriormente.   1 2 3 4 5

Los valores básicos de la Iglesia permanecen estables, pero su forma de expresión está cambiando.   1 2 3 4 5

A continuación se presenta una lista de 18 valores ordenados alfabéticamente. Estos valores tienen que ordenarse de acuerdo con la importancia para USTED, como principios que guían su vida.

Estudie la lista cuidadosamente; luego ponga el número 1 al valor que sea el más importante para usted, el número 2 para el valor que le sigue en importancia, etc. El valor que tenga la menor importancia, en relación con los demás, consecuentemente, deberá tener el número 18.

Nos damos cuenta que cada uno de los términos tiene diferentes matices en su significado. Sin embargo, ordene estos valores sin llegar a ser demasiado analítico con relación a su significado.

Piense con cuidado, y tome el tiempo necesario. Si usted cambia de opinión, tome la libertad de cambiar sus respuestas a las más apropiadas. Los resultados finales deberán mostrar lo que Ud. siente verdaderamente.

_____ AMISTAD SINCERA (compañerismo)

_____ AMOR MADURO (intimidad sexual y espiritual)

_____ FELICIDAD (contento)

_____ IGUALDAD (hermandad, igualdad de oportunidades para todos)

_____ LIBERTAD (independencia, libre elección)

_____ PAZ INTERNA (libre de conflictos internos)

_____ PLACER (una vida deleitable y despreocupada)

_____ RECONOCIMIENTO SOCIAL (respeto, admiración)

_____ RESPETO A SI MISMO (estimación personal)

_____ SABIDURIA (entendimiento de la vida)

_____ SALVACION (salvación del alma y vida eterna)

_____ SEGURIDAD FAMILIAR (proporcionar cuidados a los seres queridos)

_____ SEGURIDAD NACIONAL (protección contra ataques)

_____ UN MUNDO DE PAZ (libre de guerra y conflictos)

_____ UN MUNDO DE BELLEZA (belleza de la naturaleza y las artes)

_____ UN SENTIMIENTO DE LOGRO (una contribución permanente)

_____ UNA VIDA COMODA (una vida próspera)

_____ UNA VIDA DINAMICA (una vida activa y estimulante)

A continuación se presenta otra lista de valores. Ordene estos valores de acuerdo con su importancia en la misma forma como lo hizo en la lista anterior.

_____ AFECTUOSO (amor al prójimo)

_____ CAPAZ (competente, eficaz)

_____ COMPASIVO (dispuesto a perdonar a otros)

_____ CORTES (educado, fino)

_____ DISCIPLINADO (control de sí mismo, moderado)

_____ HONESTO (sincero, confiable)

_____ IMAGINATIVO (arrojado, creativo)

_____ INDEPENDIENTE (bastarse a sí mismo)

_____ INTELECTUAL (inteligente, reflexivo)

_____ JOVIAL (alegre)

_____ LIMPIEZA(ordenado, responsable)

_____ LOGICO (consistente, racional)

_____ MADURO (una persona moderna, tolerante, de ideas nuevas)

_____ OBEDIENTE (leal, respetuoso)

_____ PERSISTENTE (trabajador, ambicioso)

_____ RESPONSABLE (seguro, confiable)

_____ SERVICIAL (trabaja para el bienestar de otros)

_____ VALEROSO (defensor de sus creencias)

En las líneas de abajo, por favor escriba el NOMBRE de los tres delegados que Ud creé ejereieron una influencia más fuerte en ésta Congregacion General.

_____

_____

_____

MUCHAS GRACIAS

Analyse de l'organisation jésuite

Veuillez répondre aux prochaines suivantes d'après le tableau suivant:

1	Tout à fait d'accord
2	Partiellement d'accord
3	Je suis indécis.
4	En désaccord partiellement
5	Tout à fait en désaccord

VEUILLEZ N'ENCERCLER QU'UN NUMÉRO PAR LIGNE

L'élément créateur dans l'Église m'aide à approfondir ma foi chrétienne.

1 2 3 4 5

Le désordre faisant suite à Vatican II affaiblit mes propres convictions religieuses.

1 2 3 4 5

Pauvreté religieuse veut dire dépendre de la communauté pour ses besoins personnels.

1 2 3 4 5

La façon de présenter la chasteté au cours de la formation a souvent favorisé l'impersonnalisme et une fausse spiritualité.

1 2 3 4 5

Le devoir du sujet est d'obéir; il appartient au supérieur de discerner la volonté de Dieu et de dire ce qu'elle est.

1 2 3 4 5

Il est sage de recommander aux jésuites de s'intéresser à des projets d'ordre régional ou national pour lesquels ils se sentent compétents, même si ceux-ci n'ont rien à faire avec les plans de la province ou de

1 2 3 4 5

l'institution à laquelle l'individu appartient.

1 2 3 4 5

Les oeuvres et institutions de caractère international de la Compagnie doivent avoir priorité sur l'influence personnelle qu'un jésuite peut exercer au niveau de son travail.

1 2 3 4 5

Toute organisation devient avec le temps inefficace; seul du sang nouveau peut la revitaliser.

1 2 3 4 5

Un prêtre ne mérite pas le nom de pasteur s'il n'est pas tout autant préoccupé de pourvoir aux besoins sociaux de ses gens qu'à leur fournir des services d'ordre spirituel.

1 2 3 4 5

Quand j'ai à prendre des décisions dans mon travail, j'ai le sentiment que je dois essayer de prendre des décisions qui aideront à solutionner les problèmes de justice au profit de l'humanité entière. Je considère ces problèmes de l'humanité comme mes problèmes.

1 2 3 4 5

Les jésuites en pays étranger s'abstenir de se prononcer publiquement sur des questions d'ordre religieux ou social.   1   2   3   4   5

Les gens de ma province sont suffisamment soucieux de respecter les valeurs des différentes cultures dans les liturgies de groupe.   1   2   3   4   5

Il y a suffisamment de souci dans ma province pour les pauvres, les délaissés et les peu considérés.   1   2   3   4   5

Même chez eux les jésuites devraient s'abstenir de se prononcer publiquement sur des questions d'ordre religieux ou social.   1   2   3   4   5

Une province a le droit d'exiger qu'un jésuite travaille sur un projet d'envergure provinciale, même si cette tâche entre en conflit avec son apostolat ou les intérêts de l'institution dont il est membre.   1   2   3   4   5

Les préoccupations de l'apostolat individuel jésuite doivent être subordonnés au bien de l'institution ou de l'Église dont le jésuite fait partie.   1   2   3   4   5

La situation de l'Eglise doit changer; un engagement actuel est impératif.   1   2   3   4   5

Peu importe les idéaux que vous soutenez, vous ne pouvez réaliser vos objectifs qu'à la condition de mettre les pouvoirs de votre côté.   1   2   3   4   5

Quand vous y pensez, c'est la nature humaine intéressée par le gain qui l'emporte.   1   2   3   4   5

Les exigences de l'apostolat individuel du jésuite justifient ce dernier de consacrer à son travail toutes ses énergies.   1   2   3   4   5

C'est en continuant à prêcher et à enseigner plutôt qu'en expérimentant avec de nouvelles méthodes que l'Eglise accomplira le mieux sa mission.   1   2   3   4   5

En dernier lieu, la meilleure base de planification pour le futur est de faire confiance à l'expérience du passé et de baser nos décisions sur des exemples historiques.   1   2   3   4   5

Au cours des 10 dernières années, bon nombre de religieux ont évolué en ce qui a trait aux principes de base et aux valeurs auxquelles ils croyaient auparavant.   1   2   3   4   5

Les valeurs de base de l'Eglise demeurent les mêmes; seules leur expression varient.   1   2   3   4   5

Étudiez la liste avec soin. Ensuite, placez le chiffre 1
avant la valeur qui est la plus importante pour vous.
La seconde valeur par ordre d'importance recevra le chiffre 2 et ainsi de suite, de telle sorte que la valeur la
moins importante pour vous se verra attribuée le chiffre 18.

Travaillez lentement; si vous le jugez bon, changez l'ordre
de vos réponses. La classification finale devrait révéler
vos sentiments les plus profonds.

· Nous réalisons qu'entre les expressions il n'y a parfois
qu'une subtile distinction. Toutefois, classifiez ces valeurs sans trop analyser leur sens.

_____ UNE VIE CONFORTABLE (une vie prospère)

_____ UNE VIE PASSIONNANTE (une vie stimulante et active)

_____ UN SENTIMENT DE RÉALISATION (sens de la contribution)

_____ UN MONDE EN PAIX (sans guerre ni conflit)

_____ UN MONDE DE BEAUTÉ (beauté de nature et artistique)

_____ ÉGALITÉ (fraternité, chances égales pour tous)

_____ SÉCURITÉ DE FAMILLE (prendre soin des siens)

_____ LIBERTÉ (indépendance, liberté de mouvement)

_____ BONHEUR (joie intérieure)

_____ HARMONIE INTÉRIEURE (sans conflits intérieurs)

_____ AMOUR PARFAIT (intimité sexuelle et spirituelle)

_____ SÉCURITÉ NATIONALE (protection contre l'ennemi)

_____ PLAISIR (une vie agréable, remplie de loisir)

_____ SALUT (désir d'être sauvé, vie éternelle)

_____ AMOUR PROPRE (estime de soi-même)

_____ INFLUENCE SOCIALE (respect, admiration)

_____ AMITIÉ PROFONDE (camaraderie, intimité)

_____ SAGESSE (compréhension du sens de la vie)

Vous avez ici une liste de 18 qualités. Classifiez-les
d'après leur importance pour vous. Procédez de la même
façon que pour la première liste.

_____ AMBITIEUX (travailleur laborieux)

_____ LARGE D'ESPRIT (tolérant)

_____ TALENTUEUX (compétent, efficace)

_____ JOYEUX (gai d'esprit et de coeur)

_____ PROPRE (bien rangé, de bonne apparence)

_____ COURAGEUX (capable de défendre ses convictions)

_____ CLÉMENT (conciliant, capable de pardonner)

_____ SOCIABLE (désireux d'aider les autres)

_____ HONNÊTE (sincère, véridique)

_____ IMAGINATIF (créateur, audacieux)

_____ INDÉPENDANT (confiant en soi)

_____ INTELLECTUEL (intelligent)

_____ LOGIQUE (rationnel, forme d'esprit)

_____ AFFECTUEUX (tendre, aimant)

_____ OBÉISSANT (soumis, respectueux)

_____ POLI (courtois, bien élevé)

_____ RESPONSABLE (digne de confiance, fiable)

_____ MAÎTRE DE SOI-MÊME (sens de la retenue et discipline)

Dans l'espace réservé à cet effet, veuillez
indiquer les NOMS des 3 délégués qui ont eu
le plus d'influence sur la Congrégation
générale.

_____

_____

_____

MERCI BEAUCOUP

Organisatorische Analyse der Gesellschaft Jesu

Wollen Sie bitte die folgenden Fragen nach der angefuehrten Skala
moeglicher Reaktionen beantworten.

1 stimme nachdruecklich zu 4 bin bedingt nicht einverstanden

2 stimme bedingt zu 5 bin ueberhaupt nicht einverstanden

3 bin nicht sicher

Bitte kreuzen Sie **einen** Code auf **jeder** Ziffernskala an.

Die schoepferische Unruhe in der heutigen
Kirche bringt eine Vertiefung meines christ-
lichen Glaubens mit sich. 1 2 3 4 5

Die lehrte Unruhe, die auf Vatikan II folgte,
hat zur Folge, dass meine Glaubensueberzeugun-
gen allmaehlich schwaecher werden. 1 2 3 4 5

Arm sein heisst: von der Gemeinde fuer unsere
ganzen materiellen Beduerfnisse abhaengig sein. 1 2 3 4 5

Die traditionelle Weise, wie in der Priesterausbildung das Gemeinschaftsgeluebde praesentiert
wird, hat oft dann gefuehrt, dass sich unper-
soenliches Verhalten und falsche Geistigkeit
entwickeln konnten. 1 2 3 4 5

Es ist die Pflicht des Unterpfarrers zu gehor-
chen; die Verpflichtung des Oberen ist es,
Gottes Faelle zu erkennen und ihn zu verkuen-
den. 1 2 3 4 5

Es ist fuer Jesuiten ratsam, sich mit regio-
nalen oder nationalen Projekten zu befassen,
deren Aufgabenkreis sie sich gewaehlen fueh-
len. Sie sollten dies auch dann tun, wenn das
Ergebnis derartiger Unternehmen weder der Provinz noch anderen Institutionen, denen Jesuiten
angehoeren, Gutes bringt. 1 2 3 4 5

Die Aufgaben und Ziele der gesamten Gesellschaft
Jesu auf internationaler Ebene verdienen es,
allen anderen Wirkungsbereichen immer dann vor-
gezogen zu werden, wenn ein Jesuit wirksamen
Einfluss auf internationaler Ebene ausueben
kann. 1 2 3 4 5

Jede organisatorische Struktur wird mit der Zeit
zu einer drueckenden Last und muss revitalisiert
werden. 1 2 3 4 5

Ein Priester darf sich wohl kaum Hirte nennen,
wenn er sich nicht ebenso intensiv um die so-
ziale Wohlfahrt der Leute kuemmert wie um den
geistlichen Dienst zum Wohl der Gemeinde. 1 2 3 4 5

Wenn ich mich mit den Problemen meiner Arbeit
befasse, dann ueberrasche ich mich immer bei
dem Versuch, Entscheidungen zu treffen, die die
wichtigeren Fragen der Gerechtigkeit vor zum
Wohl der ganzen Menschheit lassen helfen. Die
Probleme der Menschheit sind im Grunde meine
Probleme. 1 2 3 4 5

Die gegenwaertige Lage der Kirche macht eine
Veraenderung erforderlich. Wir muessen darauf
ohne Verzug reagieren. 1 2 3 4 5

Gewisse Anlagen im Aufgabenbereich eines einzelnen Jesuiten innerhalb des Apostolats müssen der Institution oder der guten Zusammenarbeit älter Jesuiten, an der er Anteil nimmt und Anteil hat, notwendig untergeordnet werden.

1 2 3 4 5

Die Provinz hat das Recht, von einem Jesuiten Mitarbeit an den die ganze Provinz betreffenden Angelegenheiten zu verlangen, selbst dann sogar, wenn diese Tätigkeit mit den Interessen seines eigenen Apostolats und denen der Institution, der er angehört, in Konflikt gerät.

1 2 3 4 5

Selbst im Missstand sollten die SJ-Mitglieder im allgemeinen nicht zu herausfordernd Stellung nehmen zu religiösen und sozialen Fragen.

1 2 3 4 5

Die Arbeitsprogramme meiner Provinz berücksichtigen genügend die armen Leute und die niederen Klassen.

1 2 3 4 5

Die Mitbrüder in meiner Provinz haben beim Vollzug des Gottesdienstes genügend Feingespür für die Eigenworte und Fühlweisen der Einheimischen.

1 2 3 4 5

Wo SJ-Mitglieder im Ausland arbeiten, sollten sie nicht zu herausfordernd Stellung nehmen zu religiösen und sozialen Fragen.

1 2 3 4 5

Es spielt keine Rolle, wie grossartig die Ideale sein mögen, um deren Verbreitung man sich bemüht; man kann nichts erreichen, wenn man die ausgewählsichen Machthaber nicht auf seiner Seite hat.

1 2 3 4 5

Wenn man der Sache wirklich auf den Grund geht, dann liegt es in der menschlichen Natur, unter keinen Umständen etwas zu tun, ohne dabei seinen Vorteil im Auge zu haben.

1 2 3 4 5

Ein Jesuit sollte innerhalb des besonderen Apostolats, in dem er dient, den dringlichen und umfassenden Ansprüchen dieses Apostolats allem anderen voran seine wohlbedachten Bemühungen zuwenden.

1 2 3 4 5

Indem die Kirche ihre traditionelle Einstellung zu ihrer Lehrrolle beibehält, wird sie ihre Mission besser erfüllen als durch Experimente mit neuen Methoden.

1 2 3 4 5

In Grunde ist es die sicherste Grundlage einer gesunden Planung für die Zukunft, sein Vertrauen auf die Erfahrungen der Vergangenheit zu setzen und alle Beschlüsse auf Tatsachen, auf die Unverfälschten Tatsachen zu gründen.

1 2 3 4 5

Im Zeitraum der vergangenen 10 Jahre haben viele Ordensleute einige ihrer Grundprinzipien und Zertbegriffe geändert, an die sie zuvor geglaubt hatten.

1 2 3 4 5

Die Religiosen und sittlichen Grundwerte der Kirche blieben dieselben, doch deren Ausdrucksweise änderte sich.

1 2 3 4 5

Haben Sie die Güte, auf den unten gezeichneten Linien die NAMEN dreier Delegierten aufzuführen, die nach Ihrer Ansicht den grössten Einfluss auf die Generalkongregation ausgeübt haben.

_____

_____

Auf den folgenden Seiten finden Sie zwei Gruppen von Lebenszielen in alphabetischer Reihenfolge. Bitte bringen Sie diese Werte in die Reihenfolge, in die sie Ihrer Ansicht nach gehören, d.h. so wie sie für Ihr Leben wichtig sind.

Bitte sehen Sie sich die erste Liste auf Seite 3 sorgfältig an und wählen Sie das Lebensziel aus, welches Ihnen am allerwichtigsten erscheint. Schreiben Sie eine "1" in das Feld links neben dem Begriff. Dann wählen Sie das Lebensziel aus, welches Ihnen am zweitwichtigsten erscheint. Schreiben Sie eine "2" in das Feld neben dem Begriff. Fahren Sie so fort mit dem restlichen sechzehn Lebenszielen der Seite 3. Das am wenigsten wichtig erscheinende Ziel erhält dann natürlich die Nummer "18".

Bitte arbeiten Sie langsam, und denken Sie sorgfältig nach. Falls Sie Ihre Meinung korrigieren wollen, so können Sie die Zahlen durch andere oder durchstreichen und ändern. Wenn Sie fertig sind, sollten die Lebensziele in der Reihenfolge nummeriert sein, in der sie für Sie vom Wichtigkeit sind.

Es ist uns bewusst, dass jeder dieser Begriffe viele subtile Bedeutungsnuancen zulässt. Dennoch bitten wir Sie, diese Wertbegriffe in einem Rangordnung einzuordnen, ohne indessen über deren Bedeutung zu sehr analysieren zu werden.

____ DAS GEFÜHL, ETWAS ERREICHT ZU HABEN (ein dauerhafter Beitrag)

____ EIN ANGENEHMES LEBEN (ein wohlhabendes Leben)

____ EIN AUFREGENDES LEBEN (ein anregendes, tätiges Leben)

____ EINE FRIEDLICHE WELT (ohne Krieg oder Konflikte)

____ EINE SCHÖNE WELT (Schönheit der Natur und der Künste)

____ ERLÖSUNG (zum ewigen Leben) [d.h. Heilsweg]

____ FREIHEIT (Unabhängigkeit, Freiheit der Entscheidung)

____ GENUSS (ein vergnügliches, genussvolles Leben)

____ GESELLSCHAFTLICHE ANERKENNUNG (Respekt, Bewunderung)

____ GLEICHHEIT (Brüderlichkeit, gleiche Chance für jeden)

____ GLÜCK (Zufriedenheit)

____ INNERE HARMONIE (Eintracht mit sich selber)

____ REIFE LIEBE (geistig-sexuelle Vertrautheit)

____ SELBSTACHTUNG (Respekt vor sich selber)

____ SICHERHEIT FÜR DIE FAMILIE (für seine Lieben sorgen)

____ STAATLICHE SICHERHEIT (Sicherheit vor Angriffen)

____ WAHRE FREUNDSCHAFT (enge Kameradschaft)

____ WEISHEIT (ein tiefes Verständnis des Lebens)

Unten gibt es eine zweite Reihe von achtzehn Werten. Bitte bringen Sie diese Werte in die Reihenfolgegemäss deren Wichtigkeit für Sie, genauso wie Sie es schon oben getan habt.

____ EHRGEIZIG (fleissig, strebsam)

____ EHRLICH (aufrichtig, wahrhaftig)

____ FÄHIG (kompetent, wirkungsvoll)

____ GEHORSAM (pflichtbewusst, respektvoll)

____ HILFREICH (sich um das Wohlergehen anderer Kümmern)

____ HÖFLICH (wohlerzogen)

____ INTELLEKTUELL (intelligent, nachdenklich)

____ LIEBEVOLL (zärtlich, zugetan)

____ LOGISCH (überzeustimmend, rational)

____ MUNTER (leichten Herzens, fröhlich)

____ MUTIG (zu seiner Überzeugung stehen)

____ NACHSICHTIG (bereit sein, anderen zu verzeihen)

____ PHANTASIEVOLL (kühn, schöpferisch)

____ SAUBER (ordentlich, nett)

____ TOLERANT (aufgeschlossen)

____ UNABHÄNGIG (selbstgenügsam, selbstvertrauend)

____ VERANTWORTLICH (zuverlässig, verlässlich)

VIELEN DANK

ANALISI ORGANIZZATIVA DEI GESUITI

Per favore risponda alle seguenti domade secondo la scelta delle risposte :

1. Molto in favore
2. Daccordo in qualche maniera
3. Incerto

4. In favore juxta modo
5. Contrario fortemente

Per favore scelga una de queste risposte.

Oggi il fermento creativo nella chiesa consiste nell' approfondimento della mia fede cristiana.   1 2 3 4 5

La confusione venuta dopo il Vat. II e' il risultato di un graduale risveglio delle mie propie credenze religiose.   1 2 3 4 5

Poverta' significa dipendenza dalla comunita' per quanto concerne i bisogni materiali di ognuno.   1 2 3 4 5

La maniera tradizionale di presentare il voto di castita' nella formazione religiosa ha dato spesso occasioni di uno sviluppo di impersonalismo e di falsa spiritualita'.   1 2 3 4 5

Il dovere del religioso e' obbedire; e' responsabilita' del superiore scoprire la volonta' di Dio e dichiararla.   1 2 3 4 5

E' consigliabile per i Gesuiti, lavorare con progetti regionali e nazionali in quei campi in cui sono competenti per servire anche se il frutto di tale impegno non da' un risultato per la provincia o per quella instituzione Gesuita a cui si appartiene.   1 2 3 4 5

Il lavoro e la finalita' della intera Compagnia di Gesu' su un piano internazionale richiedono precedenza assoluta su tutte le altre attivita', qualora un Gesuita ha l'opportunita' di influire in tal senso.   1 2 3 4 5

Ogni stuttura organizzata diventa di peso nel tempo e ha bisogno di un rinnovamento.   1 2 3 4 5

Un prete molto difficilmente puo' dirsi pastore se egli non e' impegnato profondamente nella assistenza sociale del suo popolo come nel dare il servizio spirituale ai suoi parocchiani.   1 2 3 4 5

Quando io tratto i problemi del mio lavoro cerco costantemente di prendere decisioni che siano utili a risolvere i piu' grandi problemi della giustizia sociale etc., per tutta l'umanita'. I problemi del momdo sono molto sentiti come miei problemi.   1 2 3 4 5

La situazione attuale della chiesa richiede un cambiamento. Dobbiamo dare una risposta.   1 2 3 4 5

Alcuni lavori espletati nell'apostolato della Compagnia di Gesu' sono necessariamente di servizio all'istituzione Gesuita di cui si fa' parte.   1 2 3 4 5

La Provincia ha il diritto che un Gesuita lavori per compiti di Congregazione anche quando questo lavoro interferisce con il desiderio dell'individuo di dedicarsi al suo propio apostolato a cui si sente portato.   1 2 3 4 5

Anche quando si lavora nel propio paese i Gesuiti dovrebbero generalmente evitare di prendere degli attegiamenti forti in pubblico riguardo ad argomenti religiosi o sociali.   1 2 3 4 5

Le attivita' della mia provincia sono sufficientemente dirette ai poveri - e alle persone meno fortunate.   1 2 3 4 5

I membri della mia provincia sono sufficentemente aperti ai valori locali come pure al gusto della liturgia del loro popolo.   1 2 3 4 5

Quando si lavora all'estero i Gesuiti dovrebbero evitare di prendere degli atteggiamenti forti in pubblico riguardo ad argomenti religiosi o sociali.   1 2 3 4 5

Non importa la bellezza degli ideali che vuoi raggiungere, li puoi conseguire solo se hai le forze del potere della tua parte.   1 2 3 4 5

Nell'azione e' naturale agire anche per propio interesse.   1 2 3 4 5

Nel lavoro di un Gesuita i bisogni immediati e generali del suo particolare apostolato devono avere il primo sforzo e considerazione.   1 2 3 4 5

La Chiesa compirebbe meglio la sua missione continuando nel suo tradizionale ruolo di insegnamento, che non sperimentando sempre nuovi metodi.   1 2 3 4 5

In una analisi finale, la parte piu' forte base per un programma per il futuro sta' nel suo basarsi sull'esperienza del passato e nei fatti storici.   1 2 3 4 5

Durante i trascorsi dieci anni molti religiosi hanni cambiato alcuni dei principi e valori in cui essi precedentemente credevano.   1 2 3 4 5

I valori basilari della Chiesa rimangono gli stessi, ma la loro espressione viene cambiando.   1 2 3 4 5

Segue una lista di 18 valori. Siamo interessati nel trovare la relativa importanza di ognuno di questi valori per lei.

Prenda seriamente in considerazione la lista. Quindi metta 1 al valore che e' piu' importante per lei, poi ponga 2 al valore che e' secondo per importanza, etc. Il n. 18 sara', quindi, quel valore che ha meno importanza per lei.

Siamo perfettamente a conoscenza che alcuni valori sono similari nel loro significato. Tuttavia, li preghi in ordine senza diventare troppo analitico riguardo al loro significato. Quando ha finito di porli in ordine, dia uno sguardo di nuovo alla sua lista.

Sia libero di cambiare la lista. Prenda il suo tempo nel compilare la lista in modo che rappresenti i suoi valori.

_____ VITA CONFORTEVOLE (vita ricca)

_____ VITA ECCITANTE (vita stimolante, attiva)

_____ UN SENSO DI REALIZZAZIONE (una durevole collaborazione)

_____ UN MONDO IN PACE (senza guerra e conflitti)

_____ UN MONDO DI BELLEZZA (bellezza di natura e di arti)

_____ UGUAGLIANZA (fratellanza, uguali possibilita' per tutti)

_____ SICUREZZA FAMIGLIARE (cura per le persone amate)

_____ LIBERTA' (indipendenza - liberta' di scelta)

_____ GIOIA (contentezza)

_____ ARMONIA INTERIORE (niente conflitti interni)

_____ AMORE MATURO (intimita' sessuale e spirituale)

_____ SICUREZZA NAZIONALE (difesa da attacco)

_____ PIACERE (una vita goduta e vissuta facilmente)

_____ SALVEZZA (essere salvato per la vita eterna)

_____ AUTO-RISPETTO (stima di se stessi)

_____ RISPETTO DA PARTE DI ALTRI (ammirazione)

_____ AMICIZIA SINCERA (amicizia intima)

_____ SAGGEZZA (comprensione matura della vita)

Segue un' altra lista di 18 valori. Metterli in ordine di importanza come prima.

_____ AMBIZIONE (grande lavoratore - aspirante)

_____ APERTURA DI MENTE (mentalita' aperta)

_____ CAPACE (competente, efficiente)

_____ SORRIDENTE (gioioso, allegro)

_____ PULITO (ordinato, lindo)

_____ CORAGGIOSO (difendere le proprie convinzioni)

_____ UNA PERSONA CHE SA PERDONARE (perdonare altri)

_____ AIUTANTE (che lavora per il benessere degli altri)

_____ ONESTO (sincero, veritiero)

_____ IMMAGINATIVO (audace, creativo)

_____ INDIPENDENTE (fiducioso, auto- sufficiente)

_____ INTELLETTUALE (intelligente, riflessivo)

_____ LOGICO (razionale, coerente)

_____ AMABILE (affettuoso, tenero)

_____ OBBEDIENTE (sottomesso, rispettoso)

_____ GENTILE (cortese, educato)

_____ RESPONSABILE (attendibile)

_____ AUTO-CONTROLLO (misurato, autodisciplinato)

Nelle righe che seguono la prego di scrivere i NOMI dei tre delegati che secondo Lei esercitarono la maggior influenza in questa Congregazione Generale.

_____

_____

_____

MOLTE GRAZIE

APPENDIX TWO

ANALYSIS OF RESEARCH DATA DISCRIMINATED

ACCORDING TO CONTROL VARIABLES

The major elements of this research, its
dependent variables, included the Bulwark-
Catholic/Conciliar-Humanist polarity, the delegate value-rankings and the non-delegate value
rankings. These variables have been analyzed
for the effects of various control variables.
The results of this analysis are included in the
text of this report. However, the immediate
discussion and the tables reflecting that
analysis are collected together in this appendix.
Citations in the text direct the reader to the
sections of this appendix pertaining to the element under discussion.

Section One:

Bulwark-Catholicism and
Conciliar-Humanism Discriminated According
to Region, Age, Office, and Leadership

Controlling for region, seven Assistancies
have scores on the polarity index favoring the
Conciliar-Humanists, five have scores favoring
the Bulwark-Catholics. Four of these Assistancies group within .05 of the mean. The
Assistancies favoring C-H have an average index
score of .2546 and those favoring B-C have an
average score of -.2566. The Northern Latin
American and the French Assistancies have the
highest C-H tendency and the Italians and the
Slavic Assistancies have the highest B-C tendency. (See Table One)

Controlling for age, the forty to forty-nine

TABLE ONE

DISCRIMINATION OF ASSISTANCIES

ACCORDING TO INDEX OF B-C/C-H POLARITY

Rank*	Assistancy	Mean Index Score	Standard Deviation	Number of Respondents
1	Italian	− 0.809	0.797	11
2	Slavic	− 0.787	0.912	10
3	German	− 0.387	0.676	18
4	Spanish	− 0.024	0.706	23
5	American	− 0.011	0.930	34
6	Indian	0.005	0.771	19
7	English	0.047	0.804	20
8	Southern Latin America	0.149	0.931	15
9	East Asian	0.158	0.579	14
10	African	0.195	0.734	7
11	French	0.683	0.830	14
12	Northern Latin America	0.821	0.724	11
	TOTALS	0.004	0.874	196

* Ranked according to polarity B-C to C-H.

year old age group, which comprises forty-nine
percent of all of the delegates, inclines the
most strongly to the Conciliar-Humanist style.
The thirty to thirty-nine year old age group,
which comprises four percent of all of the delegates, have a score which tends to the Bulwark-
Catholic style. The two older groups also tend
more to the Bulwark-Catholic style.

When the ages are considered year by year,
the inclination to the Conciliar-Humanist pre-
vails in nearly all groups under fifty years of
age. The mean age of the delegates is forty-nine
years. (See Table Two)

Controlling for office yields mixed results.
Two measures of administration are compared. The
first is a measure of all delegates who presently
or in the past have served in Jesuit administrative positions. The second is a measure of the
kind of work the delegates presently engage in.

The biographical records of 112 respondents
indicate some present or past administrative
service, the records of eighty-three do not.
These administrators tend to Conciliar-Humanism
with a mean score of .103, while the non-
administrators tend to Bulwark-Catholicism with
a mean score of -0.117. (See Table Three)

Considering the work delegates are presently
engaged in, ninety-seven delegates presently
serve in administration and ninety-nine do not.
Present administrators tend slightly to Bulwark-
Catholicism with a mean score of -.01 and non-
administrators tend slightly to Conciliar-
Humanism with a mean score of .01. This is a
negligible difference.

The comparison of two measures of Jesuit
administration suggests that there is not any
strong following for one style or another which
is consistently held by the administration of
the Society of Jesus.

423

TABLE TWO

DISCRIMINATION OF AGE-GROUPS
ACCORDING TO INDEX OF B-C/C-H POLARITY

A   Age Discriminated According to Questionnaire Response
in ten year interval categories

Groups	Number	Mean Index Score
30-39 years old	9	− .059
40-49	95	.174
50-59	73	.115
60-69	19	− .357
TOTALS	196	0.004

B   Age Discriminated According to Year Born

	Groups	Number	Mean Index Score	Groups	Number	Mean Index Score
Born	1936	4	0.522	1920	9	−0.423
	1935	3	−0.057	1919	5	−0.600
	1934	3	−0.479	1918	7	0.168
	1933	6	0.493	1917	3	0.062
	1932	10	0.174	1916	10	0.094
	1931	3	0.184	1915	1	0.486
	1930	12	−0.090	1914	5	−0.403
	1929	16	0.159	1913	3	−0.003
	1928	13	0.594	1912	3	−0.282
	1927	11	0.387	1911	2	0.151
	1926	11	0.237	1910	1	−0.503
	1925	10	0.506	1909	1	−1.219
	1924	11	0.506	1908	2	−0.953
	1923	6	−0.165	1907	1	0.165
	1922	10	−0.434	1906	0	0.0000
	1921	12	−0.135	1905	1	−0.753

TABLE THREE

DISCRIMINATION OF OFFICE ACCORDING

TO INDEX OF B–C/C–H POLARITY

A   Discrimination by Designation of Administrator Scored
From Biography of Present and Past Occupations

Group	Number	Mean Index Score
Some Administrative Office	113	0.093
No Administrative Office	83	−0.117
TOTALS	196	0.004

B   Discrimination by Questionnaire Response of Present
Super-Institutional Administration or Not

Group	Number	Mean Index Score
Administrators	97	−0.006
Non-Administrators	99	0.014
TOTALS	196	0.004

Controlling for attributed leadership gives
slightly different results than controlling for
administration. Various measures of attributed
leadership are compared. The first designation
considers only those delegates who were named as
having influenced the Congregation by other
delegates after the Congregation was completed.
Thirty-five delegates are designated leaders in
this measure. The second designation considers
all delegates who were named either before or
after the Congregation by either delegate or non-
delegate respondents. Sixty-nine delegates are
designated leaders in this measure. Both measures
of designated leadership show the leaders to have
Conciliar-Humanism scores but the differences are
negligible.

Two other measures of possible leadership
were analyzed for possible influence. The first
discriminated those delegates who served on the
editorial commissions of the various documents.
The second considered only those delegates who
were elected to some General Congregation or
headquarters office by the delegates. Once
again the results were mixed and near negligible.
(See Table Four)

From a discrimination of both administrators
and designated leaders on the basis of the B-C/
C-H polarity index, no conclusive difference or
significant influence is revealed. Neither group
consistently differs from all other delegates in
respect to the transition of Jesuits from an
elite status to that of a minority.

Section Two:

Value-Rankings of Delegates
Discriminated According to Selected Variables

Administrators and non-administrators evidence similar value-ranking profiles. There are
ninety-nine administrator respondents and

426

TABLE FOUR

DISCRIMINATION OF LEADERSHIP ACCORDING

TO INDEX OF B-C/C-H POLARITY

A   Designated Leaders by Delegates Responding After the
Thirty-Second General Congregation

Group	Number	Mean Index Score
Not Designated	169	-0.009
Designated Once as Leader	11	0.389
Designated More Than Once	15	-0.055
TOTALS	195	0.0095

B   Designated As Potential or Actual Leaders by Delegates
and Non-Delegates

Group	Number	Mean Index Score
Not Designated	126	-0.016
Designated Once as Leader	35	0.017
Designated More Than Once	34	0.097
TOTALS	195	0.0095

C   Delegates Who Served on Editorial Committees of
Congregation Documents

Group	Number	Mean Index Score
Not on Editorial Committee	162	0.022
Served on Editorial Committee	34	-0.080
TOTALS	196	0.004

Table Four - continued

D   Delegates Elected to Some General Congregation
                              or Curial Office

Group	Number	Mean Index Score
Elected to General Assistant	3	0.342
Elected to Congregation Secretary	3	−0.233
Elected to Document Definitores	4	0.484
Appointed to Regional Assistant	2	−0.327
TOTALS	12	0.1614

seventy-five non-administrator respondents among the delegates to the Congregation.

Over the thirty-six ranked values, only one value differs with statistical significance at the .05 level. The non-administrators rank family security more highly than the administrators. This is a curious finding since the subtitle for the value-ranking is: "taking care of loved ones." The difference in ranking score is .94 with the non-administrators ranking it twelfth and the administrators ranking it thirteenth. Non-administrators also rank true-friendship and world peace more highly than administrators. Administrators rank inner-harmony and an exciting life more highly.

Non-administrators place the instrumental value of loving in the highest rank and place honest in fourth place. Administrators place honest in the highest ranking and loving in fourth place. Non-administrators also give higher priority to intellectual and administrators give higher priority to imaginative. (See Table Five)

Leaders resemble non-leaders in value-ranking profile. This is the case when the criterion for leadership is the designation as leader by delegates after the Congregation.

If the category of leadership is expanded to include those delegates named as either potentially or actually leaders, the value-rankings are very similar. Only the instrumental ranking of polite (in fourteenth and sixteenth place respectively) is statistically significant beyond the .05 level. The contrast between honest and helpful noted above remains strong in this larger rendering of leadership (sixty-one designated leaders). The non-leaders' higher valuation of loving also remains. Across all other value-rankings, the similarity between the smaller group of twenty-two leaders remains similar. (See Table Six)

429

DISCRIMINATION OF VALUE-RANKINGS ACCORDING

TO PAST OR PRESENT ADMINISTRATION OFFICE

Value	Delegate is Not a Jesuit Administrator N=75		Delegate is a Jesuit Administrator N=99		Probability
	R	Sc	R	Sc	
I TERMINAL					
A Comfortable Life	17	17.03	17	17.02	.905
An Exciting Life	14	13.40	12	11.60	.219
A Sense of Accomplishment	9	9.85	9	9.65	.669
A World at Peace	5	6.46	7	7.25	.604
A World of Beauty	13	12.20	14	12.55	.856
Equality	4	5.25	3	5.31	.930
Family Security	12	11.00	13	11.94	.046*
Freedom	6	6.64	6	5.73	.215
Happiness	8	9.40	8	8.19	.662
Inner Harmony	7	7.33	4	5.38	.084
Mature Love	11	10.88	11	10.13	.510
National Security	16	13.96	16	14.27	.588
Pleasure	18	17.22	18	17.51	.613
Salvation	1	1.25	1	1.34	.568
Self-Respect	10	10.60	10	10.00	.788
Social Recognition	15	13.61	15	13.15	.510
True Friendship	3	5.00	5	5.67	.562
Wisdom	2	4.04	2	3.72	.609

Table Five - continued

Value	Delegate is Not a Jesuit Administrator N=75		Delegate is a Jesuit Administrator N=99		Probability
	R	Sc	R	Sc	
II INSTRUMENTAL					
Ambitious	17	15.33	17	14.00	.615
Broadminded	6	7.60	6	6.58	.516
Capable	9	9.69	9	9.44	.856
Cheerful	12	11.25	11	10.31	.758
Clean	18	16.73	18	16.61	.894
Courageous	7	8.00	7	7.18	.536
Forgiving	5	5.63	5	6.25	.792
Helpful	2	3.57	2	3.86	.926
Honest	4	4.06	1	3.40	.588
Imaginative	11	10.71	8	9.15	.274
Independent	15	13.00	15	13.27	.894
Intellectual	8	9.44	12	10.69	.187
Logical	14	12.65	13	13.09	.598
Loving	1	3.44	4	5.00	.662
Obedient	13	12.56	14	13.11	.632
Polite	16	14.06	16	13.44	.507
Responsible	3	4.06	3	4.23	.991
Self-Controlled	10	10.00	10	9.91	.826

DESIGNATION OF LEADERSHIP POTENTIAL AND
ACTUAL BY DELEGATES AND NON-DELEGATES

	Non-Leaders N=113		Leaders N=61		Probability
	R	Sc	R	Sc	
I TERMINAL - continued					
A Comfortable Life	17	16.99	17	17.10	.515
An Exciting Life	14	12.65	13	12.00	.749
A Sense of Accomplishment	9	10.00	9	9.20	.676
A World at Peace	7	6.78	7	7.57	.894
A World of Beauty	13	12.44	14	12.40	.907
Equality	4	5.46	3	5.00	.618
Family Security	12	11.53	12	11.56	.907
Freedom	5	5.82	6	6.75	.152
Happiness	8	8.65	8	8.67	.921
Inner Harmony	6	5.89	5	6.00	.705
Mature Love	10	10.04	11	11.00	.666
National Security	16	14.31	16	13.57	.569
Pleasure	18	17.44	18	17.32	.694
Salvation	1	1.33	1	1.24	.541
Self-Respect	11	10.78	10	9.60	.295
Social Recognition	15	13.32	15	13.44	.984
True Friendship	3	5.25	4	5.75	.672
Wisdom	2	4.00	2	3.69	.866

Table Six - continued

	Non-Leaders N=113		Leaders N=61		Probability
	R	Sc	R	Sc	
II INSTRUMENTAL - continued					
Ambitious	17	14.23	17	15.00	.596
Broadminded	6	7.56	6	6.42	.302
Capable	8	9.69	9	9.13	.672
Cheerful	10	9.96	12	12.00	.054
Clean	18	16.61	18	16.75	.772
Courageous	7	8.20	5	6.40	.245
Forgiving	5	5.71	7	6.75	.584
Helpful	1	3.18	3	5.06	.056
Honest	3	4.15	1	2.81	.051
Imaginative	12	10.56	8	8.88	.538
Independent	16	13.39	13	12.38	.553
Intellectual	11	10.56	10	9.42	.586
Logical	15	13.00	14	12.71	.559
Loving	2	3.27	4	6.00	.131
Obedient	13	12.85	14	12.81	.972
Polite	14	12.86	16	14.75	.034*
Responsible	4	4.28	2	3.80	.856
Self-Controlled	9	9.89	11	10.06	.869

When the delegates are discriminated according to the social class backgrounds they were raised in, numerous differences emerge. The higher the social class, the less priority on salvation (significant at .01 level), and family security (.01 level), and the higher priority of a world of beauty (.01 level). Also, the higher the social class, the lower the priority of honesty and obedience and the higher the priority of politeness. Equality and freedom, forgiving and helpful are ranked more highly by higher social class delegates. Happiness and inner-harmony, courage and imagination are ranked more highly by lower social class delegates. (See Table Seven A)

Those delegates who responded as task-oriented differ from those who responded as person-oriented in two main areas of terminal values but in six areas of instrumental values. The task-oriented ranked national security significantly higher than the person-oriented (fourteenth compared to sixteenth place). Person-oriented ranked inner-harmony more highly than task-oriented (fourth compared to eighth place). Task-oriented ranked the instrumental values of capable, intellectual and logical more highly. Person-oriented ranked loving. obedient and ambitious more highly. (See Table Seven B)

Those who took final vows before the Second Vatican Council rank salvation more highly than those who took final vows after the Council, although both groups rank salvation as highest priority (1.20 compared to 1.63). Those who took vows before the Council rank wisdom and world peace more highly while those who took final vows later rank true friendship and mature love more highly. The more recently vowed rank imaginative, cheerful, loving, ambitious and broadminded more highly. Those who took final vows earlier rank intellectual, independent, capable, logical and responsible more highly. (See Table Seven C)

Lesser differences are evident when the

434

TABLE SEVEN

DISCRIMINATION OF VALUE-RANKINGS BY SOCIAL CLASS,
TASK OR PERSON-ORIENTATION AND DATE OF FINAL VOWS

7A Social Class Delegate was raised in · 7B Whether Delegate responded as Task-Oriented or Person-Oriented · 7C Whether Delegate took Final Vows before or after the Second Vatican Council

I TERMINAL	Lower and Unskilled N=23 R	Sc	Middle N=95 R	Sc	Upper-Middle & Upper N=56 R	Sc	Probability	Task-Oriented N=39 R	Sc	Person-Oriented N=30 R	Sc	Probability	Before N=103 R	Sc	After N=71 R	Sc	Probability
A Comfortable Life	18	17.14	17	17.02	17	17.00	.627	17	16.97	17	17.08	.283	17	17.03	17	17.03	.708
An Exciting Life	13	12.63	15	13.56	13	11.50	.569	16	13.67	13	12.17	.501	14	13.11	12	11.20	.119
A Sense of Accomplishment	9	10.00	9	9.96	8	8.50	.640	9	8.33	10	10.03	.230	9	9.40	8	7.92	.272
A World at Peace	6	6.38	7	6.75	7	7.25	.815	6	6.33	6	6.93	.828	5	6.00	11	10.09	.047*
A World of Beauty	12	11.67	13	13.31	12	10.93	.004***	12	12.20	14	12.50	.807	13	11.89	15	13.25	.171
Equality	7	6.58	3	5.29	4	5.17	.893	3	5.20	5	5.36	.942	3	4.96	5	6.13	.261
Family Security	11	10.92	12	11.00	14	12.64	.006**	11	12.08	12	11.44	.620	12	11.53	13	11.56	.895
Freedom	8	7.13	6	6.00	5	5.79	.270	5	6.29	7	5.86	.986	7	6.13	4	6.00	.787
Happiness	5	6.00	8	9.25	9	8.64	.226	7	7.92	8	8.95	.220	8	9.15	7	7.29	.133
Inner Harmony	4	5.13	4	5.46	6	7.25	.046*	8	8.20	4	5.38	.003**	4	5.55	6	6.67	.246
Mature Love	14	13.00	11	10.00	10	9.83	.081	10	10.67	11	10.17	.766	11	11.29	9	9.56	.034*
National Security	15	13.75	16	14.00	16	14.38	.767	14	13.00	16	14.44	.007**	16	14.03	16	14.29	.526
Pleasure	17	16.63	18	17.48	18	17.43	.556	18	17.38	18	17.38	.918	18	17.51	18	17.21	.636
Salvation	1	1.22	1	1.21	1	2.00	.010**	1	1.25	1	1.29	.821	1	1.20	1	1.63	.005**
Self-Respect	10	10.25	10	10.00	11	10.83	.692	13	12.38	9	9.83	.109	10	10.78	10	9.86	.673
Social Recognition	16	14.00	14	13.38	15	13.00	.348	15	13.13	15	13.50	.807	15	13.71	14	12.78	.137
True Friendship	3	5.00	5	5.79	3	4.79	.564	4	6.14	3	5.12	.129	6	6.11	2	4.22	.008**
Wisdom	2	3.92	2	3.80	2	3.93	.867	2	3.13	2	4.02	.277	2	3.36	3	4.46	.080*

Table Seven - continued

II INSTRUMENTAL	7A Social Class Delegate was raised in							7B Whether Delegate responded as Task-Oriented or Person-Oriented					7C Whether Delegate took Final Vows before or after the Second Vatican Council				
	Lower and Unskilled N=23		Middle N=95		Upper-Middle & Upper N=56		Probability	Task-Oriented N=39		Person-Oriented N=130		Probability	Before N=103		After N=71		Probability
	R	Sc	R	Sc	R	Sc		R	Sc	R	Sc		R	Sc	R	Sc	
Ambitious	15	14.00	17	14.92	16	13.50	.553	18	16.80	17	13.86	.024*	17	15.56	14	13.57	.106
Broadminded	7	8.67	6	6.86	6	7.00	.625	4	6.67	6	7.28	.726	7	7.71	5	6.44	.219
Capable	11	9.63	8	9.69	8	9.21	.756	8	7.75	8	9.97	.048*	8	9.33	10	9.78	.629
Cheerful	14	12.63	11	10.43	11	10.71	.506	13	11.75	10	10.21	.687	12	11.75	9	9.44	.061
Clean	18	17.20	18	16.70	18	16.17	.293	17	16.73	18	16.62	.786	18	16.61	18	16.75	.859
Courageous	3	5.33	7	7.80	7	7.36	.769	7	7.38	7	7.43	.895	6	7.27	7	7.88	.668
Forgiving	9	9.13	5	5.81	5	5.33	.355	6	7.00	5	5.63	.667	5	5.57	6	6.88	.650
Helpful	2	4.00	4	4.05	1	2.90	.581	3	5.33	2	3.37	.209	2	3.56	3	4.00	.806
Honest	1	2.33	3	3.75	2	4.05	.019*	2	3.29	3	3.88	.516	1	3.46	2	3.94	.591
Imaginative	6	7.88	10	10.33	10	9.83	.502	11	9.00	11	10.70	.651	11	11.05	8	8.56	.009**
Independent	16	14.33	15	12.96	14	13.17	.311	14	13.33	14	13.07	.849	14	12.82	16	13.88	.286
Intellectual	10	9.25	9	10.19	12	10.50	.867	10	8.80	12	10.77	.045*	9	8.56	12	10.84	.149
Logical	13	11.33	14	12.82	15	13.50	.575	12	11.43	15	13.21	.011*	13	12.53	15	13.71	.083
Loving	5	6.75	1	3.63	3	4.17	.543	5	6.88	1	3.15	.001**	4	4.43	1	3.75	.954
Obedient	12	11.00	13	12.43	17	13.72	.004**	15	13.92	13	12.20	.013*	15	12.85	13	12.80	.885
Polite	17	15.14	16	13.56	12	12.50	.022*	16	14.13	16	13.61	.667	16	13.67	17	14.13	.906
Responsible	4	5.80	2	3.73	4	4.21	.111	1	3.22	4	4.50	.169	3	3.87	4	5.00	.129
Self-Controlled	8	9.00	12	10.55	9	9.61	.555	9	8.33	9	10.05	.624	10	9.88	11	10.05	.772

delegates are discriminated according to the academic degrees they have obtained. Of thirty-six
values, only one rank differs significantly at
the .05 level or below. Those without a Ph.D.
or M.D. degree rank equality as second highest
whereas those with the Ph.D. or M.D. degree rank
equality seventh. Those with a doctorate rank
wisdom, inner-harmony, true friendship and self-
respect more highly. Those without a doctorate
rank mature love, an exciting life, a sense of
accomplishment and a world of beauty more highly.

Regarding instrumental values, those with
the Ph.D. or M.D. degree rank imaginative, intellectual, independent and cheerful more highly.
Those without those degrees rank courageous,
obedient, self-controlled and logical more highly.
(See Table Eight A)

Seventy-eight of the delegates, or thirty-
three percent, graduated from the same university,
The Gregorian University in Rome. This group
differs significantly from those who did not
graduate from The Gregorian University in respect
to two terminal values and four instrumental
values. Those who have graduated from The
Gregorian rank salvation first with a stronger
composite score than those who have not (1.16
compared to 1.38). Those who did not graduate
from The Gregorian rank a sense of accomplishment
eighth compared to the ranking of twelfth by
Gregorian graduates. This difference is significant beyond the .001 level of significance.

Graduates of The Gregorian rank forgiving,
intellectual, logical and obedient of significantly higher rank. Non-Gregorian delegates rank
helpful, imaginative, intellectual, cheerful, and
broadminded more highly. (See Table Eight B)

Those who have published articles or books
are significantly different in their value-
ranking of three values. They rank salvation
highest and a world of peace higher than the
others. Those who have not published rank

437

TABLE EIGHT

DISCRIMINATION OF VALUE-RANKINGS BY ACADEMIC DEGREE,
GREGORIAN UNIVERSITY GRADUATION AND NUMBER OF PUBLICATIONS

I TERMINAL	8A Sample of whether delegate has a Ph.D. or M.D. or not						8B Whether delegate was Graduate of the Gregorian University						8C Number of Publications listed for delegate								
	Attained Ph.D. or M.D. N=42		No Ph.D. or M.D. N=28		Probability		Not Graduate of Gregorian N=120		Gregorian Graduate N=54		Probability		No Publications N=79		One or Two Publications N=59		Three or more Publications N=36		Probability
	R	Sc	R	Sc			R	Sc	R	Sc			R	Sc	R	Sc	R	Sc	
A Comfortable Life	17	16.97	17	16.93	.869		17	17.00	17	17.07	.735		17	16.92	17	17.13	17	17.09	.528
An Exciting Life	16	14.00	14	11.50	.184		12	11.39	14	13.33	.137		13	12.42	12	11.13	15	13.50	.269
A Sense of Accomplishment	10	10.75	9	9.50	.151		8	8.50	12	11.70	.001***		10	10.00	8	8.00	9	10.17	.188
A World at Peace	6	6.50	6	5.75	.532		7	6.50	7	7.75	.534		7	6.45	7	7.81	4	5.50	.041*
A World of Beauty	13	13.00	12	11.25	.590		14	12.67	13	11.90	.520		14	12.57	14	12.56	12	11.50	.801
Equality	7	6.88	2	3.75	.007**		3	5.42	3	5.07	.683		6	5.88	3	4.88	3	4.90	.562
Family Security	11	11.10	13	11.50	.878		13	11.94	10	10.64	.054		12	11.32	13	11.73	13	11.75	.667
Freedom	5	5.67	5	5.50	.960		5	5.75	6	6.67	.225		4	5.46	6	6.44	7	6.63	.603
Happiness	8	8.83	8	8.83	.878		9	8.72	8	8.50	.967		8	7.20	9	9.00	8	9.93	.096
Inner Harmony	4	5.17	7	7.00	.259		6	6.14	5	5.64	.745		5	5.86	5	5.60	5	6.33	.559
Mature Love	12	11.90	10	10.00	.306		11	10.40	9	10.00	.846		11	10.25	10	9.25	11	11.00	.619
National Security	15	13.64	16	15.00	.067		16	14.38	15	13.50	.143		16	14.31	16	14.18	16	13.67	.509
Pleasure	18	17.00	18	17.57	.216		18	17.27	18	17.60	.180		18	17.42	18	17.33	18	17.40	.964
Salvation	1	1.28	1	1.43	.525		1	1.38	1	1.16	.023*		1	1.42	1	1.26	1	1.17	.084
Self-Respect	9	9.00	11	11.00	.598		10	9.95	11	11.30	.174		9	9.86	11	10.88	10	10.83	.555
Social Recognition	14	13.17	15	13.70	.533		15	13.09	16	13.94	.143		15	13.71	15	13.11	14	12.50	.505
True Friendship	3	4.75	4	5.17	.878		4	5.58	4	5.17	.699		3	5.25	4	4.94	6	6.50	.118
Wisdom	2	3.25	3	4.50	.081		2	3.91	2	3.77	.891		2	3.85	2	4.04	2	3.25	.321

Table Eight - continued

	8A Sample of whether delegate has a Ph.D. or M.D. or not					8B Whether delegate was Graduate of the Gregorian University					8C Number of Publications listed for delegate						
	Attained Ph.D. or M.D. N=42		No Ph.D. or M.D. N=28		Probability	Not Graduate of Gregorian N=120		Gregorian Graduate N=54		Probability	No Publications N=79		One or Two Publications N=59		Three or More Publications N=36		Probability
II INSTRUMENTAL	R	Sc	R	Sc		R	Sc	R	Sc		R	Sc	R	Sc	R	Sc	
Ambitious	17	15.50	17	15.00	.960	17	15.00	16	13.93	.652	17	13.56	17	15.71	17	15.83	.131
Broadminded	7	7.50	6	8.17	.732	5	6.75	6	7.75	.508	7	7.57	6	7.00	5	6.50	.636
Capable	10	10.25	9	8.50	.960	8	9.28	9	9.93	.520	10	9.81	8	9.42	8	9.00	.812
Cheerful	13	12.00	11	9.50	.306	11	9.94	14	12.00	.137	10	9.67	10	9.67	11	10.50	.696
Clean	18	16.38	18	16.70	.803	18	16.71	18	16.58	.901	18	16.77	18	16.53	18	16.75	.880
Courageous	6	7.17	10	9.50	.533	7	7.25	7	8.00	.560	6	7.27	7	7.38	7	9.00	.691
Forgiving	5	5.33	5	6.50	.598	6	6.88	5	4.93	.048*	5	6.67	5	5.19	6	6.75	.298
Helpful	1	3.07	1	3.00	.801	1	3.31	3	4.36	.130	1	3.15	1	3.63	3	4.83	.024*
Honest	3	4.36	2	3.50	.299	2	3.58	1	3.70	.846	3	3.33	1	4.00	1	3.70	.546
Imaginative	12	11.50	8	8.50	.644	9	9.43	11	10.50	.699	8	9.25	9	9.43	14	11.50	.580
Independent	15	13.30	13	10.50	.260	13	12.92	15	13.75	.556	15	13.14	13	12.67	15	13.38	.989
Intellectual	9	9.90	7	8.50	.529	12	10.90	8	9.00	.047*	11	10.57	12	10.58	9	9.17	.294
Logical	14	12.63	16	14.00	.147	15	13.24	13	11.75	.007**	14	13.13	15	13.25	12	11.33	.565
Loving	4	5.00	4	5.00	.878	4	4.67	2	3.90	.545	3	3.80	2	3.75	4	5.50	.008**
Obedient	11	11.10	14	12.25	.306	14	13.23	12	11.25	.035*	13	12.75	14	13.22	13	11.50	.271
Polite	16	14.50	15	13.83	.732	16	13.72	17	14.00	.930	16	13.25	16	14.25	13	13.83	.545
Responsible	2	4.33	3	4.00	.878	3	4.04	4	4.38	.820	4	4.33	4	4.25	2	3.83	.636
Self-Controlled	8	9.50	12	9.83	.732	10	9.77	10	10.36	.565	9	9.67	11	10.05	10	10.50	.651

happiness, freedom, friendship and helpful more highly. (See Table Eight C)

The delegates who speak more languages differ from those who speak fewer languages in giving higher priority to equality and ambition. They also place salvation in higher priority. Those who are less linguistically fluent rank freedom, happiness, and imagination more highly. (See Table Nine A)

A discrimination of the delegates for whether or not they were canon lawyers yielded only nine lawyers and 165 non-canon lawyers. Only two rankings yielded results statistically significant beyond the .05 level. The canon law group ranked family security fifth while the rest ranked this twelfth. The non-canon lawyers ranked pleasure of slightly higher priority. (See Table Nine B)

Of forty-one delegates who are teaching major areas in education as their present work, a discrimination was made into two groups, those who teach sacred subjects and those who teach secular subjects. Thirty of the sample teach sacred and eleven teach secular subjects.

The difference of the group of secular professors from the sacred professors in respect to the ranking of salvation is statistically significant at the .001 level. The secular professors rank salvation seventh (8.00) and the sacred professors rank it first (1.13). The sacred group ranks inner-harmony fourth while the secular group ranks it twelfth and they rank a comfortable life significantly higher than the secular group. The secular group ranks a world of beauty, true friendship, an exciting life, and world at peace more highly and happiness and self-respect less highly than those who teach sacred subjects.

Also, the secular group ranks ambitious significantly higher. It gives higher priority to cheerful, helpful, imaginative, and loving.

TABLE NINE

DISCRIMINATION OF VALUE-RANKINGS BY NUMBER OF LANGUAGES SPOKEN, STATUS AS CANON LAWYER OR NOT AND PURSUIT OF SACRED OR SECULAR SUBJECTS

I TERMINAL	9A How Many of the Languages of the General Congregation does the Delegate speak								9B Whether the Delegate is a Specialist in Canon Law or not					9C Whether Delegate specialized in and teaches Sacred or Secular Subject				
	One or Two G.C. Languages N=78		Three or Four Languages N=73		Five or more Languages N=20		Probability		Not a Canon Lawyer N=165		Canon Lawyer N=9		Probability	Sacred Subjects N=30		Secular Subjects N=11		Probability
	R	Sc	R	Sc	R	Sc			R	Sc	R	Sc		R	Sc	R	Sc	
A Comfortable Life	17	17.09	17	16.91	17	17.17	.147		17	17.04	17	16.80	.641	17	16.83	18	17.81	.033*
An Exciting Life	13	12.00	15	13.25	13	11.50	.210		13	12.19	16	14.00	.168	16	14.17	5	6.00	.086
A Sense of Accomplishment	9	9.75	9	9.67	10	10.50	.821		9	9.67	12	12.00	.245	9	9.83	9	8.00	.922
A World at Peace	6	6.17	7	7.43	5	6.50	.287		7	6.89	6	7.00	.882	7	6.50	4	5.67	.653
A World of Beauty	14	12.63	13	12.57	9	10.25	.209		14	12.31	15	13.25	.521	13	12.50	8	8.00	.041*
Equality	4	5.17	6	6.63	3	4.25	.012*		3	5.25	4	5.75	.882	3	5.17	3	5.00	.773
Family Security	12	11.50	12	11.59	8	9.50	.854		12	11.71	5	7.00	.006*	12	11.64	13	11.00	.922
Freedom	5	5.32	5	6.45	6	6.75	.208		6	5.94	7	7.13	.101	6	6.25	6	7.00	.922
Happiness	8	8.30	8	8.00	14	12.50	.367		8	8.54	10	10.25	.547	8	9.70	10	9.33	.922
Inner Harmony	7	6.33	3	5.43	7	7.50	.589		5	5.92	9	8.00	.773	4	5.75	12	11.00	.016*
Mature Love	10	10.00	11	11.00	11	11.00	.580		11	10.38	8	8.00	.570	11	11.00	11	10.75	.773
National Security	16	14.32	16	13.85	16	14.17	.739		16	14.17	14	13.00	.308	15	13.50	16	13.88	.677
Pleasure	18	17.13	18	17.61	18	17.50	.089		18	17.31	18	17.94	.024*	18	17.40	17	16.63	.192
Salvation	1	1.43	1	1.26	1	1.13	.066		1	1.32	1	1.06	.185	1	1.13	7	8.00	.001**
Self-Respect	11	10.07	10	10.33	12	11.50	.548		10	10.23	13	12.67	.543	10	11.00	14	13.00	.922
Social Recognition	15	13.50	14	13.05	15	14.00	.732		15	13.43	11	11.00	.570	14	13.50	15	13.67	.922
True Friendship	3	4.79	4	6.11	4	4.50	.207		4	5.41	3	5.75	.971	5	6.10	1	2.88	.129
Wisdom	2	4.30	2	3.40	2	4.00	.595		2	3.75	2	5.00	.083	2	4.17	2	3.00	.509

Table Nine - continued

II INSTRUMENTAL

9A. How Many of the Languages of the General Congregation does the Delegate speak

	One or Two G.C. Languages N=78		Three or Four Languages N=73		Five or more Languages N=20		Probability
	R	Sc	R	Sc	R	Sc	
Ambitious	16	14.30	17	15.67	13	12.25	.046*
Broadminded	6	6.79	7	8.20	6	5.50	.106
Capable	10	9.80	8	9.06	11	10.50	.520
Cheerful	9	9.75	12	11.71	10	10.50	.575
Clean	18	16.97	18	16.44	18	15.83	.181
Courageous	7	7.00	6	7.88	7	8.17	.507
Forgiving	5	6.00	5	6.40	3	4.00	.549
Helpful	1	3.67	2	3.75	1	3.00	.987
Honest	2	3.72	1	3.31	4	4.50	.600
Imaginative	8	9.10	11	10.00	12	11.50	.054
Independent	13	12.93	15	13.00	17	15.00	.708
Intellectual	12	10.83	9	9.63	8	9.17	.503
Logical	15	13.14	14	12.88	14	12.50	.768
Loving	4	4.70	4	4.08	2	4.00	.844
Obedient	14	12.95	13	12.33	16	13.50	.679
Polite	17	14.50	16	13.11	15	13.00	.100
Responsible	3	4.06	3	4.00	5	5.17	.580
Self-Controlled	11	10.28	10	9.79	9	9.50	.740

9B. Whether the Delegate is a Specialist in Canon Law or not

	Not a Canon Lawyer N=165		Canon Lawyer N=9		Probability
	R	Sc	R	Sc	
Ambitious	17	14.36	16	14.33	.942
Broadminded	6	7.13	6	7.00	.854
Capable	9	9.58	8	9.00	.971
Cheerful	12	10.46	14	12.00	1.0
Clean	18	16.67	18	16.63	.826
Courageous	7	7.29	10	16.63	.157
Forgiving	5	6.05	5	5.25	.854
Helpful	2	3.71	3	3.75	.912
Honest	1	3.70	2	2.75	.565
Imaginative	8	9.41	13	12.00	.179
Independent	15	13.06	17	15.25	.628
Intellectual	11	10.05	12	11.75	.882
Logical	14	13.04	11	10.67	.073
Loving	4	4.44	1	1.40	.547
Obedient	13	12.97	7	8.00	.109
Polite	16	13.88	15	12.25	.882
Responsible	3	4.16	4	4.25	.799
Self-Controlled	10	9.95	9	10.00	.739

9C. Whether Delegate specialized in and teaches Sacred or Secular Subject

	Sacred Subjects N=30		Secular Subjects N=11		Probability
	R	Sc	R	Sc	
Ambitious	18	16.50	13	11.75	.041*
Broadminded	7	8.00	6	6.20	.549
Capable	8	9.00	11	10.25	.549
Cheerful	13	10.50	3	5.38	.653
Clean	18	16.07	18	17.71	.129
Courageous	6	8.00	7	6.25	.549
Forgiving	4	5.21	9	8.00	.185
Helpful	5	7.00	2	3.75	.549
Honest	1	3.10	8	6.75	.185
Imaginative	12	11.50	5	6.00	.549
Independent	16	14.17	14	13.00	.549
Intellectual	9	9.30	12	10.67	.773
Logical	14	12.00	15	13.13	.258
Loving	3	5.00	1	3.00	.922
Obedient	11	10.50	17	15.80	.129
Polite	15	14.17	16	15.00	.549
Responsible	2	3.50	4	5.75	.922
Self-Controlled	10	10.50	10	10.00	.922

The sacred group ranks forgiving, honest, intellectual, obedient, and responsible more highly than the secular. (See Table Nine C)

Section Three:

Comparison of Value-Rankings
of Non-Delegates with Delegates Discriminating
for Region, Age and Office

When non-delegate value-rankings are discriminated according to the major structural variables, it is seen that they are similar to the delegates' rankings, mixed across categories for values associated with the Jesuit styles, and more sharply differentiated in some categories.

In most regions, non-delegates give higher priority to salvation, wisdom and true friendship. France and Northern and Southern Latin America rank them lowest. Also, the Spanish Assistancy ranks salvation third among non-delegates; but the Spanish delegates ranked salvation first.

Mature love is ranked lower in priority by non-delegates in most regions. The rankings for wisdom, equality, a world at peace and true friendship are mixed. Some non-delegate regions rank these higher and others lower. Happiness is ranked higher and its range of rankings is wider (from third to tenth place). This is also true for an exciting life (from fourth to seventeenth place).

Instrumental value-rankings show mixed increases and decreases when the regions of non-delegates are compared to those of the delegates. Honest, intellectual and loving decrease in priority for some Assistancies but not for all. Forgiving and broadminded also show a mixed variation of rankings. Imaginative is ranked consistently lower for non-delegates than for delegates.

Overall, non-delegate rankings are seldom
more than two or three ranks different than delegates. There is a stability with reference to
cultures measurable here. The direction of the
differences is varied in such a way that no discernible pattern emerges. (See Table Ten)

When delegates and non-delegates are compared with respect to age groups, there is a
notable change. The tendency among the small
number of young delegates at the Congregation
towards the Bulwark-Catholic style is not representative of younger Jesuits generally. The
highest rankings of values associated with the
Conciliar-Humanist style (true friendship,
equality, freedom and an exciting life) are given
by the youngest groups. Salvation is ranked fourteenth by the non-delegates who are under thirty
years of age. Wisdom is also ranked lower.
Significant differences are evidenced across all
age groups for salvation, mature love, true
friendship and equality. The non-delegates over
seventy show themselves somewhat more like the
younger non-delegates and less like the middle-
aged in the rankings of peace, world of beauty
and freedom. There is lower evaluation of self-
controlled among non-delegates than delegates
and non-delegates rank obedient, loving, and
cheerful higher than delegates in most age
categories. (See Table Eleven)

The comparison for office between delegates
and non-delegates is not a comparison of administrators and non-administrators. There are only
three super-institutional administrators in the
entire non-delegate sample compared to one
hundred in the delegate group.

The comparison of non-delegates in terms of
office and occupation show only slight differences.
This was also true comparing the various occupations of delegates. Salvation, mature love, a
world of beauty and capable are significantly
different. Eight terminal value-rankings and
four instrumental values differ across the five
categories by no more than two ranks. Only

TABLE TEN

DISCRIMINATION OF NON-DELEGATE VALUE-RANKINGS BY ASSISTANCY

I TERMINAL	French N=6 R	Sc	Northern Lat. Amer. N=16 R	Sc	Southern Lat. Amer. N=13 R	Sc	Asian N=14 R	Sc	African N=7 R	Sc	English N=23 R	Sc	Indian N=16 R	Sc	American N=42 R	Sc	Spanish N=18 R	Sc	German N=16 R	Sc	Slavic and Italian* N=10 R	Sc
A Comfortable Life	18	17.00	17	16.75	17	16.92	16	17.10	16	16.63	18	17.11	17	16.79	18	16.73	17	16.88	14	12.83	17	15.50
An Exciting Life	9	8.00	4	6.83	12	11.00	8	7.00	8	7.00	7	7.00	16	15.00	13	13.30	10	9.50	15	17.33	15	13.50
A Sense of Accomplishment	11	9.00	11	10.50	15	14.58	11	10.00	6	6.75	6	6.88	7	7.00	4	5.75	6	5.50	6	6.50	10	8.50
A World at Peace	5	4.50	9	8.00	8	8.67	8	8.50	10	10.75	15	12.88	11	10.25	12	11.50	9	9.50	15	14.00	10	8.50
A World of Beauty	12	10.00	13	11.50	14	13.63	15	13.90	12	12.00	8	8.00	15	12.88	7	5.83	13	11.30	13	11.50	14	13.50
Equality	4	4.50	1	3.00	2	3.38	3	4.83	11	11.00	10	10.75	8	8.00	5	5.83	4	5.90	4	6.00	5	6.50
Family Security	8	8.00	16	13.70	13	11.63	10	10.00	14	12.67	9	9.00	12	11.50	12	12.00	16	13.75	9	8.50	9	8.50
Freedom	3	4.50	3	5.50	5	5.25	7	7.50	9	9.00	3	5.20	4	6.00	7	7.90	5	5.50	6	7.00	6	7.00
Happiness	7	7.50	6	7.00	6	6.00	6	6.50	7	7.00	5	5.80	3	5.20	8	8.50	8	8.50	9	8.50	8	8.50
Inner Harmony	13	11.00	8	8.00	3	4.67	4	5.00	3	3.00	11	11.00	3	4.83	6	6.50	4	5.00	7	6.83	4	5.50
Mature Love	10	9.00	5	7.50	11	10.25	9	9.50	17	16.75	16	13.25	10	9.00	16	14.25	11	10.50	10	10.00	16	14.50
National Security	15	15.00	14	12.50	16	14.67	13	11.17	13	12.25	16	13.25	15	13.70	15	13.79	15	13.50	12	11.50	8	8.50
Pleasure	16	16.50	18	17.83	18	17.69	17	17.10	18	17.80	17	16.20	18	17.70	18	17.36	18	17.10	18	17.50	18	17.25
Salvation	6	7.17	10	9.00	1	1.43	1	1.38	1	1.38	1	1.38	9	8.17	17	16.36	3	4.50	3	4.50	1	1.13
Self-Respect	17	17.00	12	11.50	9	9.00	12	11.00	14	13.00	12	12.00	8	8.17	8	7.94	13	11.50	8	8.00	13	13.00
Social Recognition	14	14.50	15	13.50	10	10.25	14	12.50	9	8.25	14	12.33	14	12.50	14	13.63	14	12.50	16	14.50	12	12.50
True Friendship	1	3.50	2	3.67	4	4.88	5	6.00	4	5.00	4	5.25	6	6.50	1	3.50	1	3.50	5	6.50	3	5.50
Wisdom	2	4.50	7	8.00	7	6.33	2	2.50	2	2.33	2	3.13	2	3.17	2	2.90	2	4.17	2	3.25	2	2.10

*Slavic and Italian Assistancies are grouped together here because individually there would not be sufficient number of cases of accomplish analysis.

II INSTRUMENTAL	French N=6		Northern Lat.Amer. N=16		Southern Lat.Amer. N=13		Asian N=14		African N=7		English N=23		Indian N=16		American N=42		Spanish N=18		German N=16		Slavic and Italian N=10	
	R	Sc	R	Sc	R	Sc	R	Sc	R	Sc	R	Sc	R	Sc	R	Sc	R	Sc	R	Sc	R	Sc
Ambitious	17	16.00	9	9.83	13	11.33	18	16.50	5	7.00	17	15.25	18	16.50	18	15.90	12	11.00	18	17.50	18	17.50
Broadminded	4	6.00	5	7.50	9	9.00	6	7.17	10	9.00	7	7.67	7	7.50	10	10.25	5	5.50	7	8.50	7	8.00
Capable	12	12.00	6	8.00	5	6.67	11	10.00	12	10.25	10	10.00	11	11.50	8	9.17	8	8.50	4	6.50	4	6.50
Cheerful	9	9.00	7	8.50	8	8.75	8	8.00	9	9.00	8	8.25	9	9.00	8	9.00	13	12.50	9	8.50	9	8.50
Clean	18	16.50	16	15.00	17	14.25	17	14.83	18	15.25	18	15.67	17	16.25	17	15.50	18	16.00	17	16.00	17	16.00
Courageous	1	3.00	10	10.00	4	5.75	10	9.00	8	9.00	5	6.13	5	6.00	7	8.17	7	8.50	11	9.00	11	9.00
Forgiving	8	8.50	8	9.50	7	8.00	5	6.50	6	8.00	6	7.67	8	8.50	4	6.50	6	7.50	8	8.50	8	8.50
Helpful	2	4.00	1	1.75	6	8.00	2	3.83	2	4.00	4	4.25	4	5.50	3	5.17	1	3.00	6	7.50	8	8.50
Honest	3	5.00	4	6.50	2	3.25	3	4.50	1	3.00	1	3.00	3	4.50	1	3.75	3	4.75	10	9.00	10	9.00
Imaginative	10	9.50	12	10.50	15	13.00	13	11.50	11	11.75	12	11.75	14	12.50	14	12.50	15	13.50	1	2.50	1	3.50
Independent	14	13.50	18	17.50	18	16.75	16	14.50	17	15.00	15	13.88	15	14.17	15	13.17	17	14.30	16	15.00	16	15.00
Intellectual	11	10.00	14	12.00	12	10.13	9	9.00	16	13.00	13	12.00	11	12.50	11	10.50	11	10.25	15	14.50	15	14.50
Logical	13	13.50	15	12.75	14	12.67	15	10.50	16	14.00	16	14.40	16	12.00	16	13.30	10	10.00	13	13.00	15	7.50
Loving	5	7.50	2	2.50	1	3.25	4	6.50	14	12.00	9	9.33	1	4.00	5	7.10	4	5.50	5	7.00	5	7.00
Obedient	15	14.00	13	11.00	11	10.13	12	10.50	15	13.00	11	10.33	12	12.00	12	11.83	16	14.00	16	14.00	13	9.50
Polite	16	16.00	17	15.25	16	14.00	14	12.75	7	9.00	14	12.33	10	11.50	13	12.50	14	13.00	11	11.00	14	13.00
Responsible	7	8.50	3	6.17	3	5.67	1	3.50	2	2.25	2	4.25	2	4.50	2	4.83	2	4.50	3	3.50	12	5.00
Self-Controlled	6	8.50	11	10.50	10	10.00	7	7.83	4	5.75	4	5.33	6	6.75	9	7.50	9	9.83	10	10.83	3	6.00

TABLE ELEVEN

VALUE-RANKINGS OF NON-DELEGATES DISCRIMINATED BY AGE-GROUPS

Value	Less Than 30 N=18		30-39 N=25		40-49 N=46		50-59 N=36		60-69 N=41		70 or over N=14		Probability
	R	Sc	R	Sc	R	Sc	R	Sc	R	Sc	R	Sc	
I TERMINAL													
A Comfortable Life	18	16.94	17	16.65	17	16.79	17	16.71	17	16.63	17	16.50	.819
An Exciting Life	9	9.00	12	11.00	16	13.67	16	13.00	16	13.25	16	15.90	.179
A Sense of Accomplishment	8	8.50	8	8.75	10	9.70	10	9.50	9	9.63	11	10.00	.898
A World at Peace	7	7.50	10	9.88	6	6.50	8	8.50	8	7.33	4	5.00	.545
A World of Beauty	12	11.00	13	11.75	13	12.30	15	12.79	13	12.33	12	12.50	.337
Equality	2	4.00	2	3.75	3	4.83	6	7.50	4	5.43	7	6.50	.016*
Family Security	11	11.00	14	12.00	12	11.61	11	11.30	11	11.89	9	9.83	.780
Freedom	3	4.50	5	6.40	8	7.33	7	7.83	7	7.00	3	5.00	.195
Happiness	6	6.17	11	10.13	7	7.00	5	7.50	5	6.67	6	6.50	.131
Inner Harmony	5	6.17	7	8.75	4	5.06	4	5.50	3	5.38	8	7.50	.391
Mature Love	13	11.17	6	6.63	11	10.50	12	12.17	15	13.13	15	14.00	.007**
National Security	15	13.83	15	13.75	15	13.64	14	12.75	14	12.63	10	10.00	.829
Pleasure	17	16.50	18	17.61	18	17.17	18	17.06	18	17.29	18	17.17	.333
Salvation	14	12.00	1	3.25	1	1.50	1	1.19	1	1.32	1	1.08	.001**
Self-Respect	10	10.50	9	9.00	9	9.00	9	9.00	10	10.00	13	12.83	.149
Social Recognition	16	14.00	16	14.00	14	12.50	13	12.25	12	12.13	14	13.00	.177
True Friendship	1	3.30	3	4.29	5	5.33	3	4.38	6	6.88	5	6.50	.009**
Wisdom	4	5.00	4	4.63	2	3.67	2	3.83	2	2.80	2	2.38	.153

Table Eleven - continued

II INSTRUMENTAL

Value	Less Than 30 N=18		30-39 N=25		40-49 N=46		50-59 N=36		60-69 N=41		70 or over N=14		Probability
	R	Sc	R	Sc	R	Sc	R	Sc	R	Sc	R	Sc	
Ambitious	2	10.83	17	14.25	16	14.00	18	16.00	18	16.00	18	15.70	.175
Broadminded	6	7.00	6	7.75	6	7.17	8	9.00	7	7.88	12	9.50	.908
Capable	11	10.83	8	8.13	9	9.10	10	9.50	9	9.13	11	9.50	.317
Cheerful	5	7.00	7	8.08	12	11.83	8	8.75	8	8.67	7	8.17	.017*
Clean	18	15.75	18	15.67	18	15.33	16	15.64	17	15.56	15	14.00	.579
Courageous	8	8.00	9	9.00	8	7.90	4	5.70	6	7.88	5	6.17	.756
Forgiving	7	8.00	5	6.88	5	6.75	6	7.70	5	6.75	4	6.00	.872
Helpful	1	2.50	1	2.88	2	4.33	3	4.50	1	3.63	9	8.50	.004**
Honest	4	5.50	2	3.40	1	3.75	2	4.17	2	3.75	1	4.00	.876
Imaginative	10	10.50	10	10.00	14	12.00	15	13.17	16	14.38	17	15.50	.038*
Independent	16	14.00	16	14.00	17	15.17	17	16.00	15	13.40	16	14.50	.390
Intellectual	14	13.70	11	10.63	11	11.50	11	9.83	11	11.00	14	10.00	.645
Logical	15	14.00	13	12.88	15	13.61	12	10.50	14	11.92	6	7.50	.098
Loving	2	4.00	3	4.38	4	5.83	5	5.83	12	11.25	10	9.00	.051
Obedient	7	15.75	15	13.67	10	10.00	13	11.50	10	11.00	8	8.50	.048*
Polite	13	13.50	14	13.00	13	12.00	14	13.07	13	11.92	13	10.00	.537
Responsible	3	4.83	4	5.00	3	4.50	1	3.50	3	4.88	3	6.00	.930
Self-Controlled	9	10.50	12	10.88	7	7.50	7	7.75	4	6.13	2	5.50	.069

capable, courageous, and logical differ much
across the categories. (See Table Twelve)

The control for Congregation leadership
cannot be compared between delegates and non-
delegates since Congregation leadership is attributable only to the delegates. There is no
comparable measure available for the non-delegate
sample.

Fewer differences emerge from non-delegate
rankings than from delegate rankings in respect
to social class. A sense of accomplishment,
pleasure, honest and clean differ significantly.
In these four cases, the middle-class differs
from both lower and upper rather than ascending
or descending across all three groups. This
pattern is consistent in all but seven of the
thirty-six values. For these seven, the higher
the social class, the more value is given to
mature love, freedom, and logical and the lower
the social class, the more value is given to
social recognition, world-at-peace, imaginative
and independent. (See Table Thirteen A)

Only one of thirty-six rankings exhibits
significant difference when non-delegates are
discriminated according to task and person-
orientation. This contrasts with eight significant values among the delegate respondents.
The only significant difference among the non-
delegates appears in the ranking of pleasure.
Equality and exciting life also differ somewhat.

Person-oriented non-delegates rank broadminded in lower priority and logical and obedient
in higher priority. They also rank capable and
logical more highly which is the reverse of
person-oriented delegate rankings. Task-oriented
non-delegates rank inner-harmony and loving lower
but they rank mature love slightly higher than
person-oriented respondents. (See Table Thirteen
B)

The non-delegates' value-rankings differ

449

TABLE TWELVE

VALUE-RANKINGS OF NON-DELEGATES

DISCRIMINATED ACCORDING TO OCCUPATION

I TERMINAL	Administration or Formation N=8		University Work incl. writing and research N=38		Secondary Schooling N=31		Parish Work N=57		Other Categories N=42		Probabilities
	R	Sc	R	Sc	R	Sc	R	Sc	R	Sc	
A Comfortable Life	18	17.50	17	16.74	17	16.25	17	16.82	17	16.74	.256
An Exciting Life	15	14.00	16	13.75	13	12.25	12	11.88	15	13.38	.676
A Sense of Accomplishment	12	11.00	10	9.50	7	7.20	9	8.43	11	10.17	.083
A World at Peace	9	7.50	8	8.33	6	6.75	8	7.67	6	5.83	.347
A World of Beauty	13	11.50	15	13.30	11	11.25	16	13.19	13	11.23	.009**
Equality	3	4.50	7	6.50	4	5.80	6	6.22	3	5.00	.115
Family Security	11	10.00	12	11.67	12	12.13	11	11.85	10	9.75	.137
Freedom	8	7.50	6	6.50	8	7.63	4	5.42	7	7.00	.168
Happiness	5	6.00	4	6.00	9	9.00	7	7.13	8	7.83	.167
Inner Harmony	4	5.50	5	6.50	5	6.00	3	4.94	5	5.83	.526
Mature Love	7	7.50	9	8.83	15	13.13	14	12.63	9	9.17	.022*
National Security	14	12.50	14	13.00	16	13.38	15	12.92	14	12.50	.906
Pleasure	17	17.00	18	17.00	18	17.31	18	17.18	18	17.59	.522
Salvation	1	1.00	1	1.45	1	1.75	1	1.27	1	3.50	.012*
Self-Respect	10	9.00	11	9.83	10	9.67	10	9.40*	12	10.83	.773
Social Recognition	16	14.83	13	12.40	14	12.60	13	12.25	16	14.00	.109
True Friendship	6	7.50	3	4.25	3	4.31	5	6.00	4	5.07	.388
Wisdom	2	4.00	2	3.21	2	4.20	2	4.00	2	3.64	.758

Table Twelve - continued

II INSTRUMENTAL	Administration or Formation N=8		University Work incl. writing and research N=38		Secondary Schooling N=31		Parish Work N=57		Other Categories N=42		Probabilities
	R	Sc	R	Sc	R	Sc	R	Sc	R	Sc	
Ambitious	16	14.50	17	15.00	14	12.33	16	14.13	17	14.83	.914
Broadminded	8	8.00	5	6.25	8	8.13	9	9.00	7	7.25	.237
Capable	13	12.00	8	9.10	7	8.00	8	8.08	11	11.25	.006*
Cheerful	6	7.50	10	9.90	10	9.00	13	10.38	9	8.07	.378
Clean	18	15.50	18	16.36	17	14.80	18	15.38	18	15.17	.229
Courageous	7	8.00	9	9.25	5	6.75	4	6.31	8	8.00	.105
Forgiving	4	4.00	6	6.50	6	7.38	7	8.00	5	6.70	.214
Helpful	1	2.00	2	4.83	1	3.25	2	4.63	2	4.50	.672
Honest	2	2.50	3	4.75	2	5.67	1	3.92	1	4.50	.512
Imaginative	14	13.00	12	11.50	16	13.63	15	13.67	14	12.21	.619
Independent	17	15.50	16	13.83	18	17.13	17	14.67	16	13.83	.200
Intellectual	10	10.50	11	10.17	11	11.75	14	10.08	13	12.17	.189
Logical	15	14.50	13	11.70	15	13.58	12	10.33	15	13.61	.082
Loving	5	6.50	4	6.17	4	5.63	6	8.00	3	5.00	.384
Obedient	12	11.00	15	13.50	12	12.00	10	10.89	10	10.83	.177
Polite	11	11.00	14	12.30	13	12.33	14	12.89	12	11.50	.691
Responsible	3	4.00	1	3.75	3	4.67	3	4.75	4	5.30	.548
Self-Controlled	9	9.50	7	6.83	9	8.33	5	7.40	6	7.25	.768

TABLE THIRTEEN

VALUE-RANKINGS OF NON-DELEGATES DISCRIMINATED
ACCORDING TO SOCIAL CLASS AND TASK/PERSON ORIENTATION

Value	A. Lower or Unskilled N=34		Middle N=103		Upper-Middle or Upper N=44		Probability	B. Task Orientation N=41		Person Orientation N=137		Probability
	R	Sc	R	Sc	R	Sc		R	Sc	R	Sc	
I TERMINAL												
A Comfortable Life	17	16.87	17	16.66	17	16.69	.246	18	16.75	17	16.69	.994
An Exciting Life	11	11.50	16	13.38	12	11.00	.088	16	14.38	14	12.61	.224
A Sense of Accomplishment	7	7.13	10	10.15	8	8.17	.010**	10	9.86	9	9.91	.516
A World at Peace	5	6.00	7	7.25	9	8.25	.607	4	6.38	8	7.69	.536
A World of Beauty	13	12.10	13	12.00	15	12.83	.674	13	11.67	13	12.29	.820
Equality	4	5.00	5	6.08	4	5.25	.576	7	6.80	4	5.46	.167
Family Security	14	12.25	12	11.29	13	11.75	.583	12	11.33	12	11.58	.932
Freedom	9	8.00	6	6.69	7	6.25	.884	8	7.75	6	6.31	.675
Happiness	8	7.50	8	8.00	6	6.25	.196	5	6.43	7	7.56	.591
Inner Harmony	6	6.25	4	5.25	5	6.00	.530	6	6.63	5	5.47	.584
Mature Love	12	11.75	11	10.63	10	9.17	.694	11	11.00	11	11.11	.976
National Security	15	13.30	14	12.73	16	13.79	.359	15	13.13	11	12.92	.954
Pleasure	18	17.61	18	16.93	18	17.58	.017*	17	16.35	18	17.43	.047*
Salvation	1	1.44	1	1.37	1	1.46	.820	1	1.39	1	1.40	.910
Self-Respect	10	10.00	9	9.08	11	10.30	.564	9	9.33	10	9.75	.864
Social Recognition	16	13.50	15	12.82	14	12.50	.588	14	13.00	15	12.91	.683
True Friendship	3	4.93	3	4.85	3	5.25	.836	3	3.92	3	5.26	.664
Wisdom	2	3.90	2	3.20	2	4.33	.182	2	3.14	2	4.00	.660

Table Thirteen - continued

Value	A. Lower or Unskilled N=34		Middle N=103		Upper-Middle or Upper N=44		Probability	B. Task Orientation N=41		Person Orientation N=137		Probability
	R	Sc	R	Sc	R	Sc		R	Sc	R	Sc	
II INSTRUMENTAL												
Ambitious	14	12.50	18	15.71	16	14.71	.132	17	14.88	16	14.60	.842
Broadminded	7	6.90	10	8.91	6	6.75	.056	8	7.00	8	8.31	.298
Capable	9	9.75	8	8.43	9	9.36	.815	11	10.33	9	8.81	.660
Cheerful	10	9.83	9	8.56	10	9.70	.576	9	9.13	10	9.06	.956
Clean	18	16.50	17	14.94	18	15.70	.018*	18	15.69	18	15.36	.610
Courageous	5	6.50	5	6.47	8	8.70	.174	5	6.43	6	7.56	.887
Forgiving	6	6.90	6	7.54	5	6.33	.548	7	7.00	5	7.13	1.000
Helpful	1	2.50	2	4.44	1	4.21	.354	3	4.42	2	4.04	.822
Honest	3	5.50	1	3.04	3	5.33	.009**	1	3.88	1	4.00	.887
Imaginative	12	11.70	15	12.92	15	13.50	.234	14	13.33	15	12.57	.646
Independent	17	14.25	16	14.29	17	15.50	.592	16	14.40	17	14.67	.932
Intellectual	11	10.30	11	11.08	11	11.00	.694	10	10.00	12	11.09	.628
Logical	15	13.50	14	12.56	14	12.17	.664	15	13.57	13	12.21	.286
Loving	4	5.83	4	6.43	4	5.70	.611	4	6.40	4	5.95	.887
Obedient	13	11.83	12	11.13	12	11.17	.884	13	12.88	11	10.81	.216
Polite	16	13.64	13	11.94	13	12.07	.054	12	12.58	14	12.34	.864
Responsible	2	3.50	3	5.09	2	4.50	.296	2	4.33	3	4.75	.801
Self-Controlled	8	7.10	7	8.43	7	7.13	.236	6	6.67	7	7.78	.516

according to the language group they belong to in a pattern similar to the differences between delegates. However, there are fewer rankings on which the non-delegates differ significantly (fourteen instead of twenty-three).

The terminal values that differ in ranking are self-respect, wisdom, sense of accomplishment, an exciting life and a comfortable life. The French and Spanish-speaking non-delegates ranked salvation lower, the Italian-speaking ranked it higher. This resembles the delegate priorities. The French-speaking non-delegates ranked equality and an exciting life higher as did the French-speaking delegates. English and German delegates and non-delegates both rank self-respect higher than other language groups.

The greatest differences among the instrumental values are the rankings of loving and ambitious. The Spanish-speaking rank loving second in priority while the Italian-speaking rank it twelfth and the French-speaking rank it tenth. These rankings are similar to, though stronger than, the delegate rank order. The Spanish-speaking rank ambitious twelfth while three other language groups rank it eighteenth. The Italian-speaking non-delegates rank helpful in thirteenth place. All others rank it first or second or third. The Italians rank self-controlled higher and forgiving lower compared to the German and the English. (See Table Fourteen)

TABLE FOURTEEN

VALUE-RANKINGS OF NON-DELEGATES DISCRIMINATED
ACCORDING TO LANGUAGE VERSION

Value	English N=82		Spanish N=48		French N=21		German N=19		Italian N=8		Probability
	R	Sc	R	Sc	R	Sc	R	Sc	R	Sc	
I TERMINAL											
A Comfortable Life	18	16.94	17	16.73	18	17.00	14	13.00	18	17.50	.001***
An Exciting Life	16	14.13	9	8.00	9	6.75	17	17.29	15	13.50	.001***
A Sense of Accomplishment	9	8.10	12	10.75	7	6.67	16	13.67	11	10.00	.001***
A World at Peace	7	7.50	8	7.50	8	6.75	9	9.00	7	8.00	.912
A World of Beauty	13	12.13	14	12.36	11	11.13	13	12.25	14	13.50	.953
Equality	5	5.83	2	3.83	6	6.40	4	6.25	6	6.50	.213
Family Security	11	11.50	15	13.00	12	11.67	11	9.67	8	9.17	.004**
Freedom	8	7.63	4	5.25	10	8.00	3	5.25	9	9.50	.108
Happiness	6	7.30	7	7.50	2	5.00	10	9.25	5	6.00	.253
Inner Harmony	4	5.19	5	5.75	4	6.13	6	6.75	3	4.50	.571
Mature Love	12	11.70	10	9.75	14	12.63	8	9.00	13	12.50	.587
National Security	15	13.39	16	13.17	15	13.88	12	10.75	10	10.00	.224
Pleasure	17	16.82	18	17.67	17	16.67	18	17.40	17	17.00	.041*
Salvation	1	1.27	3	4.50	5	6.25	1	1.29	1	1.17	.030*
Self-Respect	10	8.25	11	10.50	16	15.80	7	8.38	12	12.00	.001***
Social Recognition	14	13.39	13	12.00	13	12.25	15	13.25	16	14.00	.288
True Friendship	3	5.17	1	3.79	3	6.00	5	6.58	4	5.50	.044*
Wisdom	2	2.86	6	5.90	1	3.25	2	2.88	2	3.50	.001***

Table Fourteen - continued

Value	English N=82		Spanish N=48		French N=21		German N=19		Italian N=8		Probability
	R	Sc	R	Sc	R	Sc	R	Sc	R	Sc	
II INSTRUMENTAL											
Ambitious	18	16.10	12	10.50	16	14.00	18	17.25	18	17.70	.001***
Broadminded	9	9.00	5	7.50	5	6.00	8	8.25	6	7.00	.379
Capable	10	9.94	7	7.38	8	9.67	12	11.00	3	5.00	.126
Cheerful	8	8.33	11	10.50	7	9.00	10	10.00	8	7.50	.629
Clean	17	15.70	17	14.90	18	15.75	16	14.25	17	15.50	.849
Courageous	6	6.50	8	9.17	6	6.25	6	7.00	10	8.83	.382
Forgiving	5	6.50	6	7.75	11	10.67	4	5.25	11	10.00	.116
Helpful	3	5.00	1	3.00	2	3.75	2	3.00	13	11.50	.030*
Honest	1	3.50	3	5.13	3	5.25	1	2.63	1	3.50	.038*
Imaginative	14	12.28	16	14.64	12	11.88	15	14.25	16	14.50	.522
Independent	15	13.63	18	16.50	7	14.13	17	16.75	15	14.50	.084
Intellectual	11	11.38	10	10.50	9	9.75	13	12.00	7	7.50	.561
Logical	16	13.68	14	11.83	14	13.00	14	12.75	4	6.00	.081
Loving	4	6.50	2	3.25	10	10.25	5	6.13	12	10.50	.001***
Obedient	12	11.70	13	11.00	15	14.00	11	10.75	14	13.00	.778
Polite	13	12.25	15	14.50	13	12.40	9	10.00	9	8.50	.152
Responsible	2	4.50	4	5.67	1	3.38	3	4.25	2	5.00	.672
Self-Controlled	7	7.21	9	9.90	4	5.67	7	7.33	5	6.50	.042*

BIOGRAPHICAL SKETCH

Thomas Philip Faase, S.J., was born in Milwaukee, Wisconsin in 1938. After attending a parochial grade school and public high school, he attended Marquette University for three years, turning to a sociology major in the third year.

At twenty-one years of age, he entered the Wisconsin Province of the Society of Jesus in 1959. He completed his Bachelor of Arts degree from Marquette in 1963. He then attended Saint Louis University, pursued the Jesuit course of studies in scholastic philosophy and took a Master of Arts (Research) degree in sociology which was granted in 1965. Amidst teaching part-time in the departments of sociology at Saint Louis University and Marquette University and taking graduate courses at the University of Minnesota, he served as Assistant Principal and teacher at Saint Francis Indian Mission on the Rosebud Reservation in South Dakota. In 1966 and 1967, he also assisted the Sociological Survey of the Wisconsin Province Jesuits.

He subsequently took a Master of Arts degree in theology at Marquette University in 1971. That same year he was ordained a priest in the Roman Catholic Church.

In September, 1971, Father Faase began studies for the Ph.D. at Cornell University. Having spent a summer with the Survey Research Center at the University of Michigan and completing requirements for candidacy in 1974, he moved to the Regis College Jesuit Community in Toronto, Ontario to carry on the planning, research and writing of the doctoral dissertation. The collection of data was taken in Rome, Italy between December, 1974 and March, 1975. He has an appointment as Assistant Professor in the Department of Sociology and Anthropology at Marquette University for the academic year 1976-1977.

457